ATTORNEY AND LAW FIRM GUIDE TO

THE BUSINESS OF LAW®

THIRD EDITION

PLANNING AND OPERATING
FOR SURVIVAL AND GROWTH

EDWARD POLL

Cover by Tamara Kowalski/ABA Publishing.

Printed in the United States of America

18 17 16 15 14 5 4 3 2 1

Library of Congress Cataloging-in-Publication Data

Poll, Edward, author.
Attorney & law firm guide to the business of law: planning and operating for survival and growth/by Edward Poll, J.D., M.B.A.—Third Edition.
pages cm
Includes bibliographical references and index.
ISBN 978-1-62722-351-5 (print : alk. paper)
1. Law offices—United States. 2. Law offices—United States—Accounting. 3. Practice of law—Economic aspects--United States. 4. Law offices—United States—Management. I. Title. II. Title: Business of law. III. Title: Attorney and law firm guide to the business of law.
KF318.P57 2014
340'.068—dc23

2013044571

To my father, whose energy and enthusiasm for life's adventures seemed endless and whose love and compassion knew no boundaries . . . still my role model.

CONTENTS

FOREWORD

ALAN WEISS

I've been a consultant for more than 35 years and have worked with organizations ranging from Mercedes-Benz and Hewlett-Packard to dot-com startups and charities.

But I've never worked for a law firm. Not once. Not ever.

Most organizations suffer to some degree from the "not invented here" syndrome, and many are sterling examples of the cobbler's children, who must go around poorly shod because the cobbler is so busy with his craft. But nowhere is this more evident than in the field of law.

Ed Poll is the rare individual who has been able to counsel, comfort, cajole, and otherwise consult with often-cranky lawyers who don't want to be bothered with the business side of an enterprise because they're too busy protecting the First Amendment, keeping innocent people out of jail, and safeguarding the safety and comfort of their clients.

And the law is a noble calling. Ed calls it within these pages an "honorable profession." I find it hard to blame people so passionate about their calling for being resistant to what may seem like peripheral matters. But, as any of us in organizational consulting know, a law firm is a business like any other, in that it should take in more than it spends, reward the principals for their risk and investment, retain talent, attract the correct type of clients for that firm's specialties, and otherwise operate in an efficient and effective manner.

But very few of them do. Hence, the great need for Ed, and the reason this book is in its third edition.

I believe that Ed has come upon the most painless approaches to marketing, financial management, hiring, technology, and all the other bothersome aspects of the business proposition that often undermine lawyers' ability to practice law. That's right—the great irony is that ignoring the business side of the enterprise actually blunts the legal edge.

Those who have reached this point are probably going to buy this book. I urge you to read it. Your business will be the better for it, your practice will thrive as a result, and you'll love the law more than ever, because you'll be better supported in its pursuit.

And that is a noble practice.

PREFACE

This book is the result of a lifelong attempt to combine my love for the law and my love for business.

In 1965, the year of my admittance to the Bar, our primary concern was becoming better lawyers—technically. The business side was a given. Not only did we assume that we could operate a law office well enough, but we also assumed that there would be plenty of clients, certainly enough for us to earn a handsome income. Today, both premises are under attack. Technology has become a catalyst for major changes in the way we practice . . . and the instrument that allows us to provide our services at substantially lower costs to clients than ever before.

There is a fierce battle to attain good clients who not only can afford to pay our bills but also are more sophisticated and discerning in demanding better quality and better service. At one point, the lead character of the film *Network* yells, "I'm mad as hell, and I'm not going to take this anymore!" Clients have become more empowered and will not accept shoddy service at a high price. Because clients have more choices today than ever before—and because it is the right thing to do—lawyers must treat clients with respect and must look to provide value to them. Value is defined in terms of the clients' perception, not the lawyers'. When the client perceives the lawyer is adding value to his or her world, the amount of the fee is almost never an issue.

Marketing and finance are two of the most critical elements of success in today's tough economic climate. They are the basis for our discussion about law as a business and planning for success. This book is designed to help you—lawyers and law firms, start-ups, solo and small-firm practitioners, fee-based and contingency lawyers—accept the twin principles of planning for the future and running your practices as businesses.

When law firms understand that business success means meeting prospective and current clients' needs and desires, marketing efforts become buyer-driven and yield specific and measurable results. In particular, firms must be willing to use more sophisticated marketing techniques and respond creatively to market demands—that is, they must focus on improved client relations and service.

The purpose of this book is to guide you in the planning process by addressing selected issues of importance to your success. By identifying goals, creating a marketing plan, and creating a financial plan, you will be able to look ahead for ways to solve future problems, continue to serve your clients' needs, and run your practice as a successful business.

While the practice of law has taken on more of the trappings of a business, it is still an honorable profession whose practitioners are helping and caring people seeking to aid clients in distress. When we lawyers act in a more businesslike manner, we tend to be more effective in the delivery of our services, more efficient, and more profitable, all of which benefits both the client and the lawyer. This continues to be my mission in working with lawyers around the country.

Ed Poll, J.D., M.B.A.
421 Howland Canal
Venice, CA 90291
TEL: (800) 837-5880
TEL: (310) 827-5415
FAX: (310) 578-1769
edpoll@lawbiz.com
www.lawbiz.com
March 1, 2014

ACKNOWLEDGMENTS

Few ventures can be completed by one person alone. The expression that "no man is an island" is very literally true in today's modern environment. We all depend on one another for a whole host of things we use in our daily lives, and we frequently take them for granted. Former Senator Hillary Rodham Clinton expressed the same sentiment in modern terms with her book *It Takes a Village*. As this manuscript is being completed, I begin my twenty-fourth year as a coach and consultant in the legal profession. My time was not spent alone, but rather with many people over the roads I have traveled.

To the many people who, over the years, have contributed to my growth, my learning, and my experience, I can never fully express my appreciation and gratitude. My family, and in particular my wife, who prods me toward improvement; my clients who have allowed me to help them serve their clients even better; my fellow attorneys; and those who have directly coached me along the path I have chosen to travel.

Perhaps my most significant coach and mentor was my father. Watching him toil and succeed in the bowels of the industry while maintaining high ethical standards was, indeed, the most important education I could have received. Two other "coaches" of particular importance to me were Alan Weiss, the consultant's consultant, and Jack Rosenberg and his wife, Beverly Kitaen Morse, leading psychologists in the ever increasingly complex world of mental health. Their respective teachings have made my travels easier and more fruitful.

And lest I ignore my sponsor, the Solo, Small Firm and General Practice Division has made the publication of this book possible. Not only did the members of the governing body encourage my writing and publication of the first edition of this work, the second edition, and now most importantly, the third edition, but they also gave me the resources with which to accomplish the task. Richard G. Paszkiet, the editor for the Division, is the best project manager and editor I have ever worked with in the writing of my now more than 16 books. At every turn where I saw a challenge or other hurdle that I could not overcome, he made a suggestion that completely eliminated the challenge and allowed me to move forward with my work. For this, I will be ever grateful. Thanks also to Editorial Associate Shannon Bridger-Riley for her help with this edition.

ABOUT THE AUTHOR

With over four decades of professional experience in business and law, Ed Poll is the foremost expert in law practice management. Ed has been called as an expert witness in law firm management in trial courts and appointed as trustee of law firms accused of disciplinary violations. He is a thought leader who has written and produced more intellectual property than anyone else in this field and regularly shares his insights with attorneys across the United States as a coach, consultant, and syndicated columnist. He is an award-winning legal management consultant and has been quoted in the *New York Times*, the *ABA Journal*, and other leading publications.

Ed has a law degree from the University of California, Los Angeles, and an MBA from the University of Southern California. He practiced law for 25 years as in-house counsel, government prosecutor, sole practitioner, and partner in a small law firm. He was also the chief operating officer for a midsize law firm in the greater Los Angeles region.

Since 1990, Ed has been the principal of LawBiz® Management; he collaborates with lawyers to increase their gross revenue and net profits and reduce their stress. As the foremost expert on selling a law practice, he worked to create the ABA *Model Rules of Professional Conduct* Rule 1.17 and was the catalyst for its most recent expansion.

Ed has authored an entire catalog of books and practical guides concerning The Business of Law®. His most recent books include *Life After Law: What Will You Do with the Next 6,000 Days?* (2013), *The Profitable Law Office Handbook* (16th anniversary ed. 2012), and *Secrets of the Business of Law* (2d ed. 2012). His other books include *Collecting Your Fee: Getting Paid from Intake to Invoice* (ABA 2003) and *Business Competency for Lawyers* (2006).

Ed is a fellow in the College of Law Practice Management®, a board-certified coach to the legal profession in the Society for the Advancement of Consulting®, and a charter member of the Million Dollar Consultant® Hall of Fame. He is the first recipient of the California State Bar (LPMT Section) Lifetime Achievement Award.

Ed created the LawBiz® Law Practice Management Institute; the 2014 program will focus on Women's Leadership in the Law.

Ed and his wife, Paula, reside in Venice, California. In their spare time, they like to travel in their restored Airstream trailer. Ed is also an avid cyclist.

ABOUT THE CONTRIBUTORS

Chapter 6: Denis G. Campbell is the author of seven books including *Billionaire Boys Election Freak Show*. He is the editor of *UK Progressive Magazine* and provides commentary to the BBC, itv Al Jazeera English, CNN, MSNBC, and others. He produces and hosts *World View Show* and *BookViewTV* on YouTube .com.

Chapter 9: Helping thousands of law firms to communicate more effectively since the 1980s, Hugh Griffin shares 30 years of global service and product sales/marketing, publishing, printing, and brand marketing experience with the legal profession to ensure client satisfaction.

Chapters 10 and 12: Anne Gallagher is a partner with Extreme Marketing in its Chicago office. With more than 20 years of experience in professional services marketing, business development, and training, she works with professionals and their firms to help position them to develop opportunities and capitalize on them. A lawyer and journalist by training, she received her degrees from the University of Wisconsin–Madison. Anne is also active as an actress with hundreds of on-camera and voiceover credits to her name.

Chapters 10 and 12: As founding principal of Extreme Marketing, Merry Neitlich has been successfully assisting law firms and individual attorneys develop and grow their practices for over 25 years. Merry helps firms create their unique brand distinction, develop strategic and measurable marketing and business development plans, implement change within firms, design and implement client feedback programs yielding complete loyalty and satisfaction, and develop custom social media programs to connect attorneys with potential clients in meaningful ways.

Chapter 19: Charles A. White, Jr., is the executive vice president of Business Leasing Associates, Inc., a 30-year-old commercial finance and leasing company. He obtained his undergraduate and law degrees from the College of William and Mary in Williamsburg, Virginia, and his masters in international relations from Tufts University, Medford, Massachusetts. He spent 21 years as an Army Judge Advocate General officer specializing in international law and management, and he is an active member of the American Bar Association, where he has served for 14 years as budget officer for the General Practice,

Solo and Small Firm Section. Charles has also been the chair of the Budget Officers of the Section Officers Conference for seven years and liaison to the Finance Committee of the Board of Governors for six years. He is now spending time saving clients on their communications and energy costs using the savings through ACN.

Chapter 21: Myer J. Sankary has been a solo practitioner for over 40 years. He is the former Chair of the Solo and Small Firm Section of the State Bar of California. After specializing in civil litigation, business and corporate transactions, probate, and estate planning, he has been a full-time mediator for the past 10 years. He graduated from Harvard Law School in 1965 and from Texas Christian University in 1962 (summa cum laude, BA, philosophy). Myer collaborated with accountants to customize the QuickBooks accounting program so that solo and small-firm practitioners are able to comply with the requirements of the rules of professional conduct to maintain records and reports for client trust accounting. He has lectured extensively on maintaining client trust accounts using the QuickBooks program. Myer has an AV rating with Martindale and has been named a California Super Lawyer in the field of ADR for 2013 and 2014.

Chapter 21: Dean M. Atkinson is a partner in the accounting and litigation services firm of White, Zuckerman, Warsavsky, Luna & Hunt, LLP. He has testified as an expert witness in commercial litigation and family law matters and has been involved in resolution and settlement negotiations. Dean has been a licensed certified public accountant since August 1982. He is a member of the American Institute of Certified Public Accountants and the California Society of Certified Public Accountants. He holds the AICPA's ABV designation (Accredited in Business Valuation) and the AICPA's CFF designation (Certified Financial Forensic). He is a member of the Association of Certified Fraud Examiners and holds the CFE designation (Certified Fraud Examiner). He is also a member of the American Society of Appraisers and has passed all four exams in business valuation toward becoming an Accredited Senior Appraiser. Dean holds the CAC designation (Compensation Analyst Credential) from Economic Research Institute. He has conducted numerous continuing education classes on the use of computer software in litigation accounting applications and implemented computerized litigation software and systems.

Chapter 24: Annie G. Goldman Reed, M.A., J.D., has taught in higher education since 1985 in the areas of labor relations, human resource management, career development, contracts, constitutional law, and civil rights. She currently serves as ombudsperson and dean responsible for student discipline at Los Angeles Valley College, one of nine colleges in the Los Angeles Community College District.

Chapters 25, 26, and 27: Patricia S. Eyres, contributor to the second edition, speaks and consults nationwide on legal issues for business leaders. Her in-depth workshops help managers, supervisors, and human resource professionals develop skills to enact and enforce effective policies, prevent costly lawsuits, and develop defensible documentation.

Chapters 25, 26, and 27: Rebecca Torrey reviewed and edited Patricia Eyres's materials for this third edition. Rebecca is an equity partner at the national law firm of Manatt Phelps & Phillips. She is experienced in all aspects of employment law, with an emphasis on defending employers in single plaintiff and class action cases in state and federal court. She advises employers in the full range of employment matters. In addition to her work with clients, Rebecca is a leader in her firm and currently serves on Manatt's board of directors, the firm's management committee. She also serves on the advisory board of Hastings Leadership Academy for Women, an executive education course that prepares women law firm partners and in-house counsel for the highest levels of success in their firms and organizations, their communities, and the legal profession.

Chapter 29: Cookie Lewis, M.S.L.S. (Askinfomania), has been an independent law library consultant for 35 years, providing law firm management best practices in the area of law library information audits for cost reduction, negotiating database contracts, writing cost recovery policies so a firm can maximize ROI on its investment of resources, and reengineering library functions so law firm management and library staff can save time, space, and money to affect their bottom line and profitability. Askinfomania is an outsource research company providing firms without professional library staff strategic legal and business research to aid them with litigation research, law firm marketing research, corporate due diligence, industry trends, analysis and competitor intelligence, and research for strategic and business plans. Cookie uses her expert research and writing abilities to write blogs for firms that do not have the time or staff to communicate on a regular basis with existing or potential clients.

Chapter 31: Samuel J. Harris holds a B.A. in government administration and an M.S. in public administration and was a licensed property and casualty insurance broker in California for eight years. His 40 years of experience include municipal management, executive management of national law firms, and management consulting, and he currently is the CEO and senior consultant for his company, Paradigm Strategies, which provides organizational development, human resources, and management consulting services. Samuel served on committees for various professional organizations and lectured for the International City Managers Association, the Association of Legal Administrators, the Young Lawyers division of the ABA, and various state bar associations. He taught paralegal certification at California State–Los Angeles, legal management at the UCLA Extension, and municipal management in Pennsylvania and the DeVry Institute in Orange County, California.

Chapter 32: Ruth Davey received her B.A. in linguistics from the University of California at Berkeley in 1979 and her J.D. from the University of Southern California Law Center in 1984. She is licensed to practice law in Arizona, California, Colorado, and New Mexico. She is Area Chair for the College of Criminal Justice and Security at the University of Phoenix southern Arizona campus. Ruth teaches ethics, juvenile justice, and other classes to many students who are the first in their family to go to college. She also teaches online masters classes, where she interacts with students from Iraq to Guam. Ruth also advocates for abused and neglected children as a court-appointed special advocate in Tucson, Arizona.

Chapter 33: Stacy D. Phillips is a certified family law specialist and founder and managing principal of Phillips Lerner, A Law Corporation, a full-service family law firm in Los Angeles. She is the author of the book *Divorce: It's All About Control—How to Win the Emotional, Psychological and Legal Wars*, now in its sixth printing. Stacy represents business executives, entrepreneurs, and sports, entertainment, political, and religious figures, as well as other high net worth individuals. She was designated by Martindale-Hubbell with its highest AV rating, listed in *The Best Lawyers in America*, selected to the list of *Southern California Super Lawyers* as a Top 10 and Top 50 Women, and named to *Lawdragon's* 500 Leading Lawyers in America. Stacy co-authored Senate Bill 924, which extended the statute of limitations period for victims of domestic violence to sue their abusers in civil court. She graduated from Dartmouth College, cum laude and with high distinction, and received her J.D. from Columbia University School of Law.

Chapter 34: Bruce Breire is an Organizational Consultant who in 2014 began his thirty-seventh year of working with and presenting to busy people in all kinds of leadership, executive, and management positions. As a facilitator, advisor, strategist, and coach, Bruce provides very practical suggestions to better manage time, paper, projects, interruptions, e-mails, and all situations regarding people. He also does an extensive amount of business planning facilitation, helping growing companies and organizations to continually define, articulate, and communicate goals and strategies for organizational growth. Bruce has been a resource speaker for Vistage/TEC (The Executive Committee) since 1985, and by the end this, his thirtieth year as a speaker, he will have presented to well over 900 member groups on two topics: *The Organized Executive* and *The Goal-Setting Executive*. He has thus addressed and worked with close to 15,000 executives and senior staff Vistage members during his career.

PART I

Creating the Business Plan

CHAPTER 1

Law Is a Business

Law is an honorable profession, but it is also a business. The two concepts are the yin and yang for the delivery of quality legal services.

—Author Unknown

Failure to plan is planning to fail.

—John Wooden

Chapter Checklist

- o Law Is a Business
- o The Three Competencies
- o Warning Signs
- o Why Plan?
- o Action Plan

Brad Waters was really upset. He had just received the notice from the state bar. A doctor involved in a case that was settled had filed a complaint with the bar claiming that Waters had not sent him his check. Yes, it was true, but Waters was going to send the check as soon as he could get around to it.

He was busy. Very busy. He was the sole lawyer in his seven-person private practice. Here he was with very large gross revenues each year from his small law firm, but he just did not seem to have enough time. And he could never figure out where the money was, nor did his accounts receivable ever seem to get smaller.

"Why," he thought, "am I getting so bogged down? I just want to do what I do best—practice law."

Although the name is fictitious, the scenario is not. Waters's complaint from the doctor is merely the symptom of a much larger problem. In recent years, there has been an explosion in lawyer discipline complaints. In California, this increase mirrors the surge in the number of the state's lawyers—more than 150,000 in 1994. As of that date, before political differences between the governor of the state and the bar nearly destroyed the integrated (mandatory) bar, 75 percent of the State Bar of California's annual budget was allocated to its lawyer discipline system. And in 1991, for example, that state's bar received 76,858 complaints, investigated 6,447 of them, and prosecuted 1,345 cases. These figures mirror what is happening in every state in the country, even today.

By far, the most common complaints (39 percent) concerned lawyers' performance—mostly failure to perform, delay, abandonment, or failure to communicate. And one of the main reasons that small firms or solo practitioners get into trouble—with their state bar or with their own cash flow—is an inability or unwillingness to run the business of the practice efficiently.

Let's admit it: most lawyers (and I am one of them) are egocentric. They are also very bright. They require that the control of a matter remain in their hands. *Client control* is a favorite phrase among lawyers (the concept is well ingrained as early as the first year of law school). Therefore, lawyers believe that they also know how to run their offices.

Lawyers may know how, but when faced with the logistics of taking care of their primary task—advocating their clients' interests—it becomes clear that the management of a law practice takes a secondary position. The problem is that if lawyers are not able to take care of their own business, they obviously are not going to do a very good job of taking care of their clients. And that attitude leads to trouble.

During my more than twenty years of law practice, I have observed that a few lawyers and law firms are acutely conscious of the business aspects of running a practice. They deliver legal services with a view to the costs and benefits of those services—that is, they try to balance the benefits to be achieved for the client with the cost of delivering those benefits.

But, unfortunately, most are not very business savvy. Some, like the lawyer in the example above, are frequently overworked, unorganized, and lacking in the basic business skills to make their practices run more efficiently. Are these lawyers delivering "quality" legal services?

Successful law firms pay attention to the needs and desires of their clients. Successful law firms are able to communicate this awareness of and sensitivity to the client's wishes to the client. Successful law firms deliver their services at a price that does not offend the client. And finally—and critical to the other aspects of success—successful law firms know how to run the business of their practice.

§ 1.01 Law Is a Business

Most lawyers would now agree—although some grudgingly—that law is a business. This recognition indicates a dramatic change from recent times. Today, most acknowledge that law is a professional service business and that there is a need to pay attention to business factors previously ignored or given little public expression. Factors like marketing, collection of accounts receivable, write-offs, cash flow, and leverage that make the business more efficient and profitable are beginning to be popular topics of study among lawyers today. Yes, law is an honorable profession, but it is also a business. The two concepts are the yin and yang (complementary halves) of the delivery of quality legal services.

Most professionals were not prepared to deal with the economic downturn of the early 2000s. Lawyers witnessed or experienced the go-go days of the 1980s and the resurgence of the late 1990s, which saw the gigantic explosion of regional firms into meganational law firms with hundreds of (and now more than a thousand) lawyers. There were rumors of huge partner draws. Almost everyone painted pictures that were rosier and rosier. Yet, during that heady time, most firms were not addressing certain basic economic issues. And those moments of inattention inevitably led to trouble (and will do so again when similar circumstances arise). Feeling the new economic pressures, law firms that failed to have sound basic economic policies in place began to crumble. Some lawyers had come to believe that it was their inalienable right to increase their own personal economic well-being each year, but other factors emerged that began to thwart that belief. Some realized that they were not able to collect what was owed to them because of their clients' economic woes, or they could not get new clients, or they found it tougher to compete with an increasing number of lawyers fighting for a decreasing number of solvent clients/customers. Then came the highly publicized breakups or demergers of several major national firms, such as Finley Kumble.

The economic turmoil that faced the legal profession is still being felt by all lawyers, not just the big firms, which has led to all lawyers asking themselves serious questions about the economics of their practices:

- "How can we collect our accounts receivable?"
- "Should we hire an outside executive director to manage the practice?"
- "How do we attract more and better clients?"
- "How can I better manage my practice?"

These are all legitimate business questions, but before lawyers can begin to answer them, they need to understand how businesses—including law practices—function.

§ 1.02 The Three Competencies

All businesses—whether they are law firms, pickle factories, sheet metal fabricators, or swimming pool cleaning services—have to do three things to survive and grow:

- Get customers.
- Do quality work.
- Get paid.

I call these the three dimension of law practices, or the three-dimensional lawyer.

If you fall down in any of the three areas, you will ultimately fail. You can package the best-tasting pickles in the world, but if you cannot find enough customers or those customers do not pay you on time, you will soon be out of business.

It is no different in the legal field. Getting—and keeping—customers is called *marketing* or *practice development*. Doing the work is the technical part of lawyering, and getting paid is the financial part (and some would say the best part).

Here, then, is the basic structure of a legal business in terms of the three basic competencies:

- Marketing (get the customer)
- Technical (do quality work)
- Financial (get paid)

§ 1.02.1 Marketing Competence

As recently as the 1970s, law schools gave little or no instruction in marketing competence, or getting—and keeping—the customer. Aside from a course or two in client relations, not much was done about marketing. In the 1980s, law schools started to put more effort into this area, but not until the beginning of the 1990s did we begin to see a serious effort, at least at the practitioners' level, aimed at marketing. Law schools, generally, have still not yet addressed this issue appropriately, though some are teaching client relations as part of courses in ethics.

However, such marketing concepts as pricing and differentiation have now become critical to the survival of firms, and we will discuss them at length later in this book.

§ 1.02.2 Technical Competence

In the 1960s and 1970s, the only issue of concern to the profession was technical competence, or, as I like to say, doing quality legal work. Law schools structured their curricula to provide students with the greatest amount of knowledge in substantive law. It used to be that lawyers thought only about lawyering, or doing a good job for the client—creating an estate plan, putting a brief together, arguing a case, etc. But now we need to expand our definition of *technical competence*.

Today, we know that doing a good job includes service, and that service includes new concepts (or old concepts merely renamed), such as improved client relations, "bonding," quality, etc. Successful lawyers have been attuned to the idea of service from the beginning, but for many others this is new ground. While substantive law is outside the scope of this book, some of the client relations aspects of a law practice are appropriate for our discussion because they impact the other two areas: marketing and finance. More about these later.

§ 1.02.3 Financial Competence

Currently, issues concerning financial competence are beginning to appear in the legal press. Undoubtedly, the most apparent reason for this is that the economic pressures that clients have experienced during the last several years (dating at least from the Crash of '87) are, finally, being passed on to professionals such as lawyers and accountants.

Low realization remains the biggest financial problem for most lawyers. Failure to have a 95 percent realization rate means that even as the firm pays expenses at 100 cents on the dollar, it is earning less. This is lost cash flow, and it leads to disaster if it continues.

Financial competence is, of course, more than your collection of fees or your contingency recovery. Financial competence is the ability to manage the affairs of the law firm relating to money, either personally or through designated people. In the end, being financially competent means that you are able to make and keep more money than you spend.

Marketing and finance are two of the most critical—yet, to most lawyers, mysterious—elements of success in today's tough economic climate. They are the basis for our discussion about law as a business and planning for success.

§ 1.03 Warning Signs

Since professional service businesses must now face the test of the market along with everyone else—due to more competition for fewer and more sophisticated clients (consumers of legal services), changing economic forces, and a maturing market, among other factors—it is important to analyze specific warning signs in the context of The Business of Law®.

Most lawyers begin to realize that they are in trouble only when the money ceases to come in the door. However, cash flow cessation is usually the last symptom of a downward spiral that started long before.

Here are some basic indicators that may signal that the business of your practice needs some first aid:

- Deteriorating firm financial performance
- Lower partner draws (taking less money home)
- Poor firm cash flow—that is, not enough money coming in compared to money going out
- Clients taking longer to pay (aging accounts receivable)
- Fewer clients (especially fewer financially healthy clients)
- More noticeable competition for new clients

- Working more hours but feeling as if you are falling behind
- Shrinking practice areas
- Increases in client complaints
- Lack of trust among partners
- Compensation, management structures, and management teams that change every few years
- Poor morale among associates and staff
- High turnover among lawyers

Your law practice is like an athlete who is exercising in hot weather. Hydration—maintaining adequate body fluids—is critical to an athlete's performance and even his health. In fact, dehydration (losing water) can lead to serious medical problems like heat exhaustion, heat stroke, and ultimately death. In hot weather, when athletes are competing vigorously for extended periods, it is common for water loss to exceed water intake. As dehydration sets in, the body diminishes its sweat rate to conserve remaining water supplies. When this happens, the body starts to overheat because sweating is how the body cools itself. Unfortunately, the body's ability to detect dehydration is slow. When athletes first begin to feel thirsty, their body weight has already decreased 0.5 to 2.0 percent from loss of fluids. In other words, there is a lag time between when the body starts to become dehydrated and when it sends a signal (thirst) for the athlete to head to the nearest water fountain to do something about it. Knowledgeable athletes anticipate this problem by drinking plenty of fluids before and during exercise even if they are not thirsty.

A law practice works the same way. The point at which the cash has stopped coming in the door is much too late to start wondering if you may have a problem. You do. The seeds of the problem were undoubtedly sown weeks, months, or even years earlier. Like our overheated athlete, you need to think about your practice's business before you run into problems. This is usually called planning ahead, and the point of this book is to help you plan now so that you will not find yourself in the middle of the race without a drinking fountain in sight.

§ 1.04 Why Plan?

In a scene from Lewis Carroll's *Alice's Adventures in Wonderland*, Alice, trying to find her way, encounters the Cheshire Cat sitting in a tree:

> "Would you tell me, please, which way I ought to walk from here?"
> "That depends a good deal on where you want to get to," said the Cat.
> "I don't much care where," said Alice.
> "Then it doesn't matter which way you walk," said the Cat.
> "So long as I get somewhere," Alice added as an explanation.
> "Oh, you're sure to do that," said the Cat, "if you only walk long enough."

Or, as Yogi Berra, the famed New York Yankees catcher, said, "When you come to a fork in the road, take it."

In today's economy, however, walking long enough to get to an undefined destination is a recipe for disaster. The path to nowhere in particular is the path to failure. Any journey should include a plan.

A road trip is a good analogy. Driving from Los Angeles to Chicago requires a plan. You could just take off in a northeasterly direction and hope for the best, but a better strategy is to open up a road map of the United States and plot the best route to get you to your destination. The map; your objectives (scenic versus shortest route); and your program for stopping to sleep, eat, and refuel all constitute your plan.

In addition to consulting with law firms, I also teach regular business and entrepreneur classes. One difference that I have noticed between the two groups (lawyers and business students) is that, in general, the lawyers are leery of planning, but the business students of today accept planning for the future as a natural and necessary topic of discussion. Why do lawyers seem to have so much trouble accepting the concept of business planning? There are four main objections, or "excuses."

First, believing that the law is an "honorable profession," lawyers somehow think that attention to the business side of the practice is demeaning or "unprofessional." Worrying about the money is somehow considered beneath them, a necessary evil that would best be left to its own natural actions or to private thoughts. But an open discussion or, heaven forbid, actual planning for the firm's success—now, that is giving the subject way too much visibility and importance. How crass. How dishonorable. Sound familiar?

Second, lawyers feel they do not have the training to handle business decisions. And many just do not want to. After all, if they had wanted to learn about business, they would have gone to business school, not law school, right? Although law is a caring, helping profession and lawyers are generally quick learners, most lawyers already spend so much energy, time, and effort learning the substantive areas of their practice that they have little or no time or desire to learn business skills.

Third, planning is complex, intimidating, and just plain boring. There probably is not one of you who is reading this book who has not thrown up your hands in disgust and had your eyes glaze over after trying to muddle through a complex business-plan format, a cash flow textbook, or a planning treatise. This stuff is basically horrible torture, is it not?

Fourth, there just is not enough time to spend on nonlegal matters these days. Everyone seems to be working ten-, twelve-, or fourteen-hour days as it is. How can anyone squeeze any more time out of the day?

Let's counter these criticisms directly. First, business is not dishonorable at all. Doctors do it, architects do it—every successful person does it. In fact, and as stated before, law is a business. Anyone who does not understand that is living in the past. Second, with regard to training, any reasonably intelligent lawyer can learn the basics of planning and business without getting bogged down by the details. Third, while it is true that traditional studies on this subject have been anything but user friendly, it does not have to be so; and one of my goals is to make all of this gibberish simple and understandable. Fourth, and I know this may sound threatening, you had better find some time to think about the business of your practice, or time may be all you will have left!

The world has changed, and the practice of law has changed right along with it. Make no mistake about it: the stick-your-business-head-in-the-sand approach to the practice of law is dead, if it ever existed. Lawyers who have been slow to accept the concept of business planning are now paying the price. The old way of a firm just rolling along at the whims of its strongest partners—without a cohesive vision or plan that binds all of the partners, associates, and staff—is obsolete. In our current treacherous economic waters, if all of the crew members are not rowing in the same direction, the boat is very likely to sink!

No matter how you measure your success, whether it be in business terms, personal terms, or both, a failure to plan is a plan to fail. The future is not a result of choices among alternative paths offered by the present but a place that is created—created first in the mind and will and created next in activity. The future is not someplace you are heading but a place you are creating. The paths to it are not found but made.

The opportunity for utilizing the primary tool of good management—effective business planning—is here and available. The purpose of this book is to guide you in that planning process. The question is, What do you plan to do about planning for your success?

§ 1.05 Action Plan

- Continue to chapter 2.
- Get ready to plan for your journey to success.

CHAPTER 2

First Steps in Starting a New Practice: Initial Checklist

Whenever you see a successful business, someone once made a courageous decision.

—Peter Drucker

The chief business of the American people is business.

—Calvin Coolidge (speech, 1925)

Chapter Checklist

- o Skills for Success
- o Initial Checklist: Starting a New Practice
- o Initial Checklist: Making a Lateral Move
- o Action Plan

Starting your own practice is, first and foremost, an emotional process. You must want to do so, or you must believe that you have no other alternative. In either case, the level of stress is high. The psychic income of being your own boss is poor compensation for the loss in real dollars that usually accompanies the first years of practice. While the early years may be leaner, the hope and expectation is that the future results will compensate for the early efforts.

Starting a new practice or making a move is seldom easy, and it always brings challenges. Proper advance planning and candid communication with soon-to-be-former colleagues go a long way toward lessening the risks of your move. Engaging someone in the profession with experience in making such a move can further ease your concerns and provide you with a turnkey operation.

As the "boss," the new law firm practitioner must be a juggler and wear many, if not all, the hats: CEO, COO, marketing director, personnel manager, collections manager, technology expert, janitor, and chief bottle washer. You do not have to perform all of these functions yourself; you may delegate many of them to others skilled in the respective areas. But you must be the manager (project manager) to ensure that these tasks are completed properly and when required.

(See other chapters in this book for more starting-out steps, including hiring staff, library needs, and other aspects of setting up your own office.)

§ 2.01 Skills for Success

This book focuses on The Business of Law® and a number of skills in the operation of a law practice that will make you more successful. The skills discussed apply to the new practitioner, to the practitioner who is moving laterally from one firm to another, to the practitioner who is moving his office, and to the practitioner who is continuing in the practice but wants to be more successful in its business aspects—that is, the practitioner who wants to be more profitable!

It has been said, and with good reason, that starting your own practice is even more risky than life itself! However, putting your life's savings, soul, and energy into the new venture can be emotionally and financially rewarding if you understand your objectives and work your plan. That's what this book is about: guiding you in the planning process and addressing selected issues of importance to your success.

Before we start, however, one word of caution is necessary: as you plan for your successful journey, be sure to include and get the enthusiastic support of your significant other. His or her emotional support and understanding will be essential during times of stress in your early phases. As the military learned, a battle on one front can be managed; a battle on two fronts (front and rear flanks) is almost a sure guarantee of failure.

§ 2.01.1 Strengths of the Entrepreneur

There are many skills and characteristics that are needed for a successful lawyer and firm, particularly a start-up. The self-employed or entrepreneurial lawyer will exhibit some or all of the following traits:

- *Motivation to achieve*. The single most important word in the entire process of operating your own law practice is *commitment*. You must be committed to succeeding—that is, to providing quality legal services to meet clients' perceived needs so that they are well served and you are rewarded (profitably).

- *Focus on goals and ability to bring others into his sphere of influence and enthusiasm.* Being a leader of your staff is important. Most important is being the leader of yourself. Knowing what your goals are and planning the strategy and tactics appropriate to achieve those goals is essential to delivering quality services to satisfied clients for a fee that will exceed the cost of delivering the services.
- *Tendency to be a reward seeker.* While most lawyers are perceived as financially successful, this tends not to be the primary reason for people to become lawyers.
- *Perspective that the reward need not be only money.* Law is an honorable and caring profession. Serving people, addressing their legal needs, and protecting them against unfair odds are the springboard for most people entering the legal profession. Remembering that without clients there would be no reason for lawyers is an essential ingredient to the success formula.
- *Fortitude to take calculated risks.* Being a solo or small-firm practitioner is a risk in today's environment. However, I believe that it is a calculated risk worth taking when compared to the good that lawyers provide to their clients and society at large.
- *Organization.* Lawyers generally have the ability to organize matters for their clients even if their own offices may look like a war zone. The better lawyer, however, can also organize his own office and, where appropriate, employ the principle of delegation.
- *A healthy outlook.* The younger generation more often talks about a "balanced life," and maintaining a balanced life serves not only the lawyer and his family but also the client. That does not mean that this lawyer is lazy or fails to work long hours but rather that this lawyer finds ways to exercise, eat correctly, and spend time with his family. While this seems more and more difficult today, it is possible.
- *Optimism and ability to recover quickly from unexpected challenges.* No matter what your background, this characteristic goes a long way toward keeping you healthy and able to overcome the periodic ruts in the road that we all face.
- *Commitment to clients.* Most clients seek this trait from their lawyer. They want to know that their lawyer is on their side no matter what. This does not mean that they expect their lawyer to lie for them or tell them a sugarcoated story. It does mean that the lawyer must keep his client informed and pay attention to the client's concerns, both stated and unstated. The process of communication is essential to the successful lawyer-client relationship.
- *Industriousness—that is, doesn't mind spending long hours to achieve goals.* I know of no lawyer who works few hours; most lawyers work very long hours on client matters in addition to those hours that are necessary to market and organize their practice.
- *General good health, excitement about the work, and enthusiasm in conversations about daily activities.* Being sick and out of the office will not get

the work done. Don't treat yourself like an object, but do what is necessary to plan, organize, market, and create your successful practice in whatever format is appropriate for you.

- *Acceptance of personal responsibility.* Few people who perceive themselves to be victims are successful.
- *A take-charge attitude.* The successful lawyer doesn't blame but fixes problems. He enjoys the perspective that success is determined by actions and finds ways to overcome challenges. This is the lawyer who does not merely say no but instead says that the current approach won't pass muster and that this other approach is better.
- *Persistence and perseverance.* There is a difference between persistence and stupid doggedness. Sometimes we cannot tell the difference until after the fact, and by that time our life's savings and energies may have already been poured into the effort. We must take the time and seek the assistance of those we trust and respect to understand the difference. A quote from Albert Einstein might help put this in perspective: "Insanity is doing the same thing over and over, yet expecting a different result." Be sure to evaluate your efforts and the ensuing results to know whether you are being appropriately persistent or merely foolish in your continuing efforts.

§ 2.01.2 Weaknesses of the Entrepreneur

The above are some of the primary traits of the entrepreneurial professional. There are also some weaknesses of this group:

- Works quickly and sometimes without a plan
- Fails to do the due-diligence study necessary to uncover hurdles before they become roadblocks

§ 2.02 Initial Checklist: Starting a New Practice

After completing the self-analysis suggested by the foregoing and determining that your personality will permit you to accept the challenge of starting a new practice and be successful at it, the fun begins. The following is only a partial list of the next steps to consider:

- Know yourself.
    - Look at your strengths and weaknesses.
    - Do a SWOT (Strengths, Weaknesses, Opportunities, and Threats) analysis for yourself and your practice (regardless of whether your practice is ongoing or a start-up).
- Know why you want to start your own practice.
    - Create a business or strategic plan as outlined in this book.
    - Know who your target market is: What type of clients do you want to serve?

  - Look for space to house your practice. When you are not certain of your future, consider subleasing, renting space with only a short-term or no-term obligation, or working out of your residence.
- Rent or purchase a telephone system.
- Obtain a phone number that is transferable with your next move.
- Purchase, rent, or lease equipment.
  - Consider new options available with new technology.
  - Have access to a library and a knowledge management system.
  - Rent or purchase furniture, fixtures, and cabinets.
- Purchase supplies.
- Determine personnel needs and hire or outsource appropriate personnel.
  - Delegate all functions possible, retaining only your core competencies: lawyering and marketing.
  - Bring your staff into the planning process.
- Develop a marketing plan.
  - Create and obtain stationery, business cards, announcements, and related items.
  - Determine and create a database for your initial professional networking efforts.
  - Create a database for your initial announcement mailing.

The foregoing, as noted, is only a partial listing but includes some of the more important elements of opening a new office. See other chapters in this book for further, and expanded, elements of the successful operation of a law practice, whether start-up or continuing.

§ 2.03 Initial Checklist: Making a Lateral Move

Those of you who are reading this book because you have decided to leave an existing law firm and go it alone have a number of additional issues to handle when making your move. These issues are as important as those that we have already reviewed, as well as other considerations discussed elsewhere in this book, and must be considered before you make a move.

§ 2.03.1 Make a Considered Decision

There are plenty of positives for lawyers who have decided to leave one firm for another, provided that the decision is made with eyes wide open. The starting point for a lawyer's successful lateral move is a careful evaluation of the prospective new firm to ensure that the move will be worthwhile. Will the lawyers at the new firm be colleagues who are supportive and easy to work with? Will the financial rewards at the new firm make a move worthwhile? Does the new firm take a shared approach to compensation and clients (or is it every lawyer for himself)? Affirmative answers to these questions define a high likelihood of a positive move.

§ 2.03.2 Review the Existing Partnership Agreement

Before you decide to leave your law firm, review the existing partnership/shareholder agreement, contract, or other written document that binds you to your current law firm. You will have obligations to your former firm if and when you leave, and you will need to understand what those are and how they affect you legally and financially. Employing a lawyer, law practice management consultant, and/or accountant to provide an impartial review should be considered. Depending upon your current firm's financial-management program and the requirements set forth in the agreement, there will be a best—and worst—time to depart. You need to know both before you make a final decision.

§ 2.03.3 Know Your Financial Obligations

As mentioned in section 2.03.02, there is a best time and a worst time to depart from your existing law firm. Generally, you will have a financial obligation to your current law firm when you leave. This might be a minor obligation in the long-term scheme of things, but it very well could have a significant and immediate impact if and when you announce your intention to leave. Therefore, know in advance what your obligations and rights are before you announce your departure.

§ 2.03.4 Establish a Relationship with Your Bank and Banker

You will need a line of credit, a credit card, banking services (wire transfers, escrow accounts, trust accounts, etc.), and long-term loan services from a bank. You may need assistance in structuring your financial obligation to your former firm. At some point, you will need to establish loans and other banking services for a client, so establishing a sound banking relationship before you decide to move is essential. In fact, this factor may be the most critical to your decision to leave your current firm. You should meet with several bankers to see what they can offer you before you make a decision. Do some homework ahead of time so that you are prepared to ask the right questions and elicit the right responses from the bankers you interview. (See and review chapter 18 about banks and loans.)

§ 2.03.5 Select an Accountant

Because you will need an accountant when you are on your own, it will be easier on you to establish this relationship before you decide to move. A good certified public accountant can help you understand your financial obligations to your current firm and what you will undertake with your own firm. The accountant's input will be invaluable in getting you started on the right financial footing.

§ 2.03.6 Establish a Relationship with an Insurance Broker

You are going to need insurance and insurance-related benefits when you start your own firm. These benefits may include (1) health, (2) life, (3) disability (long- and short-term), (4) professional liability, (5) workers' compensation, (6) employment practices liability (7) property and general liability, and (8) communications liability (see more about insurance in chapter 20). Again, you should know what the requirements are for these various coverages and what the costs will be before you make the decision to leave your firm and before you meet with your banker. You should look for an insurance professional who understands law firms and who has an excellent reputation within the insurance and legal communities. You might consider your current firm's insurance professionals after you announce your decision to leave, or you can contact lawyers you know in other firms for referrals.

As with bankers, you may want to interview several insurance professionals for the right fit.

§ 2.03.7 Create a Business Plan

No one should consider starting a law firm (or any other business, for that matter) without a business plan. No successful organization or business can continue to exist and prosper unless it has a clearly defined plan. When you take on a new case, you review all of the relevant information, consider the issues, consider the facts, and then develop a plan to proceed (or not). Starting your own law practice is no different from taking on a new case. When you meet with the banks and others in preparation for your new practice, they will be impressed by the fact that you have established a business plan; this will definitely work in your favor.

§ 2.03.8 Develop a Forms File

Going out on your own, you probably will be permitted to leave your current firm with your personal (nonfirm-related) files, client files for those clients selecting you as their counsel on your departure, and your own forms file. If you do not have a forms file now, prepare one before you leave. You will soon need your own resources. Cautionary note: Do not remove any document or form that is proprietary to the firm without prior permission.

§ 2.03.9 Review and Select Technology

Technology is critical in today's practice. Functionality, expandability, compatibility, costs, and availability of technology choices all must be considered before you leave. You will require word-processing software; database-management software; accounting software; other specific practice-related software; and fax, telephone, and other related equipment on the day that you start your new practice. Therefore, you cannot wait until after you move.

§ 2.03.10 Develop Your Client and Related Files List

Do not wait until you leave to develop your client and related files list. Plan your file transfer well in advance because when you announce your intention to leave the current firm, the relationship will change immediately, and that which was readily available no longer may be available. You will need to plan for the transfer of files and for their storage (active versus closed).

§ 2.03.11 Develop a Case File–Numbering Scheme

Using your current firm's system as a guide, determine the file-numbering system that you will use in your new firm. This should include a policy on how you will open new files and the format of all new files when opened. You will need to establish a "file tickler system" as well; this system, whether manual or electronic, will alert you to due dates and deadlines.

§ 2.03.12 Determine Which Clients/Matters Will Go and Which Will Stay

Bear in mind that the clients and matters that you would like to take and the ones that you ultimately do take may not be the same. You will need to think this through and have a list prepared, including the rationale for why you should be able to take certain clients/matters to your new firm. Again, remember that your relationship with your firm will change upon your announcement to leave; and no matter how amicable your departure may seem, when it comes to clients and related matters, expect to have to fight for your list. Of course, the final decision remains with the client. Your actions, however, must minimize the risk of claims of interference with contractual relationships.

§ 2.03.13 Draft a Client Contact Letter

Be prepared with the draft of a letter to be sent to clients advising them of your decision to leave the firm. You and your existing firm should agree on the final form of this letter, and, in fact, the firm may wish to send a letter on its own. If possible, both you and your firm should agree upon the contents of both letters in order to present a unified, clear, and understandable statement to the clients who are being given the opportunity to go or to stay. If the firm does not agree to present a united front, you may still send your announcement.

The letter should address the client's opportunity to go with the departing lawyer or stay with the existing firm. Clients should not be left ignorant of who their lawyer will be following a lateral move. Without clear communication, clients may well engage a second law firm just to make sure they have legal representation while their lawyer moves to a new home. Be careful, though, how you solicit clients of the firm. Obtain legal guidance before you send your announcement.

The letter should also address client permission for client files if the client intends to move with the lawyer. Although clients can request copies of their own files, the departing lawyer cannot do so with the explicit intent to use them for taking clients from the firm. In some instances, even if the lawyer personally created work product, the copyright protection on client files may attach to the documents and reside with the law firm. Client permission is needed to move a file, and it is only ethical to suggest that a client make that request if the client intends to continue working with the departing lawyer.

§ 2.03.14 Develop a Retainer Agreement

You will need a retainer agreement, and you should have it ready before you leave.

§ 2.03.15 Prepare a Letter to Colleagues in the Firm

You will want to present this letter for approval when you make your announcement to depart. It is essential that you create an amicable departure with the firm and with your colleagues, if at all possible. The letter will likely be in your words if you prepare the initial draft.

§ 2.03.16 Know When Enough Is Enough

In the effort to excel, made more intense by the pressure of economics, lateral moves can cause problems for lawyers. Generally, lawyers are successful because they are competitive. However, if they don't know when to stop and keep moving from firm to firm in order to come out on top and in control, striving for success can be counterproductive.

§ 2.04 Action Plan

- Understand the commitment that is required for you to succeed.
- Enlist the support of your significant other and other family and friends for your journey along the path of success.
- Do a SWOT analysis.
- Focus on your strengths.
- Review, in particular, chapter 3.

CHAPTER 3

The Planning Process

For everything, you must have a plan.

—Napoleon Bonaparte

Dig a well before you are thirsty.

—Chinese Proverb

Chapter Checklist

- o What Planning Is and Is Not
- o The Basic Steps
- o Secondary Plans
- o Agreeing to Plan
- o Who Plans?
- o The Logistics of Planning
- o Gathering the Relevant Information
- o Looking Ahead
- o Action Plan

Law is a business as well as a profession, and planning should be the first responsibility of business owners. Yet, during the Great Recession, many previously successful business organizations with detailed and elaborate planning processes failed. Some drew the conclusion that planning is not possible in these volatile times and that the best any organization can do is a form of white water rafting—riding the rapids to cope with events as they happen. Regrettably, such an attitude is too prevalent in law firms.

Most people are fearful of change. One of the beauties of planning is that it helps mitigate this fear by giving you more control of those changes that are certain to come. Change is something you can count on. The question is, Do you want to control it, or do you want to have it control you?

The hardest part about planning is starting to do it. After the initial struggle to get the ball rolling, it is much easier to keep it going. Remember, as John Wooden said, a failure to plan is a plan to fail.

§ 3.01 What Planning Is and Is Not

A plan is a scheme or program for making or doing something; it is a detailed method, formulated beforehand, of proceeding on a course of action.

Since what we are discussing here is the business of the practice of law, our plan is appropriately called a business plan. Some call this a strategic plan.

By whatever name, a good business plan has the following attributes:

- Is simple to understand
- Requires effort and time to create, though less than most fear
- Is ongoing and evolving, capable of being changed as circumstances change and more accurate information is gathered
- Is based on shared beliefs
- Is agreeable to and supported by all those with responsibility to act—staff as well as lawyers

A bad business plan has the following attributes:

- Is overly complex and intimidating
- Is academic, without practical applications
- Is "carved in stone" and inflexible
- Has limited support

Business planning is an idea and an action that can be accomplished regardless of the nature of the substantive area of your practice. This process applies to transactional work (usually based on hourly billing, fixed/flat fee, etc.) and to contingency practice such as personal injury or debt collection (usually based on a percentage of the fee recovered without reference to the time invested by the lawyer).

Contrary to what many people think, a business plan does not need to be a thick document with a fancy binder. The problem with most business plans is that they are too complicated and too intimidating. Consequently, they are typically and quickly put on a shelf, never to see the light of day again. A plan that is not used is no plan at all.

The most difficult part of creating any plan is getting started. What information is required? How do you proceed? What are the steps to take? A certain amount of fear is common with this kind of big-picture planning, and lawyers are not immune to feeling it.

You do not need to feel frightened about business planning, however, even if you have never done it before. As mentioned in the previous chapter, planning should first and foremost be simple and understandable. It should also be logical.

§ 3.02 The Basic Steps

Rather than being afraid of planning, lawyers should actually feel confident since they are trained to think logically about problems and solutions. Planning is merely one form of problem solving. And like all problem solving, the business-planning process has certain steps. Although there are plenty of twelve- and fifteen-step planning processes out there, I believe that they are too complicated or abstract for the average lawyer to put into practice. My goal is to simplify the process of running a successful law practice by breaking it down into its essential elements. To accomplish this, we will be using "Poll's Basic Business-Planning Steps," as listed below:

Poll's Basic Business-Planning Steps

- Prepare to plan (agree to plan and gather information).
- Identify your goals.
- Create the marketing plan.
- Create the financial plan.
- Evaluate and compare the results with your goals and revise the plan(s) as and when necessary.

I call these five steps taken together *a business plan*, and the most important steps are setting goals, creating a marketing plan, and creating a financial plan. In other words, you need to decide where you are going and what you want to be (goals), you need to set into motion marketing actions to get you there (marketing plan), and you need to manage the financial resources to make it all happen (financial plan). In later chapters, we are going to spend more time concentrating on these steps because they hold the key to your practice's business success.

Let's take a brief look at each of the five steps.

§ 3.02.1 Prepare to Plan

In a law firm, it is important for all of the key players to agree on the direction of the firm. If the partners are not clear about the overall goals as well as specific objectives and strategies, then the planning process is bound to be sabotaged and ineffectual. Partners need to "buy in" to a plan. Solo practitioners are not immune from this requirement, either. They must get a spouse or significant other to accept the general direction of the firm. That is why the first element of any plan is to agree to make and abide by the plan.

You need to gather a certain amount of historical information so that you can analyze it and start thinking about realistic modifications for the future. Plans for the future need not mandate growth; in a stagnating economy, planning to stay at the present level of revenue or size may be the most that a lawyer can expect. You will be primarily interested in marketing and financial data in the form of documents; statistics; reports; survey results; and, when there is nothing else, your best guesses. All of this data will give you a snapshot of your firm's marketing and economic health in the present. Once you can see where you have been, it is much easier to see where you can go. Later in this book, we will talk about the specific marketing and financial information that you will need.

§ 3.02.2 Identify Goals

If you do not decide what type of practice you want, you will wind up with one reflecting whatever walks in the door. Serendipity or whim may make you successful, but it is doubtful. You need to decide what you want to be and what you want to do, both professionally and personally. Remember Alice and the Cheshire Cat. We will go into more detail about goals in chapter 4.

§ 3.02.3 Create the Marketing Plan

Since your practice is dependent on customers, or clients, then getting them and keeping them is obviously critical to your success. A marketing plan helps you see who these elusive people are and how to attract them to your door. Marketing is absolutely crucial to any business, and law practices are not exempt.

The marketing plan begins by creating a profile of the firm's ideal clients. The firm can increase revenue dramatically by focusing on the demographics, occupation, location, financials, and other characteristics of clients who will provide the desired work. That said, the number one place to find these ideal clients is on the current client list. Conventional wisdom says that 80 percent of a typical firm's revenue is produced by 20 percent of its clients—the large heavy hitters. It follows logically that such clients should be the focus of the marketing plan. Don't, however, fixate on these large clients to the exclusion of pursuing ideal targets; make sure that no single client exceeds 10 percent of total planned revenue because the loss of a large client is a major risk.

We will discuss marketing at length in chapter 5.

§ 3.02.4 Create the Financial Plan

The financial plan is the culmination of all of your earlier information gathering, thinking, and planning. The financial plan is the statement, in financial or monetary terms (the language of business), of your dreams and goals.

One component of the financial plan is cash flow. In other words, firms should plan for profits by prioritizing, anticipating, and allotting the revenues and expenditure of funds. Cash flow includes the firm's revenue inflow; expenses, which are the uses of the revenue; and outflow of money. The cash flow should cover a rolling period of twelve months into the future and ideally should be revised weekly (and no less often than monthly) to spot developing problems and take remedial action.

Another component of the financial plan is collections. The key here is integrating how many hours the lawyers bill with how much money they collect. The goal is to have a high collected-to-billable ratio—well over 90 percent. Plan this realization on two levels: the billed-to-billable ratio (the percent of billable or booked hours billed) and the collected-to-billed ratio (percent of billed work collected). Promptly identify all clients who are not paying their bills and take immediate and necessary action.

We will go into more detail about the financial plan in chapter 13.

§ 3.02.5 Evaluate and Revise the Plan

For some firms, the biggest objection to a plan is that it locks the firm into rigidity at a time when flexibility is needed. But good planning is not static; it is meant to be a guide against which you can judge actions or outcomes. The beauty of a flexible plan is that it can be revised to better reflect the reality of your specific situation and to help you get to your desired outcome.

Recognize that your first efforts to plan may not be perfect; no one ever took on a new task and executed it flawlessly the first time. For example, the "first pass" of your marketing and financial plans will require modification as experience tells you where you were too optimistic or pessimistic in your predictions. This is a normal result of this process, and you will get better and become more accurate in your projections as time passes. Lack of perfection (especially in the beginning) is not a reason to refuse to make the effort to create your business plan. Experience and educated guesses (best efforts) are the most effective teachers.

Planning is an ongoing process. If a certain aspect of a plan is not working or needs some adjustment, change it. Making adjustments from time to time is quite appropriate, just as people make alterations to an estate plan as family circumstances change. Even junking a strategic plan is acceptable when circumstances and assumptions warrant. However, a replacement strategy should be developed in its stead, not just a series of jumps from here to there.

How can you tell if your plan is working? If you think that you have been making some progress in reaching your goals, here are seven signs to show you if you are right:

1. *Results that are in sync with your planning process.* You will be meeting the goals, required actions, deadlines, and responsibilities outlined in your original action plan.
2. *Performance that parallels projections.* It is not realistic to expect every line of the financial statements to match your projections, but the results as shown in your cash flow revenues and expenses should be close to your forecasts.
3. *Good communication between lawyers and staff.* Let staff members know that you are open to their ideas for improving the business. And be sure to share good news so that they can see the progress being made.
4. *Improved cash flow.* This is the obvious—and some would say only—indicator of success.
5. *Controlled credit.* Are you up to date with your creditors? If not, let them see your improvements or proof that change is coming.
6. *Maintenance of customers.* Are you satisfying your clients? Are you gaining clients, or are they fading away?
7. *Employee morale.* Staff members know when changes are working. Their morale is an accurate barometer of progress.

§ 3.03 Secondary Plans

The broad strategic plan should encompass secondary planning efforts, such as a disaster-recovery plan and a succession plan. Like the overall strategic plan, such secondary plans should identify the desired business outcomes within a given time period, define what is necessary to achieve those outcomes, and work toward them consistently.

§ 3.03.1 Disaster-Recovery Plan

The goal here is more than disaster recovery; it is business survival and continuity. Before creating a disaster-recovery plan, review each practice area and staff function in the firm separately. Ask how long it can afford to be "out of business" and what resources it would need to get up and running. Conduct a firm risk assessment to review readiness and look for weakness, an effort that should include reviewing insurance policies to determine whether they cover natural disasters and crime in addition to general liability. Create a comprehensive internal emergency communication system, plan for temporary space, and back up all computer data and store data backup as well as important records and documents off-site. Finally, prepare a plan manual that creates a disaster-recovery team and spells out who does what no matter what level and type of disaster takes place.

§ 3.03.2 Succession Plan

Failure to plan for how clients will be taken care of as a lawyer approaches retirement age can, according to some authorities, be construed as a reckless disregard for client welfare—a true ethical violation regardless of the size of the firm. In large firms, planning and structuring client service teams, with senior lawyers involved as team coordinators of a multidisciplinary team composed of lawyers at various stages of career development, is perhaps the most effective way to begin the transitioning of client service responsibilities. The issue of client transitioning is just as important in small firms and solo practices. Planning options can include simply closing or selling the practice, grooming a successor by hiring an associate to learn the practice, or merging with or hiring a lateral with the option to sell the practice to him.

§ 3.04 Agreeing to Plan

Business planning in a law firm requires a commitment from all of the key individuals. These key individuals need to "buy into" the planning process. If some are lukewarm to the idea, you need to do your best to "sell" the planning idea to all concerned. Provide key decision makers with planning articles and books, planning documents, white papers, and other reports on industry and professional trends and forecasts. Maintain a constant stream of planning information and materials. Someone—and it might have to be you—may need to promote the importance of planning to the firm. It may be in your best interest.

§ 3.05 Who Plans?

Who should be involved in the planning process is an important question.

If you are a solo practitioner, the answer is easy: you are the planner. But the solo who has no other staff also has the disadvantage of having no one else to talk to or to get feedback from. In that case, solos should consider involving a spouse or significant other or consider accountants, bankers, or even outside law firm management consultants who have some understanding of the legal field and whose judgment they trust.

In small firms with more than one lawyer, all lawyers, whether partners or associates, should be invited to participate in planning. If not, someone who is not a part of the process can, and probably will, attack the outcome.

What about including staff? Opinions are split on this question. Reasons to include staff in the planning process include the following: they have a better idea of the practical, day-to-day activities of the office; they will be more motivated if they have input into the planning; and it is proof that you value their contributions and that you think they are worthy of your trust. Reasons not to include staff include the following: lawyers may feel inhibited about "telling it like it is," the staff will have access to confidential information, and staff should not be involved in the overall direction of the firm.

The best choice is to include your staff in the planning process. All employees want to feel that they are part of the team. And when they feel that they are part of the team because they had some input into the process, they will usually act more responsibly. Staff, especially in a small firm, have knowledge and insight into the firm that owners or partners frequently do not. An administrator or manager, if there is one, is a good example of a staff member who should be involved in the planning process. Administrators usually have a unique perspective and significant practical information about the firm. Also, when staff members understand the goals of the firm, they may be more inclined to help generate revenue through their own network of contacts.

Two people on a tandem bicycle can go faster than one person alone, so try to include other "riders" on the planning vehicle.

§ 3.06 The Logistics of Planning

It is important to consider various logistical details of planning such as confidentiality, location, and management.

What about confidentiality? Although full disclosure is the best way to discuss the direction of the firm accurately, firm owners are sometimes reluctant to reveal to associates or staff financial information like gross receipts, expenses, salaries, or draws. In my experience, associates and staff intuitively know this information—maybe not precisely, but closely enough to warrant opening up the real data. One solution, however, is to convert all of the sensitive facts to percentages or averages.

Where do you plan? For the small firm, a series of meetings or a weekend conference is the best option. In either case, it is important to get away from the daily interruptions of the office. In fact, it sometimes helps to get as far away as possible. Most of you know the feeling of being able to see your business in a different perspective when you are away from it. If you cannot go away on a retreat-type weekend, consider a conference room with no telephone or office interruptions. A planning meeting requires complete focus.

How do you run a planning meeting? Other than the principals, there are two specific people needed: a facilitator and a reporter. The facilitator's job is to encourage and assist the flow of communication. Consequently, the facilitator should not be the strongest partner or the most dominant person in the firm; otherwise, he will impose his opinions on the rest of the group. If that happens, the meeting will be a waste of time. The reporter documents all of the discussions and decisions so that no one forgets what was accomplished.

The main point about the actual meeting or meetings is that they should be nonthreatening; no one should dominate. The purpose is to come to a consensus that includes everyone's input. Strong partners need to step back to allow others the chance to articulate their contributions. The whole group should understand and practice a nonjudgmental policy; no put-downs and no ridicule are allowed if open communication is to be encouraged.

§ 3.07 Gathering the Relevant Information

Now is the time to gather the appropriate historical information about the firm's marketing and financial issues that will serve as the starting point for discussing the future. This information will come from both inside and outside the firm. (See chapters 5 and 13 for more detailed information on marketing and financial issues.)

Try to gather as much of the following firm financial information and general marketing information as possible:

Firm Financial Information

- Financial statements of the law practice for the last five years, or less if you are a new practitioner (these statements are normally prepared by the firm's bookkeeper or accountant and usually consist of documents such as a balance sheet, an income statement, and, possibly, cash or cash flow statements (more about these later))
- Tax returns of the law practice for the last five years (if available), which may include your Schedule C, the law partnership tax return, or the professional law corporation tax return
- Aging of accounts receivable, if any
- Billing records, including ledger cards showing billings and payments over time by individual clients
- A checkbook register showing all checks written, the names of the payees, and the amounts and types of expenses
- Previous plans or projections prepared by or for you
- Bank statements for your general account
- Bank statements for your client trust accounts

General Marketing Information

- Articles/statistics about legal marketing trends
- Law firm surveys from bar groups

- Basic demographic information about your current client base showing the number of clients, types of business, scope of services, legal requirements, etc.
- Basic demographic information about your prospective clients, such as industry, size, and type of services required

You are encouraged to add to the above by gathering additional economic information that will help you fill in the gaps in picturing your firm:

- How many people were employed at your firm at the end of last year? Break it down by partners, associates, of counsel, etc.
- How many contingency versus fee-based lawyers?
- What is the average hourly rate for partners/shareholders? For associates?
- What was the average number of billable hours for the same groups for last year?

Use the Law Firm Economic Survey form (see Figure 3.1) to help obtain this information. Copy it, and encourage lawyers and staff to fill it out as honestly and completely as possible. Add to the questions or change them if you like, but get this kind of information! The more information you have, the easier it will be for you to see weaknesses, strengths, and areas for improvement at your firm.

While you are gathering all of this information, keep a portion of your attention open to the future. If you see obvious problem areas or areas of opportunity, jot them down. In fact, make up a sheet, call it something like "Changes/Needs/Opportunities," and jot down any fact or observation that strikes you as important. This will ensure that you will not forget important ideas or "flashes of enlightenment." You will be able to pull them out for discussion at the appropriate point later.

§ 3.08 Looking Ahead

Too many good attorneys are so busy with immediate concerns that they cannot look forward for ways to solve future problems. This applies not only to the lawyer's practice but also to clients' needs. Make yourself invaluable by going the extra mile and providing a service that clients feel they must have. Know your clients' business and anticipate their future problems. Suggest articles or webinars on new business trends. When you become truly invaluable to a client, you will always compete successfully for their business. And as long as you're competing, you have the opportunity to succeed.

§ 3.09 Action Plan

- Get the agreement and commitment to start the planning process.
- Schedule the planning meetings.
- Gather relevant information and fill out the Law Firm Economic Survey (see Figure 3.1).

FIGURE 3.1

Law Firm Economic Survey

BUSINESS STRUCTURE

1. How many of each of the following were employed at your firm as of December 31, 20XX? (fill in number of all that apply)
   _____ Partners/shareholders
   _____ Associate lawyers
   _____ Of counsel
   _____ Paralegals
   _____ Secretaries
   _____ Administrative staff
2. Which of the following describes your firm's business structure? (check only one)
   _____ Professional corporation
   _____ Partnership
   _____ Sole proprietorship
3. Which of the following do you have? (check all that apply)
   _____ Managing partner/shareholder
   _____ Management committee
   _____ Number of members
   _____ Nonlawyer chief executive officer
   _____ Full-time executive director
   _____ Part-time executive director
4. Does your firm have a partnership or shareholder agreement?
   _____ Yes
   _____ No
   If so, is it written or oral? _____

FINANCIAL INFORMATION

5. 20XX annual gross billings $ _____
6. 20XX annual gross receipts $ _____
7. 20XX annual expenses (estimate where needed):

   EMPLOYEE SALARIES
   Partners'/shareholders' compensation $ _____
   Associate lawyers' compensation $ _____
   All other payroll $ _____
   Rent $ _____

   ALL OTHER EXPENSES
   Supplies, travel, postage, phone, professional services, client disbursements written off, depreciation of furniture/fixtures, etc.
   $ _____

8. How much office space does your firm occupy? _____ sq. ft.

NET WORTH

9. What was the amount of unbilled time (work in progress) at your regular hourly rates at the end of December 31, 20XX? (do not include pro bono work) _____ hrs.
10. What was the amount of time written off (either as unbillable or through reduced rates) during the year? _____ hrs.
11. What were the "clients' costs advanced," outstanding at the end of December 31, 20XX? $ _____
12. What was the amount of billed accounts receivable at the end of December 31, 20XX? $ _____

HOURLY RATES/SALARIES

13. Which one of the choices below most closely describes how your hourly rates are determined? (check only one)
    _____ Costs
    _____ Competition
    _____ Arbitrary
    _____ Other (please specify) __________
14. Fill in the chart below to compare lawyers' salary rates, billing rates, and billable hours by years of experience and position in the firm.

Years in Position	**Average Annual Salary**	**Average Hourly Rate**	**Average Number of Billable Hours per Year**
Partners/ Shareholders			
1–4 years			
5+ years			
Associate Lawyers			
1–2 years			
3–4 years			
5+ years			

15. Who determines employee compensation? (check all that apply)
    _____ All partners
    _____ Committee
    _____ CEO
    _____ Managing partner
    _____ Other (please specify) __________

16. For which of the following expenses do you bill clients? (check all that apply)
    _____ Photocopy time
    _____ Telephone time
    _____ Clerical time
    _____ Incoming fax charges
    _____ Outgoing fax charges
    Are the above billed at cost or marked up? _____
    If marked up, what percentage? _____

MANAGEMENT

17. Does your firm hold partner/shareholder meetings?
    _____ Yes
    _____ No
    If yes, how many times per year? _____
18. Does your firm have a written business plan?
    _____ Yes
    _____ No
19. Does your firm utilize a formal cash flow statement?
    _____ Yes
    _____ No
20. How many lawyers do you expect to ADD to your firm in 20XX + 1?
    _____
21. How many do you expect to DROP from the firm in 20XX + 1?
    _____
22. How many lawyers do you expect to ADD to the firm in the next five years? _____
23. On average, how many years does it take a first-year associate to be admitted to partnership on a normal track? _____ yrs.

MANAGEMENT INFORMATION SYSTEMS

24. Are you currently using a computer system?
    _____ Yes
    _____ No
25. Who manages your computer system? (check all that apply)
    _____ Lawyer
    _____ Bookkeeper
    _____ Systems manager
    _____ Office manager
    _____ Outside consultant
    _____ Other (please specify) __________

26. For which of the following are you using your computer system? (check all that apply)
    _____ Word processing
    _____ Time and billing
    _____ Accounts receivable
    _____ Calendar and docket control
    _____ Document management
    _____ Payroll
    _____ Accounts payable
    _____ General ledger

27. How has the system affected staff size? (check only one)
    _____ Increased it
    _____ Decreased it
    _____ Remained the same

GROWTH

28. In the last year, how has the volume of work changed? (check only one)
    _____ Increased
    _____ Decreased
    _____ Remained the same

29. In the last year, how has staff size changed? (check only one)
    _____ Increased
    _____ Decreased
    _____ Remained the same

CHAPTER 4

Setting Goals

If you don't know where you're going, you might wind up someplace else.
—Yogi Berra

Chapter Checklist

- o SMART Formula
- o Identifying Personal Goals
- o Identifying Law Firm Goals
- o Identifying Work-Life Balance Goals
- o Action Plan

It is important to have goals because only when you have goals can you make plans.

Goals are specific statements describing results that you want to achieve. There is no paucity of treatises and theories defining and elaborating on concepts such as values, missions, goals, and objectives. In keeping with my belief in simplicity, I am going to condense them all into one term in this chapter: *goals*.

An example of a personal goal is to retire by the age of sixty and never have to work again. A law firm goal might be to become the largest family law firm by revenue in the city. Both of these goals are specific and capable of being evaluated by some objective criteria. Statements such as "To be the best" and "To be proud of my profession" are not specific enough and, by my definition, not truly goals. How will you know when you are the best? Or when you will be proud?

§ 4.01 SMART Formula

There are smart and foolish ways to start a practice. The smart way is to plan. Every law firm is a business, and a business that grows without a clear idea of overall goals and specific strategies will wind up reflecting whatever walks in the door. Foolish growth relies on whim and serendipity—not the best paths to success.

An excellent acronym, SMART, describes what's required for a smart growth plan:

- *Specific*. The issue is not more money but how much, not more clients but what kind.
- *Measurable*. If you can't measure your growth, you'll never know what you've achieved.
- *Achievable*. Set near-term targets that are realistic; don't set yourself up for failure with unreasonable income expectations.
- *Relevant*. Your goals should be aligned with the firm's objectives.
- *Timely*. Give yourself an adequate time frame, but one that still imparts a sense of urgency.

If you are a lawyer in a solo firm, the SMART formula helps you decide where you want to go as you grow. Once you do, there is a greater likelihood of achieving a satisfying practice—and life.

§ 4.02 Identifying Personal Goals

I once knew a tax practitioner who had a traditional accounting background (business school, accounting firm) and who, after passing the bar, naturally gravitated to tax law. But after several years, he found himself pushing pencils and not really enjoying his work. When he asked me to consult with him about his practice, he confided that his law practice was stagnant and that he was not happy in his career.

My advice began with a simple question: "What do you want to do?" He said that he had never really thought about it; he had just drifted into the work he was doing. I suggested that he might want to start a goal-setting process by answering personal and firm-related questions that you should also be thinking about, such as the following:

- What do you want to be when you grow up? (You might think that this is a ridiculous question, one that is only asked of children or young adults; but like my friend above, some people are never asked this question and so never think about it.)

- What is it about the law that you really like?
- What don't you like?
- Do you have a passion for the law that keeps you practicing it?
- What kind of firm or practice do you want—small, medium, or large?
- Do you want to specialize, or do you like being a general practitioner?
- Are you a full-service law firm or a boutique? Contingency or fee-based?
- Do you seek business or individual clients? Sophisticated or unsophisticated clients?
- What do you want your geographic orientation to be—local, regional, or national?
- What about your image—high-profile or understated? High-powered or low-key?
- Do you want to be viewed as progressive or traditional?
- Do you want to optimize profits or lead a more relaxed lifestyle?

It is never too late to set goals, and you can never revise or restate them too many times. The more thought that you give to your goals, the better. You need to decide what you want to be. You need to be realistic. And then you need to stay focused on whatever you decide.

A now-well-known psychologist—let's call him Bill—was a college instructor making less than $20,000 per year. Deciding to change his life and to make more money, he wrote his desired annual income goal—$125,000—on the bathroom mirror in lipstick. Every morning and every evening he looked at the mirror and focused on his goal. Soon he saw an opportunity to share his knowledge of people and what makes them tick with corporate clients. He began actively marketing himself to corporations, and his growing business was soon bringing in $40,000 annually.

Still looking at his mirror and focusing on his goal, Bill decided to expand even more. He wrote a general-interest psychology book on his own and began looking for ways to let people know about it. He investigated advertising in large publications like *Reader's Digest* but found the ad rates much too expensive. But he did not give up looking for opportunities to publicize himself and his book. One day, he met a writer at a party who was intrigued by the psychologist's ideas. After an interview, the writer wrote an article about psychology for the *National Enquirer*, mentioning Bill and his book. The book soared in popularity, and Bill went on a speaking tour to promote it.

Only when his income reached $400,000 did Bill erase the lipstick from the mirror.

§ 4.03 Identifying Law Firm Goals

Personal goals usually deal with things like money, retirement, family time, travel, personal satisfaction, etc. Law firm goals typically include topics like firm size, revenue/profits desired, personnel size, firm image, practice areas, type of clients, etc.

The smaller the firm, the more intertwined the personal goals of the lawyer and the goals of the firm become. For the individual lawyer to endorse the firm's goals, those goals must also support the individual's goals. It works both ways. Let's say that the majority of a firm's four partners believe that their mission is to help the indigent and the needy. Does that mesh with the desires of Lawyer A, who has a large family and who is concerned only with taking home the largest draw or salary possible? Probably not, and eventually the partnership will have to resolve the conflict. It is important to find out in the planning stage whether the personal goals of the principals are consistent with the firm's goals. The two need not be the same, but they cannot be in conflict with each other.

Approach this goal-setting procedure in two parts. First, have each lawyer and staff member answer a list of thought-provoking questions about themselves personally and about themselves professionally (see Figure 4.1, Personal Goals Questionnaire). This should be done before the first planning meeting. The purpose is to get the participants to start thinking about their goals and how they fit into the bigger picture of the firm. The answers to the questions are to remain personal—that is, no disclosure to the other participants. People should be encouraged to share this process with their families or others closely involved in their lives since they have something at stake here, too. Solo practitioners especially will want to consult their spouses or significant others since unknown or contrary goals can quickly lead to tension and conflict in a relationship.

Then, have the same individuals answer questions about the firm itself (see Figure 4.2, Law Firm Goals Questionnaire). By thinking about and answering these questions (questions can be added or subtracted as needed), each person will give some thought to the major areas of concern to the firm so that when the whole group first meets to delineate and refine the company's goals, the groundwork will have been done.

The priority, then, of the group's first meeting is to agree on the firm's goals. Simply go topic by topic down the firm questionnaire; discuss the various responses and opinions; and write the final, agreed-upon goal statements. If you need more than one meeting to do this, so be it. Everyone needs to understand and agree on the firm's goals before you can proceed. However they are framed, the goals belong to you and the firm—they are your own story, they are your dreams, they are your future!

By going through this procedure, you will discover very quickly if you and your partners see eye to eye on the direction of the firm. Only when the big picture of your practice's goals is clearly defined can you take advantage of the opportunities that will inevitably come along to move you down the road to success. And because of this planning process, you will tend to become more focused; and once focused, you will be more likely to see and understand and take advantage of the opportunities that pass in front of you, just like our psychologist with his lipstick.

Once your vision of your overall goals is clear, it is time to work on your marketing and financial plans, which are discussed in subsequent chapters of this book.

§ 4.04 Identifying Work-Life Balance Goals

No discussion of goals would be complete without touching on work-life balance goals. Lawyers are always concerned about having enough client demand in the pipeline, but being overextended is just as great a worry.

Several years ago, I participated in a discussion where solo lawyers expressed reluctance about marketing their practices and getting more business. Some feared losing time for professional and personal obligations; others feared less flexibility in their schedule. All believed in setting limits on how much they could and wanted to do. Such work-life balance is a long-term assessment that every lawyer must make. In the short term, there is really no such day-to-day phenomenon as balance: at any given moment, the lawyer is doing just one thing—either working or engaging in personal pursuits. The broader perspective is how much cumulative time is devoted to each and what you value more.

All successful people work long hours and are focused and passionate about what they do. In the effort to excel, made more intense by the pressure of economics, trying too hard can cause problems for lawyers. Generally, successful lawyers are competitive lawyers. But if a lawyer doesn't know when to stop and has to come out on top and in control even for little things, the striving for success can be counterproductive. Lawyers wanting to maximize their billable hours while maintaining a sense of balance in their lives should take a deep breath and assess their time and money wants (desirable but not necessary) and needs (fundamental requirements). Successful lawyers can get past the distractions and stress, define what matters, and then put their focus on what they value most.

§ 4.05 Action Plan

- Understand the basics of the SMART formula.
- Create a written list of personal goals for the next year and the next five years.
- Create a written list of professional goals for the next year and the next five years.
- Review the two lists and confirm whether there is harmony (or, at least, no conflicts) between the two lists.

FIGURE 4.1

Personal Goals Questionnaire

This questionnaire is for your benefit and will not be disclosed to anyone else. The purpose of answering these questions is to help you analyze your personal goals and put them into context with the goals of the firm. We encourage you to share this process with your spouse or significant other.

1. What have been the most satisfying and the least satisfying work-related activities in your life?
2. What have been and what are the most satisfying and the least satisfying aspects of your personal life?
3. How does your work-related life currently impact your personal life?
4. Do you feel that you spend enough time with your family and friends?
5. Do you plan to retire? When?
6. How much money are you currently making? Do you want to make more? How much more?
7. What aspect of the practice of law has been the most satisfying to you?
8. What would you like to be doing in your work-related and non-work-related life in five years?
9. Why did you go to law school?
10. What percentage of the goals that you wanted to achieve by practicing law when you graduated from law school have you actually achieved?
11. Which field of law interests or satisfies you the most? How much time (by percentage) do you spend in that field?
12. What part of your law practice do you love the most, and what part do you hate the most?
13. What other complaints do you have about your practice?
14. What one thing would you change to make your law practice more satisfying? Why haven't you changed it? How can you go about changing it?

FIGURE 4.2

Law Firm Goals Questionnaire

This questionnaire deals with your view of the activities and the performance of the firm. The purpose of answering these questions is to help determine problem areas and areas of opportunity for the practice. These answers should be shared with all involved in the planning process.

1. What is the image of this firm? Should the image be different? How?
2. What are three of the firm's strengths? Three weaknesses?
3. What are the major threats facing the firm?
4. What are the main opportunities facing the firm?
5. What current and future trends are affecting or will affect the firm?
6. Where is the firm headed in the next five years? Where should it be headed? What changes within the firm will need to be made to accomplish this change in direction? Should the firm add/delete practice areas in the next five years?
7. Do you think the firm is too large, too small, or just about right in size? What is the optimum number of lawyers for the firm presently and in five years?
8. How would you rate (good, average, bad) the firm in terms of each of the following?

   Personnel policies/procedures
   Financial performance
   Administration/management practices
   Clients/marketing activities
   Practice development

9. What improvements can you suggest for the firm in each of these same areas?

   Personnel policies/procedures
   Financial performance
   Administration/management practices
   Clients/marketing activities
   Practice development

PART II

Marketing Paradigms

CHAPTER 5

Creating the Marketing Plan

Marketing is an attitude, not a department.

—Phil Wexler

Most barriers to your success are man-made. And most often, you're the man who made them.

—Frank Tyger

Chapter Checklist

- o Marketing Defined
- o Components of a Marketing Plan
- o What Clients Want
- o The Marketing Mix
- o Embrace Marketing
- o Action Plan

Forget all of the textbook definitions of *marketing* that you may have read over the years. It is really very simple: *marketing* means getting and keeping customers, or clients. Marketing begins from the moment you awake to the moment you go to sleep. It is an activity—not a department—that is continuous.

Any action that helps you get and keep clients is marketing or, as some call it, practice development. Some, like advertising, are obvious, but others are not. Leading seminars, public speaking, publishing brochures and newsletters, the manner in which your office staff answer the phone, handling complaints, client relations, differentiation, quality—these are all marketing considerations since they help you or hinder you in reaching out to your prospective clients and in holding onto their business once you have it.

§ 5.01 Marketing Defined

The most common misconception among lawyers is the belief that marketing is the equivalent of advertising. *Advertising* is defined as any paid form of nonpersonal presentation and promotion of legal services by a law firm. Typical advertising activities include television or radio advertisements, Yellow Pages advertisements, newspaper advertisements, etc. Advertising is often used as a mechanism for strengthening the public's awareness of a lawyer or law firm.

Marketing, on the other hand, is much broader than advertising and encompasses a wide variety of activities, including the creation, pricing, promotion, and distribution of legal services. More specifically, *marketing* can be defined as the process by which a law firm creates and exchanges products and services of value to others. Therefore, marketing is the underlying process by which lawyers and law firms determine their whole set of strategies for delivering legal services. Marketing involves decisions such as which practice areas a firm should emphasize, which clients or groups of clients the firm will primarily seek out, how the firm will price its legal services, and how the firm will deliver its legal services. Marketing is the process by which a firm defines itself and differentiates itself from its competitors. In the grand scheme, advertising is but one type of marketing activity.

§ 5.02 Components of a Marketing Plan

Since marketing activities can cost a significant amount of money, it is crucial that marketing be considered very carefully and that it be planned. Unfortunately, it is very common for law firms to make decisions to spend money on advertising or brochures or other items on the spur of the moment. Usually, a partner has just seen an ad by a rival firm or reads an article about the latest marketing gimmick in a legal publication and decides to commit scarce resources to try out the idea. This is not the way to do it! A well-thought-out marketing plan takes into account the firm's goals and direction (see chapters 3 and 4) and considers all of the marketing options in coming up with the most appropriate strategy. There are, of course, unforeseen opportunities that may come up, but they can be judged against the marketing plan and incorporated or dismissed.

A marketing plan is one of the main components of the business plan and is usually created and revised on an annual basis, although it can be reviewed at shorter intervals if it needs changing. A simple marketing plan answers these questions:

1. What is your current situation?
2. What are you trying to accomplish?
3. Who are your target customers, or clients?
4. What is your strategy for reaching them?
5. Who does what, when, and for how much money?
6. How will you know if you are successful?

Let's look at each of these marketing plan elements in depth.

§ 5.02.1 What Is Your Current Situation?

This is an assessment of your practice and of the legal market that pertains to you. It is the where-you-have-been, where-you-are-now, and who-you-are-now analysis. It is both qualitative and quantitative in terms of the type of information required.

The qualitative side is composed of opinions and attitudes about marketing issues held by the lawyers and staff of the firm. The relevant issues and questions to be answered include the following:

- What services do you offer?
- How are you providing those services?
- What is the need for those services?
- Are those needs changing?
- Who else provides those services (competition)?
- What do you think your strengths and weaknesses are? What are the strengths and weaknesses of your competition?
- Are you likely to face competition from large firms or from smaller, boutique firms?
- What are the practice area trends in your community or in general?

The trends apparent in the economy, both national and local, allow you to spot opportunities and shift practice areas. For example, because of the real estate slump in many areas of the country, firms are getting more involved in foreclosures. The same can be said for bankruptcies, services for the elderly, and environmental law. Each region or subregion will have its own peculiarities, strengths, and concerns. Use sources such as the American Bar Association and your state and local bars for law firm statistics and general information about current conditions in the legal industry. The *Martindale-Hubbell Legal Directory* and other similar directories can help you research such questions as the number of firms and individual lawyers in your area and the percentage that are small, medium, or large.

The quantitative information is more statistical and factual:

- Can you identify the sources of referrals and business?
- Who are they and what percentage of your overall business do they contribute?
- Can you identify the type of clients you currently have by number and by percentage? How about by practice areas?

- Are the clients individuals or businesses?
- Can you identify the clients that provide the bulk of your revenue?
- Can you identify all of your fees by source?
- How has your volume of work changed in the last year? Has it increased? Decreased?
- How has your revenue changed in the last year?
- How has your staff size changed in the last year?
- How much advertising have you been doing and where?
- What was the response to those ads?
- What were the total fees and/or contingency recoveries collected for the last three to five years? From what sources did you receive this business?

Much of the firm-specific information can come right out of the accounting and billing records that you have already gathered or noted in the Law Firm Economic Survey in chapter 3. To help you with a framework for completing your situation review, I have created a Marketing Situation Questionnaire in this chapter (see Figure 5.1). Have each lawyer fill out whatever is appropriate for him. Include staff personnel to bring in their points of view regarding issues about which they are knowledgeable. This valuable information can then be summarized and shared during the planning meetings. A clearer picture of your firm's current situation will emerge, and the steps you need to take to change your situation will become more evident.

§ 5.02.2 What Are You Trying to Accomplish?

What are the marketing objectives that will drive the practice in a specific direction? The quantitative information from the situation review can be your guide. Based on what you already know about your firm, what revenue objectives by client type would you like to achieve? How would you like to shift the practice area balance? What sort of image would you like to project to the world?

This is where you plug in any of the marketing- or practice-oriented goals from the previous chapter. But you now need to do more—you need to come up with specific objectives to help you reach those goals. And those objectives should be quantifiable. For example, a marketing objective could be "To reach out to 1,000 prospective new clients and retain fifteen of those within one year" or "To have at least five articles in regional legal publications mention our name in a positive light."

Refer to the Marketing Strategy Grid (see Figure 5.2), and use the information from the previous section to come up with a few specific objectives for your firm. If you feel that you do not know enough yet, create a few objectives anyway, even if they are preliminary. You can revise, refine, and add to them as needed.

§ 5.02.3 Who Are Your Target Customers, or Clients?

Target clients can include existing as well as prospective clients.

Before looking for new clients, market to existing ones. Besides the fact that existing clients are always your best source for additional business, it is cheaper to keep a client than to get a new one. Other industries—the mail-order catalog business is a good example—know this very well. Advertising, buying mailing lists, creating promotional material, paying postage costs, etc., in order to reach prospective clients can be very time-consuming and expensive. Why not go to the clients who already know you and with whom you already have a relationship? They can bring in new clients as well as their own added business. Sometimes, all they need is a reminder from you that you are available to do additional work like estate plans and wills, corporate minutes, judgment renewals, lease negotiations, contracts and options, expunging of prior criminal records, or other work appropriate to your particular expertise.

In order to successfully market to your existing clients, you should be able to answer the following questions:

- Who, exactly, are your clients?
- What businesses are they in?
- Are there any expected changes in those businesses that could affect your business with them?
- How similar are these clients to each other? How different?
- What kind of legal work are they looking for?
- What are their needs now, and what will they be in the future?
- What do they think about you and what you offer them? What do they think about the competition and what it offers them?

If you do not know the answers to these questions, you need to find a way to ask. A survey form handed out or mailed, a brief interview with new clients, your knowledge of your client base, or even research by an independent research company are all appropriate. The more you know about your clients, the better you will be able to deliver the services that they want.

In addition to existing clients, consider expanding your client base by marketing to prospective clients. To do this, you need to consider market segments. Market segments are large, identifiable groups of individuals or parties within the market for legal services that are looking for specific types of legal expertise. For example, within the legal market there might be the following market segments:

- Administrative and agency
- Antitrust and trade regulation
- Bankruptcy
- Civil rights
- Construction
- Corporation and general business
- General practice
- Employment
- Securities
- Trial practice

- Immigration
- Wills, trusts, and estate planning

Of course, this is not a comprehensive list, but it illustrates the point.

The first step for a firm or lawyer is to determine which market segments it is competent to service and wants to pursue. Finding your market segments is as simple as knowing which practice areas are a fit for the firm's lawyers (i.e., the lawyers are competent to practice in those areas) and offer profit margins to justify the effort. Therefore, market segmentation can be a fairly simple decision.

A niche, on the other hand, is a subset of a market segment that has a special set of needs within that segment of services. A good example of a niche market in the general corporate and securities segments is the entrepreneurial start-up company. The start-up company needs the same level of legal expertise as a large established corporation, but it has dramatically different needs regarding payment of legal services. Since start-ups are cash poor, they cannot typically afford to pay premium up-front hourly fees. Several marketing-savvy Silicon Valley law firms successfully altered their mix of services in order to specifically meet the needs of the start-up companies in the area in the 1980s and 1990s. These innovative firms experienced dramatic successes with their niche strategies and became choice providers for members of the entrepreneurial niche. Currently, many large law firms offer highly specialized, full-service legal services to a large number of market segments but do not spend enough time determining the needs of selected niche groups within those market segments.

Niche marketing requires a law firm to do a substantial amount of research in order to find the right mix, or solution, that creates super satisfaction in the smaller niche subsets of a market segment. Successful niche marketers must continuously evaluate the niche's needs and alter their service mix if those needs change. Niche marketing is relationship focused and requires an intimate knowledge of the market. The benefits of niche marketing are significant, however, and often result in positive long-term relationships with clients who are not hesitant to utilize the firm's services when legal issues arise.

Of course, in today's Internet-driven world, there are few geographical limitations to distribution—that is, the methods by which a lawyer or law firm makes its services available to potential clients and delivers its services to existing clients. At one time, lawyers were limited to local or regional clients because they did not have the means to market their services to potential clients outside of their geographical vicinity. Nevertheless, a cautionary note: Be very careful not to engage in the unauthorized practice of law by providing legal services to clients in a jurisdiction in which you are not authorized to practice.

Using the quantitative information from the first section plus any new data or thoughts, describe your current and intended client base.

§ 5.02.4 What Is Your Strategy for Reaching Your Target Audience?

Promotion should be aimed at educating the targeted markets about the firm. The overriding purpose of promotion is to communicate to the targeted groups of clients in their language how the firm will serve their legal needs better than its competitors.

Promotion can be performed through the typical channels such as television, newspaper, radio, weekly or monthly newsletters, lectures, the Internet, etc. Communications is the nitty-gritty of marketing. Some think, erroneously, that communications *is* marketing. The main categories of marketing communications are as follows:

- *Advertising*. *Advertising* means sending paid messages via the media. The days of lawyers not advertising are over. It is a question of whether you think it is appropriate for you and which is the best vehicle to get the message out to the target audience. Do not be limited to thinking only of Yellow Pages ads. Trade magazines, radio, and cable television are becoming popular vehicles for legal advertising. Make sure that you review the rules of professional conduct in your jurisdiction regarding advertising.
- *Public relations*. Public relations involves getting mentioned in the media, but for free. Get press mentions by becoming an expert on a specific legal subject and promoting that expertise to newspaper and magazine editors. You can be the one who is quoted when articles are being written. Someone has to do it!
- *Other*. The "Other" category is composed of whatever is left over:
  - *Writing articles in legal publications*. These publications are usually in need of quality articles and will be more than willing to accept your contributions.
  - *Speaking at conferences and before industry groups*. Make sure that you are speaking to groups of prospective or potential clients or colleagues who may refer business to you.
  - *Joining targeted trade associations and charitable organizations*. Get involved by joining the membership committee, where you will meet more people and be recognized as making a contribution to the growth and health of the organization. Or get involved by joining the finance committee or a similar committee that will allow you to learn quickly about the inner workings of the group and will place you near the seat of power of the organization.
  - *Conducting presentations and seminars*. This is a great way to communicate your expertise, your enthusiasm in a specific field, and your availability.
  - *Creating brochures and newsletters*. Realize that while a brochure needs to be created only once (until it is obsolete), a newsletter requires a regular commitment. Brochures can be fancy or straightforward, but their value is not necessarily determined by the cost of production. Either of these promotional materials will put information about your firm directly into someone's hands.
  - *Promoting client and law firm referrals*. Satisfied clients, when reminded, are usually happy to make referrals to colleagues, friends, or relatives. Many law firms make referrals of matters about which they feel unqualified or in which there may be a conflict of interest.

Make other firms aware of your expertise and availability. Participating in your bar association's activities is an excellent way to become known by other members of the profession.

- *Networking*. Participate in networking gatherings, breakfast "lead-sharing" meetings, etc. But be sure that the participants are potential clients or colleagues who may refer business to you.
- *Preparing mailings.* Prepare mailings to potential clients, in accordance with the rules of professional conduct in your jurisdiction. There is an almost-infinite number of sources for names, including mailing-list brokers who do nothing else. If you can identify a target client group, there is undoubtedly a list of those people available. Mailings can highlight a new practice, a new service offered, changes in personnel, a change in the economy—almost anything can be the reason for a mailing. One effective technique is to highlight a change in case law or legislation that may impact your clients. Your analysis or a summary of the change provides a valuable service in addition to creating awareness of your legal services.
- *Creating firm letterhead, building signage, announcements, etc*. Realize that these items are also marketing pieces. They communicate something about you and the firm. Make sure that they say exactly what you want them to. (See chapter 9 for more on this topic.)
- *Maximizing the Internet*. Internet marketing encompasses much more than creating an online advertising brochure through a law firm website or maximizing the number of "hits" to the firm's web page. In addition to promotional activities, the Internet can actually be used to enhance the services that a law firm offers if it is used as a regular means of communicating or exchanging information with clients and other parties to a legal transaction. (See chapter 7 for more on this topic.)
- *Starting a blog*. Blogging (or blawging, as some say) provides an opportunity to display your expertise, offer your opinions, and suggest new alternatives for clients to consider. (See chapter 8 for more on this topic.) Generally, it is wise to focus on your practice area(s) and leave personal comments to social media platforms like Twitter and Facebook.
- *Cross-selling*. It is a marketing rule of thumb that it is much easier (and less expensive) to sell more services to an existing client than it is to find a new client. Promote other appropriate legal services to all existing clients.

Which marketing strategies and communications techniques will you use to get the word out about your practice and to achieve your objectives? As an example, let's look at the sample objective mentioned earlier: to reach one thousand prospective new clients and retain fifteen of them. If the practice area is personal injury and the target audience is individuals, one strategy would be to utilize print advertising in the Yellow Pages. People who are looking for personal injury lawyers frequently flip through the Yellow

Pages looking for an ad that strikes them. The marketing strategy then would read: "Place one ad of XX size in the XX Yellow Pages to run for XX months." Another target audience with the same objective could be middle-market corporations that need outside corporate lawyers. A different strategy could be to utilize a direct-mail campaign to reach the CEOs of these corporations and to convince them of your expertise. A marketing strategy would read: "Create and mail one thousand direct-mail packages by November 1 to corporate CEOs obtained from the XX mailing list."

One firm in Los Angeles seeks its clientele from outside its local area; in fact, this firm does no advertising at all in Southern California but spends heavily for advertising in the midwestern and eastern parts of the United States, from which it gets its business referrals.

The size of your firm, its practice areas, and its desire to grow are important considerations in the development of your marketing strategy. The correct selection of media or methods that make up a marketing mix is the art of marketing. No one can tell you exactly what will work and what will not. It takes intuition, a hard look at the facts, and experience to do it right. If you are new to marketing, you will just have to try different strategies and pay attention to what works and what does not.

Using the Marketing Activity Checklist (see Figure 5.3), choose the most promising activities to reach your target audience to achieve your specific objectives. One way to represent this visually is to make a grid sheet for each client type like the sample in Figure 5.2.

§ 5.02.5 How Much Time, Staff, and Money Will Be Required?

This is where you allocate who is responsible for what (whether your marketing will be done internally or through an outside agency or consultant), when it is going to happen, and how much it is all going to cost (see Figure 5.4, Marketing Action Plan).

There are advantages and disadvantages to using an outside source such as a consultant or an ad agency to help implement your marketing plan. Outside sources have, or should have, the marketing and communications expertise that you may not. They have staff and resources that most law firms do not have. They also bring an outsider's fresh, unbiased viewpoint to the procedure. This is sometimes the main advantage for firms with strongly held but equally split opinions by partners on how to market the firm. The downside is that outside agencies charge for their services (surprise!), although an hourly fee for an outside creative consultant is usually less than your legal fee.

One way to justify the added expense of hiring an outside firm or consultant to work with you on your marketing is to engage it only for specific tasks that you cannot do. An example would be a firm brochure. You could write it and hire an agency or design firm to do the layout and production coordination. As in many areas of life, it usually pays to hire someone who is an expert in a specific field—even if you have to pay top dollar—and get the job done right. The money it takes to carry out all of the marketing activities can be estimated by your experience or actual price quotations from designers, printers, etc. These marketing expenses must then be plugged into the paid expenses cash flow form under the "Marketing and Public Relations" category (see chapter 13).

§ 5.02.6 How Will You Know If You Are Successful?

Only by setting up specific marketing objectives that are quantifiable can you honestly evaluate whether you have succeeded or not. Did you receive the five editorial mentions? Did you, in fact, retain the fifteen new clients? When the objectives are specific, it is easy to know if you have reached them. Keeping track of the results can be as simple as making notes or check marks on the Marketing Action Plan (see Figure 5.4).

§ 5.03 What Clients Want

If marketing is getting and keeping clients, then it makes sense to discuss what clients are looking for in a lawyer. The better you know what clients want, the more services you can provide. The clients will be happier, and your relationship will be stronger. Most clients look for five main ingredients in a law firm:

- *Expertise in the area of specialty.* Quality has always been a key factor in the purchase of goods and services, and it is especially important in a tough economy. Do you have the knowledge and ability to advocate for the client's interests? Do you provide the best legal services that you can? Do your services meet the expectations of your clients?
- *Knowledge of the client and his business.* Do you have hands-on knowledge of the client's business or industry so that you can offer the best advice based on the client's situation?
- *Imaginative advice.* Clients appreciate advice that offers aggressive and creative approaches to business problems. Today, we call this being proactive to client circumstances. This creates an even stronger bond between client and lawyer. On the other hand, if you are merely reactive, the client may believe that you are only a technician, and a technician is a commodity that can be changed based on pricing of the service, school credentials, and size of firm, among other factors.
- *Service.* At first glance, it may appear that law firms and lawyers cannot easily differentiate their legal services from those of their neighbors competing in the same market segments. After all, each firm offers highly competent lawyers who are well respected in their practice areas. The lawyers in each of these firms also produce high-quality legal work in a professional manner. So what makes these firms and lawyers different from the client's perspective? This is an important question for a firm to ask. Clients often place as much emphasis on nonlegal characteristics of a firm—firm atmosphere, use of technology, lawyer availability, understanding of the industry, responsiveness, and communication—as they do on the actual legal services performed.

- *Timeliness.* Dealing with the client in a prompt, timely manner, without having to be pushed, is essential to retaining client loyalty. Do what you say you will do, in the time frame that you establish. Clients want to feel important. The client will feel like a second-class citizen if he has to wait for services for a long time or if services that were promised at an earlier time are delayed. In the long term, the client will deal only with providers who act as though they believe that each client is important.
- *Responsiveness.* How quickly do you return telephone calls and respond to letters? If you are unable to respond because you are in court, preparing for another client, on vacation, or otherwise unavailable, a secretary, paralegal, or other associated lawyer must respond quickly. The response may be nothing more elaborate than saying that you are presently unavailable and will return the call or letter by a certain date. If the need of the client is such that an immediate response is necessary, the lawyer's office should make other arrangements to resolve the matter.
- *Communication.* Explain the process to the client, and demystify the judicial system so that the client will know what to expect. Tell the client immediately if and when unexpected events occur and what the events mean to the overall objective of the client and the game plan previously established. Clients also appreciate communication or explanations that do not make them feel stupid or unknowledgeable.
- *Handling Complaints.* A specific part of service—and another element of marketing—is the handling of complaints. Complaints can be a learning as well as a marketing (keeping the client) tool; you can find out if there is a gap between what you are promising (as perceived by clients) and what you are delivering. Here is what you should do when this client-relations problem crops up:
  - *Log the complaint.* This helps determine whether there is a steady or consistent pattern that needs to be dealt with. Frequently, one problem in isolation, even if repeated, may not make us aware of a pattern that needs further treatment.
  - *Look into the problem.* Determine all of the relevant facts. If the issue relates to billing, do not send another statement until the issue is cleared up; that would only compound the problem and confuse things further. If the bill is the issue, you must determine whether further work is to be performed before the matter is settled.
  - *Respond to the client.* Tell the client that you are reviewing the matter and will respond to him by a certain date. If you take longer than expected, call the client and tell him that you will be later than expected but that you will respond by X, a new target date. Do not let the client believe that you are ignoring his concern, that you are too busy to handle the matter, or that you do not care about money (if the billing is in question). This latter perception may permit the client to further delay payment of future bills.

- *Determine the solution*. The solution must be perceived by the client as fair, and it must be consistent with previous firm policies. Alternatively, you may want to change firm policies to reflect new thinking raised by the client's complaint. There should also be a way for the client to "save face"—that is, to be reassured that his concern was legitimate even if it could not be handled in the way that the client desired.
- *Communicate and explain your decision*. Even if the response is adverse to the client, he must understand the basis of the decision; this may be the only way to preserve the goodwill of the client.
- *Follow up*. Has the matter been resolved to the satisfaction of the client? If the answer is yes, the follow-up will reinforce goodwill created by a satisfactory response. If the answer is no, determine what problem still needs to be addressed. If it can be resolved, do so quickly.

- *Value.* Are your rates reasonable? Does the client receive good value for the money charged? Does your service contribute to the client's bottom line by either saving money or making money? Price is an important component of legal services. Oftentimes, traditional methods of pricing legal services may not meet the needs of clients within various markets. The standard hourly fee does not always represent a useful mechanism for valuing certain types of legal services. This is not to say that the billable hour is dead or that law firms should completely discard their traditional pricing models. Rather, the firm must analyze whether current pricing models are alienating certain types of clients that the firm would like to service.

§ 5.04 The Marketing Mix

It is easy to understand how difficult it can be to successfully market a firm's services to the right group of clients because there are so many factors involved. The firm not only must properly segment its potential markets and determine which markets it wants to pursue but also must develop a proper mix or solution to satisfy the special needs of each targeted group.

If even one element of the marketing plan is altered, the firm's service may become less (or more) valuable to a certain market. Many different firms offer clients expertise in the same practice area—tax law, for example. The legal expertise is likely to be technically similar, but other factors differ, such as responsiveness, knowledge of the client, and price, all of which are part of the service offered by the firm. Price is a good example of a component in the mix that affects the value of legal services in different client markets. Some clients, such as very wealthy individuals or large corporations, may be willing to pay a premium dollar to ensure that the lawyer's research and tax advice is thorough and bulletproof. Others who are more price sensitive are more concerned with receiving adequate tax advice for moderate prices. Despite the similarities in what is technically being offered, differences in the other components to the total mix can make the service more valuable to some and less valuable to others.

Of course, a firm's promotion of these other components can certainly alter clients' willingness to utilize the firm for its tax advice. It is imperative that the firm understand precisely what it is offering in its product mix and communicate that accurately to the appropriate target market. If the firm understands its market well enough and offers the right product mix, or solution, it will successfully attract and retain clients. If there are incongruencies in its product mix, a firm will fail to attract and keep clients.

§ 5.05 Embrace Marketing

Some lawyers run the other way whenever the word *marketing* comes up. They are afraid of not knowing what marketing is and what to do about it, or they feel that marketing is somehow sleazy or distasteful. In fact, lawyers frequently disguise their discomfort by using the term *practice development* instead of *marketing*. But with the information presented in this book, along with other reading and investigation, you will learn to recognize and implement sound marketing activities that make sense for you.

As for the "sleaze" factor, you will not necessarily be associated with the late-night legal hucksters on television simply because you are advertising your services. Advertising—as well as any other form of marketing—can be accomplished in a tasteful and dignified manner. Since the landmark *Bates v. State Bar of Arizona* decision, 433 U.S. 350 (1977), marketing and being a professional legal service provider are not incompatible concepts. Professionalism and sound business practices that include a thoughtful approach to marketing go hand in hand.

Do not forget, everything that you do and every contact that you have with a client—a letter, a phone call, a report—is a form of marketing whether you think so or not. Do not be afraid of marketing—take control of it!

§ 5.06 Action Plan

- Have all of the key planning people go over the six elements of the marketing plan and answer the six corresponding questions as completely as possible. To help you do this, review the Marketing Activity Checklist (Figure 5.3), and fill out the Marketing Situation Questionnaire (Figure 5.1), the Marketing Strategy Grid (Figure 5.2), and the Marketing Action Plan (Figure 5.4).
- Create your marketing plan. It need not be more than three or four pages long. Modify the forms in this book as needed.
- Create a separate month-at-a-glance calendar for your marketing activities only. Keep it on your desk for frequent review.
- Allocate the resources (time, money, people) to carry out the marketing plan.
- Hire outside professionals—ad agency, public relations agency, design firm, marketing consultant—if needed. (Make sure that you add the expenses to the cash flow plan as described in chapter 13.)
- Monitor every marketing activity to evaluate its effectiveness.
- Make changes to the marketing plan as appropriate from time to time.

FIGURE 5.1

Marketing Situation Questionnaire
Answer the following questions to determine your firm's current marketing status.

1. Does the firm currently have a written marketing plan?
2. Does the firm have a full-time or part-time marketing director?
3. Indicate the percentage of new business that comes from the following marketing techniques:

   Referral ____%
   Seminars/speeches/articles ____%
   Direct mail ____%
   Firm newsletter/brochure ____%
   Advertising ____%
   Other ____%
   TOTAL: 100%

4. Indicate how much is being spent annually on each of the following marketing sources (list year by year):

   Referral $____
   Seminars/speeches/articles $____
   Direct mail $____
   Firm newsletter/brochure $____
   Advertising $____
   Other $____

5. What is the annual percentage of total marketing expenses (from above) compared to revenue?
6. List all clients by type, number, dollar volume, and percentage of revenue.
7. List the top ten clients who have produced the highest revenue for the firm (annually).
8. List the percentage of gross revenue to the law firm from annual service clients compared to one-time clients.
9. Identify what partners, associates, and staff have done in the past year to help market the firm to existing or potential clients.
10. What has the firm done to determine its clients' current and future legal needs?
11. What type of client or client segment is the most profitable for the firm? (State how *profitable* is defined.)
12. Who will be the clients of the future? What services will they need? Which practice areas correspond to those needs and hold the most promise for future opportunities (i.e., what are the practice areas of the future)?

13. Does the firm have a policy of cross-selling services (promoting other firm services to existing clients)?
14. Which current services should the firm strengthen? Which new services should the firm offer? Which services should the firm eliminate?
15. Who are the three major firms that compete with yours for the same practice areas? What are their strengths compared to your firm? What are their weaknesses?

FIGURE 5.2

Marketing Strategy Grid

<table>
<tr><th colspan="2">Client Type:
Example:
Corporate CEOs in Industry X</th></tr>
<tr><th>Objectives</th><th>Strategies</th></tr>
<tr><td>Example:
Reach 1,000 prospects and retain 15.</td><td>Example:
Mail 1,000 packets to the prospects by November 1.</td></tr>
<tr><td>Example:
Receive 5 mentions in local press.</td><td>Example:
Send press release to local magazine/newspaper editors. Subject: Importance of finding outside corporate counsel.</td></tr>
</table>

FIGURE 5.3

Marketing Activity Checklist

Marketing for law firms includes many appropriate vehicles or techniques. Here are some alternatives that you may want to consider:

1. Write articles in your field for legal publications and industry trade journals.
2. Speak before appropriate conferences and industry-related groups.
3. Join targeted trade organizations.
4. Join the professional arm of a charitable organization.
5. Participate in networking gatherings.
6. Prepare mailings to potential clients.
7. Cross-sell to current clients.
8. Encourage client referrals.
9. Promote law firm referrals.
10. Advertise.
11. Conduct seminars for clients, prospective clients, and sources of referrals.
12. Consider producing a firm brochure or newsletter.

You can use several of these specific techniques in combination to achieve the desired marketing communications result.

FIGURE 5.4

Marketing Action Plan

Who is responsible?	**What will be done?** (strategies from the Marketing Strategy Grid)	**When is the target date?**	**How much will it cost?**
Example: Paul Johnson	*Example:* corporate CEO mailing	*Example:* November 1	*Example:* $2,000

CHAPTER 6

A Solo and Small-Firm Practitioner's Marketing Renaissance

Success seems to be largely a matter of hanging on after others have let go.

—William Feather

Never, never, never, never give up.

—Winston Churchill

Chapter Checklist

- o Cultivate Clients
- o Serve the 99 Percent
- o Action Plan

You went to bed last night a successful partner in a two-hundred-lawyer, full-service firm. Yesterday, you had a very full plate: 2,400 guaranteed chargeable hours; a staff of associates, paralegals, and secretaries to whom you could delegate tasks; a guaranteed income with a decent chance at good performance bonuses (amazing in this economy, right?); cases that challenged you to perform at the very highest level of your craft; hallways filled with like-minded peers whom you could ask for an opinion or assistance on an issue of law; two-hour lunches; committee meetings; firm politics. . . .

. . . and you were never more miserable in your life. You hated it. Your soul was crying out for freedom and the chance to build something for yourself. It is, after all, the American Dream. So you wake up this morning a solo practitioner, and you are sitting in your three hundred square feet of freedom (loosely translated: a "B" class leased office suite with a telephone, PC, message machine, fax machine, and photocopier). But while you didn't act precipitously—you have a few files and projects to get started with—the realization is beginning to sink in that when these projects are done, you are going to have to learn to hunt and kill your own work to survive.

The bad news is that even though you are busy, you do not have the luxury of waiting until these files close before finding new work. The really bad news is that the clock is ticking, and every moment spent not trying to find new work is a lost opportunity.

When you were in that wonderful "hotel for lawyers," work magically appeared under your door every night (much like the chocolate mint that the maid leaves on the pillow). Now you have to compete to earn it, and if you wait until you finish Project X, you will then have to live through a period of time where no money is coming in at all while you beat the bushes looking for new work. If this sounds pretty bleak, it is—and it gets even worse. So . . . where do you start?

Management consultants have faced this dilemma for years: "I'm too busy doing the work to be out there mining for new work." And the higher the price and value of the service, the longer the selling cycle takes and the greater the need for developing a sales-sorting mechanism to keep generating opportunities and moving them through the pipeline. Most solo practitioners have work flow charts that are filled with peaks and valleys. In doing the work, there are many fourteen-or-more-hour days; and then the valleys occur when the work is done, and it is time to find new work.

This chapter proposes that the solo practitioner focus his marketing energies on creating an ongoing, long-term, and disciplined system of cultivating clients and serving the "99 percent."

§ 6.01 Cultivate Clients

The most important step is getting contacts and building contact lists on your smartphone, computer, etc. Without contacts, you remain extremely talented—but out of sight and out of mind. Statistics have revealed that when in a crisis, people will call the last person with whom they have made contact during the previous ninety-six hours who has the ability to solve the problem. How many times have you encountered a business associate or client who told you of a case another lawyer was handling that was an absolutely perfect match for your skill set and then said, "You know, Dave, I was so involved in the moment that I forgot and didn't think of you"? Chances are that the other lawyer was in contact with that person within those ninety-six hours.

Every contact with another human being could lead to future business. If the key in real estate is location, location, location, then the key to business development and marketing is meet a lot of people, meet a lot of people, meet a lot of people. And once you meet them, you must find a way to creatively stay in touch with them.

You are now on your own and know that the profession has long viewed marketing and selling as slightly less than a necessary evil, but you must be able to build a comprehensive and extensive network to feed this pipeline. First, though, you must get clear in your own mind that doing these activities is not only highly professional but necessary for your survival.

§ 6.01.1 Step One: Make Yourself Visible

Relationship development is a marathon, not a sprint, and it starts with getting into the public eye. There are many ways to do this that involve little, if any, expense. Some examples include writing articles, attending bar association functions, checking the local bar referral services for targeted prospect engagements, and establishing a presence on the Internet.

In addition, there are two marketing strategies that work particularly well for solo and small-firm lawyers: "Five Calls" and "Three Feet."

The Five Calls strategy is used by many successful lawyers. At the beginning of each week, go to your contact list and mark the names of five individuals with whom you have not had contact in a while. You must then commit yourself to calling or otherwise contacting one person each day for the entire week. By increasing your number of contacts, you increase the chance of being on their radar screen when trouble strikes. Some lawyers immediately react and say that they could make five times that number of calls, but the fact is that they will not. Five calls a week where you are simply making contact will be difficult enough.

Once on the phone, the purpose of the call is to simply touch base, not to sell. Remember: Rule 7.3 of the ABA *Model Rules of Professional Conduct* prohibits "in-person, live telephone or real-time electronic contact [to] solicit professional employment from a prospective client" when the solicitation involves "coercion, duress or harassment" or when "a significant motive . . . is the lawyer's pecuniary gain." You can update the contact on what you have been doing since your situation changed. However, the real purpose of the call is to find out what is happening in the contact's business life. This simple idea means that 250 calls a year are being purposefully made by hundreds of lawyers. The millions of dollars in fees that this simple idea generates continues to astound many lawyers.

(Note: The Five Calls Rule used to be called the *Five Cards Rule* back in the day when a fat Rolodex was the symbol of success. The point is that regardless of the technology that is or will be used in the future for keeping track of contacts, this rule can be adapted with the same end result.)

The other strategy is the Three Feet Rule, which, simply stated, is that if you come within three feet of someone, take it upon yourself to engage that person in conversation and find out what he does for a living. In that talk, you will also mention what you do for a living, and you will hopefully exchange business cards and continue to converse using the Five Calls Rule.

Be prepared with an "elevator pitch," small brochure, and business cards at all times.

§ 6.01.2 Step Two: Find Opportunity and Push It into the Pipeline

Opportunity knocks everywhere. It might be a simple conversation in which a prospective client says, "Call me." Or you might be invited to submit a proposal. Or you might get a phone call inviting you to come by and "talk." Regardless, your pulse should quicken because these situations represent an opportunity for you to get closer to new work.

So, you grab your briefcase and head on over to the client. One question: Have you prepared yourself fully for this meeting, or are you planning on "winging it" once you get there?

Would you go into trial without preparing? Of course not. You would write detailed trial outlines, prepare witnesses, and spend your time anticipating and defending opposing counsel's strategy. So, why would you not in this case—where thousands of dollars in potential fees are hanging in the balance—gather some field intelligence data on this company, review analyst reports on the health of the organization, and prepare to ask specific questions of the client?

Asking questions does not mean that this is an interrogation or a cross-examination. The purpose of these meetings is to gather information about the issues affecting the client. For many years, lawyers and other professionals have practiced a selling methodology referred to as "show up, throw up": they want to ensure that the client knows everything about the firm, so they throw everything ever done up against the wall of the client's office to see what will stick. What we know now is that the client has invited you because he thinks that you can do the work, so your credentials have been preapproved. The purpose of the meeting, therefore, is to find out what is on the prospective client's mind. And since a great deal of the client's decision in choosing a lawyer has to do with your personal interaction with the client, establishing a relationship of rapport and trust and demonstrating an ability to listen to the client's concerns are key.

While I do not advocate a list of trial memo questions, spending a few moments before visiting the client to develop a list of a few key questions is very beneficial. There is no other area in your business life where you would not prepare before calling on the client, yet this area repeatedly suffers.

§ 6.01.3 Step Three: Bring That Opportunity to Closure

Notice that the above subhead does not say "Closing the Sale." We have been instructed in too many courses to "ask for the order." That simply does not work in professional selling situations, especially when it is a solution you are selling. The client will decide on his own whom he wants to engage as a lawyer, and your job is to give him all of the information needed to make a decision. When you use consultative skills, clients are allowed to come to the conclusions themselves, and they usually make a decision in that manner. Although you must sell work to eat, you are not a salesperson; and an attempt to pass yourself off using the trial close, preclose, close-close, or any other technique will come across as just that—a technique.

When we say *closure* here, it is in direct relation to determining what the next step in the process is and how long a process it will be. This is unique to professional services. You cannot force a decision into closure. This is something that will occur only when the client is ready to make a decision. Your role is to help guide the client along that path to closure.

Many times you are asked to participate in a so-called beauty contest, where your skills are matched against those of several other lawyers, and many times one "contestant" is leaving just as you arrive. Or you have an opportunity to build a relationship with a client and the result is not immediate work for you, but the client says to you, "Keep in touch." How many times does your ego get in the way and say, "Well, to heck with him; he didn't see my obvious talent and hire me—it's time to move on"?

Research has shown that those lawyers who recognize, even in the face of the original "defeat," that a relationship is being built here and that it takes time to develop trust and rapport end up with tremendous future opportunities for work. Trust is the basis of any interpersonal relationship. As a business owner, why would I entrust the legal well-being or the future of my company's welfare to someone I do not know? You should not expect to walk out of the door every time with an assignment; it does not always work that way.

Finding a creative way to stay in touch is the ultimate challenge. However, by following the Five Calls Rule, speaking with the prospect three to four times a year, sending him pertinent articles and information, writing personal notes, and finding other creative ways to communicate, you are never completely out of sight or mind; and when the right opportunity arises, you will be called.

Remember that you must stop treating business development as a sprint race when it is often a marathon.

§ 6.01.4 Step Four: Follow Up, Follow Up, Follow Up

When the potential client does call with an issue, how high a priority do you make it? Do you return all calls within three hours? Eight hours? Twenty-four hours? What is the right level of follow-up, and how important is it? Follow-up is critical and key to the survival of any aspect of your business development effort. The question is, What is the best way to do this?

In terms of following up on issues, we are learning that the client's level of patience and service expectations are moving in directions that make lawyers uncomfortable. A lawyer once remarked, "I hate technology. It used to be easy to draft a document and place it in overnight mail and move on to another issue. Now, with fax, e-mail, cellular phones, and other tools, the client demands that I revise four and five times in a single day. I am worried about the quality of my legal work under those circumstances." The profession has been dragged into the twenty-first century—kicking and screaming.

In terms of following up with regard to general communication, although many people use e-mail and the telephone, there is still nothing as strong today as that handwritten note of thanks and appreciation for the client's time. Even more creative executives include something that is meaningful to the client. If you know that a client loves tennis and you notice that *Tennis* magazine has just published a list of the fifty top tennis resorts worldwide, why not tear the article out and send it to the client? It shows you were listening, and that skill is extremely important to clients. Do not do anything that seems uncomfortable or disingenuous to you. But do something to stay in touch in a creative way.

§ 6.01.5 Step Five: Discipline Yourself

We are essentially lazy when it comes to marketing. We are so busy in our lives and in our jobs that we tend to avoid anything "outside the box" (like marketing) that requires a different and newer skill set. Successful professionals, however, develop a system of calls, checks, and balances that they use daily to achieve their objectives. If Five Calls does not work for you, find a system that does and consistently apply it. The absolute hardest part of the process is looking for work, making phone calls, and following up on leads, especially when you are working fourteen hours a day. You cannot do this unless you tell yourself when you get up in the morning that you are going to make those calls—and that those calls are the most important task today, not the task to do when everything else on the list has been completed.

§ 6.02 Serve the 99 Percent

The legal profession has reached a point where upheaval is the new normal. Certainly, large law firms are changing in response to recession, technology, and client demands; those firms that don't change quickly enough, like Dewey & LeBoeuf, are doomed to swift failure.

Some wonder if the solo and small-firm practitioner will survive this kind of turmoil. The answer is that although big law firms serve the "1 percent" of the corporate world, there is enormous potential for solos and small firms to thrive by serving the "99 percent" of our society. These firms focus on small to midsize businesses and individuals, and the volume and fundamental nature of their legal matters and issues will continue as long as people need lawyers. There will be substantial work available for those smaller firms that are attentive enough to their clients and flexible enough in their business processes to be competitive.

§ 6.02.1 Guarantee Satisfaction

No lawyer can ethically guarantee a result, but an effective marketing technique for small-firm lawyers is to guarantee exceptional effort—which does not violate Rule 7.1 of the ABA *Model Rules of Professional Conduct*

("Communications Concerning a Lawyer's Services") because it deals with factors within the lawyer's own control. Such a guarantee presented when discussing an engagement, especially when combined with a budget, reduces clients' feelings of risk so that they feel comfortable moving ahead.

There are firms that affirmatively embrace such a "satisfaction guaranteed" approach. Chicago's Ungaretti & Harris has for well over a decade offered clients this assurance: "We cannot guarantee outcomes; we do guarantee your satisfaction with our service. If we do not perform to your satisfaction, inform us promptly. We will resolve the issue to your satisfaction, even if it means reducing your legal fees." Again, there is no ethical problem with guaranteeing that the firm will make every effort to satisfy clients—and then standing behind and in front of that effort.

§ 6.02.2 Establish Alliances

A sophisticated, effective marketing strategy is an ongoing alliance with another small firm, with customized service packages and billing arrangements.

An excellent example is how two small Chicago-area firms (nine-lawyer Varga Berger Ledsky Hayes & Casey and ten-lawyer Collins Law Firm P.C.) have for more than a decade partnered to represent plaintiffs in environmental pollution cases. Four key lawyers, two from each firm, have secured millions of dollars in monetary settlements and remediation actions for their clients. These lawyers call themselves a team, publicizing their capabilities together on their own website, www.pollutionlawwatch.com.

Beyond such a focused alliance, firms can maintain joint retainer arrangements with allied lawyers for help if a need outside the normal field of expertise arises.

§ 6.02.3 Embrace Technology

In the 99 percent world of today, a firm's competition is not just the other law firms in the Yellow Pages. Competition also includes "onshore" legal staffing companies that hire lawyers in lower-cost areas in the United States and pay them less compensation for repetitive work, which is provided through a virtual online relationship. There are also the many do-it-yourself websites purporting to offer advice, research, and forms in such areas as family law, probate, real estate closings, and even patent filing. Against this kind of competition, the successful firm must market by adopting technology to reduce costs and then passing those savings on to the client.

A detailed consideration of technology's application to the production function shows what the successful smaller firm of the future must do. Clients continue to demand cost efficiencies, but these can no longer be had by cutting overhead—whether that means people or infrastructure. After years of recession, there is not that much left to cut. The real need is not cost cutting but rather efficiency. And that means using technology as a competitive tool.

This is a trend well advanced in litigation. Even many smaller firms use case-management software, and now new e-discovery software can analyze documents required for litigation discovery in a fraction of the time for a fraction of the cost when compared to using lawyers for the task. Profitability for the firm comes from swiftly analyzing the millions of equivalent paper pages that electronic documents represent.

This is the model for the future production function. It reduces overall legal costs, not the lawyer's hourly rate. Some or all of this cost reduction can be given to clients as savings. The law firm that does so will be able to work out billing alternatives that make such savings profitable as it eliminates inefficiencies, duplications, and unnecessary services. The leverage from technology is the small firm's production advantage.

§ 6.03 Action Plan

- Make five calls per week.
- Maximize opportunities.
- Bring opportunities to closure.
- Follow up, follow up, follow up.
- Discipline yourself.
- Distinguish your services from those of the big firms serving the 1 percent.

CHAPTER 7

Using the Internet to Market Your Legal Services

. . . God hath made man upright: but they have sought out many inventions.

—Ecclesiastes 7:29

What good is a newborn baby?

—Benjamin Franklin (when asked what good was served by the first balloon ascension)

A tool is but the extension of a man's hand and a machine is but a complex tool. And he that invents a machine augments the power of a man and the well-being of mankind.

—Henry Ward Beecher

Chapter Checklist

- o Benefits of Internet Marketing
- o The Law Firm Website
- o Designing and Maintaining the Firm's Website
- o Electronic Mailing Lists
- o LISTSERVs and Other Discussion Groups
- o Internet Communities
- o Action Plan

Many law firms have created an Internet presence for themselves by making information available about their lawyers and practice specialties on a public website. The general idea is that individuals who are in need of a lawyer can merely search for *law firm, lawyer, attorney,* or some specific practice area on an Internet search engine, and pull up the firm's website. Many lawyers and law firms that created websites for this purpose have come to realize that their initial expectations of instantaneous marketing success may have been misplaced. Other lawyers and law firms have had excellent results from their Internet marketing efforts.

The truth is that the Internet is the Internet—nothing more and nothing less. It is not a yellow brick road that instantly leads to overnight client-development success stories or hordes of clients that will beat down the door. In order to succeed on the Internet, a lawyer must renounce the "If you build it, they will come" mentality. It may have worked for Kevin Costner and his baseball field, but it certainly does not work for lawyers and their websites. However, despite the Internet's lack of magical powers, lawyers can successfully use the Internet to develop a more formidable reputation, attract new clients, and make their current clients happier. The key to remember is that the Internet is only a different medium for communication—although a uniquely powerful one.

Through the Internet, lawyers are able to promote their services to prospective clients who were not previously within their reach. Lawyers can also utilize the Internet to enhance their delivery of legal services to existing clients through private websites. Each lawyer's success or failure with Internet marketing depends upon his understanding, strategy, and execution in mastering the tools available in this new world of virtual communication. Many lawyers' long-term professional success may depend upon how well they adapt to the Internet as a prevalent medium for business communications.

§ 7.01 Benefits of Internet Marketing

Although marketing principles remain the same for marketing activities performed through the Internet, the Internet offers lawyers tools that have never before been available. The Internet permits you to promote your legal services to clients located in areas that previously may have been out of your geographic reach. You can utilize the Internet to distribute information much more efficiently to larger groups of clients than ever before. Furthermore, the results of Internet marketing activities are often much easier to measure than results obtained from other forums. For example, it is often difficult to count the number of new clients that a lawyer obtains from speaking at a local conference. Web pages, however, can utilize software to measure precisely how many hits a website is generating. Additionally, these hits to a firm's website can be categorized and subcategorized to include much useful information. Check out Google Analytics at www.google.com/analytics for such tools. *Google for Lawyers* by Carole A. Levitt and Mark E. Rosch is also a useful resource.

Marketing success over the Internet requires a lawyer to have a comprehensive and well-thought-out plan that is aimed at addressing the needs of his particular target market or markets. The Internet has become an essential tool that has changed the way lawyers practice law. Innovative lawyers who are willing to embrace some of these changes can differentiate themselves from their competitors. Clients always appreciate superior service, and they will reward lawyers who find better ways to meet their legal needs.

Before making the decision to incorporate the Internet into your marketing plan, you should have a practical understanding of all of the marketing tools available via the Internet. If these tools are used strategically, you will bolster your reputation as well as your law practice.

§ 7.02 The Law Firm Website

The World Wide Web has certainly become the most popular Internet tool for marketing purposes. Thousands of law firms have created websites and have placed them on the web for public view.

The success of these websites varies greatly. Many firms have created a website without any underlying purpose or strategy. However, a website is a marketing tool that should be created to achieve certain predefined marketing objectives, although the specific objectives may vary from firm to firm. Successful websites come in all different colors, sizes, organizational schemes, and levels of sophistication. Above all, though, the site must be designed to adequately perform the specific functions that it was intended to perform. This is a principle that cannot be altered by larger investments of money, flashy graphics, or all the promotion in the world.

When implemented properly, websites offer a great place to publish information that prospective and current clients can access through the web. Depending upon a law firm's particular marketing strategy, the information placed on a site will vary. The more useful the information contained on the website is to the law firm's targeted groups of clients, the more effective the site will be in attracting new clients.

As with all marketing plans, it may take time before a site generates the amount of traffic that the firm desires. If the firm plans well and continually makes adjustments to its content and presentation, it will find the right combination that will enable the firm to achieve its marketing goals. The key is to remain patient, keep trying new ideas, and thoroughly integrate the firm's web marketing activities into the overall marketing plan.

Descriptions of the three primary types of websites follow.

§ 7.02.1 Brochureware Websites

Brochureware websites are the most basic websites available, and most law firms' websites are likely to fall under this category. These websites are generally used as an alternative medium for communicating basic promotional information about the firm and often are merely online versions of glossy pamphlets or brochures that firms would typically hand out to new or prospective clients. The primary purpose of this kind of site is to educate new or prospective clients about the firm's lawyers, services, and philosophy. It is important that these sites communicate the firm and its offerings in a manner that is consistent with the needs of the particular markets that the firm is targeting. Typically, these sites contain the following information:

- *Firm history.* Firms with a long or unique history should consider placing this information on their websites, particularly if the firm has made an impact or been very active in the local community. Not all firms have been around for a long period of time, and this information can distinguish a firm from its competitors.
- *Firm practice areas and specialization.* All law firm websites should contain information relating to the particular legal skills of lawyers within the firm.
- *Fees for services.* Though done rarely, you may want to discuss the issue of fees for specific services as well as any alternative billing arrangements that may be available. Also, this would be the time and place to discuss client satisfaction issues and guarantee of satisfaction with the process and lawyer-client interactions, if the firm offers such a guarantee.
- *Lawyer biographies and profiles.* Most law firms provide specific information and pictures of each lawyer. This information often describes the lawyers' educational background, experience, legal expertise, jurisdictions in which the firm is authorized to practice, and other information generally contained on a résumé. It is also generally recommended that an e-mail link be placed by each lawyer so that clients can contact lawyers conveniently and quickly.
- *Geographic location of offices and directions.* Firms with multiple offices often provide information relating to the geographic location of each of the firm's offices as well as an address and a link to a site such as http://maps.yahoo.com/py/maps.py that will provide the client with a map and customized directions to the firm's office location. You should also indicate whether the firm services clients locally, nationally, and/or internationally.
- *List of representative clients.* Many firms list their largest clients on their website and may even place links to the clients' websites. This client list is used to establish the credibility of the firm. However, the firm should obtain clients' approval before placing their name and uniform resource locator (URL) on the firm's website. There also is, among some, the concern that using clients' names is a violation of the rule requiring confidentiality. In addition, it could be argued that while this may be a good tactic for selling some professional services, it may not be good for lawyers; after all, we are not selling soap or facelifts. Consult your state's rules of professional conduct and your own feelings of propriety before using testimonials.
- *Links to other useful sites.* Often, a law firm will want to place links within its site to direct its clients and prospective clients to sites that

contain useful information. This is a beneficial practice, but it is imperative that the firm regularly check the links on its site to ensure that they remain active. A site that has inactive links presents a poor image to visitors whose searches are interrupted by outdated links.

- *"What's new" section.* The "what's new" section of the website offers a firm the opportunity to communicate items of interest to potential and existing clients, such as the addition of a new lawyer to the firm, a major legal success that the firm recently achieved, recent awards, new services offered to clients, etc. At some point, new information becomes old information, though, and a law firm must make sure that this page remains current.
- *Differentiating information about the firm.* Some firms also place information on the firm website informing potential clients of special services or characteristics that distinguish it from the multitude of other firms offering the same practice specialties. Types of information that fall under this category include technological innovations utilized by the firm, firm community service or pro bono activities, and particular accomplishments of the firm or lawyers within the firm.

Brochureware websites have received a lot of negative press in the past few years, caused in part by unrealized marketing expectations. The creators of this category of website should not expect these sites to attract multitudes of anonymous web surfers or to generate new clients of their own accord. There are thousands of law firm websites available on the Internet, and most web surfers will not stop to read a law firm's web brochure unless they have some special reason for doing so.

Potential clients on the Internet browse websites for two reasons. First, they search sites for valuable information that may provide insight into a legal situation that they are facing. Web surfers often look for explanatory information prior to looking for a lawyer, and sites that do not offer useful information regarding legal issues do not generally attract a lot of traffic. The second reason that web surfers might seek out a website is if another person directed them to the site, such as a lawyer within the firm or a referring client. Since brochureware websites do not contain much information beyond the firm's practice information, they can generally be successful only if the law firm promotes the website as part of its traditional marketing campaign. For example, all business cards and other materials should contain a law firm's website information. When a lawyer meets a prospective client, he should think about referring that person to the firm's website instead of handing out a glossy brochure. Existing clients, if aware of the website, may also refer their friends and colleagues to the site when providing "word of mouth" referrals. When used in this manner, brochureware websites can be a very useful source of supporting material for firm marketing efforts. You would never expect a glossy brochure to generate new client leads; neither should you expect your brochureware website to generate new client leads. You and your referring clients will be the ones who generate the traffic to the website by promoting and directing prospective clients to the site as a means of learning more about the firm's services. In a sense, a brochureware website requires you to push new client prospects to the website.

§ 7.02.2 Information-Hub Websites

Information-hub websites generally have all of the information contained in brochureware sites as well as other information that is useful to clients. Eventually, if the site contains the right kind of information, it will attract web surfers looking for the information contained on the site; and it may become a favorite resource for clients, who will periodically return to the site for new information.

Information-hub websites should be specifically designed to attract particular groups of prospective clients to the website by providing high-quality information that is useful to those individuals. As you can see, this type of site utilizes a much different strategy than the brochureware website. It is designed to pull or draw in the desired individuals by knowing what information is important to them and providing it free of charge. These individuals find the site by searching for the information on an Internet search engine such as Google or Yahoo! and then browsing through the listed hits. If the law firm's site contains useful information, the web surfer will browse through the site and hopefully bookmark it for future reference. Once the site is bookmarked, the law firm has achieved a major online success. However, this success will be short-lived if the firm does not regularly provide new information to keep these interested individuals coming back on a regular basis.

To illustrate how information-hub websites are perceived by existing and potential clients, think of the site as an alternative medium for communicating information that is often contained in legal newsletters, bulletins, and live presentations. Lawyers who successfully use these vehicles to market their legal services should consider using this type of website because it offers similar benefits: if a lawyer effectively provides information to people who find the information useful, they will often seek out his services when they are in need of legal counsel. Remember, though, that just as a lawyer must continually produce new newsletters or provide new information in presentations, he must be committed to providing new substantive content for the website, though this information may be the same as that provided in lectures or newsletters.

Blogging, discussed in chapter 8, is typical of this type of site. This is a significant tool for communicating not only your expertise to potential clients but also both changes in the law and your perspectives to existing clients. This is also a subtle tool that forces you to remain current.

The time and resources required to keep such a site current and useful to prospective clients can be significant. But firms that make this commitment and provide the right combination of information on the site can experience excellent results over time as the site gains popularity and begins to pull in more traffic.

Another advantage of using websites is the ability, as previously mentioned, to use software to track the number of hits that the website or even a page within the website receives over selected periods of time. This tracking software can serve as a useful marketing tool to begin to understand which information creates the greatest impact on the firm's respective targeted markets. For example, if an article is placed on the site and the number of people viewing that article doubles or triples the normal traffic, you may want to provide more information on that particular topic because of its apparent popularity with your targeted audience. This kind of feedback can be very useful if analyzed regularly. You can react quickly to your target markets by customizing the information on the website to meet clients' information needs.

As with all marketing efforts, the primary goal of information-hub websites is to attract new clients. You must view this site as a client-development process and have faith that your efforts will pay off in the long run. In fact, the timing of this process is similar to the timing of results obtained by writing newsletters or speaking in seminars. Potential clients often do not contact a lawyer immediately after seeing him speak in a seminar. Rather, they often make contact weeks, months, or even years later—when they have a specific need for your expertise. The more you publish useful information that is seen by potential clients, the greater your name recognition will be and the more likely that it will be your name that potential clients will remember when they need a lawyer.

§ 7.02.3 Websites for Conducting Private Communication

The previous two categories of websites are used primarily as promotional or "client-getting" tools. This third type of site is different because it is not used to communicate promotional information to potential clients. Rather, websites falling under this third category are used as a means of enhancing the delivery of legal services to existing clients. Rather than containing promotional material that is available to the general public, private websites or extranets are used as virtual offices in which law firms are able to securely and privately make a client's legal information available to him. For example, a client would be able to obtain documents, briefs, discovery material, and other important case-related information by pointing his web browser to this secure site and performing the authentication requirements. Additionally, these extranet sites are often capable of facilitating dialogue and other communication between the lawyer and the client, which can dramatically reduce the need to play phone tag in order to exchange information or coordinate last-minute changes on legal documents. Extranets can save law firms and clients thousands of dollars by reducing their need for overnight delivery, faxing, mail, and courier services.

Extranets are an important marketing tool because they offer you the ability to differentiate yourself from competitors by providing a value-added service. Extranets are a standard communication tool for exchanging confidential information with clients. Firms that take proactive steps to utilize these private websites can develop a reputation for innovative and leading-edge client service. These extranets can be obtained from third-party developers who have created sophisticated solutions that are both inexpensive and tailored to meet a law firm's communication needs. Another benefit of these solutions is that they can be implemented and fully functional in a very short period of time.

§ 7.03 Designing and Maintaining the Firm's Website

Much literature has been written about what features every good website should include. While there are some common principles to follow, much of what goes into a site should depend upon the particular marketing strategy of the firm creating the site. After all, this website will exclusively represent the firm's image to all who come to its virtual doorstep. If a firm makes use of the following guidelines, it should be able to successfully create a website that effectively serves its purposes.

§ 7.03.1 Step One: Determine the Marketing Purpose of the Website

The first step in designing a website is to determine what function and purpose the firm wants the website to perform. For some firms, it may make sense to begin by constructing a simple brochureware website to serve as an online brochure. Later, the firm can upgrade to an information-hub website when lawyers within the firm are ready to make the commitment to regularly publish new information on the site. There is no right or wrong approach, but a firm should understand that a brochureware website is not likely to have as much marketing impact as an information-hub website. Likewise, the firm must educate its lawyers on how to properly utilize the site to achieve its intended purposes.

§ 7.03.2 Step Two: Design the Layout and Content

After determining which type of website the law firm wants to develop, the firm should engage the services of a professional web developer or assign this task to a qualified developer in-house. WordPress currently is a low-end way to create and modify a website with limited development skills. However, I still prefer engaging the services of a web developer, who should possess

- HTML programming and page layout skills,
- expertise in writing small animation programs (called Java applets) or in scripting languages that enable the page to capture information about visitors and store it in a database, and
- graphics-development abilities.

If the web developer is not proficient in all of these areas, he must be able to bring the right people to the project when these skills become necessary.

The web developer can provide a firm with some layout ideas, but the individual (or group) within the firm who is responsible for the website should also look at other websites to develop his own ideas and preferences.

While a firm's subjective preferences with respect to a website are important, there are several nonnegotiable principles of web development that are critical for a successful site. The most important principles include the following:

- *Establish your own domain name, such as lawfirm.com.* Having your own domain name establishes credibility and makes it easier for prospective clients to remember your web address and e-mail addresses. To find out whether your preferred domain name is available, go to www.networksolutions.com or www.godaddy.com to perform a search.
- *Do not include too many pictures, graphics, and animations.* Although these items are necessary to some degree to make the site look professional and catchy, too many graphics can make a website very slow to upload. The website's visitors are there primarily to obtain specific information, not to look at pictures and graphics. Therefore, use nonessential graphics and pictures sparingly. Your visitors will not wait around if your web page takes too long to load.
- *Create a logical and consistent structure to the site so that it is easy to move from section to section.* A common toolbar at the left or top of the page that contains all of the major links to the different sections in the site is helpful because it permits the visitor to jump immediately to unrelated sections of the website. If the website is not organized in a logical fashion, visitors can become confused and will not take the time to find the information. Use your structure to make it easy to obtain information on the site.
- *All firms are equal in the virtual world.* The website visitor cannot tell the difference between firms with lots of resources and firms with few resources. The website is the only means that visitors have to judge the competence of a firm. For this reason, it is essential that each law firm internally develop the content for the firm's website. Lawyers within the firm understand the firm's philosophy and services best and will promote themselves better than an outside professional. The content of the website will help determine whether the visitor feels comfortable hiring the firm to handle his legal needs. If the site does not adequately describe the firm's competence, culture, and service philosophy, the website visitor may not find the firm interesting enough to contact in person.

§ 7.03.3 Step Three: Make the Website Available to the Masses

Once you have built a site, there are only two ways in which individuals can find your site on the World Wide Web.

The first method requires firm personnel and others to promote the site by providing interested parties and potential clients with the precise URL of the website. One way to further this strategy is by placing the website's URL on all business cards, letterhead, and other promotional material that is sent to clients and prospective clients. In this manner, interested parties can type the URL into their web browser, which will then load the web page for viewing.

The second way that interested parties can find a firm's website is to search for the site through an Internet search engine. It is important that a firm think about the strategy involved in making its website retrievable by a search engine. First, a firm will want to register its website with all of the popular search engines. This registration ensures that these search engines will include the firm in its database of information, making the website available to individuals who use the search engine to find information contained on the site. Second, the firm should carefully consider what key words and terms it wants to associate with the website so that web surfers searching for those terms will find the firm's website. Some search engines will look through the text of a website to find key words that are used frequently and will rank the firm's website according to the number of times the terms are used in the site. Other search engines analyze a site according to meta tags, or hidden information that is programmed into the web page but is not viewed by the browser. In this case, it is important that the web developer include these key terms in the hidden code programmed within the firm's site. For search engine optimization purposes, it could also be useful to check out how competitors' websites are faring; see www.compete.com for tools to help you conduct this type of analysis. Most sites will rank high when the site grows organically by adding new content regularly and frequently. This is an important consideration in developing your marketing strategy.

§ 7.03.4 Step Four: Maintain the Website

Website maintenance is just as important as the initial development and creation of the site. Many law firms make the mistake of treating the website as a static document and, once published, believe that their work is complete. Firms need to maintain and update their websites regularly, even if only to update their lawyer biographies. Sites that contain obsolete information reflect poorly upon a law firm because visitors to the site base their perception of the firm on the quality of the site that they are visiting.

Maintaining a website can be troublesome if the law firm has to hire an outside webmaster to make all of the changes to the site. Not only is it expensive over time, but often outside webmasters are slow to respond to the firm's requests or fail to make the changes at all. An answer to this dilemma is to train at least one person in the firm to act as the webmaster who makes the updates to the site. Currently, most sites require the use of FTP (file transfer protocol) to make changes to the site. FTP is not a terribly difficult Internet communication protocol, but it is not a tool with which most people are familiar, and the firm must pay for a special FTP account with the firm's Internet service provider as well as invest time and training for someone to become familiar with the process.

Another alternative to hiring a webmaster allows nontechnical people to easily add or change site content without knowing the technological details required by HTTP (hypertext transfer protocol) and FTP. Individual lawyers or other personnel having responsibility for the content in various parts of the site can manage their area of responsibility by literally dragging files to the website through their browser. A lawyer who publishes a weekly newsletter on the website could easily add the document to the site directly from his local computer or network drive. This solution may be appropriate for lawyers who want to create an information-hub site but do not want to expend the resources required to hire a webmaster. Even more important, by eliminating the prior barriers to web content management, a firm can more easily encourage the lawyers within a firm to create a dynamic hub of information in which new content can literally be added on a daily basis by all lawyers wanting to do so.

§ 7.04 Electronic Mailing Lists

Electronic mailing lists are group e-mails that contain useful information presented in a newsletter or bulletin format. As with web pages, lawyers can target any specific group of individuals with these mailing lists. However, it is essential that the firm understand precisely which niche groups of clients it is targeting with its mailing lists and narrowly focus the type of information to meet the specific needs of the targeted groups.

Recipients of mailing lists generally want this information to be concise. They want the mailing list to keep them abreast of new developments in the market and provide them with information about forthcoming legal issues. The law firm gains from its efforts because recipients of the mailing list will presumably call the firm if it faces any related legal issues. Examples of information that can successfully be contained in electronic mailing lists are as follows:

- Weekly mailings containing the jurisdiction's supreme court case decisions
- Monthly mailings containing the latest developments in a certain technical area of law, such as employment law, workers' compensation, securities law, etc.
- Practical solutions to common legal dilemmas
- Administrative law decisions in areas such as labor law, environmental regulation, etc.

The information contained within these mailing lists is similar to or the same as information that a firm could choose to place on its website. In fact, it is often wise to offer a web-page version of this information as well as the mailing list service. Some individuals prefer to have certain information pushed to them through e-mail rather than browsing for it, though. Electronic mailing lists are generally best utilized in conjunction with the firm's site because a law firm should never send the electronic mail to any individuals who did not specifically request the information. This type of unsolicited mailing constitutes "spamming" in the virtual world and is harshly criticized. The firm's site should contain a form that allows interested people to register for the service by providing their name and e-mail address.

Electronic mailing lists do not offer a law firm the opportunity to interact directly with its targeted clients, but they do give the firm a chance to offer a valuable service to these prospective clients with little out-of-pocket expenditures. Because the information is sent to the recipients electronically, the firm does not have to pay for the costs of physically printing the material or buying postage to mail it to the desired people. The only expenses in providing this type of service are initially setting up the website to handle the registration process and the lawyers' time to compile the information. The marketing results from this service can be very profitable for firms that understand their targeted clients' information needs. These clients are often appreciative of the service and tend to be more loyal to the firm.

§ 7.05 LISTSERVs and Other Discussion Groups

LISTSERVs and other discussion groups, such as LinkedIn, are Internet tools through which a lawyer can interact with other niche groups of lawyers and/or targeted groups of prospective clients. There are literally thousands of discussion groups already established on the Internet. Each of these forums is generally limited to communication relating to one particular topic or subject. For example, there are discussion groups dedicated to discussing technology in the practice of law, intellectual property law, criminal law, constitutional issues, crime, securities law, patents, trademarks, and virtually any other topic that an individual might want to talk about. People interested in a particular topic will join the LISTSERV or discussion group that deals with that particular area of interest. In this way, lawyers know that other people corresponding within that particular forum are likely to belong to the lawyer's target market.

The difference between a LISTSERV and other discussion groups is not in function but in the manner of delivery. Both of these tools permit members to post inquiries or comments in a forum where they can be viewed by other members. The communication between members is not in real time, but members read and respond to the comments when it is convenient. LISTSERVs are typically administered through e-mail; each member's communication is e-mailed to all of the respective members. Discussion groups are generally web based, meaning that a member can access the communications by going to a certain web page or utilizing the discussion function in his browser.

These discussion groups offer you the ability to interact directly with your target markets because group members can read posted comments and inquiries. Additionally, you may selectively respond to particular inquiries posted by other members. Through these interactions, you are able to market your legal expertise to other members of the group. You not only have the ability to interact directly with prospective clients but also can interact with other lawyers to create referral relationships. Those members who are very active in these forums create strong name recognition and respect when their contributions are valuable to the group. Of course, it is imperative that you avoid providing specific legal advice within these forums and use discretion when communicating legal principles to the other members.

When communicating in these forums, you should use the following guidelines:

- *Refrain from actively contributing to discussions for a few weeks after you join.* This inactive participation will provide you an opportunity to understand the culture and protocol of the group. Making political mistakes early on, even if innocent, can quickly earn you a bad reputation.
- *Always use a professional and friendly tone even when the discussion becomes heated.* If another member directs derogatory remarks in your direction, refrain from responding. However, if you feel as though you need to respond in order to protect your reputation, consider your remarks carefully. An angry outburst may tarnish others' perception of you even if your comments are justified. Another point of caution: Even if you direct a message to another member privately, you have no assurances that he will not forward your message to the group. So use discretion in all of your communications.
- *Keep your comments concise and to the point.* Other members may become annoyed if your contributions are too lengthy.
- *Only contribute if you have something meaningful to add.* Many discussion groups generate a large number of messages, and incidental comments can become burdensome.
- *Do not be aggressive when marketing your services.* The motivation behind your interactions should be to provide assistance to the group. However, if you feel as though someone might want more information, consider sending that individual a private message. In some cases, it may be better to speak with this person on the phone. It is best to merely make the offer and let the other person decide whether he would like to communicate outside the forum.

Finding the right group may require a little research. You can search www.listserv.org and LinkedIn for legal forums that may serve as a useful starting point. You can also run a search on one of the popular web search engines to find a discussion forum that addresses a more particular area of the law. For a search term, use *LISTSERV* to locate the list of discussion groups.

In some cases, it might make sense to create your own discussion group. Creating a discussion group requires an initial investment in the firm's site plus the costs of marketing the discussion group and handling the automatic registration of new members to the group. In addition, you must make some policy decisions about the role you will play in moderating the discussion. Moderating a discussion group can be time-consuming and difficult. On the other hand, some discussion groups are completely open and unmoderated;

however, in such groups, there is a risk of members posting messages that are off-topic and sometimes derogatory.

§ 7.06 Internet Communities

Internet communities, sometimes called chat rooms, are another great way for you to interact with targeted groups. Internet communities are different from discussion groups because they offer live interaction among members: members simply type messages into a browser in a manner that allows others to view comments and respond while online. A great feature of Internet communities is the ability of members to hold a conversation with literally hundreds of people at one time. These communities are generally structured like discussion groups in that they are organized by substantive topics, and members of each community limit their conversations to these topics.

The primary advantage of these communities is the ability to interact simultaneously with others, which often allows for more dynamic and spontaneous communications. However, this is also a disadvantage in that a member must be online at the same time as the other members. Expect to see Internet communities become more and more popular communication forums because of their unique ability to bring large numbers of geographically dispersed individuals together to collaborate on topics of common interest.

§ 7.07 Action Plan

- Determine the marketing purpose and strategy of the website.
- Design the layout and content.
- Make the website easily accessible.
- Maintain the website.
- Participate in the electronic community by joining an appropriate LISTSERV or other discussion group.

CHAPTER 8

Using Social Media to Market Yourself

Every seller praises his wares.

—Yiddish Proverb

Chapter Checklist

- o Marketing Benefits
- o Maximizing Social Media Use
- o Measuring Returns
- o Need for Personal Contact
- o Bar Association Regulation
- o Formulating Policies
- o Special Concerns About Blogging
- o Action Plan

Social media platforms—such as Facebook, Twitter, LinkedIn, and blogs—are marketing opportunities that should not be overlooked. Social media marketing efforts are typically designed to generate awareness and to get potential clients to initiate contact. A social media presence is more than advertising; it also educates the public about lawyers and what they do.

Clients can make an educated decision in determining whether a lawyer's skills match their needs. Once prospective clients start to gather the names of lawyers—either directly through Internet searches or via personal referrals—they can use social networking resources to check out the lawyers' credentials, experience, and testimonials. They can use social media to get feedback from current clients and even to get a personal feel about the lawyers based on what the lawyers reveal on these sites about family, hobbies, and opinions. Because the Internet is an equal opportunity medium, social media levels the marketing playing field among all firms, small and large.

It's no coincidence that in the American Bar Association's *2011 Legal Technology Survey Report*, which included a wide cross-section of ABA members, 42 percent of respondents said that their firms maintain an online presence in social media, compared to 17 percent in 2010—and 65 percent of individual respondents said that they personally have an online professional presence.

§ 8.01 Marketing Benefits

Law firms and lawyers that use social media experience positive marketing results. Website visitors translate into more people to convert to leads and new business. Blogging or active Twitter feeds in particular will likely increase the number of calls you receive from reporters, who are extensive searchers of blogs and other social media tools for sources. Blogging and other social media initiatives frequently lead to an increase in the number of speaking invitations that attorneys receive. This is important for one reason above all: visibility. The more that your target market sees your name and knows who you are, the more likely it is to call you.

The ultimate payoff from a social media presence is "marketing gravity." This means having enough material in varying social media that you become perceived as a thought leader in your field. Thus, in a scenario, for example, in which an individual is charged with a criminal offense, he would follow this thought process:

1. I need to get a lawyer.
2. I need to get a criminal defense lawyer.
3. I need to get the specific lawyer I have seen quoted in a column in the newspaper or in a blog on the Internet.

In this example, the client goes from knowing that he needs a lawyer to knowing that he needs the thought leader and top performer in the field, which happens to be you. Clearly, it is beneficial for you to use social media to specifically create a reputation as a leader in a given field.

Bear in mind that social media platforms are really a conduit that can lead to a variety of channels for becoming a thought leader. Establishing an online reputation can become your passport to writing articles for local and national publications in your field, writing a commercially published book (the gold standard of marketing success—that is, only someone important would appear in a commercial publisher's venue), speaking at conferences, creating teleseminars, creating a video, doing podcasts, or sending out an electronic newsletter. These are only a few of the available channels of communication. You must be all over because you never know who will see and be influenced by a certain channel and thus make the phone call to engage you.

Although creating new clientele is important, when pursuing social media, lawyers should never forget the necessity of continuing to bond with existing clients.

§ 8.02 Maximizing Social Media Use

It's essential for any lawyer who does have a social media presence to maintain it and integrate it with the full range of online marketing tools. There are fundamental rules for maximizing social media use to increase marketing benefits:

- Do constant follow-up by responding to inquiries and incorporating posted material into articles, speeches, client updates, and so on. Make an effort to further the marketing application of social media posts beyond the social media itself.
- Incorporate social media into your daily professional routine. Occasional posts are simply not effective. Establishing a regular posting routine keeps you engaged with prospects and ensures that your content is fresh.
- Create blog topics that demonstrate thought leadership.
- Don't give away the store on a blog or Facebook page. The wisest course is to suggest your firm's knowledge and capabilities rather than to fully display detailed information and allow your followers to make full use of it.
- Make your tools interact with each other—don't build silos. Ensure that LinkedIn, Facebook, and Twitter content is consistent and feeds into both blogs and your own biographical profile on the firm's website.
- Make your blog attractive enough that others will link to you organically because of the value that you provide to readers.
- Register your blog with blog directories and legal blog lists to increase your exposure to potential clients.

§ 8.03 Measuring Returns

Social media has rapidly become the new seductive tool for approaching clients—not just through websites and blogging but via all of the new and constantly expanding social networking innovations. However, such media are "broadcasting" in the purest sense of that now-quaint word. They may reach potential clients, but they also reach many more people who don't have the slightest interest in a given lawyer or law firm. And the firm is paying for all those disengaged listeners in terms of not only a few up-front costs but also the time that consistent online marketing requires. If you can't measure your marketing efforts by the specific number of contacts made, clients added, and billable time gained, you'll never know if your efforts have been worthwhile.

Social media results are, in fact, measurable in certain ways—for example, how many followers you have on Twitter, the number of "like" designations on your Facebook page, and the range of connections you've made on LinkedIn. These measurements, however, are merely starting points to show that you have opened contact with potential clients.

Lead generation and new business secured from those leads are the only valid measurements of whether social media marketing works. Attracting more followers and online connections is worthwhile only if they lead to in-person meetings. Online marketing has to produce new files and new revenue, or ultimately it's just a hobby, not a business-development tool.

In measuring benefits, cost has to be taken into account. For the most part, building an active presence on social networking sites does not require a large up-front investment. The main expenses include such tools as blog hosting services and standard technical assistance and maintenance offered by outside providers of blog support. However, there is also lawyer time involved, which makes measuring business gained even more important; this time investment is the number one return-on-investment metric for social media.

Making frequent tweets or Facebook or blog posts and providing responses to others' posts can definitely take time. Let's say it's just two hours per workweek. If we assume fifty workweeks per year for ease of calculation, two hours per week, and $200 per hour billable value for an attorney, the total cost is $20,000 of billable time. Thus, it's essential to provide a return on investment.

Of course, you may leverage the efforts of others. There is nothing wrong with using a ghostwriter or having staff members do research for your social media content. Their contributions free more of your time to do what you do best and what only you can do—practice law.

§ 8.04 Need for Personal Contact

Social media—whether it encompasses blogging, a LinkedIn or Facebook page, a Twitter post, or any number of other new iterations—constitutes a powerful marketing tool for lawyers by combining personalized observation with facts and insights from the lawyer's area of focus to help create new client relationships.

However, it is important to understand that social media should not be used to actively recruit new clients. Rather, social media should be used to expose you and your services to people who might need your expertise and will thus choose to engage your services. The ABA's Commission on Ethics 20/20 Working Group on the Implications of New Technologies recommended in 2011 that social networking should not be used to solicit clients and should be viewed as general communication to educate potential clients.

This is as it should be. From blogging to social networking, technology has given lawyers more marketing tools than ever. There is a real danger, however, in becoming so infatuated with the tool that you forget the objective. Marketing legal services isn't about speed or worldwide presence. It remains fundamentally about identifying the people most likely to hire you for the work that you want to do, communicating with them to let them know who you are, and developing close relationships with these people so that they choose you to be their lawyer.

Social media relationships are no substitute for in-person relationships and more personal contact. Never forget that personal contact at meetings, on the phone, and through handwritten notes remain effective outreach tools. Using such methods today, when so many lawyers are scurrying about online, becomes a differentiating factor that gets a lawyer noticed. And getting noticed—with social media use as a key strategy but not the only one—is the foundation of effective marketing.

§ 8.05 Bar Association Regulation

In terms of social media, bar associations seek to regulate lawyers in ways that other governing bodies do not attempt for such professionals as doctors and accountants.

Disclaimers are one area in which bar associations have implemented regulations. For example, the Virginia State Bar in 2011 charged a lawyer with professional misconduct for talking about his own completed cases on his blog without adding an advertising disclaimer that results depend upon factors unique to each case and that results in one case do not predict similar results in others.

In addition, bar associations are looking more closely at character as evidenced on social media sites. Several years ago the Florida Board of Bar Examiners' Character and Fitness Commission recommended that the board consider expanding its review of personal websites during background investigations as necessary and decided to adopt a policy allowing a case-by-case investigation of social networking websites. Applicants' Facebook pages and similar social media sites could be reviewed in cases where there is previous evidence of substance abuse, where flippant reference is made to alcohol or drug consumption, or where candor is in question. These situations are a far cry from major ethics concerns like dipping into client trust accounts. In today's society, no one (including lawyers) is exempt from scrutiny and questioning about personal conduct as revealed on social media.

Avoid giving commentary on cases. Remember, social media platforms are generally public forums open to all. An online criticism of an expert witness or an adversary in a current case could become an ex parte communication if the judge hearing the case reads your criticism. Your opinion may have ramifications well beyond your own social media use, so use discretion.

Finally, avoid openly soliciting clients on your social media as this could expose you to disciplinary action.

§ 8.06 Formulating Policies

By now, most of us have heard horror stories of employees being reprimanded or even fired over the content of their personal or business-related social media sites. Many large companies and firms have implemented formal policies to help employees navigate the minefield of ethical, legal, and loyalty issues that can arise from social media. Even small firms can benefit from a formalized policy to protect the firm's integrity and reputation—and to prevent employees from making career-limiting social media posts of their own! Rather than being viewed as a Big Brother imposition, the policy should be developed collaboratively in the best interests of both the firm and individual lawyers.

§ 8.07 Special Concerns About Blogging

Blogging is a type of social media that is a particularly effective marketing tool for lawyers. As a dedicated blogger myself (http://www.lawbizblog.com), I have found the experience to be a powerful form of communication that continually connects me to actual and potential clients in ways that I never anticipated. When done right, a blog can be a living, detailed entity that represents you to the world.

§ 8.07.1 Marketing Tactics

To blog effectively, employ the following strategies:

- Create a profile of your ideal client, and develop a marketing strategy that focuses on this target, not everyone.
- Make sure that your blog supports your market and strategy. If your target market is consumers who are not sophisticated enough to regularly search the web, then blogging is not very meaningful to them and may not be a worthwhile marketing strategy for you.
- Prepare your blog postings to visualize and address your market so that recipients will learn what your value to them can be and why they need you and your services.
- Express your knowledge and opinion in your practice area; if the goal is business development, then this is not a personal journal.
- Write your blog posts with the intention of carrying on a conversation with this ideal client, whom you can't yet meet face-to-face. Be informal and conversational, and show that you have something meaningful to say.

§ 8.07.2 Technology Concerns

There's no getting around the fact that blogs require some technological investment—and even technological expertise. However, there is no need to go to extremes on either score. The following strategies can keep the technology cost manageable:

- Purchase software that is inexpensive and easy to use if you want to do blog posts yourself.
- Many developers today use WordPress.
- Avoid fancy graphics.
- Avoid complex navigation. Blog posts should be in straightforward chronological order with the most recent first. If you want to archive your older posts, it may be best to group them into categories—but do not group your current ones.
- Create links from your blog to your website, if you have one. By doing that, the frequency of your blog posts can improve your website's standing in the search engines.
- Link your blog to other blogs, and encourage bloggers to link to you. External linkage is another driver of search engine rankings, which are a measure of your blog's popularity.
- Consider hiring someone to manage the technical aspects of your blog: posting your content, tracking replies to posts, and working on search engine optimization. The expense may be far less than the time you spend yourself in updating and managing.
- Focus on your core competency—writing about your legal practice area—and delegate the blog maintenance to others.

§ 8.08 Action Plan

- Determine the social media platforms that might fit into your marketing plan.
- Create a social media presence.

CHAPTER 9

Using Business Cards, Stationery, and Print Media to Support Rainmaking Goals

I see where several of our politicians are predicting a return of prosperity as soon as business picks up.

—Anonymous

Chapter Checklist

- o Establishing Your Firm Image
- o Business Cards
- o Firm Stationery
- o Other Basic Paper Items
- o Large Mailing Envelopes and Mailing Labels
- o Firm Announcements
- o Firm Brochures and Seminar and Direct-Mail Printing
- o Action Plan

Business cards, stationery, and basic printed supplies to open a new office need not be expensive. Recognize that these materials will be seen by clients and therefore should also serve your marketing or rainmaking goals. They are not simply office supplies.

§ 9.01 Establishing Your Firm Image

In each of the following sections, the value of a consistent, professional identity is emphasized. If you are unfamiliar with the process of establishing a professional image, do not panic. Professional legal printers are highly experienced in helping you with the essentials of type style, layout, and wording. Some provide free sample booklets to demonstrate options, and a few provide comprehensive free art and design services.

§ 9.01.1 Selection of a Vendor

Select a knowledgeable vendor who will assist you in identifying issues; provide complimentary proofs; and help you achieve the final, coordinated look without up-front costs or obligation. Good vendors understand the technical, archival, authentication, and graphics/marketing issues affecting your profession. Traditional printers should not be expected to be cognizant of the issues surrounding legal practice, so if you choose a general printer, you take full responsibility for the accuracy and performance of each printed item.

§ 9.01.2 Graphics Issues

Considering that most law firms need to scan, photocopy, or fax documents on a regular basis, your type style should be appropriately sized to reproduce clearly. Although you can control the quality of your office equipment, you have no control over the quality of someone else's facsimile machine. In order to prevent future problems, always presume that your information is going to someone with lower technology.

Your choice of type and graphics can also demonstrate your appreciation of client needs. For example, if your practice is concentrating upon estate or elder law, it is thoughtful to increase type sizes as these clients are more likely to be visually impaired to some degree.

A good printer or engraver is usually willing as a courtesy to give you camera-ready artwork with your firm name in the established type style. This is something that you will want to have handy if you plan to have signage made for your entrance. It is also useful if you plan to advertise. Wherever your firm name appears, it is in your best interest to ensure that a consistent brand image is used.

§ 9.02 Business Cards

Establishing a good first impression with engraved business cards should cost around $50. For this outlay, you should be able to get five hundred high-quality cards and receive complimentary design and layout suggestions for your entire firm image (as it will be built upon this foundation). As an independent practitioner, you need to convey professionalism and attention to detail. These characteristics are instantly measured by potential clients and referral sources, so making a strong first impression is no luxury—it is essential.

Consider adding your photo to your business card. Nothing makes a more immediate impression than a personal photo on a business card. However, that impression can cut both ways. If the photo is engaging and current, it can create a strong connection with the viewer; conversely, a photo depicting a smug or hostile expression or a photo that is woefully out of date can do more harm than good. The latter phenomenon is all too common: male and female lawyers alike believe that a decades-old photo conveys a young impression when it merely shows the lawyer as outdated and potentially out of touch.

§ 9.03 Firm Stationery

Firm stationery (letterhead paper and envelopes) should be purchased in the minimum quantity of one box each (five hundred pieces). For a cost of about $100 total, you can have these items engraved with matching black ink. Letterhead stationery, in particular, serves as more than a communications function in the legal arena. You need to be able to authenticate originals, documents may require archival life, and every professional communication must support your objective of building credibility for the practice. Use only paper with genuine watermarks for security reasons. Envelopes should match the letterhead (same paper color, quality, and process).

Desktop stationery (all laser printed) is not wise. Although it may seem more efficient and economical, long-term savings are negligible. More important, statistical evidence has repeatedly demonstrated that "desktop firms" are six times less likely to be selected in competitive situations. Avoid looking indifferent by sending sensitive documents with an upside-down or backward watermark. Competency does not differentiate your practice, but it does define it. Your firm's identity is a tangible asset, and it should be managed to reflect your style of practice.

§ 9.03.1 Maximize the Value of Your Letterhead

In addition to the obvious use for letterhead, you can laser print firm statements on first-page letterhead (remember to include your tax ID number on them as a courtesy to clients). You can also use professional-quality letterhead as a direct-marketing tool. A well-written, one-page letter outlining your practice (features and benefits) is an effective "next step" after sending professional announcements.

Recognize that your identity projects your values to a wide audience: potential and existing clients, referral sources, bankers, employees, media, and even vendors. Repeated and consistent use of a professional identity builds awareness of, and confidence in, your firm. A lack of attention or an indifferent attitude toward your professional image can be very costly.

§ 9.03.2 Plain Paper

Purchase a single box (five hundred "plain" sheets) of the same paper used to engrave your first-page letterhead and envelopes. This ensures that all letters and documents longer than one page present a consistent image. Letterhead paper should typically be 24-pound weight for a "pleasing feel" and have at least 25 percent cotton content for archival life purposes. This paper works well in all desktop printers. You can expect to pay around $18 for five hundred sheets of matching, high-quality plain paper (depending on your personal quality standards and taste).

In this price range, you have a wide choice of colors and finishes. While paper color has no bearing on cost, paper weight, as reflected in the thickness and feel of the sheet, does. The feel of your paper also makes a tangible and significant statement about your attitudes and values. Most successful law firms use good-quality, 24-pound laser paper with recycled content (this has no cost impact and demonstrates a responsible attitude).

Most of your billable work will not result in tangible product. Therefore, you should ensure that when someone handles your communication or work product, however briefly, the impression conveyed is consistent with the quality of service that you provide. Think of paper and engraving as a "wardrobe" for your business; treat them with the same amount of attention that you give to your personal appearance, and you'll be less likely to suffer embarrassment.

§ 9.04 Other Basic Paper Items

Depending on the style of your practice, there are a few other inexpensive paper items that you may need. For example, if you are going to be preparing original court filings, note that virtually every jurisdiction has an expressed preference for 20-pound paper (to reduce filing bulk). Further, many courts now **mandate** recycled paper with a minimum of 30 percent postconsumer waste content and 25 percent cotton content in original filings. A ream of bright white, 20-pound, 25 percent cotton content, 100 percent recycled content (30 percent postconsumer and 70 percent preconsumer content) laser paper should cost around $16. Bright white is the preferred color for court filings because it is easier to read. Observing these specifications will eliminate any risk of conflict with standing rules.

You can purchase preprinted pleading paper from competent legal printing vendors who are knowledgeable about the court rules in your area; however, if you are computer literate, you can save a bit of money by creating a software macro feature that automatically drafts the "rules and numbers." Contact the clerk of the court where you expect to be filing for information on the court's rules and guidelines. Many jurisdictions have local rules in place that do not work well with generic software, so be careful about purchasing "pleading software." Confirm that it meets your specific margin, rule, and numbering needs before purchasing. The number of "lines per page" and page margins are variable by location, and some court systems have different formats for first and continuing pages.

§ 9.05 Large Mailing Envelopes and Mailing Labels

Large mailing envelopes and labels are common needs in practices where large or bulky documents will be exchanged. Do not waste money purchasing printed large envelopes. You can buy preprinted mailing labels (or perhaps plain ones if you are skilled enough to prepare a label macro on your computer) to eliminate the cost of printing the envelopes themselves. When you affix preprinted mailing labels, your return address will automatically appear.

If you shop for mailing labels at an office supply store, pay attention to the format that it is promoting. You are best served by purchasing a version that can be desktop printed "as documents are created." Typically, stores promote "six-up" versions (six labels per sheet/one hundred sheets to a box). Unless you expect to be printing six mailing labels at once, that format creates needless waste and expense. In addition, such formats often require special software for use. Worse still, large sheets from which you have removed only a few labels have a tendency to jam when refed through some desktop printers. The goal in most law offices is to spend as little as possible and maximize the productivity of basic office equipment.

The fastest-growing desktop mailing label solution at present is a "two-up" version, which feeds like an envelope. These eliminate all jamming issues and the need to use any special software for label printing. You simply feed them like an envelope and use the envelope-printing instructions in your existing software. Better still is the cost: five hundred two-up laser mailing labels that have been preprinted (in your matching type styles) will be around $60. This is half the cost of using a six-up version.

As with most printed or engraved items, there are substantial savings when you order one thousand pieces versus five hundred at a time. However, you should only take advantage of those savings at your first reorder point. When setting up an office, never assume that all the information you've been given is correct. Lease, telephone, and postal information are typically spelled out at the last moment (and unexpected changes are common). Take time to confirm these before having anything printed, and avoid overbuying initial supplies. Do not confuse "quantity discounts" with good cash flow management. Storing unneeded supplies is not the best use of operational funds, it requires more space, and it is potentially risky.

§ 9.06 Firm Announcements

Firm announcements should be mailed to launch a new practice; but once they are received, the indication is that you are open for business. Therefore, all of the foregoing items need to be in place by the time announcements are sent out.

The first step in preparing announcements is evaluating your contact list to develop an accurate count or quantity needed. Reviewing that audience also helps you focus on the wording of your message. In general terms, less is more. Trying to state too much reduces the likelihood of someone reading everything, so keep your message succinct.

Another common mistake is the addition of a date on the firm opening announcement. Placing a date on the announcements denies you the utility of using some later where appropriate. A well-crafted announcement makes a great handout later provided that it is not out-of-date. This is to your benefit in terms of purchasing as well.

Professional announcements can be purchased in any quantity, but the setup costs are high. The more you create, the lower the cost per piece. If your mailing list is 225, it is wise to get 250. You will have a few extras to hand out or mail when an unexpected referral source appears. Going back to the printer for a small handful of announcements after the initial printing results in twice the setup charges. As a rule of thumb, get at least 10 percent more than your mailing list count.

§ 9.06.1 Envelopes

Addressing your announcement envelopes is a time-consuming task if done correctly. You do not want a commercial, junk-mail label on these because that reduces readership. Therefore, ask your printer to furnish the announcement envelopes as early as possible. That way, the addressing can be handled in advance. This helps you stay on schedule and may help you recall other useful contacts (another reason to make sure that some extras are available).

If you have not had steady contact with those on your mailing list, it is wise to have your business return address engraved on the announcement envelope flaps. This ensures that undeliverable mail will be returned by the post office, at which point you should update your contact list accordingly. Not knowing that your message was misdirected is a potentially expensive mistake.

§ 9.06.2 Announcement Content

The following is an example of effective wording in a firm-opening announcement:

EDWARD POLL
ATTORNEY-AT-LAW
(FORMERLY WITH SUCH & SUCH LAW FIRM)

IS PLEASED TO ANNOUNCE THE OPENING OF HIS OFFICES

AT

1462 BEVERLY DRIVE
SUITE 700
BEVERLY HILLS, CALIFORNIA 90210

TELEPHONE 310.827.5415
FACSIMILE 310.578.1769
E-MAIL: EDPOLL@LAWBIZ.COM

MR. POLL'S PRACTICE IS LIMITED TO ENTERTAINMENT AND INTELLECTUAL PROPERTY MATTERS, SPECIFICALLY DIGITAL GAMES AND ONLINE MEDIA.

The inclusion of a practice description is important. In the example given, the lawyer's goal is to focus very narrowly on a niche expertise, thus establishing a boutique or specialty firm. More typically, the goal is to detail the areas that reflect the breadth of your expertise, increasing the likelihood of referrals. Describing your practice emphasis is the only way to ensure that your audience recognizes all of the situations in which your services might be appropriate.

In this one area, less isn't more. The statement should be brief but fully descriptive. Educational and other credentials are sometimes included, but more important is the clear expression of what type of matters you are well qualified to handle.

Avoid the use or misuse of the word *specialization* unless you are indeed a board-certified specialist. Check with your state bar if you feel that an expression such as *specializing in* provides more clarity to readers. Make certain that the use of any form of *specialization* is approved if you intend to use it in your practice description. Alternative expressions that work include *concentrating in the area(s) of, emphasizing, focusing upon,* and *practice limited to.* Again, the latter expression would indicate that you are not seeking a volume of matters but rather a specific type of matter.

When future announcements are created to recognize additions to the firm or to announce a relocation, always use those opportunities to state the firm's practice description to maximize your return on investment. A professional announcement mailed directly to your target(s) has a phenomenally higher likelihood of being read, whereas print ad versions typically have very low visibility and "recall" value.

§ 9.07 Firm Brochures and Seminar and Direct-Mail Printing

Firm brochures and seminar and direct-mail printing come into play when you begin to develop an integrated marketing plan. They are not typically needed when opening a new office. When establishing a new law firm, fundamental items like business cards and stationery should form the basic foundation of your firm image. Future items should be built upon that established identity. A mistake to avoid is reversing this order. Firms attempting to "back" a sophisticated brochure image into their everyday identity/practice needs typically suffer higher cost and slower service.

Firm brochures and like items can be costly if not well thought out. You want to be confident that your address and contact information are correct and are not going to change anytime soon before paying for a large press run of supplies that will last eighteen to twenty-four months at a time. "Ready, fire, aim" can have devastating consequences for a tight budget.

If you do not have experience in developing or buying these types of items, seek professional help at the outset. Good identity management ensures that your business essentials support "just-in-time" purchasing and service needs by design. This gives you maximum flexibility for changes. If you plan your image correctly, it will express key attributes about your firm, the expense should comprise no more than 1–2 percent of your total operating costs (whereas rent and compensation typically account for 80–85 percent of total operating costs), and your investment will yield an identity that is a tangible asset.

§ 9.07.1 Law Firm Brochures: Two-Pocket Folders

Law firm brochures are currently popular, but their use is a direct function of the type of law that you choose to practice. A high-quality, two-pocket folder prepared with your firm identity engraved on the front cover would be a good strategic purchase. These folders have many uses: you can insert marketing information inside and use them as handouts, you can use them at seminars with highly targeted content, and you can "package" work product for clients in these folders when furnishing their copies. Well-packaged work product conveys "value received" to many clients.

If you avoid printing address and contact information on folders, they do not fall out of date when a telephone area code change surprises you, they do not "spoil" if you relocate, and you avoid the temptation to place a tacky label over changed information (subtly conveying that poor judgment was used earlier). A good nine-by-twelve-inch, two-pocket folder should have die-cuts on at least one inside pocket where you can insert your professional business card (and always have current contact information with low-cost flexibility).

High-cost, fully printed, and bound law firm brochures with photographs are typically best suited for large, established firms courting corporate clients or very large buyers of complex legal services. These items are complex enough themselves to justify a stand-alone book. In briefest terms, potential clients react to these in ways that many lawyers do not understand. An expensive and elaborate firm brochure does not automatically create an impression of "successful"—it may express "too expensive" to many people. Brochures are communications tools, not sales tools in the sense that simply handing one out or mailing one is going to secure a new client (by itself). A good, effective brochure should support the relationship-building effort, provide enough depth to demonstrate capability, and reflect good judgment (in look, feel, and expense) on the firm's part.

§ 9.07.2 Law Firm Brochures: Alternatives to Two-Pocket Folders

Pocket folders or roll folders are less costly tools that can be created to accomplish many of the same tasks as more complex and expensive pieces. Again, the proper tool is a function of your practice and sensibilities. These two items are expressly designed to fit inside standard No. 10 envelopes (letterhead-size envelopes). This makes them practical to store, carry, and mail. The reduced size also increases the probability that someone will take the time to actually read them fully.

Pocket folders are typically designed to hold inserts that describe separate areas of practice. Some feel that "shingle-cut" inserts, much like a bank lobby folder, are clever. Consider, however, that if someone removes a single insert from a folder, the remaining material looks used and incomplete.

A roll folder is one of the most cost-effective tools that a small firm or practice group can develop. If you simply take a standard sheet of letterhead paper, turn it sideways, fold the right-hand third of the sheet in toward the center, and then fold the left third over the center, the result is a 3.6-inch wide, 8.5-inch tall folder. This format gives you six panels to present information. It fits in a standard (letterhead-size) envelope, and the printing cost is minimized because you are simply printing two sides of a standard-size piece of paper prior to folding. Professional help with layout and copy is recommended. There are margin concerns and other graphic features that must be considered given the size of each panel after folding. Professional printers are very familiar with this type of job.

Consider using digital printing for roll folders because you can purchase any quantity, and they can be addressed "as printed" (from your data list) and mailed for you when targeting a large audience.

§ 9.08 Action Plan

- Create your personal design/image.
- Consult a printer experienced in dealing with legal professionals.
- Select quality paper and print style.
- Purchase only what you need for the first order.
- Create a contact list for mailing announcements.
- Mail your announcements.

CHAPTER 10

Branding

Be yourself. Everyone else is already taken.

—Oscar Wilde

Chapter Checklist

- o Unique Selling Points
- o Internal Acceptance
- o Management and Marketing Issues
- o Why Brand?
- o Action Plan

A brand is a "claim of distinction." It is nothing more and nothing less. In a world where business executives as well as consumers are bombarded with thousands of messages a day, a brand identity can help a firm distinguish itself in the marketplace.

For some lawyers, the whole concept of branding smacks of marketing gimmickry. But for those firms who have successfully undertaken the process, branding is more akin to strategic planning than most any marketing endeavor that they have undertaken. Done well, a branding program not only identifies a firm's unique "essence" but also sets the course for its future as a law firm. In the process, a successful branding initiative brings to light some critical management and marketing issues.

This chapter provides insight into the branding process and details the five most common management and marketing issues that result from it.

§ 10.01 Unique Selling Points

Branding development is the process of identifying a firm's unique essence, or brand distinction. Small, medium, and large firms must look introspectively with the assistance of brand development consultants to discover what is unique about their firm and then winnow the options to find their true unique selling points (USPs).

As an example, let's look at Mulcahy LLP, a boutique firm located in Southern California that specializes in franchise, antitrust, and vertical distribution law nationally. The firm wanted to attract more attention from larger companies. It needed to create a strong brand essence and marketing campaign for the firm. The brand would became *the* message under which all marketing and business development efforts would fall.

The firm engaged Extreme Marketing consultants to facilitate a half-day branding session and requested that all firm partners be involved. During the session, the firm focused on the essence of its business and the characteristics that distinguished its practice from all other firms. In part, the branding session forced Mulcahy LLP to make hard decisions about what it really stood for as well as the areas that it didn't want to focus on. In the brand development process, the firm came up with its USPs:

- Incredible depth of franchise, antitrust, and vertical distribution experience
  - "Wrote the book" (literally)
  - Helped to create the franchise expert test for the state bar
  - Frequently called upon for national speaking and publishing opportunities
  - Significant jury trial experience
  - General counsel and outside counsel expertise
- Judgment and litigation fearlessness
  - "I know your business."
  - "We'll find an out."
  - "We'll come after you aggressively in court."

These two areas became the foundation for the firm's brand essence. In addition, there were a number of supporting facts that surfaced during the brand development process that helped reinforce the strength of the franchise/antitrust brand. The firm had a profound commitment to its craft and combined these facts to paint a picture that offered a distinctive approach to franchise and distribution law. Each of these components communicated who Mulcahy LLP is and what its unique brand of lawyering could do for its clients.

Two weeks after the session, the consultants returned and unveiled positioning line options that reflected the firm's brand distinction. The firm quickly decided on a positioning line that truly represented the firm's brand essence and offered a unique platform on which to design a strong marketing and business development plan with specific and measurable results built in: "Mulcahy LLP: A firm approach to franchise law." (Over the years, the firm maintained its brand essence but changed its tagline to "Mulcahy LLP: A firm approach to competition litigation" to provide a broader view of its capabilities.)

To make the brand work, the firm committed to the time and to both hard- and soft-dollar costs to make the brand come alive throughout the marketplace. The firm would also need someone to manage the new activities. The business development plan put the partners in front of both business owners and general counsels of many large organizations. This would be the start of the relationship-enhancement process that began with the brand and continued to be reinforced through example, experience, time, and commitment.

§ 10.02 Internal Acceptance

A brand, particularly a law firm brand, will have more profound implications internally than it will to its external audiences. This is because brands must begin internally to be successful. Done well, brands bring cohesion and structure to a firm's strategic planning and marketing efforts. Executed poorly or merely as a splashy external program of advertisements and mailings, a brand will fail because the people who must make it work—the lawyers—will invariably think that it is just marketing gimmickry. Without buy-in and commitment to the branding process from within the firm, a brand effort will lack consistent and substantive effort.

The crucial test of a law firm brand is twofold:

- Does it truly represent the essence of the firm and its lawyers?
- Does it become one and the same with the firm through a structured program to both internalize and externalize it?

Today, the substantive mettle among the many but "real" law firm brands in the marketplace is impressive. Firms with such hallmarks boast buy-in from managing and marketing partners, new operating credos, enhanced internal morale, and a clearer sense of direction.

§ 10.03 Management and Marketing Issues

For all the positive attributes that a brand can bring (i.e., increased morale, stronger market presence, higher billing rates, etc.), it still will raise a firm's most complex issues.

At most companies, there is a common maxim about the underlying aspects of marketing issues. When you take the three issues of time, cost, and activity and initiate effort in any one area, the other two areas simultaneously begin moving. When a branding initiative is added to the equation, an additional dynamic occurs. While time, cost, and activity are in motion, so, too, are a host of firm-management issues, rearing their heads throughout the process with unmistakable force.

Typically, branding initiatives are the delegated province of specially empowered law firm marketing committees. Yet, in every instance where a branding initiative is properly administered, it will raise the most thorny and controversial management issues within a firm. In this respect, most firms are not fully prepared for the implications of their own branding exercises. In a strange but positive way, however, the fact that a firm's skeletons happily pop from their closet doors is an asset in the most profound sense as it gives firms the opportunity to make themselves stronger internally and externally.

In the years since *Bates v. State Bar of Arizona*, 433 U.S. 350 (1977), when law firm advertising and marketing gained a legal toehold in the marketplace, most firms have equated marketing issues as somewhat important but not necessary to their survival. Experience in the branding area has led to a perceptible shift in this attitude. Marketing and management issues are becoming increasingly intertwined. In many respects, the prevalence of law firm branding initiatives is leading the way simply because it so thoroughly raises issues of firm direction, commitment, and leadership.

The five most common management and marketing issues that arise in branding situations include the following:

1. Strategic marketing plan
2. Marketing costs
3. Lawyer time and activities
4. Negative fallout from the brand
5. Firm leadership

While these issues can be firm- or situation-specific, the means of addressing them are similar. To make a branding or marketing initiative work, a law firm must be open to receiving constructive and often critical feedback from within its own ranks and have either the leadership and infrastructure in place to manage it or the commitment to "do what it takes" to create success as a firm.

§ 10.03.1 Strategic Marketing Plan

Once the brand is created, the next logical step that a firm should take is the development of a strategic marketing plan. This plan will turn ideas into actionable, specific, and measurable goals and objectives. An effective plan turns the more right-brained aspects of the branding process into left-brained concrete and observable accomplishments. When firms do not develop a strategic marketing plan following a branding exercise, it foretells their lack of commitment to building their presence internally and externally.

Of course, there was a time when firms created strategic plans and marketing plans separately. But no longer. Certainly it is difficult to picture a strategic marketing plan today that does not include management and reward systems, law practice management issues, growth prospects, new practices, marketing plans, and more.

Logically, the brand acts as the umbrella for the plan. All activities, plans, and tasks should fall under the direction of the brand rather than the brand being a separate component of the plan. Everything that the firm does—from building a website to reorganizing practice groups; managing public relations and advertising; and designing a logo, stationery, and collateral materials—should be executed with the brand in mind.

One of the more tactical issues arising from brand development is consistency within a firm's identity and collateral materials. Firms are well advised to review for consistency the firm-wide use of typefaces, layouts, colors, and graphic representations. Many firms, even large, well-run operations, fall prey to partners in disparate offices using completely different business cards. In a meeting recently, partners in a large Chicago-based firm were providing their business cards to their outside consultant when they noticed for the first time that one had an e-mail address on it and the others did not. This disparity occurred with partners who were working in the same physical office and who participated on the same marketing committee at the firm. Whether it is an inconsistent business card or, more significantly, partners from the same firm describing their service offerings with utter disparity, the brand promise fails.

Firms can also run into dangerous territory by believing that once a branding initiative is created, brand management can simply be relegated to the marketing department or outside consultants. When this issue arises, it is a signal of problems within the firm—most often partnership squabbles highlighting the partners' level of commitment (or lack thereof) to marketing. Firms with a commitment to marketing understand that the right ongoing mix of time, costs, and activities will help the brand and the firm evolve in the marketplace. In every instance of a successful brand, the initiative relies on a multiplicity of efforts.

§ 10.03.2 Marketing Costs

One thorny issue arising from branding is the inevitable discussion of the costs involved. The branding process typically involves resource review and allocation. Most often, this culminates in the hiring of additional staff or outside resources to help manage the marketing function, even in law firms with effective marketing departments.

The threshold issue that law firms face is how they can best bring their brand to market in a way that will most likely be heard by their clients and prospects. Contrary to some notions, creating a brand does not have to cost millions of dollars and does not have to involve advertising expenditures. If a firm has both the budget and the inclination to bring its brand to a mass audience, the costs will be proportionately large, as will the need for mass marketing techniques like advertising and direct mail. However, law firms can travel a less expensive route; they can successfully communicate their brand distinctions directly to their top clients. Using a combination of technology to identify client buying patterns and historical expenditures and anecdotal knowledge about a firm's best clients, a very targeted, cost-effective marketing program can be developed that will show specific, measurable results.

§ 10.03.3 Lawyer Time and Activities

A common myth in the legal community is that marketing is the series of activities that "marketing people" handle while lawyers go about the valuable business of billing time and serving clients. More sophisticated lawyers understand, of course, that good marketing and good lawyering are the same thing. Branding is an attitude and a feeling as much as it is a position. To execute a brand, the partnership not only has to believe in it, it has to live it.

Beyond issues of brand agreement in a firm, there must be an understanding that with a commitment to a brand comes a corresponding responsibility for lawyers to devote time to building the brand. Certainly, there are a number of areas in which marketing directors, managers, and staff support brand activities. However, there are any number of activities that lawyers must incorporate into their workdays to make the brand credible, real, and effective.

For example, an international firm, as a result of its branding efforts, believed that the cornerstone of its essence was its ability to provide an "integrated offering" to clients. Without the corresponding ability of all partners to truly provide integrated services to clients, the "brand promise" would fail. The firm therefore orchestrated a series of client meetings, some designed to assess client satisfaction but all created to identify whether clients actually know about the firm's service offerings. In nearly every instance thus far, when a partner talks about the services provided, clients invariably associate the firm only with the particular service that it received. This has been true even where clients have had long-standing and close relationships with individual partners. "If you are meeting with a client for any reason other than this type of assessment, then the client only focuses on the work at hand," one partner noted. "When you meet specifically to explore client service issues, then you can really hear whether a client is aware of the breadth of service we are offering."

In this scenario, as in others, there is a training implication involved. While most partners intimately understand their own practice areas and marketing initiatives, they typically do not understand the full range of services that their own firms can provide. To cross-market effectively as well as to "sell" the brand, all of the partners in a firm need to have a full understanding of the services that they can offer. Internal training sessions can help solve this issue, as can communication methods such as internal newsletters and "brown-bag" lunches with partners, associates, and staff to talk about the types of work they are handling.

Regardless of the particular solution, lawyers must spend more time in nonbillable marketing activities than before the brand was developed. For many firms, the issue of adding time and activities to lawyers' work flow can be enough to effectively stifle the brand. It is an issue that should be addressed at the outset of a branding initiative.

§ 10.03.4 Negative Fallout

Negative fallout might be defined as the heightened, and perhaps increased awareness of, marketing- and compensation-related problems in a law firm.

The act of branding does not actually create negative fallout. However, it may highlight or even intensify the depth of internal disagreements—while often generating possible solutions for them.

For example, most firms grapple, at some level, with unproductive practice groups and partners. Through the branding process at one two-hundred-lawyer firm, the firm's executive committee was motivated to deal with both of these issues, using the brand as its starting point.

At the outset of this firm's branding initiative, the firm identified one of the core issues as its inability to charge "premium" rates for certain types of legal work, including insurance defense work. The firm's hope was that the brand process would lead the partnership to a more coherent understanding of how it could enhance profitability for the future. By identifying its essence, the firm also identified its new and more specific direction away from the insurance defense industry and into higher-level litigation work. According to one of the partners who participated in the process, "Our new brand provided focus for our firm. Once we understood what we didn't want to be, we could decide with clarity exactly how we could achieve our vision of the future."

With existing insurance defense lawyers, the firm developed a program in which it provided both relationship and sales training to partners in this practice group as a means of helping them attract new litigation clients. All of the training and marketing tools used the brand to assist these lawyers in communicating a clear and consistent message about the firm.

Gradually, the firm folded the more profitable areas of this practice group into a more general litigation practice area. Over an eighteen-month period, the firm also "cut loose" a significant handful of clients that were unwilling or unable to pay fees that the firm considered market rates for its services.

At other firms, issues regularly arise about specific, usually prominent, partners whose goals are at odds with the institution's long-term marketing and branding goals. At a midwestern firm with seventy professionals, this situation arose with "Bob," a partner who was a recognized expert in his field and who received a lot of personal publicity from writing a book. Unfortunately for the firm, Bob did not understood how to leverage this publicity to attract clients. When the firm's brand was developed, all partners, including Bob, were charged with new marketing responsibilities. Bob was resistant to these efforts because they were taking him away from personal efforts to promote his book.

In tandem with the development of the brand, the firm was also in the process of revising its partner compensation structure. To encourage partners' work on brand-related efforts, the new compensation formula provided direct financial rewards while changing the previous formula that promoted Bob's efforts in the past. Rather than a punitive measure directed at Bob, the revised compensation structure was developed more as a means of supporting the new brand efforts. It did, however, have the additional effect of changing the cultural standards for marketing activities.

Even at new law firms, compensation is a significant issue in branding efforts. Without a compensation system that provides incentive for all partners (and perhaps associates), a brand stands little chance of success. The existence of unproductive partners and their burden to the firm must be addressed. Dealing with the potentially unpleasant issues of compensation and unproductive partners is unavoidable in a successful brand implementation.

Another common area of negative fallout comes from lawyers who may not see the value of the brand in their practice area. Despite the many positive aspects of a brand, a firm may have to contend with partners who do not see that "a rising tide lifts all boats." Those whose work is removed from the epicenter of the new branding focus may feel an emotional pang when their colleagues seem to get a disproportionate share of the spotlight. As a result, management's challenge is at least threefold in this context: (1) remind lawyers regularly that they all play important roles within the firm, (2) help all lawyers grow and develop strong reputations in their own right, and (3) find ways for all lawyers to leverage the dynamic growth to be created by the new branding efforts of the firm.

§ 10.03.5 Firm Leadership

Strong firm leadership is a critical factor for the success of a firm-wide branding and identity campaign. Lack of firm commitment and leadership is the most common reason that identity and branding programs fail. The successful firms are almost always the firms that have strong buy-in from firm management.

Typically, the managing or marketing partner who can "sell" the concept of branding in the firm is a leader in the truest sense. And when such firm leaders define and reward the behaviors that they want to see from their partners and associates, real change occurs. While it seems intuitive that firms will have strong leaders to guide them, this tends to be the exception rather than the rule. More than one law firm has suffered because a partner or committee simply could not create firm-wide consensus.

Unfortunately, the law firm business climate is rife with mixed messages. As one consultant noted, "[l]awyers can't be expected to simply emerge from years of a 'profits above all else' philosophy into a 'profits plus other things' mind-set without serious evidence that the 'other things' will be counted. This doesn't happen without serious leadership to take them there."

§ 10.04 Why Brand?

Given all of the issues that a strategic branding process raises, why would any firm undertake such a ritualistic cleansing? The reasons are obvious and include differentiation, the ability to charge a premium price for your product or service, unifying the members of your firm, and creating an entity that becomes larger than its parts.

In a parity-defined marketplace, the only real differentiating feature that any firm or company can bring to its clients is what those clients believe about the firm, product, or service and their relationship with the brand. Branding at its best can help to build the equity behind and inside the law firm.

§ 10.05 Action Plan

- Determine the essence of your firm.
- Create/modify collateral materials that reflect this essence.
- Focus your marketing resources on this essence.
- Address the management and marketing issues that crop up in order to strengthen your firm.
- Define and reward the behaviors that your firm wants to reinforce.

PART III

Marketing Beyond Advertising

CHAPTER 11

Rules for Improving Client Relations

Customers would be the scourge of the business world except for one thing: They're the ones with the money.

—Gene Perret, *Business Humor*

I knew one business person who had the right idea. He always spelled "customer" with a dollar sign in front of it.

—Gene Perret, *Business Humor*

Chapter Checklist

- o Believe That the Client Is Number One
- o Return Phone Calls
- o Make Sure That Staff Members Know the Names of Clients
- o Communicate Regularly with Clients
- o Build a Team Concept
- o Make the Client Feel Like Part of the Team
- o Visit Clients
- o Advise Clients About Changes in the Law That Impact Them
- o Be Realistic in Forecasting Work
- o Ask Clients for Feedback
- o Action Plan

It is not a secret that the public at large—and prospective and current clients in particular—has misgivings and complaints about the legal profession. And this goes far beyond the usual lawyer-bashing jokes or newspaper cartoons. In fact, the results of state bar association focus groups have exposed the foundations of this widespread distrust of the legal community. For example, when the California State Bar asked probing questions, clients ranked lawyers for honesty and integrity just ahead of prostitutes and behind garbage collectors and cab drivers! And one of the most frightening results of these studies is that the more clients are involved with lawyers, the less they like them.

What that really means is that lawyers are doing something wrong. And it is not the other side's lawyer or the publicity that the local bar association does or does not do that can be blamed. Instead, it is what lawyers do one-on-one with their clients that affects their ability to satisfy them and improve the impression that clients have about lawyers.

Clients are not concerned about competence—that is presumed. They are not even so concerned about your fee. Their concern is whether you are resolved to help them and whether you are communicating with them so that they can understand what is truly happening with their matter. If you are dedicated to them and use good "bedside manners," clients will be satisfied.

When law firms understand that business success means meeting prospective and current clients' needs and desires, marketing efforts become buyer-driven and yield specific and measurable results. In particular, firms must be willing to use more sophisticated marketing techniques and respond creatively to market demands—that is, they must focus on improved client relations.

The following sections detail some "rules of the road" to help any lawyer develop good client relations. If you put this advice into practice, your client relations will be far superior to what they are today. Not only will your clients come back to you time after time and refer you to their friends and associates with a big smile, but perhaps you can help move lawyers up a notch or two on the integrity scale.

§ 11.01 Believe That the Client Is Number One

Think of the department stores or other retail outlets where you like to shop. You keep going back primarily because of the customer service, right? Lawyers, likewise, need to take a customer-service approach to dealing with clients. This may be a new concept for lawyers brought up on the idea of "client control," which basically means that the lawyer is the boss and the client better stay out of the way!

Client control is an antiquated concept, and it has no place in the modern practice of law. Today's lawyers need to realize that the client is the boss. When this shift in attitude occurs, clients intuitively sense and appreciate it.

§ 11.02 Return Phone Calls

Sounds simple, doesn't it? Yet the single most frequently registered complaint with state bars across the country is the failure of lawyers to return telephone calls.

I know one lawyer who has a very large, successful practice and who keeps getting return clients. I asked him how he did it, and he let me in on his secret: he makes a point of returning all telephone calls within four hours.

Here is how this busy lawyer does it: Client names are divided into alphabetical units (A–G, H–O, P–Z) by last name, with one staff person responsible for each unit. When a phone call comes in, the name is taken and the caller is switched over to the appropriate staffer, who handles the question or request. That staff person is a paralegal or secretarial or clerical type, not a lawyer, since most clients are not asking for legal advice but are usually asking about the status of their case. If a caller needs legal advice, the staff person will take a message, and the lawyer will call back later in the day or no later than the following morning. In this way, every client is contacted; every client is responded to; and if the lawyer is in court or otherwise unavailable, arrangements are made for later follow-up.

It is amazing what returning telephone calls can do, and I recommend that all lawyers live by this rule.

§ 11.03 Make Sure That Staff Members Know the Names of Clients

One of the worst things that a client can experience is being asked to spell his name when he calls his lawyer.

I recently had the opposite experience when I called someone in another state whom I had spoken to only a few times before. The person on the other end of the line said that my party was not available, but she would take my name and communicate the message that I had called. I said fine, and as I was starting to spell my last name, the staff person said that I did not have to spell it because she knew exactly who I was. Did that make my day!

By simply knowing who your clients are, your staff will make them feel welcome and important.

§ 11.04 Communicate Regularly with Clients

Since clients typically have an involvement with the law only once or twice in their lives, they really do not understand the process that you live with day in and day out. That is why it is important to let them know what is happening by communicating regularly with them.

One way to do this is to photocopy and send to your clients all relevant documents pertaining to them that come in or leave your office. In addition to benefiting the client, there is a very selfish reason for doing this. If the client sees all of the work that you have done to resolve a matter, he will appreciate not only your skill, which is sometimes taken for granted, but also the effort that you have gone through and the amount of work and time that you have put into the process.

Another way to communicate with your client is to send status reports on a regular basis. Even if there is nothing much to report, tell the client. Say that you are on target, that things are going as projected. The last thing that a client wants to see is a surprise. And if costs—depositions, expert witnesses, etc.—are accumulating, then the client will not be shocked when it is time to settle up.

Think of regular communication as a way to educate your clients about the process and as an opportunity for cementing your relationships.

§ 11.05 Build a Team Concept

Experience suggests that clients ultimately hire law firms and not lawyers. And when clients increasingly want to see a dynamic shift toward a model of commodity services provided by a legal team, the momentum can be hard to resist. The best way to do that is through a service approach that emphasizes the firm's entire range of capabilities and value-added resources.

Serving clients through teams rather than just a single rainmaker allows the firm to identify and provide needed practice specialties that reflect the full range of a client's concerns. A billing attorney coordinates the service provision according to a strategic plan and can give clients a complete and virtually seamless service package. The client receives "one-stop shopping" from a group of lawyers who are chosen to address specific needs in terms of both practice specialties and billing rates. And because the team is the portal through which the firm's counsel is provided, clients are spared the worry that their lawyer might leave or otherwise be unavailable.

Under a team concept with client service as the focus, client relationship management (CRM) databases are used to facilitate client transitions from senior partners to more junior members of a client service team. This process facilitates the existing professional relationship while providing better service to meet the client's needs and wishes.

§ 11.06 Make the Client Feel Like Part of the Team

This is a corollary to the rule stated in section 11.05. You can be much stronger in your delivery of quality legal services to the client—and gather valuable information in the process—when he feels like part of the legal team. Lawyers are more than technicians. They need to weigh complex factors and make important decisions about any case. The benefits of the team approach is that the client has a greater understanding of, and less frustration in dealing with, the judicial system. A client team member can also contribute valuable information to the matter. And, if nothing else, a team member is less likely to resist paying the bill when he has been involved in the entire process.

§ 11.07 Visit Clients

You can learn a great deal about clients (and prospective clients) by visiting them in their environment. In many instances, the spoken word is only one part of the communication process. In order to really understand clients, you need to learn about the territory in which they live and work. This is particularly true of business clients.

Understanding your clients' industry and business will allow you to use the terminology of their business and to better understand the clients' issues. Clients feel better about dealing with lawyers who know the problems of their business and their particular situation.

By visiting the client, you will have an opportunity to ask questions in a way that bolsters the lawyer-client relationship. Lawyers too often slip into adversarial questioning, but a visit to the client's habitat is conducive to a much more supportive approach. Lawyers who use effective questioning strategies show empathy and develop rapport while marketing themselves (asking questions that get people thinking about business solutions that involve the lawyer's services).

Neil Rackham developed an effective questioning technique in his book *SPIN Selling* (McGraw Hill 1988). The acronym *SPIN* identifies four kinds of questions:

- *Situational questions.* At the start of a client meeting, it is appropriate for the lawyer to ask questions to gather background information. Although situational questions have an important fact-finding role, successful service providers do not overuse them. Too many such questions will bore clients and make them feel that their time is being wasted. Situational questions thus are used merely to set the stage. Examples: "What are your plans for corporate growth?" "What recent changes have had the largest impact on your firm?"
- *Problem questions.* Once sufficient information has been gathered about the (potential) client's situation, successful interviewers move to problem questions. Examples: "Are you concerned about litigation trends in your industry?" "Have changes in manufacturing worked out with expected labor demands?" "Have you lost market share as a result of your impending merger?"
- *Implicit questions.* The third type of question, which is more complex and sophisticated, helps the (potential) client understand the seriousness or urgency of a concern. Examples: "How will this affect your future profitability?" "What labor problems do you anticipate will follow this merger?"
- *Need-payoff questions.* The most important use of need-payoff questions is to get the client to tell you the benefits that your solution could offer. There is a strong correlation between asking need-payoff questions and having the client ask for your assistance in solving a current or potential legal problem. Examples: "If putting in new contractual assurances to your clients could increase business by 12 percent,

> would that be a significant increase?" "If these labor guidelines could reduce litigation by 20 percent, would that offer enough to the bottom line to solve the legal budget problem?"

By using this approach, your clients will have greater trust in you, and they will more likely understand the information that you need to better serve them. A better outcome for the client will always result, and a happier client will always pay the bill more quickly.

Do not charge for the site visit. While clients will appreciate your interest, they will not appreciate paying for it. But show the visit on your next billing statement—as a "no charge."

§ 11.08 Advise Clients About Changes in the Law That Impact Them

It seems that every year, legislators seek to justify the income that they receive from taxpayers by passing new laws. Consequently, at the end of each legislative session, there is usually a book or summary of this new legislation that is prepared by one or more of the major law publishers. A quick review will highlight changes that have occurred in your area of expertise. Send a brief summary of such changes early in the year to your clients; they will always appreciate it.

Also, at other times of the year, if there are changes such as new tax regulations likely to occur, let your clients know about them. Do not let them hear the news first at the local barber shop or salon or over the fence from the neighbor. Make sure clients hear it first from you.

When you send a note, clipping, or letter, clients will know that you are up-to-date and that you care about them because you took the time to remember that this was an issue of concern to them.

This is also a great marketing opportunity. By sending clients information about related matters, you can let them know that you also perform services in these other areas.

§ 11.09 Be Realistic in Forecasting Work

Use your common sense and be realistic about the amount of time that it will take to complete any work. And do not be afraid to communicate the truth to your clients. If you are going to do an estate plan for the client and you think that it will take a total of ten days, do not tell the client that it will take seven days merely to impress him. Instead, say it will take fourteen.

Except in the unusual circumstances where you are dealing with statutory or filing deadlines, clients usually do not care exactly how long it will take you to resolve a matter. But they do not want to be told one thing and delivered another.

§ 11.10 Ask Clients for Feedback

Why don't lawyers do what most other product manufacturers and service providers do—that is, ask customers or clients how satisfied they are with the product or service and if they have any suggestions for improvement? (See chapter 12 for more on this topic.)

Lawyers should be asking clients questions such as the following:

- "How am I doing?"
- "Is there anything that you'd like to see done differently?"
- "Is there an issue that I have not spent enough time on for you?"
- "Is there an area of this matter that is more important to you than another?"
- "Has my staff been friendly and courteous to you?"
- "Are we doing what you want us to do?"

It is easy. Take your client out for coffee, and simply ask the questions. If you are in a larger firm, it sometimes helps to have somebody else in your firm do the questioning so that the client feels freer to be honest.

Do not think that clients will not answer you because they will if given the opportunity. They will tell you the good and they will tell you the bad, which is exactly what you need to hear.

Part two, of course, is showing that you were paying attention and have taken the steps needed to address the issues that the clients raised. The worst thing that you can do is nothing. Be sure to let the clients know that you were listening by calling or writing them later to explain what improvements you have made. (See chapter 12 for more on this topic.)

§ 11.11 Action Plan

- Change your attitude; the client is your only reason for being.
- Create a policy to return phone calls within twenty-four hours or sooner.
- Communicate regularly with your client.
- Ask the client for feedback.

CHAPTER 12

Listening to Clients

The world is not run by thought, nor by imagination, but by opinion.
—Elizabeth Drew, *The Modern Novel*

You can observe a lot by just watching.
—Yogi Berra

Chapter Checklist

- o The Client Satisfaction Survey
- o Presentation Skills
- o Listening Techniques
- o It Pays to Ask Questions
- o Following Up
- o Action Plan

Companies like Nordstrom, FedEx, Ritz-Carlton, and British Airways are well known for delivering services precisely the way their customers want them. British Airways, in fact, spends more on customer satisfaction than on advertising. "Companies like these," said Steve Barrett, formerly the national marketing director of Perkins Coie LLP, "have led business people to expect extraordinary services."

Law firms are catching on. They are acknowledging that if they want to sustain client loyalty at a level comparable to the intense loyalty of Nordstrom or FedEx customers, they must focus on client services and satisfaction just as sharply as successful businesses do. To be successful in this market-driven reality, law firms must take the initiative and ask their clients, "What can we do to create complete satisfaction in our relationship?" And then law firms must be prepared to follow up and make sure that all clients get what they have asked for.

Failure to deliver what a client requests can lead to disaster in a relationship. Clients may look to other service providers to meet their expressed needs. In fact, according to some research, the majority of clients who switch to other service providers are not dissatisfied; they are simply not delighted with the service provided.

§ 12.01 The Client Satisfaction Survey

Client satisfaction is determined only by the client. Keeping clients completely satisfied is how a law firm maintains current business and obtains new business.

The client survey, or audit, is a critical step in benchmarking the quality of the service that your clients, prospective clients, and referral sources feel that they are getting (see Figure 12.1 for a sample survey). The key component in conducting the survey is to focus on the needs of the client: What does the client value in the delivery of legal services? How well is the firm delivering what the client values? Are referral sources receiving positive feedback from clients they refer to the law firm?

(Note: The client survey process works equally well with potential clients. Imagine how impressed a potential client will feel when a lawyer asks at the outset of a potential relationship for help in structuring that relationship based on the client's needs and requirements. Success will follow the firm that trains a team to present a proposal response meeting with a big chunk of time reserved for asking the clients questions about their needs instead of telling them how good the firm is and what they'll get.)

§ 12.01.1 Survey Types

Client satisfaction surveys can be conducted in writing, over the telephone, or in person. The response rate is directly related to how the survey is conducted: mail-in surveys yield the lowest response rate, and in-person surveys yield the highest. A mix of the three survey types—written, phone, and in-person—works best in providing information to clearly assess clients' needs.

Survey questions can be shaped to elicit predefined responses, from a simple *yes* or *no* to a continuum response. A continuum response is made by selecting from a scale of 1 to 6, for example, where 1 means "rarely satisfied" and 6 means "completely satisfied." (Using a scale from 1 to 6—or any even number of choices—forces the respondent to be on one side or the other of the middle.)

Questions drafted to elicit set responses like *yes* or *no* lend themselves to computer analysis. Open-ended questions that require the client to make more detailed responses can provide a deeper level of information as well as topics for follow-up questions.

The more often a firm elicits client feedback, the more up-to-date such feedback is. Although surveying is a time-consuming activity that does not always generate immediate revenues, surveying clients is important, even essential, in order to survive in today's economy. Firms need to plan carefully for the commitment that this marketing tool requires.

§ 12.01.2 Written Survey

Written surveys are most useful when a firm wants to get more general feedback from a large number of clients at one time. A practice that deals with one-time users—that is, clients who seek legal assistance for personal injury, workers' compensation, debtor's bankruptcy, or family issues—can include a brief survey at the end of the matter to gauge client satisfaction. Firms whose practices are based on ongoing relationships may want to conduct written surveys from time to time to see how things are going.

To improve the response rate, the questionnaire should be kept as short and as focused as possible. A rule of thumb would be two pages and ten minutes to complete.

Because a written survey has the lowest response rate, at least two mailings are necessary for maximum response. The more follow-up that is executed, the greater the response rate. If confidentiality is not an issue, a staff member can establish a log of respondents and do at least one follow-up request for a response two weeks after the initial mailing.

Another technique for improving response rate is to reward respondents. A discount or credit against future legal services ($50 off the next bill, for example) not only gets the survey back but also sets the stage for future representation.

If the survey consists primarily of continuum questions, support staff can compile the responses. The firm's lawyers, however, should review the survey forms, looking for written comments, which can be very revealing.

Open-ended questions, which provide very specific feedback, are also suitable for written surveys. It is necessary to plan for personal, one-on-one follow-up to these "essay questions," especially for those who provided lengthy responses.

§ 12.01.3 Telephone Survey

Telephone surveys yield a more significant response than do written surveys because clients can easily expand their answers and respond to follow-up questions. This is a good way to enhance client–law firm relationships. Nonverbal communication, however, is lost in telephone interviews; and if the phone interview is conducted for the convenience of the law firm and not the client, the firm sends a signal that the client is not important enough to merit the presence of the lawyer.

Telephone surveys are a good way to get feedback while a matter is pending. A client can be asked, "Are you satisfied with the amount of information that you're getting on your case?" or "Are your calls and letters being promptly answered in language that you can understand?" The client's answers communicate his needs before problems develop and the relationship is damaged. If the firm is already providing satisfactory service, brief telephone surveys boost the relationship by sending the message that the law firm cares about its clients.

§ 12.01.4 In-Person Survey

A face-to-face interview between the lawyer and the client yields the most significant response rate. There is, in fact, no better tool for building a good client relationship because the in-person interview demonstrates sincere commitment. Interviewing an ongoing client offers an opportunity to cement the relationship and often opens the door to new business.

Always conduct thorough research before going on interviews. Learn about the company through a variety of mediums, including, among others, Google searches; databases such as Hoovers, if applicable; LinkedIn Profiles; and aggregator software such as Manzama. Be sure to conduct some due diligence on competitors, the industry, and related areas. This is called *competitive intelligence.* Depending on the size and importance of the client, focus your research accordingly.

Because in-person interviews are time-consuming for both law firms and clients, an appropriate amount of time should be scheduled to meet this commitment, as for any other major legal work. Ten questions with their follow-up components can be covered in about forty-five minutes to an hour. Follow-up questions are a must, and the interviewer should engage in active listening and ask clarifying questions that draw out more specific answers.

The rules of thumb for conducting an in-person survey include the following:

- Acknowledge to the client that he is doing a service by participating in the interview. Firms should make sure that clients understand that the law firm is not billing for this process.
- Set a clear time limit, usually no more than one hour, so that both the lawyer and the client can schedule appropriately.
- If possible, meet at the client's office. This is a courtesy that will emphasize the value that the firm places on the client's business.

It is also useful to survey clients who do not have an active matter at the law firm. This will give the firm the opportunity to resolve past issues or concerns perhaps not expressed by inactive clients. Surveying inactive clients can become a stepping-stone to new business.

To create a list of survey questions that will be pertinent to various client segments, be sure to address issues that are relevant to the following:

- Major clients or referral sources that make up 10 percent or more of the firm's gross revenues
- Key clients or referral sources that offer potential for real growth
- A cross-section of clients (taking into account services used, fees generated, size of business operation, geographic location, and length of relationship with the firm)
- Third parties from the community who can become referral sources, including bankers, accountants, real estate brokers, and other professionals

§ 12.02 Presentation Skills

Presentation skills are the effective techniques used by successful speakers. They are designed to increase audience participation, increase audience retention of your content, and motivate the audience to want to remember and learn your content. In addition to learning the skills and tricks to increase audience participation, retention, and desire, the trained presenter learns to involve the audience by using appropriate questioning techniques, humor, and activities. The trained presenter also uses audiovisual aids, including PowerPoint presentations, overhead slides, and charts on a stand.

These techniques can help lawyers increase their effectiveness with many different types of audiences. A lawyer or other interviewer who has mastered presentation skills will be more successful on a one-to-one basis, such as in a client interview; when presenting to a small group; when responding to a proposal; and when giving a speech to a large peer group.

§ 12.03 Listening Techniques

When asked, clients will offer a frank assessment of the services that they receive, but the interviewers must be ready and able to really listen. When lawyers listen attentively to clients, those clients perceive that the lawyer and the firm that he represents can provide a level of service that distinguishes the firm from others. Savvy firms, therefore, are now training their partners and marketing directors in optimum listening techniques, including active listening, gender listening, and paying attention to nonverbal communication.

§ 12.03.1 Active Listening

Active listening is the process of listening carefully and paraphrasing what the speaker says. It is similar to what psychologist Carl Rogers called "reflective listening." For example, in a client interview, if the client states that he is feeling ill at ease with the bill, the lawyer should reflect the client's feelings by repeating key phrases or words that he hears the client say and elicit clarification by asking, "What parts of the bill make you uncomfortable?"

Other active listening skills include the following:

- Sitting forward in the chair, which signals attentiveness and care
- Taking notes
- Not interrupting the interviewee or showing other signs of impatience
- Nodding, making consistent eye contact (without, of course, staring at the interviewee)
- Making comments like, "It sounds as though you have a few reservations about . . ."
- Asking open-ended questions to get more information

§ 12.03.2 Gender Listening

Gender listening, which means listening differently depending on the sex of the speaker, is based on the work of experts like Deborah Tannen (*Talking from 9 to 5* (Avon Books 1994)), who researched the different communication styles of men and women.

During a conversation, women, for example, tend to nod their heads to show that they understand what is being said. Men interpret this nodding, however, as agreement with what is being said and are often surprised to learn that all is not well. Women will say, "I'm sorry," meaning "It's too bad that such and such happened." Men tend to view the "I'm sorry," however, as the woman's apology—as if she feels responsible. It is also true that women often tilt their heads and smile, two gestures meant as courtesy; men tend to consider them submissive. Finally, women tend to be more intuitive and better listeners, whereas men tend to lecture to others and interrupt more. The law firm interviewer who understands gender listening will pick up on these clues and cues and gather more and better information than an interviewer who is unaware of such gender distinctions.

§ 12.03.3 Paying Attention to Nonverbal Communication

Going beyond early research in body language, gestures, and other forms of nonverbal communication, the work of Professor Albert Mehrabian of the University of Southern California defined three essential components of personal presentation: verbal (what we say), vocal (how we sound), and visual (how we look when we speak). The effectiveness of a speaker is, Mehrabian found, 55 percent visual, 38 percent vocal, and only 7 percent verbal. Nonverbal communication may therefore be as vital during a survey as the words spoken, and the interviewer should both hone his own nonverbal skills and remain alert to the interviewee's nonverbal communication. It is necessary to pay close attention to eye contact, gestures, posture, facial expressions, and other signals.

§ 12.04 It Pays to Ask Questions

Although many lawyers are concerned that prior mistakes or misunderstandings between themselves and their clients may surface during the survey process, client satisfaction surveys are, from a marketing perspective, opportunities for lawyers to reinforce relationships with their clients, in particular because the comments made by clients and prospective clients are, almost without exception, constructive, specific, and productive.

Mistakes are a part of life. They are a part of business deals as well as legal matters. It is the recovery process of righting a wrong that is a lawyer's chance to demonstrate that he is willing to deal with an error, correct it, and stand behind the relationship. The recovery of an error is one of the strongest marketing opportunities that exist.

A few examples follow:

- Through gentle but strong probing during a face-to-face interview, a client finally revealed that the in-house department had been very disappointed with a weak coverage memo written two years earlier by the law firm. The client had been so disappointed with the memo, in fact, that it had retained another firm to write a second opinion, but the client had never complained to the first firm about either the problem or the fee. Chagrined to learn about this blunder and its consequences, the law firm decided to compensate by providing four free hours of coverage work to the client, to be used anytime that the in-house lawyer deemed necessary. This solution pleased the client and resulted in a significant amount of new litigation being sent to the law firm over the following months. The relationship continues to this day.
- When the managing partner of a law firm visited a privately held, father-and-son-owned company, he was greeted with accolades and great war stories. When the son was asked whether there was anything that the law firm could do to make the service even better, however, he peered over his glasses, paused, and said, "Well, I wasn't going to say anything about this because it's embarrassing. But you know that litigator you've been bringing around? The one who will replace your retiring partner?" The managing partner nodded. "Well," the son continued, "Pop hates him." He added that they had been interviewing other litigation boutiques to take over that part of the work. The very next day, the law firm's managing partner brought a

new litigator to meet the father and son, thus salvaging the relationship.

- A managing partner met with the in-house counsel of a Fortune 500 electronic company to discuss the company's views on the services that the law firm had been providing for over twelve years. As the interview progressed, the managing partner was shocked to learn that this client, who had been using the firm exclusively for corporate and intellectual property matters, had no idea that the firm had a litigation department. A meeting was set up to cross-market the litigation practice group, and within six weeks litigation matters followed.
- A large paper products manufacturer had been working with a law firm for eight years. During an interview, the interviewer was surprised to learn of the company's annoyance about billing. The company's billing format had changed, and on three separate occasions instructions had been sent to the law firm regarding future billings. The company's representatives expressed their anger over the law firm's continued disregard of the new formatting instructions and said they were contemplating ending the relationship. It turned out that the billing department had been filing the requests, but no one was acting on them. The situation was rectified immediately, and the relationship was saved.
- A market penetration research interview was conducted with a potential client, an emerging biotechnology firm in Silicon Valley. The company provided all of the specifics about how outside counsel were selected; what the working relationship should be; and how the company preferred to engage one of their ten in-house lawyers to work directly with the outside lawyers, thus forming a cohesive team. The company even provided a bridge for the law firm by detailing the experience that a firm must have and how that information should be relayed to the general counsel in order to be considered for future matters.

§ 12.05 Following Up

Merely surveying clients is clearly not enough to maintain and develop client relationships. After the firm finds out what the client requires, expects, or demands, partners and lawyers must be prepared to meet those requirements, expectations, and demands to implement genuine changes. If such action is not taken—and taken promptly—the client may go elsewhere for legal services.

At the conclusion of the survey, if conducted via telephone or in person, thank the client for his time and participation. Follow up with a thank-you letter to the client that reflects the specific issues raised during the interaction and what changes you, the attorney(s) and the firm, will be making in order to completely satisfy the client.

When responding to global changes, such as the aggregated information from a written survey or group of phone surveys, send a letter to all respondents that summarizes changes taking place in the firm as a result of the survey process. Changes may include offering a direct electronic hookup with clients who want it, systematizing procedures for sharing litigation documents, adding another dedicated fax line, sending out practice group brochures, setting up alternative fee arrangements, and exploring precisely what "partnering" means.

Even where changes cannot or will not be made as the clients request, be sure to respond and tell them. There is nothing worse, or more damaging to client–law firm relationships, than either not telling the clients what action will or will not occur from their requests and recommendations or telling them what changes you will make and then not implementing them.

The past several years have demonstrated to the legal community at large that law firm survival depends on responsiveness. Longevity of a relationship is no longer any guarantee of the continuity of a relationship. Clients want more than *satisfaction;* now, just like the customers of Nordstrom, FedEx, and Ritz-Carlton, they demand *delight.* Spend most of your marketing dollars on plans for satisfying and delighting existing clients, and then watch your firm's business base expand.

§ 12.06 Action Plan

- Determine which clients you want to keep.
- Create interview questions.
- Interview the clients you want to keep.

FIGURE 12.1

Sample Client Satisfaction Survey

The following is a sample client satisfaction survey using the continuum model. It is appropriate for mail-in and telephone interviews but may be best used with in-person interviews so that follow-up questions may be easily asked.

I. Please circle the number that best represents how you feel about each of the following.

1 = rarely satisfied; 6 = completely satisfied

A. How satisfied were you with the turnaround time on the work we performed for you?

1 2 3 4 5 6

B. How satisfied were you with the amount and timeliness of information given to you regarding the status of your matter?

1 2 3 4 5 6

C. How satisfied were you with the amount of attention given to your matter?

1 2 3 4 5 6

D. How satisfied were you with our timeliness in responding to your telephone calls and/or letters?

1 2 3 4 5 6

E. How satisfied were you that the lawyer was accessible on short notice?

1 2 3 4 5 6 N/A

F. How satisfied were you with how we listened to your concerns?

1 2 3 4 5 6

G. How satisfied were you that we understood your business and/or personal goals?

1 2 3 4 5 6

H. How satisfied were you that your matter was appropriately staffed with respect to the work performed by the lawyer and the work performed by the paralegal or legal assistant?

1 2 3 4 5 6

I. How satisfied were you that our written communications were clear, concise, and in understandable language?

1 2 3 4 5 6

J. How satisfied were you with the amount of information given on our billing statement?

1 2 3 4 5 6

K. How satisfied were you with our responsiveness to billing comments that you made?

1 2 3 4 5 6 N/A

L. How satisfied were you that we were cost-conscious in handling your work?

1 2 3 4 5 6

M. How satisfied were you that we understood your preferences with respect to the delivery of legal services?

1 2 3 4 5 6

N. How satisfied were you with the amount of your legal fees and costs given the quality of the services that we provided?

1 2 3 4 5 6

O. How satisfied were you with the ability of this office to meet your legal needs?

1 2 3 4 5 6

P. How satisfied are you that we keep you informed of legal changes that might affect your business?

1 2 3 4 5 6

II. Please answer the following questions.
  A. Please tell us what we should keep doing for you.
  B. Please tell us what we should stop doing.
  C. Please give us your suggestions on how we can improve our service to you.
  D. Please tell us about any instance of anyone from our office not relating well to you and your staff.

III. Please mark with an X the legal services that you have used from this firm.

___ General civil litigation
___ Personal injury
___ Family law
___ Real estate
___ Estate planning
___ Business law
___ Bankruptcy
___ Criminal law
___ Banking/credit union law
___ Employment/labor law
___ Tax law
___ Intellectual property
___ Environmental law

IV. Please mark with an X the legal services that you anticipate needing in the future.

___ General civil litigation
___ Personal injury
___ Family law
___ Real estate

___ Estate planning
___ Business law
___ Bankruptcy
___ Criminal law
___ Banking/credit union law
___ Employment/labor law
___ Tax law
___ Intellectual property
___ Environmental law

Thank you for taking a few minutes to complete this survey. The information that you provide will help us give better service to all of our clients.

PART IV

Financial Management

CHAPTER 13

Creating the Financial Plan

My difficulty is in reconciling my gross habits with my net income.

—Errol Flynn

Chapter Checklist

- o Key Financial Terms
- o Introduction to Cash Flow
- o Creating the Collected Revenue Cash Flow Form
- o Creating the Paid Expenses Cash Flow Form
- o Creating the Summary Cash Flow Form
- o Final Thoughts on Cash Flow Plans
- o Action Plan

The most important element of the business plan is the financial plan. Ironically, this is the step on which most firms spend the least amount of time. The financial plan is the true guide to the firm's success or failure.

The basis of a financial plan is the historical facts of the business up to the point of making or revising the plan. What the revenues and expenses have been comprise the firm's financial history. The natural tendency is for history to repeat itself—and therefore for the firm to continue along as it always has. The problem is that those who are mired in the past will never move ahead. But because you are reading this book and starting to think about planning, you are probably not satisfied with your performance history to date. You probably want to improve your firm's and/or your personal financial situation.

History does not necessarily *have* to repeat itself—the act of planning can create new directions and effect substantial improvements in a firm's finances. Planning involves taking the facts of the past but changing some of the assumptions and altering some of the financial and marketing elements to affect the future. To put it another way, the financial plan begins with the history of the firm's performance and allows you to take steps that will positively change the future.

So what exactly is a financial plan? What does it look like, and what does it do? Although it could involve many kinds of charts, budgets, and statements, the simplest and most powerful plan of all—and the only one that really counts in a professional service business like a law firm—is the cash flow statement. The cash flow statement is a three-page schematic or document that spells out exactly where and how the firm will spend its money in the next twelve months. The cash flow statement (also called a *cash flow budget, statement of cash,* or *forecast*) is a *forecasting* tool that is the key to financial planning for lawyers.

The main principle to keep in mind for a cash flow plan is KISS: Keep It Short and Simple. As mentioned in other contexts, unless the process is simple, it will not be used. The key is to make a chart that is no more than three pages long: one page projects the firm's revenue, one page projects the expenses, and the last page summarizes the previous two. No long treatises, no binders, no colors. Just three one-page charts, with supporting data if desired. For examples of these charts, filled in with information from a hypothetical firm, see Figures 13.1, 13.2, and 13.3.

A cash flow schematic or form can be created in a number of ways. Use any standard spreadsheet computer program (Microsoft Office, Corel, QuickBooks, etc.) or one of the law practice management programs that have cash flow schematics, or simply copy the blank forms in this book and fill them in—using a pencil *with an eraser* until after the process is completed and you have finished making adjustments.

My plan for this chapter is to take the forms that comprise the cash flow plan, break them down row by row, and help you understand how to fill them out. By the end of this chapter, you should be able to take the three blank forms in appendix A—along with the financial information that you have already gathered and some careful consideration—and fill out your own cash flow statement.

§ 13.01 Key Financial Terms

Before we look at the specific forms, let's learn a little about the terminology of the financial accounting world. The financial world has its own language, and while this book is not a financial accounting primer, a working knowledge of the main terms and their definitions will be helpful to you. More definitions can be found in the glossary in the back of this book.

- *Accounts payable.* Money you owe others (usually expenses) that you have not yet paid out.
- *Accounts receivable.* Money owed to you for work done that has been billed but not yet received.
- *Accrual versus cash accounting.* Accrual records reflect income irrespective of whether cash has been collected. In other words, accrual accounting reflects billings, work in progress (work partially done but not yet billed), and accounts receivable (work billed but not yet collected). Cash accounting, on the other hand, reflects only collections, never billings or work in progress. Almost all small law firms operate on a cash basis—that is, accounting for cash as it comes in and goes out. Larger law firms maintain both cash and accrual records.
- *Aging.* This refers to analyzing how long a client has owed you money for work performed and billed; shows how old each billing is (see the accounts receivable aging forms in appendix B).
- *Expenses.* Expenses are uses of the firm's cash; they reduce the cash available. These are all of the checks written or charges made for salaries, rent, taxes, supplies, utilities, insurance, etc.
- *Financial statements.* These are reports that summarize the results of a business's transactions during a specific period of time. There are three basic reports, or statements, of which you need to be aware:
  - *Balance sheet.* This is a breakdown of the assets and liabilities of a business as of a certain date. It is a static measure, or a snapshot, of the firm at one moment in time. The balance sheet, in the context of a professional practice, is generally not very important. It does not give any indication of where the business is going. A law firm is not capital- or equipment-intensive; the real assets of the firm—its people—are not balance sheet items.
  - *Cash flow statement.* Cash is the grease that makes the wheel turn; without enough of it at the right times, your whole business grinds to a halt. While income statements and balance sheets do provide valid information, the cash flow statement is the most important working document for a law firm as well as for any other business. A business needs a cash flow statement because of the time differential between the expenditure of funds and the receipt of cash revenues. This cash-back-to-cash cycle takes time. Before the first cycle is concluded, the second cycle has started. Thus, a business needs additional cash to keep the firm operating and must plan for cash flowing both in and out. This is true even in cases where advance, initial retainers are received. Such retainers ease your plight or shorten the cycle, but they do not eliminate this overlap of cycles.
  - *Income statement.* The income statement—also called the *profit and loss statement*, or *P&L*—is moderately important. It tells you how well the firm did financially for a given period of time (see example in appendix C). Using the accrual (versus cash) method of accounting, the income statement tells how much revenue has been billed,

how much expense has been accrued, and how much net income or profit resulted. The income statement is usually prepared on a monthly, quarterly, and annual basis. This statement, however, does not tell us how much cash was collected or spent. That is done by the cash flow statement.

- *Income and profits*. These are two different terms frequently used to mean the same thing in accrual accounting; they have little relevance to small law firms. They both refer to what is left over after expenses are subtracted from sales or revenues. However, most professional service businesses are operated on a cash basis. This figure, if it is positive, is usually taken out as a lawyer's salary (payment to an associate or staff person) or draw (payment to an equity lawyer as a prepayment of compensation, which will be adjusted at the end of the year based on the firm's compensation system and formula). (I do not want to confuse the issue with "gross" or "net" profits at this point; but if you are interested, the profits that I am talking about here are net profits after federal income taxes are paid.)
- *Revenues*. Revenues are any sources of cash to the firm; they increase cash available. For lawyers or other professional service providers, the revenue that matters is the revenue that is collected, not billed. It is the fee or recovery that has actually made it through the door that counts.

§ 13.02 Introduction to Cash Flow

The cash flow plan is not a historical document to be preserved for posterity in firm files. It is an ongoing management tool that requires constant updating as new information becomes available from the operations of the firm. It is a financial guide that a manager uses to plan for profits by prioritizing, anticipating, and allotting the revenues and expenditure of funds. Cash flow analysis is the most important management tool at your disposal for contemplating future activities and controlling the firm's financial affairs.

Let's follow a calendar timeline to see how the cash really flows—or slows to a trickle. On days 1 to 30, you perform legal services such as negotiating and writing a contract for your client. On day 30, if you are paying attention to the lessons of this book, you will send out your billing statement to the client. In the meantime, between days 1 and 30, you have expenditures connected with this matter, such as rent, salaries for secretarial and other staff, insurance, etc. Somewhere between day 31 and day 120—let's make it day 63—the client sends you partial payment. On day 48, you start to work on another matter for that client. This matter, for example, is a breach of contract trial that requires the expenditure of additional costs, including more rent, more salaries, etc. At the end of the trial, you send out a new statement to the client even though you have yet to receive full payment for the first task. Thus, there is a lag in the cash-back-to-cash cycle.

In order to keep your firm financially healthy, you need to plan for such lags by completing a cash flow plan, which is comprised of three charts: a revenue chart, an expenses chart, and a chart summarizing the other two charts. You need to concern yourself with this cash flow statement on a weekly, if not daily, basis.

Keep in mind that when working with cash flow forms, you are to fill in amounts in the month that they are collected or paid out. Also, fill in all of the boxes across the page for each row. The cash flow statement covers a period of at least twelve months into the future. As you forecast for months farther away from the present, the figures may become more conjectural. That is OK because more information will become available as you get closer in time to those months. The plan should be revised at least monthly so that you can alter directions and spot problem areas when things do not go as you have planned. I call this a rolling twelve-month cash flow budget: every thirty days, you knock off the oldest month, make appropriate revisions, and add a new month at the point farthest out in time. (Figures 13.1, 13.2, and 13.3 cover a twelve-month period. When you become more comfortable and proficient with this kind of planning, I suggest that you extend the process to eighteen months.)

The amount of time that you spend on this planning process will depend on how precise you want the cash flow budget to be. I suggest that you not worry about preciseness, especially the first time that you prepare the plan. An error factor will always exist; our world is not perfect, and you will not be perfect the first time that you use this process. It gets easier with time and experience, though.

If you do not have the time to do this kind of detailed cash flow work yourself, or if you feel less than proficient with numbers, get someone you trust to put together all of the figures and do the clerical work. An accountant, bookkeeper, trusted employee, or adviser is appropriate. But do not forget that you must be involved in the development of all of the assumptions that go into the making of this plan and that you are responsible for all of the decisions that result from it.

§ 13.03 Creating the Collected Revenue Cash Flow Form

The first part of the cash flow statement describes the "inflow," or revenue coming into the firm on a month-by-month basis during the next year. To start creating the elements that will become the completed revenue cash flow form (see Figure 13.1 for an example and the blank form in appendix A for completing your own), assemble all of the financial facts that you have gathered as described in chapter 3. For this part, you will need all of the revenue information available to you. (See also chapter 14, "Methods of Determining Revenue," for related information.) Then, fill in each row as described in the following subsections.

§ 13.03.1 Row 1: Cash Retainers Collected for General Account

One source of cash inflow is cash retainers (cash includes checks). Cash retainers are split into two parts: the "nonrefundable retainer," which is given for the privilege of having access to you and which goes into your general account; and the remaining portion, which is considered an advance payment for work to be done and which is put into a client trust account. Row 1 concerns only the nonrefundable retainer.

There is no precise percentage or amount that constitutes a nonrefundable fee. The amount depends on the size of the retainer, your experience, and your common sense. You should be aware that at the time of this writing, some bar associations are reviewing this issue, and I expect that a rule of professional conduct addressing this issue will soon be developed.

Look at your historical information and make a total of the nonrefundable portion of your retainers from all of last year (or the most recent twelve-month period). Now evaluate your goals and your marketing strategies and come up with a percentage of change or a new total amount for this category. Take that new desired total for the next year and divide the number by twelve. You now have the average nonrefundable cash retainer that you are expecting each month. Fill in that number in each square of the first row of the revenue cash flow schematic. Do not forget to include the total at the end.

If every business ran with Swiss-watch perfection, you would be done with this section. But business activities have a habit of varying during the year depending on clients coming and going, staff vacations, etc. So while keeping in mind your experience with seasonality and all of the ebbs and flows that you could reasonably expect for your business in the next year, take that same row and, month by month, make adjustments by increasing the amounts for some months and decreasing others.

The total at the end should be the same *unless* during the course of this exercise you decide to change your mind about some of your assumptions. That is OK! Thinking about this process—maybe for the first time—will allow you to consider new ideas, new clients, and new strategies that affect your revenue. Just make sure that you jot down how and why your assumptions changed.

When you are satisfied that this first row of numbers reflects your nonrefundable cash retainers, stop. You have now completed the first step of your cash flow plan. Congratulations.

§ 13.03.2 Row 2: Transfer of Funds from Trust Account per Client Instructions

The portion of the retainer that is placed into the client trust account is the advance payment to be applied against future billings that, according to your state bar regulations, is refundable if the work is not completed and the fee not earned. Fee deposits that are placed in the client trust account represent unearned, advance payment to be applied against expected future fees.

Row 2 represents those trust account funds that have been earned during the month in question, irrespective of the source or the time of deposit into this account. When your fee is considered earned *and* the client has authorized you to withdraw funds from this account for payment of your fees, you are entitled to transfer funds from the client's trust account to your general account. Without both earning the fee charged *and* receiving written client authorization, you normally cannot transfer fees.

For safety's sake, client authorization should be specific and should be obtained in writing for each fee payment to be made from the client's trust account. However, some lawyers prefer to get an overall, general authorization rather than contact the client each time. This general authorization should be set forth in writing, and the written fee agreement that is signed at the very beginning of the representation should contain it.

Following the same procedure as used in Row 1, take your information from last year; add your desired changes, your experience, and your best guesses for the future; and fill in the new numbers across this row.

§ 13.03.3 Row 3: Contingency Fees Collected

Another revenue source is collected contingency fees. Lawyers working on contingency cases usually handle personal injury, debt collection, workers' compensation, or major antitrust matters. The handling of other matters may also be compensated on a percentage basis. These fees increase your cash in the month in which they are collected.

In the same manner as before, take the information that you have, make appropriate adjustments for the future, and fill in the boxes in Row 3.

If you are a contingency-based lawyer, you may think that projecting revenues applies only to hourly or other fee-based lawyers, but you can do it, too. You know more about your potential revenue than you think. Most contingency matters take anywhere from eighteen months to five years to resolve. Although you may not know exactly when a case will be settled or tried, you should be able to estimate when the matter is likely to be resolved and what the likely outcome will be. By going through all of the cases in the office, you can plot out your expected revenues on the basis of your jurisdiction, the matter, your recovery arrangement with the clients, and your past experience. This is no less accurate than the method that hourly-based fee lawyers use when they estimate what their revenues will be on the basis of previous history and work expected in the future.

§ 13.03.4 Row 4: Collected Accounts Receivable

The next source of inflow comes from the collection of accounts receivable. Accounts receivable refers to all of the money that is owed to you for work done that has been billed but not received, over and above any trust account transfers. In the cash-based method of accounting that I recommend (as opposed to the accrual method), the moment that you receive money owing to you and deposit it is the moment that you account for it and declare it as revenue. This is an increase in cash, and it goes into Row 4 in the appropriate box. (For a discussion of specific collection tips for decreasing your accounts receivable and speeding up your cash flow, see chapter 17, "Credit and Collections.")

Again, take the information that you have, make appropriate adjustments for the future, and fill in the boxes in Row 4.

§ 13.03.5 Row 5: Funds Collected from Sale of Assets

This row represents the money that you collect from the sale of used equipment or other assets, such as a used car, a used computer system, a personal computer, or a telephone system.

§ 13.03.6 Row 6: Miscellaneous Collected Funds

This row is for funds received from a variety of other sources, such as the interest on checking accounts or anything else that may be specific to your firm.

§ 13.03.7 Row 7: Total Operating Funds Collected

In this row, add up the amounts that you entered for each month in the first six rows, and put the grand total for the year in the far right box.

§ 13.03.8 Final Rows

You will see two more items after Row 7: Row 8, "New Equity Funds Collected"; and Row 9, "New Debt Funds Collected." These amounts come from the summary cash flow form described below. New equity funds represent money to start your new practice or to keep your existing practice on an even keel. This is money that is invested in exchange for ownership—or equity—in the firm. New debt funds are either short-term or long-term loans from a bank, a relative, or another source to whom you will owe these funds.

These two rows are not part of the operating revenue because, at this point, you do not know if you are going to need them. Only after you have worked through the summary will you know if you require additional funds as either new equity or short-term/long-term loans. Although this will be actual cash that you receive, you do not need to account for it on this form; the items are listed here only as reference information. The actual figures are accounted for on the summary form.

§ 13.04 Creating the Paid Expenses Cash Flow Form

Expenses are uses of cash, and the next part of the cash flow statement describes this "outflow" of money from the firm (see Figure 13.2 for an example and the blank form in appendix A for completing your own). If you have not already done so, assemble all of the pertinent financial facts relating to your expenses.

Expenses can be predicted with greater certainty than revenues because in a professional practice setting the expenses tend to be limited in kind and repetitive. The repetitive nature of expenses and the control that the professional has over them are the key reasons for the greater certainty in predicting what future expenses will be.

Expenses include such items as payroll, library, continuing legal education, rent, auto, dues and subscriptions, insurance (errors and omissions, general liability, etc.), telephone, and utilities. In addition to these expense items, outflow includes capital expenditures such as equipment and furniture purchases, but these infrequent expenses are covered on the summary chart described later in the chapter.

Many of the expenses cannot be controlled or reduced once set in place. These items include rent and insurance (although in today's fluid economy, even rent is not as fixed as we used to think). Some items, on the other hand, can be reduced, such as library expenditures (you can share a library or use the county law library in your local jurisdiction), payroll (to a more limited extent, especially if you are a solo practitioner), and dues and subscriptions. Savings in these three areas alone can be substantial in many cases. Further, if you know when to anticipate low and high cash flow periods, you can postpone or advance equipment purchases. (For more cash flow tips, see chapter 22, "Improving Your Bottom Line.")

If you do not have the needed historical facts for filling out the expense cash flow chart, there are industry standards or guidelines that may speed up the process for you. Several organizations have published statistical surveys showing averages of their collected data. According to one such recent study, the expenses of the average law firm can be estimated as follows:

- Staff (including paralegals), 45 percent (not including draws or partner compensation)
- Occupancy (rent), 17 percent
- Equipment (on summary chart), 6 percent
- Malpractice insurance (errors and omissions), 4 percent
- Outside professional services, 2 percent
- Library, 2 percent
- Marketing and public relations, 2 percent

The total in this study is 78 percent, a high percentage that leaves only 22 percent for the lawyers as draws or salaries. Currently, many firms are reporting nonlawyer operating expenses of over 70 percent. However, while some lawyers are taking only 20 percent for themselves as draws or salaries, others are taking home up to 80 percent. Keep in mind that projected expenses based on industry averages are just that—averages for firms that may or may not be close in nature to your firm. In fact, these averages are usually based on larger firms. Using these averages as anything more than a benchmark or reference point is dangerous.

For the paid expenses cash flow form, I have separated expenses into standard categories. Feel free to modify these headings to reflect your particular needs.

§ 13.04.1 Row 1: Employee Salaries

The single most important (i.e., largest) expense for a law firm is salaries. Salaries are comprised of two categories: employee salaries and partner draws or shareholder salaries. Employee salaries concern employees such as secretaries, receptionists, telephone operators, clerical personnel, etc., but not lawyers. Row 1 is for employee salaries only.

Many small firms and solo practitioners are successful in maintaining a low ratio of personnel to lawyers; that is, fewer personnel are required in today's technological environment than at any time in history. In addition, many tasks today can be outsourced—that is, there are companies that act as independent contractors and specialize in specific tasks such as accounting, secretarial work, and even lawyering. The advantage of such outsourcing is that you incur expenses only when and as they are required. The disadvantage is that it is sometimes hard to predict when that will be.

Outsourcing expenses should be forecast in reference to the anticipated revenue strategies determined in the collected revenue chart already created. By contrast, if you maintain a regular staff, the expenses related to staff salaries are readily known and predictable.

So, for Row 1, fill in the anticipated employee salaries using the same procedure as before. Be sure that these figures reflect any changes in staffing due to new marketing strategies, downsizing or growth plans, extra projects, or the need for additional help around vacation time. For example, in a one-secretary firm, when the secretary goes on vacation, the work still needs to get done. You would probably have the expense of one temporary plus the normal pay for the permanent secretary on vacation. Adjust the amounts in the months in which they will be paid.

§ 13.04.2 Row 2: Employee Taxes

Employee taxes are an important category and should be considered separately. Failure to pay payroll taxes is not only a civil offense that carries a stiff fine, but it may also be a criminal offense under certain circumstances. There is no excuse to forget this category, and there must be no temptation to "temporarily" borrow the tax money until that expected "check in the mail" arrives. Too many times that check does not arrive, and then there are no funds available to pay the payroll taxes. This process can be compounded until the hole is too big to crawl out of and the professional faces the worst of consequences. In some jurisdictions, such a violation is deemed to be moral turpitude and, apart from civil and criminal penalties, is reason for disbarment.

The tax generally approximates one-third of employee salaries. This is not applicable to partner draws until such time as the draws are converted to salaries. The tax does apply to shareholder salaries when the salaries are paid.

§ 13.04.3 Row 3: Partner Draws / Shareholder Salaries

While the salaries of staff are often fixed (already determined), partner draws and shareholder salaries are not, or at least should not be, fixed. Fixed expenses are constant and usually do not change regardless of what the firm is doing or not doing. Variable expenses can vary with firm activities or decisions.

The single largest expense that *should* be variable is the partner's or shareholder's draw or salary (see chapter 22, "Improving Your Bottom Line," for more about this). Although many lawyers act as though they believe that they are entitled to a particular draw or salary and that this sum should be increased each year, I believe that lawyers must now approach their draw or salary as a variable expense, not as a given. As in any business, lawyers who own their practice should be the last ones to be paid. Whatever is left over is available to pay the draw or salary of the lawyer(s). The financial focus of the firm should be on the success of the business, not the enrichment of the lawyer(s) at the expense of the firm. After all, without a healthy business, there will not be any salary to draw!

§ 13.04.4 Row 4: Rent

Typically, the second largest category of expenses is rent.

Usually, rent is a fixed obligation based on a previously signed lease or rental agreement. The only variables are "escalations" or "pass-throughs" (including common area maintenance), which are charges that the landlord is entitled to add to the base rent set in the first year of the lease term and that are based on a formula set forth in the lease. But even when a portion of the rent is unknown until the end of the year, a very close estimate of the amount that will be due and when the amount will be payable can be figured by referring to your previous experience with the landlord or the experience of other tenants in the building. This information is readily available. If there are no anticipated changes, fill in the boxes with the same rent amount for each month for the entire year. (For more about reducing your rent expense, see chapter 22, "Improving Your Bottom Line.")

Fixed costs like rent (occupancy costs) tend to be higher in the West than in other parts of the country because the rates per square foot are greater and the office spaces tend to be larger. Also, the proportion of this expense to revenue is greater because western law offices tend to use more staff per lawyer.

§ 13.04.5 Rows 5, 6, and 7: Insurance

The next three rows concern insurance. Row 5 is for health insurance expenses. Row 6 is for general insurance expenses, including general liability, business interruption, fire (at replacement value), office package (replacement of valuable papers), personal property, workers' compensation, and a general umbrella policy. Row 7 is for errors and omissions (malpractice) insurance. Fill in the appropriate amounts for all insurance costs.

§ 13.04.6 Row 8: Marketing and Public Relations

Marketing and public relations can be a large expense category. Advertising is not cheap, and neither are mailings.

The old rule of thumb was that marketing is the first expense to cut when things are tough. I believe in the counterargument that when times are tough and everyone else is cutting back on marketing, *that* is the time to keep your marketing efforts strong. You will stand out from the crowd (one of the purposes of marketing) and establish yourself in the market.

My suggestion is to keep your marketing costs somewhere between 1 percent and 5 percent of total operating costs. However, this is merely a guideline. It clearly has no relevance when you first open your practice. Then, much of your time and a high percentage of your expenditures will be for marketing.

As before, make sure to figure your payments in the month that they are to be paid out. For example, if you are running an ad campaign through an advertising agency, your expenditure for a November newspaper ad may be due in advance or on a net 30 basis, depending on the agency's policies.

In general, ad agencies tend to charge a monthly retainer plus hourly billing for services rendered on a net 30 basis. Outside expenditures made on your behalf may be billed in advance. Public relations agencies mostly work on an advance monthly retainer. Design studios tend to charge on a project basis, with a 50 percent advance and the balance due on completion or billed net 30.

§ 13.04.7 Rows 9 and 10: Office Expenses

Row 9 is for office or miscellaneous supplies.

Row 10 is for another large expense category: telephone charges, fax copies, and photocopies. In a larger firm, photocopying costs can be a major expense.

While many firms bill clients for the expenses in Row 10, sophisticated clients are now objecting and arguing that the lawyer should absorb such costs. These clients are saying that such expenses are normal, are part of the overhead of a law firm, and should be included in the hourly or other fee being paid by the client.

Thus, the best way to handle most of these miscellaneous expenses is to increase your hourly billing rate. Most clients do not mind an increase of $5 to $15 in the hourly billing rate, and this added revenue usually will create a net increase in revenues even after you have paid for the above-listed cost items. Only special items and large per-item costs, such as a large photocopying job and deposition transcript fees, should be billed to a client.

§ 13.04.8 Row 11: Professional Dues

Row 11 is for professional dues. If you practice in a state with an integrated or mandatory state bar participation, you will undoubtedly have to pay annual dues. Fill in the amount(s) in the month that you pay the dues; do *not* spread out the fee over twelve months. As an example, if you reside in California, show payment of dues of $500 to the California State Bar in November (when the fee is due) and dues of $300 to the American Bar Association in August.

§ 13.04.9 Row 12: Continuing Legal Education

Row 12 is for continuing legal education (CLE). Education for lawyers has become big business, and there is no shortage of CLE programs available. In at least thirty-seven states, CLE is mandatory. Some providers charge an annual fee—the California Continuing Education of the Bar, for example, provides a program "passport" for $1,500, payable in January—while others charge on a per-use basis. You could set aside a specific sum (e.g., $100 per month) for all educational programs.

§ 13.04.10 Row 13: Library

Row 13 is for library expenses. Most publishers are willing to bill lawyers on a monthly basis. Consider this category as constant throughout the year.

§ 13.04.11 Row 14: Professional Services

This category includes accountants, law firm management consultants, marketing consultants, and any other *outside* professionals who provide services to the practice.

§ 13.04.12 Row 15: Travel and Entertainment

This category is for official firm travel and entertainment of clients.

§ 13.04.13 Row 16: Loan Repayments

Loan repayments include not only principal but also interest. Any loans that you receive (see the cash flow summary section for details) must be paid back—with interest. Since this is cash out the door, fill in the appropriate amounts, if any, in the months that the payments occur.

§ 13.04.14 Row 17: Total Operating Expenditures

Total the amounts for each month in this row, and put the grand total in the lower, far right box. Congratulations—you are now two-thirds of the way through the cash flow plan.

§ 13.05 Creating the Summary Cash Flow Form

The third, and final, chart is the summary cash flow form (see Figure 13.3). It combines what we have already done in the revenue and expenses forms with new information and provides an overview of the cash flow for the firm. This is the critical schematic to evaluate on a regular basis to keep on top of the firm's economic health.

§ 13.05.1 Row 1: Beginning Cash Balance

Row 1 is titled "Beginning Cash Balance." The beginning cash balance (in the first box of Row 1 in the upper left corner) is the opening capital account for the first day of the office or practice. This is the amount of money with which you start the practice.

If the practice is presently an ongoing venture, then use the "book" cash balance (what is showing in your checkbook) as of the first day of the month when you begin this analysis. Be careful to distinguish between the book cash balance and the cash balance according to the most recent bank statement. These two figures will be different.

§ 13.05.2 Rows 2 and 3: Increases and Decreases in Cash

The next two rows refer to either an increase or a decrease in the cash based on the revenue and expense charts that you have already completed. Simply take the monthly totals and pencil them into these rows: revenue in Row 2, "Plus: Increases—Collected Revenue"; and expenses in Row 3, "Less: Decreases—Paid Expenses."

§ 13.05.3 Row 4: Cash Balance

By adding Row 2 to Row 1, and subtracting Row 3, you now have the numbers for Row 4, "Ending Cash Balance."

§ 13.05.4 Row 5: Short-Term Loans

To the extent that the ending cash balance will generally be less than the desired working cash balance, you may need to obtain a short-term loan, which will be entered in Row 5.

Depending on your comfort level and how much you like to sleep at night, the rule of thumb is that in any new law practice, the principals should have an adequate reserve of cash to cover living expenses for six to eighteen months *if no draws or salaries are available to take out of the firm*. In lieu of such a cash supply or a large enough ending cash balance, you may want to consider a short-term loan.

A short-term loan may be a loan from friends or family, it may be loans on your credit card, or it may be a revolving bank loan or line of credit. But it is intended to be *short-term*—only long enough to get you over a temporary shortfall in the cash flow of the firm.

§ 13.05.5 Row 6: Cash Available

Row 6 is the total cash available for a given period. The total of the short-term loan (Row 5) and the ending cash balance (Row 4) will produce the total cash available for that given period of time.

§ 13.05.6 Row 7: Capital Expenditures

Next, you need to account for capital expenditures, if any, such as equipment, furniture, redecorating, etc. Consider equipment a variable or flexible element. This should be one of the first items to cut or reduce if the cash flow picture is looking bleak. You could also finance a major purchase to spread the payments over time or delay the purchase until cash flow is restored.

§ 13.05.7 Row 8: Balance of Cash

The difference between cash available (Row 6) and equipment purchases (Row 7) results in the balance of cash in Row 8.

§ 13.05.8 Row 9: Long-Term Loans

If the balance of cash is negative in one or more months, then you must look for long-term loans to increase the level of cash. Long-term loans are identified in Row 9.

Long-term loans are usually either new equity funds or new debt funds. New equity funds are received in exchange for ownership—or equity—in the firm. New debt funds are loans from a bank, a relative, or another source to whom you will owe these funds.

Since these funds are actual cash receipts, you need to account for them on this form. These figures are also noted for reference at the bottom of the collected revenue cash flow form.

§ 13.05.9 Row 10: Free Cash Flow

When you add Row 9 to Row 8, the net result is free cash flow, which is documented in Row 10.

§ 13.05.10 Row 11: Savings

Row 11 is a deduction of cash for savings. Law firm savings take two forms: (1) savings for the "valleys," or lulls of the practice, or for unexpected emergencies in the practice; and (2) personal savings, savings for retirement, or savings for unexpected personal emergencies. This is, of course, a variable use of cash.

§ 13.05.11 Row 12: Net Free Cash Flow

Subtract Row 11 from Row 10, and you now have the amounts for Row 12, "Net Free Cash Flow." Although nothing in life is actually free, this is the cash that is available for your use.

§ 13.05.12 Row 13: Extraordinary Use of Cash Flow

There always seems to be another pull on your hard-earned cash, but Row 13, "Less: Extraordinary Use of Cash Flow," is the last one. *Extraordinary use of cash flow* means any extraordinary, specific project like purchasing a new computer system, relocating the office, or redecorating the office. If you have got the cash, this is the place to use it!

§ 13.05.13 Row 14: Monthly Cash Totals

The last row, Row 14, "Net Free Cash Flow Carryover," now shows the monthly cash totals for the practice, with the twelve-month grand total in the lower right box.

Note the significance of the term *carryover*—that is, the last number in the first column is the first number in the next column, etc. At any point where you want to stop this schematic and start a new one, any of these bottom-line figures will then "carry over" and become the next period's beginning cash balance.

Congratulations—you have now completed the first run-through of a complete cash flow statement. These figures provide an instant view of the cash flow health of the firm.

§ 13.05.14 Addressing the Issue of Negative Numbers

By reviewing the summary form, you will see that the negative numbers, if any, will start showing up in Row 4 ("Ending Cash Balance"), Row 6 ("Cash Available"), and Row 8 ("Balance of Cash"). If, after Row 9, you have not changed these negative numbers to positive numbers, then your ability to do anything about Row 11 and Row 13 is severely restricted.

One of the goals of creating and evaluating a cash flow plan is to spot upcoming cash problems and adjust the firm's activities so that the cash is always flowing in the right direction—a positive direction. Any dips toward zero—and, in particular, a negative—need to be seriously evaluated (see Figure 13.3). You can and should fine-tune all of the rows in these three schematics—and, of course, the firm's activities that give you the figures—so that you end up with positive figures in Row 14 in the summary form. The grand total needs to be a positive number because you cannot live in a negative cash flow world for long!

§ 13.06 Final Thoughts on Cash Flow Plans

The hardest part is over; from now on, as you gain experience with your business and with this plan, the fine-tuning and revisions will get easier and easier. And your guesses about the future will turn out to be much closer to reality. (For the next level of analysis, see appendix D for forms that go into more depth by allowing you to analyze the projected figures, the actual figures, and the variance (how far off you were).)

Remember that this is a working plan—you will never actually *complete* it, but you will continue to revise it, evaluate it, and learn from its steady use. The remainder of this book will present additional information to help you in thinking about your practice and the cash flow and marketing plans.

§ 13.07 Action Plan

- Using the three blank cash flow forms in appendix A, go through the entire process of filling in the numbers as described in this chapter. Plan to spend as much time as needed for this—it can take many hours or even days to complete.
- Review, adjust, and revise the forms as needed depending on how the figures work out. One of your goals should be to limit or reduce all negative numbers.

FIGURE 13.1

Cash Flow Projection Form: Collected Revenue

Cash Flow Statement: Revenue													
2013													
Revenues	**Jan.**	**Feb.**	**Mar.**	**Apr.**	**May**	**June**	**July**	**Aug.**	**Sept.**	**Oct.**	**Nov.**	**Dec.**	**Totals**
Cash Retainers Collected for General Account (Not Trust Account)	$ 25,000	–0–	$ 15,000	$ 22,000	$ 32,500	$ 7,200	$ 3,200	$ 4,900	$ 3,350	$ 10,000	$ 15,000	$ 45,000	$ 183,150
Transfer of Funds from Trust Account per Client Instructions	100,000	2,000	25,000	100,000	5,000	10,000	–0–	32,000	45,000	–0–	2,500	4,500	326,000
Contingency Fees Collected	–0–	–0–	–0–	–0–	10,000	8,000	33,000	–0–	25,000	4,200	–0–	23,000	103,200
Collected Accounts Receivable	134,000	125,000	112,000	145,000	133,000	122,000	135,000	188,000	189,000	150,000	165,000	130,000	1,728,000
Funds Collected from Sale of Assets	–0–	–0–	–0–	–0–	–0–	–0–	–0–	–0–	–0–	12,500	–0–	–0–	12,500
Miscellaneous Collected Funds	125	–0–	–0–	–0–	1,500	–0–	–0–	4,500	–0–	–0–	–0–	–0–	6,125
Total Operating Funds Collected	$259,125	$127,000	$152,000	$267,000	$182,000	$147,200	$171,200	$229,400	$262,350	$176,700	$182,500	$202,500	$2,358,975
New Equity Funds Collected	–0–	–0–	–0–	–0–	–0–	–0–	–0–	–0–	–0–	–0–	–0–	–0–	–0–
New Debt Funds Collected	5,000	500,000	–0–	305,000	–0–	230,000	455,000	300,000	110,000	150,000	500,000	–0–	2,555,000

FIGURE 13.2

Cash Flow Projection Form: Paid Expenses

Cash Flow Statement: Revenue													
2013													
Expenses	**Jan.**	**Feb.**	**Mar.**	**Apr.**	**May**	**June**	**July**	**Aug.**	**Sept.**	**Oct.**	**Nov.**	**Dec.**	**Totals**
Employee Salaries	$125,000	$100,000	$113,000	$120,000	$118,000	$119,000	$121,000	$121,000	$119,000	$118,500	$124,000	$123,500	$1,422,000
Employee Taxes	12,500	10,000	11,300	12,000	11,800	11,900	12,100	12,100	11,900	11,850	12,400	–0–	129,850
Partner Draws / Shareholder Salaries	130,000	$130,000	$130,000	$130,000	$130,000	$130,000	130,000	130,000	130,000	130,000	130,000	260,000	1,690,000
Rent	20,000	20,000	20,000	20,000	20,000	20,000	20,000	20,000	20,000	20,000	20,000	20,000	240,000
Health Insurance	8,000	7,500	8,000	8,000	7,750	7,750	7,500	7,500	7,750	7,750	8,000	8,000	93,500
General Insurance	10,000	2,000	–0–	–0–	–0–	10,000	2,000	–0–	–0–	–0–	–0–	4,500	28,500
Errors and Omissions Insurance	5,000	4,000	4,000	4,000	4,000	4,000	–0–	–0–	–0–	–0–	–0–	–0–	25,000
Marketing and Public Relations	1,000	1,000	1,500	1,800	2,000	1,000	3,000	2,500	1,200	1,000	1,300	1,250	18,550
Supplies	3,750	550	1,500	1,650	1,875	600	1,300	2,050	2,150	7,400	2,500	1,600	26,925
Phone/Copy/Fax	2,500	3,000	2,750	3,300	2,750	2,300	2,450	2,200	3,200	3,000	2,800	2,750	33,000
Professional Dues	250	250	250	250	250	250	250	250	250	250	250	250	3,000
Continuing Legal Education	1,500	–0–	–0–	1,500	–0–	–0–	1,500	–0–	–0–	1,500	–0–	–0–	6,000
Library	150	150	150	150	150	150	300	–0–	150	300	–0–	150	1,800
Professional Services	2,000	2,000	2,000	2,000	2,000	2,000	2,000	2,000	2,000	2,000	2,000	2,000	24,000
Travel and Entertainment	7,500	2,500	5,000	6,000	5,500	7,000	5,750	6,000	2,500	3,000	2,750	5,000	58,500
Loan Repayments	10,000	10,000	10,000	10,000	10,000	10,000	10,000	10,000	10,000	10,000	10,000	10,000	120,000
Total Operating Expenditures	$339,150	$292,950	$309,450	$320,650	$316,075	$325,950	$319,150	$315,600	$310,100	$316,550	$316,000	$439,000	$3,920,625

FIGURE 13.3

Cash Flow Projection Form: Summary

Cash Flow Projection: Summary													
2013													
	Jan.	Feb.	Mar.	Apr.	May	June	July	Aug.	Sept.	Oct.	Nov.	Dec.	Totals
Beginning Cash Balance	$100,000	($105,025)	$124,025	($138,425)	$ 12,925	($221,150)	($269,900)	($62,850)	$45,950	$ 3,200	($86,650)	$179,850	($418,050)
Plus: Increases—Collected Revenue	259,125	127,000	152,000	267,000	182,000	147,200	171,200	229,400	262,350	176,700	182,500	202,500	2,358,975
Less: Decreases—Paid Expenses	339,150	292,950	309,450	320,650	316,075	325,950	319,150	315,600	310,100	316,550	316,000	439,000	3,920,625
Ending Cash Balance	19,975	(270,975)	(33,425)	(192,075)	(121,150)	(399,900)	(417,850)	(149,050)	(1,800)	(136,650)	(220,150)	(56,650)	(1,979,700)
Plus: Short-Term Loans	5,000	–0–	–0–	5,000	–0–	–0–	5,000	–0–	–0–	5,000	–0–	–0–	20,000
Cash Available	24,975	(270,975)	(33,425)	(187,075)	(121,150)	(399,900)	(412,850)	(149,050)	(1,800)	(131,650)	(220,150)	(56,650)	(1,959,700)
Less: Capital Expenditures	25,000	–0–	–0–	–0–	–0–	–0–	–0–	5,000	–0–	–0–	–0–	–0–	30,000
Balance of Cash	(25)	(270,975)	(33,425)	(187,075)	(121,150)	(399,900)	(412,850)	(154,050)	(1,800)	(131,650)	(220,150)	(56,650)	(1,989,700)
Plus: Long-Term Loans	–0–	500,000	–0–	300,000	–0–	230,000	450,000	300,000	110,000	145,000	500,000	–0–	2,535,000
Free Cash Flow	(25)	229,025	(33,425)	112,925	(121,150)	(169,900)	37,150	145,950	108,200	13,350	279,850	(56,650)	545,300
Less: Savings	100,000	100,000	100,000	100,000	100,000	100,000	100,000	100,000	100,000	100,000	100,000	100,000	1,200,000
Net Free Cash Flow	(100,025)	129,025	(133,425)	12,925	(221,150)	(269,900)	(62,850)	45,950	8,200	(86,650)	179,850	(156,650)	(654,700)
Less: Extraordinary Use of Cash Flow	5,000	5,000	5,000	–0–	–0–	–0–	–0–	–0–	5,000	–0–	–0–	–0–	20,000
Net Free Cash Flow Carryover	($105,025)	$124,025	($138,425)	$ 12,925	($221,150)	($269,900)	($ 62,850)	$ 45,950	$ 3,200	($86,650)	$179,850	($156,650)	($674,700)

CHAPTER 14

Methods of Determining Revenue

Remember, that money is of a prolific, generating nature. Money can beget money, and its offspring can beget more, and so on.

—Benjamin Franklin (letter to "My Friend, A.B.," 1748)

Chapter Checklist

- o Revenue Pattern Analysis
- o Turnover Ratio
- o Aging Analysis
- o Payment Pattern Analysis
- o Action Plan

In chapter 13, you learned that revenues are sources of cash to the firm—they increase the cash available. A big question that many lawyers ask themselves is, "How can I accurately determine how much revenue to forecast in my cash flow plan?"

As noted in chapter 13, the most obvious way to do this is to look at your historical records; take what you received last year; and, thinking about what will happen in the next year, simply adjust the revenue expectations up or down accordingly. These expectations are based on a number of factors, including new cases, contracts, or retainers; anticipated engagements, based on affirmative or positive responses to your marketing efforts; and expectations of competitive pressures within the legal profession in your particular area of practice. To be accurate in these projections (and you can be), you must know your clients well enough to anticipate their needs. As an aside, this close relationship also will ensure that you are the lawyer from whom the clients will seek all of their legal needs.

But for the more arithmetic-oriented person, there are other mechanisms for projecting future revenues. Four of them are revenue pattern analysis, turnover ratio, aging analysis, and payment pattern analysis.

§ 14.01 Revenue Pattern Analysis

First, by looking at the financial information that you have gathered, prepare a *year-by-year* schedule indicating the revenue that you received in previous years. Now start looking to see if there are any apparent patterns that stand out.

The patterns may be as simple as the following examples:

- You received at least 10 percent more revenue each year for the last three years.
- Your flow of annual revenue fluctuated up or down in proportion to the amount of time and energy you spent in bar association activities.
- There was no apparent pattern for the growth (or decline) of your revenue.

Next, by looking at the same information, prepare a schedule that shows the revenue that you received on a *monthly* basis within each of the previous years. Again, look for patterns.

For example, say you receive a similar percentage of your revenue in the second and third quarters of the year (April-May-June and July-August-September), the largest percentage in the first quarter (January-February-March), and the smallest percentage in the last quarter (October-November-December). Your revenue flow has probably fluctuated up or down in relation to the seasonality of your major clients' industry patterns or in proportion to some other identifiable variable. What is that variable?

Take family law as a practice area example. In the month of December, because of the approaching holidays, new court filings will decline considerably, although visitation or custody disputes may actually increase. In agricultural law, spring may be busy with planting contracts with processors and summer with collection efforts against processors who fail to pay in a timely fashion. Almost every practice area has a certain degree of seasonality associated with it, and it is different for each area. This will be reflected in your revenues and cash flow.

§ 14.02 Turnover Ratio

Where no apparent revenue pattern is observed, try some simple accounting and arithmetic techniques that will help guide your decision-making process.

The typical accounting measure, frequently used by accountants and bankers to determine whether there is a problem in the collection of accounts receivable, is the "turnover ratio" or "average days billings outstanding." The turnover ratio will, on average, tell you that you can expect to receive payment for your billings X number of days after the client receives your billing statement.

This ratio is determined by dividing the accounts receivable balance by the result of last month's billings divided by the number of days in the month:

$$\text{TR} = \frac{\text{Accounts Receivable Balance}}{\text{Last Month's Billings / Days in Month}}$$

Let's look at a hypothetical example. Say you are doing this analysis at the beginning of February, and the accounts receivable balance at the end of the previous quarter (October-November-December) was $200,000. Taking January's total billings of $75,000 and dividing it by the 31 days in January equals $2,419. Dividing $200,000 by $2,419 equals a turnover ratio of 83 days. This means that your average bill "turns over" every 83 days; or, saying it another way, it will take you 83 days on average to collect your bills.

Even more frequently, the formula is stated in annual terms (last year's sales or billings):

$$\text{TR} = \frac{\text{Accounts Receivable Balance}}{\text{Annual Billings / 365 Days}}$$

Using the above example, $200,000 is the accounts receivable balance at the end of the year, annual billings are $900,000, and there are 365 days in the year. Plugging the numbers into the formula gives you a turnover ratio of 81 days.

As you can see by our examples, the turnover ratio is normally different depending on which of these two formulas is used. Which is correct? Both are. You decide which is the most appropriate method for your practice.

The national average for law firms, according to one survey, is between four and five months, or 120 to 150 days. Implicitly, this should tell you that you need to capitalize your firm with funds sufficient to "carry" your clients for at least six months of billings if you do not want to face serious cash pressures in the interim.

The turnover ratio—whichever formula is used—is an accounting procedure that nonservice businesses have been using for years. There is no reason why law firms cannot make use of this excellent method to help them project their revenues. Remember, though, that this is only a guide and should be tested against your own experience.

§ 14.03 Aging Analysis

The "aging analysis" is another accounting measure that may be helpful in predicting when you can expect to receive cash.

First, review your accounts receivable aging chart or schedule or prepare one if none existed before (see Figures 14.1 and 14.2 as examples and the blank form in appendix B for completing your own). A quarterly general ledger can also show this information (see the general ledger example in appendix E).

The accounts receivable aging schedule (see Figure 14.1) will show how old each client's billing is by how much money that client owes for each period of time (thirty-day periods are standard). The first column (0–30) represents the first thirty days after the billing cycle (this is typically considered a current bill that is not yet due). Each column thereafter represents another thirty days from the original billing date.

Obviously, the longer the bill is owed or the older the bill is, the less likely it is that you will ever collect it. Therefore, it is important to pay close attention to your accounts receivable aging analysis.

Looked at in another way, Figure 14.2 shows the status of billings by percentage per period of time. This schedule is based on the preceding year, on a quarterly basis. Look at the numbers at the end of each quarter and determine how "old" the receivables were. Prepare a schematic as shown in Figure 14.2 (use the blank form in appendix B), using the monthly totals for each aging period.

You could make the presentation even more complete by doing it on a monthly basis, using the information supplied in your accounts receivable aging schedule for each of the respective months. (Use the blank form for accounts receivable aging by percentage by month in appendix B.) Greater accuracy would be achieved by using as many months as are available—even up to two to three years.

Trends and patterns can usually be observed by analyzing these schedules. An average or high and low benchmarks can be determined that will be useful in predicting how much of each month's future billing will be collected in cash.

High growth rates and volatile billings can make these measures less accurate for projections of future revenue, but they are still valid guides when nothing else is available.

§ 14.04 Payment Pattern Analysis

The previous two methods of determining accounts receivable liquidity are usually adequate, but they are not perfect, especially if your practice is growing rapidly or if it has a highly seasonal revenue pattern. A more accurate way of forecasting when the cash from future billings will be received is the "payment pattern analysis" (PPA).[1]

My variation of this theory goes like this: Based on billings in each month, determine for the last year what percentage of the monthly billings were paid in each *succeeding* month. This can be done by percentages of the

1. Payment pattern analysis was first described by Professor Bernell K. Stone, *The Payment Pattern Model to Forecasting and Control of Accounts Receivable*, FIN. MGMT. 65 (Autumn 1976). Stone stated that if the pattern of the source event (billings) can be predicted, then the pattern of the event's cash flow can be accurately predicted. This pattern can best be used to monitor the payment pattern of individual clients. In fact, when the lawyer has several major clients, the analysis can most effectively be applied to the individual clients to determine when cash payment can be expected.

total billings (see Figure 14.3 as an example and the blank form in appendix F to complete your own).

You can go through your case files and determine when each client has typically paid the bill. Mr. Smith usually pays in the third month, Mr. Jones in the second, Mr. Johnson in the fifth. The results of this analysis adjusted to the amounts of each client's bills will give you a good basis for filling in the percentages in a payment pattern analysis schedule (see Figure 14.3). This may be the most informative and complete method of learning current payment patterns. With this information, projections will be far more accurate. However, this method is also time-consuming and difficult, especially in a high-volume practice.

A quicker, down-and-dirty way of doing it is to refer to your accounts receivable aging schedule (see Figure 14.1). The "total" at the bottom of each column would be the numerator; the denominator would be the total receivables for the month. Figure the percentage of the total for each period (i.e., 0–30, 31–60, etc.), and simply assume that these amounts owed will roughly equal when they were paid.

For example, 15 percent of the billings may be owed in the first month (0–30 days) after billing. Then let's say that 20 percent is owed in the second month (31–60 days) after billing. And so on. Once you have all of the percentages, you can fill in the appropriate figures month by month in your payment pattern analysis (see Figure 14.3 as an example and the blank form in appendix F to complete your own).

After you fill in your payment pattern analysis chart, based on your firm's past experience, you may notice that the percentages change in certain months. For example, the percentage of collections may be lower in the months of April, August, and December. If this is the case for you, the reason may reflect a slowing down of bill paying around tax time (April) and also around the winter holidays (December). The August fluctuations may result from vacation time for you or your clients in the earlier months of June or July. While collections from previous bills should hold steady, the billing amounts during this time are likely to go down since some people are not there to do the work (either in your office or in your client's accounts payable department), and the lower amount of payments from that low-billing period will not show up until several months later.

This analysis would—and should—also adjust for any other factors that are specific to your practice, region, or situation.

It is even more accurate and revealing if you perform the same analysis on a client-by-client basis. To do this, refer to the ledger sheet maintained by the firm for each respective client.

§ 14.05 Action Plan

- Analyze the payment patterns of those clients responsible for 80 percent of your revenue.
- Prepare and frequently review your accounts receivable schedule.

FIGURE 14.1

Sample Accounts Receivable Aging Analysis

Accounts Receivable Aging Analysis						
November 2012						
Name of Client	**0–30**	**31–60**	**61–90**	**91–120**	**121–150**	**150+**
A		5,000	3,000	3,000		
B				6,000	500	
C				5,000		
D						3,000
E					2,000	
F		7,500	5,000			
G		4,000				
H		15,000				
Totals	–0–	$31,500	$8,000	$14,000	$2,500	$3,000

FIGURE 14.2

Sample Accounts Receivable Aging Schedule by Percentage by Quarter

Accounts Receivable Aging Schedule by Percentage by Quarter				
2012				
Days Outstanding	**1st Qtr. (Jan.–Mar.)**	**2nd Qtr. (Apr.–June)**	**3rd Qtr. (July–Sept.)**	**4th Qtr. (Oct.–Dec.)**
0–30	40%	45%	50%	53%
31–60	34%	20%	18%	14%
61–90	15%	18%	20%	24%
91–120	6%	5%	4%	4%
121–150	3%	8%	3%	-0-
151+	2%	4%	5%	5%
Totals	100%	100%	100%	100%

FIGURE 14.3

Sample Payment Pattern Analysis (by Averages)

Payment Pattern Analysis (by Averages)							
2012							
Month of Billing	**First Month After Bill**	**Second Month After Bill**	**Third Month After Bill**	**Fourth Month After Bill**	**Fifth Month After Bill**	**Sixth Month After Bill**	**More Than Six Months After Bill**
Jan. Sample %	10%	20%	30%	15%	15%	5%	5%
Jan. $	$	$	$	$	$	$	$
Feb. %							
Feb. $	$	$	$	$	$	$	$
Mar. %							
Mar. $	$	$	$	$	$	$	$
Apr. %							
Apr. $	$	$	$	$	$	$	$
May %							
May $	$	$	$	$	$	$	$
June %							
June $	$	$	$	$	$	$	$
July %							
July $	$	$	$	$	$	$	$
Aug. %							
Aug. $	$	$	$	$	$	$	$
Sept. %							
Sept. $	$	$	$	$	$	$	$
Oct. %							
Oct. $	$	$	$	$	$	$	$
Nov. %							
Nov. $	$	$	$	$	$	$	$
Dec. %							
Dec. $	$	$	$	$	$	$	$
Totals	$	$	$	$	$	$	$

CHAPTER 15

Pricing Legal Services

Money isn't important, but it's the only way to keep score.

—Anonymous

Chapter Checklist

- o Basic Ways to Set Prices
- o Specific Pricing Methods: Hourly Rate Pricing
- o Specific Pricing Methods: Alternatives to Hourly Rate Pricing
- o The Future of the Billable Hour
- o Cost Disbursements as an Element of Pricing
- o The Use of Nonlawyers
- o Price Sensitivity and Raising Rates
- o Action Plan

Price is the marketplace's barometer for telling you how it values your service. Price also determines your profitability. The extent to which you make a profit depends on how much of what you get for your service is above your costs of providing that service.

One of the most difficult tasks facing any new business enterprise is setting the price for its products or services. The practice of law is no different. New lawyers struggle with this concept, and even experienced lawyers are challenged by setting the right fees and prices, especially in a competitive legal and business environment.

The following discussion will provide the basis for making a more reasoned decision in determining or adjusting your pricing or billing.

§ 15.01 Basic Ways to Set Prices

How is pricing determined? The old standard was the "Rule of Three," which stated that one-third of the fee was meant to cover overhead; one-third was for employee compensation; and one-third went to profit, or the amount drawn or paid to the lawyers or partners. A quick way to estimate a pricing or billing rate using this rule of thumb is to take a person's salary or draw and multiply it by three. The total is then divided by the number of hours billed for the year. The result is a rough estimation of the billing rate per hour. But because of changing economic circumstances, the Rule of Three no longer can be relied on. There are now two basic ways to set legal service prices or fees: (1) cost plus a markup and (2) market price.

§ 15.01.1 Cost-Plus Pricing

Cost-plus pricing involves determining your operating costs per billable hour and adding an amount to each hourly sum to total your desired salary.[1]

The key to the cost-plus pricing method is understanding what the cost of running your law practice is. Most firms are finding that their costs are eating up anywhere from 50 percent to 70 percent of the fees collected. Therefore, going through the process of determining exactly what your firm's annual operating costs are is well worth the time and effort. This should not be too difficult. In small firms, the costs are available from the check register; and in larger firms, from computerized accounting programs. If no other records are available, look at your tax return for the previous year.

Next, determine the number of hours billed. This number is obtained by reference to your time sheets. In contingency- or fixed-fee agreements, time records are not generally kept; however, in order to determine the overhead per hour, records must be kept of time spent even in matters where hourly billing does not apply.

If there are no time records available, then you need to refer to an effort or workload standard. For example, national bar studies have indicated that the average American lawyer bills approximately 1,500 hours each year. In some of the larger metropolitan firms, the standard expected of associates is 2,000 billable hours; and, in still others, it has moved up to 2,200 hours per year. A total of 2,200 hours means that the lawyer must bill seven hours per day, six days per week, fifty-two weeks per year—a very demanding workload.

---

1. Material in this segment of the chapter related to this concept is derived from the work of Wesley P. Hackett Jr. and is used with the permission of Hackett.

Of course, these are net hours billed after some hours are written off. Client goodwill, learning time that should not be charged to the client, and lawyer inefficiency are examples of reasons for the lawyer to write off hours.

Determine the additional hours written off because of bad debt or noncollection of fees billed. Not all billings are collected. Some clients do not pay all or part of the bill. Looking at your past history, determine the percentage of bad debt in your office. Some firms experience uncollected fees as low as 1 to 2 percent, others as high as 12 to 15 percent. (The percentage of billings actually collected is also called the "realization rate," i.e., what is actually realized as collected income.)

Taking the net hours billed less any hours allocated to bad debt or uncollected fees, you now have the total number of net billable hours per year.

Now you can calculate the overhead cost of running the firm by taking the annual cost of operating your firm and dividing it by the number of net billable hours. As an example, let's say a lawyer has a solo practice that costs $100,000 per year in overhead to operate. If he bills 1,125 hours (net), then the cost of overhead per hour is $89. This figure may vary from year to year, but the variation will not be significant.[2]

When you know the cost of overhead per hour, you can add an amount to the hourly fee—this is the "plus" part. How much you add will depend on what level of earnings you want to achieve from the practice.

Let's look again at the math of our lawyer billing 1,125 net hours. He knows that the annual overhead is $100,000. If the goal is to have income *after* overhead of $125,000, then another $111 per hour must be added to the overhead cost, resulting in a total of $200 per hour of cost-plus pricing.

Another way to arrive at the same point in cost-plus pricing is with this formula: Take the office overhead and add the desired compensation. To this subtotal, add an additional 25 percent to cover the amount of billings normally written off and uncollected. The total is the billing or pricing goal.

The pricing or billing rate derived from the cost-plus method should be compared to the competition. If the hourly rate is above what other lawyers are charging, you must look at the costs of your operation and find ways of becoming more efficient. It is axiomatic that you cannot sell services at a rate that is higher than the competition unless there is a perceived difference in the quality of the service being provided. If the fee is below the market rate, you should seriously consider raising your hourly fee. This will provide more profit and allow you to save some of the difference (in fees received) for promoting future legal services.

With this cost-plus information, lawyers can look at billings in an entirely new light. For example, if you take pro bono cases, you can calculate the exact amount of your contribution by multiplying the hours expended by

---

2. Hackett placed several years of his financial statements on computer. He calculated the overhead costs annually and confirmed that the variance is small between one year and the next. If the firm grows dramatically by adding lawyers or significant administrative staff, the overhead costs will be modified accordingly. However, such growth will probably produce sufficient revenue to overcome the added overhead costs incurred.

your overhead-cost-per-hour rate. After all, pro bono work also requires the operation of your office and the services of your office staff. And if you want to promote your legal services by giving a bonus or special discount to a current or prospective client, you will know the level below which you cannot go in your fee arrangement because of the cost factor.

§ 15.01.2 Market Pricing

A market-oriented price is based on the fees customarily charged by lawyers in your community or in the same area of specialty practice.

In earlier times, fee schedules were published by local bar associations. These schedules indicated what the standard or average fee was for given types of work and what average hourly rate was being charged in the local community. Such fee schedules have been declared to be in violation of the antitrust laws, and bar associations discontinued the practice.

Today, you can find the average rate or fee by having discussions with colleagues and by learning from clients what other lawyers are willing to charge them in order to get their business.

As with any other service or product, price is dependent on supply and demand, among other factors. The greater the demand, the greater the price or fee that can be charged. The greater the supply (or competition from other lawyers), the lower the fee charged. The reverse is also true.

In addition, case law and the rules of professional conduct in many jurisdictions require that a lawyer's fee be reasonable. Here are some factors to consider in determining the reasonableness of a fee:

- The time and labor required
- The novelty and difficulty of the questions involved
- The skill required to perform the legal service properly
- The likelihood, if apparent to the client, that the acceptance of the particular engagement will preclude other engagements by the lawyer
- The fee customarily charged in the locality for similar legal services
- The amount involved in the controversy
- The results obtained
- Time limitations imposed by the client or the circumstances
- The nature and length of the professional relationship with the client
- The experience, reputation, and ability of the lawyer performing the legal services
- Whether the fee is fixed or contingent
- Awards in similar cases
- The "undesirability" of the case

Ultimately, of course, it is the client's (buyer's) perception of value that determines whether the price is reasonable for the service provided—that is, the value of your service is determined by the client.

The market-rate fee is the "suggested retail price" for legal services. But this market-based, asking-price concept is coming under attack both by the legal profession and by consumers or buyers of legal services. As a result, many variations of market pricing are developing. Here are several alternatives:

- Market fee per hour less a promotional discount for the first year of work, but not less than cost plus a lowered profit markup
- Market fee per hour less a promotional allowance based on various factors such as volume or cash discounts

§ 15.02 Specific Pricing Methods: Hourly Rate Pricing

The "time-and-billing-rate" (hourly) method of pricing for legal services came into vogue in the early 1900s at the time when manufacturing facilities became enamored with time and motion studies to improve the efficiency of the production line. Knowing the amount of time spent on each legal file could help determine whether that particular matter was profitable for the law firm. The hourly rate is still the most frequently used pricing technique.

With this method of pricing, the lawyer computes the time expended on a given matter and multiplies that total by an hourly rate. The result is the amount billed to the client for the lawyer's fee. Costs are often billed separately (see discussion in section 15.05). Time is normally computed on the basis of a minimum time unit charged—or minimum billing unit—of 1/10 or 1/4 hour.

You should continue to keep time records even if alternative billing methods are used. The original purpose of such records—knowing whether a profit is made on each file—can be accomplished only if accurate time records are kept.

An hourly rate is best used when there are variables that cannot be predicted with adequate certainty, when no reasonably fair alternative method can be determined, when the lawyer is not willing to accept any risk, or when court approval is required and the court is accustomed only to hourly fee billing.

The advantages of the hourly rate pricing method include the following:

- It is familiar to both law firms and clients.
- Rates can be set, quoted, and compared by clients.
- The client pays only for time expended—a subjective judgment of value is not required.
- Timekeeping systems are in place and automatic.
- The risk is placed on the client; the lawyer bears only the risk of nonpayment.

Some disadvantages of hourly pricing include the following:

- An hourly rate discourages efficiency and better ways to provide legal services at a reasonable cost to clients.
- Clients are frequently surprised by the bill because it is difficult for them to know in advance what the total charges will be.
- The client accepts all of the risk, including lawyer inefficiency.
- It promotes client resistance to the perceived high cost of legal services.

- The fee may have little relationship to the value of the services to the client.
- The lawyer is not compensated for results in high-value or high-responsibility cases.
- It frequently does not recognize extraordinary or emergency services.
- It puts a cap on gross income based on the number of billable hours and the rates charged.

Nevertheless, there is a seductive simplicity to the hourly fee that causes both clients and lawyers to accept its faults and disadvantages.

§ 15.03 Specific Pricing Methods: Alternatives to Hourly Rate Pricing

Fixed fees based on the task and alternative methods based on results date back to the 1800s; and although the hourly rate is still the most popular pricing method, we are beginning to come full circle. Because clients are increasingly more sophisticated and because of greater competitive pressures, alternative pricing measures are becoming more prevalent. Today, consumers once again seem to want (1) the assurance of knowing the maximum that they will have to pay for legal services and (2) the lowest possible price for those services.

An important lesson that many lawyers have learned only recently is the need for greater understanding of the client's needs and appreciation of the client's perceptions of the legal services being offered and delivered. The client is the customer, and the client ultimately determines how legal services are priced.

There are many alternatives to the billable hour. Choosing the right alternative is ultimately a business matter for both the firm and the client. There is no universal best billing alternative. Client preferences and each firm's operations differ, and each project or case has a multitude of factors that could accommodate billing options.

However, in all of these alternative pricing methods, the bottom or ending point is the overhead, or the cost of operating the law practice, including a reasonable payment to the lawyer. If the fee dips below the cost, it is obvious that the lawyer is paying for the privilege of representing the client. This may work for a little while in pro bono cases, but it will not work in matters that are intended to produce profit.

The following subsections detail the predominant alternative pricing methods employed by law firms across the country.

§ 15.03.1 Blended Hourly Rate

A modification to the normal hourly rate is the blended hourly rate, in which the client is charged one fee per hour irrespective of who in the firm works on the matter. The partner, whose hourly rate is substantially higher, will bill at the blended rate, as will the associate, whose hourly fee is normally lower. This is one way to market or promote legal services at an apparently lower hourly rate.

Obviously, a law firm will make more money if the client is charged the normal hourly rate of the lawyer. However, the client may be more comfortable with a blended rate. With the blended hourly rate, the law firm will make more money if associates rather than the partners can work on the matter.

The main advantage of the blended rate is that it may encourage more delegation of duties, something that encourages law firm efficiency. The main disadvantage to the client is that there may be a disincentive for a partner or senior associate to work on the matter.

§ 15.03.2 Fixed or Flat Fee

This is a fee that is determined in advance of the engagement of counsel, before the lawyer and the client say yes to the representation. The fee is set and a figure is agreed upon that will not vary no matter how much time you expend as the lawyer or what the result is for the client.

A flat or fixed fee encourages the use of systems, delegation, and technology to make the work process as streamlined as possible. It had better be if the lawyer wants to make a profit. It is best used for routine services or if the lawyer is comfortable accepting the risk that costs might exceed the fee.

The main advantages of a fixed fee are that it forces agreement between you and the client, the client knows what the fee will be in advance of the engagement (no surprises at the end), and there is no energy spent in time accounting. In addition, depending on the rules of professional conduct in your jurisdiction, the entire amount of the fee can be deposited into the general account upon receipt, improving your cash flow.

The disadvantages relate to law firm profitability. A fixed-fee arrangement will not be profitable if services are performed inefficiently, if the cost of providing the services exceeds the estimated cost, if the work is not clearly defined, or if unforeseen difficulties arise.

§ 15.03.3 Value Pricing

This pricing method attempts to correlate the cost of the legal services rendered with the results obtained.

In a commercial matter, one firm recently agreed to perform services at one-half its normal hourly rate if the result anticipated by the lawyer did not occur, and three times the normal hourly rate if the result turned out as expected. By lowering the rate and "participating" in the process, the lawyer was able to demonstrate that (1) he believed strongly in the case; (2) he was willing to share in the consequences of that belief; and (3) the cost to the client, if the lawyer was wrong, would be substantially less than normal.

One of the difficulties of value pricing is deciding what the value is and who determines it. Frequently, the sequence of events is as follows: An estimate of value is determined by the lawyer; the client disagrees; and the court becomes the arbiter in a second, unrelated action by the lawyer against the client for fees. Value pricing is best used when the lawyer and the client have confidence in each other's fairness and when the value can be determined by a formula in advance.

The advantages of value pricing are that it rewards efficiency and creativity, it is innovative, and it spreads the risk between the firm and the client.

The disadvantages are several, including the following:

- It is unfamiliar territory for most lawyers.
- If payment is delayed until the end, when the result is known, cash flow is uneven. Responsibility for advancing the costs of carrying the legal representation needs to be discussed with the client in advance of representation.
- It may be unprofitable if the law firm is inefficient or spends more time than anticipated.
- The risk is spread between the lawyer and the client (this can be an advantage or disadvantage, depending on which side of the fence you are standing on).
- It does not encourage lawyers to monitor their costs.

§ 15.03.4 Contingent/Percentage Fee

Another version of value pricing is the contingent, or percentage, fee, where the amount of the fee is based on the value of the recovery for the client, usually a percentage of a favorable result. It is typically used in personal injury, collection, and related types of cases.

Contingent/percentage fees are best used when the client cannot afford legal representation for an interesting or lucrative matter or when the lawyer is skilled at analyzing and screening cases so that there is a high likelihood of success.

The advantages of contingent/percentage fees are as follows:

- The client pays only in the event of a favorable result.
- It can be lucrative for the lawyer or firm because it is not time dependent, and it encourages efficiency by the lawyer and the firm.
- Most cases are settled without trial.

The disadvantages are as follows:

- The law firm assumes the risk of providing services without being paid.
- Expenses, usually advanced by the law firm, may not be recovered if the result is other than expected.
- There is a possible conflict of interest between the client and the lawyer as to whether and when a matter should be settled or otherwise resolved.
- There may be uneven cash flow since it is more difficult, though not impossible, to estimate the amount and the timing of money received.
- Statutes in different jurisdictions may limit the contingency percentage recoverable by lawyers in certain matters.

§ 15.03.5 Premium Pricing

This is a form of value pricing or billing where an hourly or other method is used as a base, and, depending on the result, a premium or added value is charged. Some firms, particularly in complex or high-dollar-value cases, feel justified in assessing such a premium when a particularly good outcome is achieved.

Premium pricing may limit the number of clients who can afford a higher rate, but if the marketplace perceives that you are worthy of it, you may be able to command it.

Sometimes, although rarely, you can assure the client that because of your expertise, the number of hours will be reduced significantly, keeping the total cost at a level comparable to the cost of a less efficient lawyer who would charge a lower hourly rate.

This method has the same advantages and disadvantages as value pricing except that the law firm will be paid a minimum fee even in the event of a "bad" or unexpected result.

§ 15.03.6 Retainer

This method sets up a fixed-fee-per-time cycle (frequently monthly) for a designated time period (frequently one year). It is sometimes used as a one-time payment to guarantee the availability of the lawyer or firm at a future date. At other times, the retainer is used as a deposit against future services. When an hourly fee is used, the retainer acts as a minimum billing per month.

The advantages of the retainer are the security of knowing the amount and timing of cash flow into the firm, the fact that the client is not paying by the hour, and the potential marketing opportunity for work not covered by the arrangement. For example, clients on retainer frequently bring in additional work for which the lawyer might be entitled to extra billing (depending on the limitations in the retainer agreement).

The disadvantage is mainly that the client may request more services than the retainer fee would warrant if the fee were computed by the hour. If the retainer is a minimum fee to guarantee availability, then there is no disadvantage.

§ 15.04 The Future of the Billable Hour

One legal services question raised, but not adequately answered, by the Great Recession is whether the billable hour as it has long been known is dying. A recent survey by a major U.S. law firm consultant reported that almost 73 percent of 2009 outside counsel fees were based on arrangements other than the standard hourly rate, up from 66 percent the year before. It is clear that law firms are scrambling with deals to retain clients. But is it also an inescapable conclusion that law firms are moving away from the standard hourly rate?

Certainly, the much-maligned concept of billing for legal services by time increments has negatives that the recession's cost pressures have emphasized. As clients regularly point out, more hours billed do not mean that a lawyer is more productive or harder working. Reaching the correct solution is the objective, and the lawyer who takes five minutes to do so instead of three hours produces better value for the client.

However, many clients don't really want to become involved in creating their own pricing arrangements. Paying the standard billable hour rate without question puts all of the burden on the shoulders of the lawyer to solve the problem. The client's response becomes a detached, "That's what I'm paying you for."

Furthermore, if the lawyer uses a different method of accounting, such as value billing or fixed fees, and does not explain the billing, clients are likely to misunderstand what the lawyer did and how it helped them. Fee controversies are too often the result.

Even if the client accepts the concept of value billing, lawyers may be safer, despite whatever billing methodology is employed, if they keep track of time expended. When billings come into question, the tried-and-true method of demonstrating what was done usually comes back to hourly metrics.

The fact is that the larger corporations whose general counsel are more senior lawyers and often come from large law firms are imbued with the hourly rate mentality. Law firms have been built on the hourly rate and the ease of increasing fees by a small percentage increase here and a small percentage increase there. And the smaller or individual client, too, understands the idea of hourly rates.

Hourly rate billing will only disappear when lawyers begin to understand the cost of doing business and can create a "laundry list" of unbundled services for established prices, each of which is determined in a way that produces a reasonable profit for the law firm and a fair price for the value delivered to the client.

Will we reach that point in the near future? Possibly. More effort is being placed on teaching lawyers professional service cost accounting, more law firms are engaging professionals in other fields to help them understand the needed processes, and more lawyers are learning project-management techniques. When these skills come together, we may see a de-emphasis on the billable hour and the delivery of legal services based on the value received by the client.

§ 15.05 Cost Disbursements as an Element of Pricing

Most matters require that the lawyer advance some costs on behalf of the client. Costs are of two types: external and internal.

External costs include messenger services, filing fees, deposition transcripts, and expert witness fees. These are charges that are external to the operation of the office and relate specifically to the individual client's matter. All firms charge clients for the external costs, usually at the fee charged without a markup.

Internal costs include photocopying, postage, telephone, and fax. Many firms charge clients for these costs *plus* a markup. For example, if the hard cost for copying is 7.5 cents per page, the firm may charge 10 to 25 cents per page in an attempt to make a little extra money.

More and more firms, however, are absorbing these internal costs. Many clients are beginning to object to these not-so-subtle costs, and competitive pressure is forcing lawyers to revisit this issue. The trend is toward the philosophy that internal costs should not be a profit center. In the corporate world, they are part of overhead and part of the sales price for the product or service. In the lawyer's world, too, charging for these costs has become a less acceptable way of raising the fee. Many are using their lack of charging for these costs as a marketing ploy, telling clients that costs will not be charged except for external fees.

Whichever way you choose to handle this, make sure to discuss the issue at the very beginning of representation.

§ 15.06 The Use of Nonlawyers

The use of nonlawyers—paralegals and legal assistants—can be a factor in your pricing strategies. *Legal assistant* has been defined by the American Bar Association as

> a person, qualified through education, training, or work experience, who is employed or retained by a lawyer, law office, governmental agency, or other entity in a capacity or function that involves the performance, under the ultimate direction and supervision of a lawyer, of specifically delegated substantive legal work, which work, for the most part, requires a sufficient knowledge of legal concepts that, absent such assistant, the lawyer would perform the task.[3]

These nonlawyers are used not for secretarial work but for creative legal work such as meeting with clients, meeting with court personnel, deposition summaries, drafting pleadings, contracts, and investigations.

Here is a quick look at the financial impact of using lower-cost legal assistants and charging the standard or blended fee of the office:

---

3. *Current ABA Definition of Legal Assistant/Paralegal*, AM. BAR ASS'N (Aug. 14, 2008), http://www.americanbar.org/groups/paralegals/resources/current_aba_definition_of_legal_assistant_paralegal.html.

Use of Nonlawyers			
Billing Person	**Cost Based on Hourly Rate**	**Blended Fee**	**Profit or Loss**
Partner	$175	$150	($ 25)
Associate	90	150	60
Legal Assistant	50	150	100

The impact of these economics may be even more dramatic in a contingency matter. You can reduce the cost of handling the matter by delegating as much of the work as is reasonably practical to legal assistants. This will allow more time for the lawyer either to do other work that will produce higher total revenue for the firm or, if there is insufficient work for the lawyer, to do marketing to improve the total caseload and revenue for the firm. Delegating as much work as possible makes for greater efficiency in the firm.

Here are two examples of the effect that using legal assistants has on firm billings:

Example A:

Assume that a typical firm involvement in a client matter would be the following:

10 lawyer hours at $100	=	$1,000
4 legal assistant hours at $40	=	160
Total amount of bill		$1,160

Example B:

Assume that one variation of the above allows the lawyer to reduce direct involvement and raise his hourly rate. Even if more time is required by the assistant, the cost to the client normally would be the same or less than in the above example:

4 lawyer hours at $150	=	$600
14 legal assistant hours at $40	=	560
Total amount of bill		$1,160

No matter how you play with the numbers to achieve a particular result, the principle remains accurate in practice—that is, delegating work to the lowest economic level capable of performing the task will result in the greatest revenue and net profits for the firm.

Here is another way of looking at this: If the lawyer is required to dedicate ten hours to each file, he can then handle only 180 files per year (based on 1,800 billable hours per year). If the lawyer can reduce the file time to four hours, then the same lawyer can handle 450 files annually. If the lawyer is working on a contingency basis, there is a greater opportunity for increased revenue. And if the lawyer is billing based on hourly rates and can now demand higher hourly rates, the total revenue increases both because the hourly rate is higher for the lawyer and because more cases are being handled (with the help of the legal assistant).

§ 15.07 Price Sensitivity and Raising Rates

To the average client, there is little price sensitivity in choosing a lawyer. That is, the choice is made not because of the fee being charged but because of other factors, such as ability. Usually, the client is in your office because of a referral from a trusted source. Only if the fee difference is very significant (e.g., $50 per hour or more) will the client pause to reflect. Because of this lack of sensitivity, you can raise hourly rates to new clients by $10 to $15 per hour without fear of client resistance.

The same is not necessarily true of existing clients because written notice must be given to existing clients before increasing the billing rates, and such notice will probably cause the client to be aggravated, if not irate, considering the belt-tightening that many clients are experiencing.

Therefore, if you want to raise your rates, a good approach might be to increase the rates for new clients and, if you continue to be busy, increase the rates on new matters for existing clients. Keep existing rates for present matters until they are concluded unless it is a matter of long duration and there is a provision in the engagement agreement permitting you to raise the fee.

For ongoing retainers, consider the benefit of regular payments from existing retainer clients—they should be entitled to the benefit of being the last to have their rates increased.

Based on the rule that increased demand can lead to increased fees, the busier you are, the easier it is to raise your hourly rate or increase the fixed fee for any task.

On a related note, do not lower your fees (except for discounts for timely payments on a previous bill—see chapter 17). When lawyers are temporarily not busy or when a client tells a tale of woe, lawyers sometimes lower their fees. Guard against this inclination. Clients generally do not appreciate, even sometimes do not know, that you are lowering the fee.

§ 15.08 Action Plan

- Review your pricing model(s).
- Consider your clients' preferences.

CHAPTER 16

The Billing Process

If there's anyone listening to whom I owe money, I'm prepared to forget it if you are.
—Errol Flynn

Chapter Checklist

- o Importance of Billing Process
- o Clients and the Billing Process
- o Who Should Do the Billing?
- o What Should Bills Look Like and Contain?
- o When Should Bills Be Prepared?
- o When Should Bills Be Sent?
- o Responses from Clients
- o Action Plan

Pricing refers to the fee, or amount of compensation, you initially ask for, and billing refers to the actual amount charged for the services rendered. Billing is the total compensation, including all hourly rates, expenses, mark-ups, etc. But there is much more to billing than that.

§ 16.01 Importance of Billing Process

The billing process is important for two reasons, one obvious and one not.

First, you cannot get paid until you bill. The average national accounts receivable cycle for lawyers' services is 4.3 months. What this means is that it will take, on average, about four and one-half months from the date that any bill is received by the client for you to receive the funds. Therefore, any expediting on your part in getting the bills out will ensure that this time lag is kept to a minimum.

Another, less obvious function of a billing statement is that it serves as an important marketing tool if used correctly. Since marketing describes how you relate to and communicate with clients, then the billing process is a natural channel for marketing. It is part of the ongoing, two-way communication process between you and the client, and it is one of the easiest ways to reach existing clients and let them know that you are doing a good job for them.

It is very important to continue marketing to existing clients. Marketing to your current clients is both more effective and less expensive than marketing to prospective or new clients. The 80/20 rule of thumb puts this idea into perspective: on average, 80 percent of your business comes from 20 percent of your existing clients. And your billing statement is one of the easiest ways to reach those existing clients.

With effective billing communication, there is a greater likelihood of "bonding" with clients. Bonding is the relationship that develops when you care about clients and they know it. You connect with clients on a personal level by understanding their true needs and problems and by delivering more than they expect. Complete billing statements let clients know that you are working hard for their interests and that you care.

§ 16.02 Clients and the Billing Process

It is important for the client to understand the billing process. Explain it to the client at the initial meeting or at the time that the engagement is being negotiated.

The billing process should then be explained again, in writing, in the letter of engagement. In most jurisdictions, it is required that the letter of engagement be in writing.

§ 16.03 Who Should Do the Billing?

The lawyer responsible to the client should do the billing. That lawyer should review and revise, if necessary, all time records of other lawyers and staff members who work on the client's matter.

Even if some records are computerized, billing should not be a mechanical process; much subjective analysis should go into the preparation of billing statements. Bills can be "written down"—or written off—at the discretion of the billing lawyer if the work done for the client cannot be justified either because of inefficiencies in the process of preparation or because of learning curves that the client should not pay for. Bills can also be written off for client goodwill.

§ 16.04 What Should Bills Look Like and Contain?

§ 16.04.1 Appearance

The actual appearance of the billing statement is a personal matter. There are many quality formats in use today; only the imagination of the lawyer limits the statement's appearance. Obviously, though, the statement should be dignified and in keeping with the tone of the office and the type of practice.

Standard computer billing programs limit the aesthetic possibilities. If the format of a computer program is not appropriate for your practice or does not project the image that you want to convey to your clients, find a computer consultant to modify and customize the program for you.

If modifying a standard computer program is impractical or not economically feasible, combine original typing with the information gathered from the computer. While you may be duplicating efforts to some extent, you will save time and money, and you can produce the statement format of your choice.

§ 16.04.2 Content

There are three basic types of bills: a simple statement, a time breakout of activities with brief descriptions, and a narrative. The simple statement (see Figure 16.1) merely states that the client owes a certain amount for legal services; there is no description and no detail. The brief description version (see Figure 16.2) lists what actions were taken, when they were taken, and how much time they took to complete. The most complete format is the complete narrative description (see Figure 16.3); it details your accomplishments, it is action-oriented (uses sentences beginning with verbs), it provides a monthly recap of your activities, and it is complete. (At a minimum, it is important to check your local rules of professional conduct to determine how much description is required.)

Ask the client what style or format of billing he prefers. This is particularly important for corporate clients because the corporate counsel may require the billing statement to be in a particular format to enable the accounting department to process your bill.

If the client has no preference, the narrative billing statement will serve you much better than either of the other two styles. Since the billing statement is a prime marketing tool, it can and should communicate in the most tangible manner possible what you have done during the month to justify asking for the fee that is in the statement. In other words, it should be more than a recitation of the copies of documents received and sent from your office. The contents of the billing statement should be complete enough to describe the work done so that clients have an appreciation of the effort expended on their behalf. A narrative bill communicates to the clients that you have taken the time to tell them how hard you have been working for them. Clients appreciate this kind of effort in communication.

Needless to say, billing statements should also be accurate. Clients do not like sloppiness from their lawyers; it undermines the client's confidence in the lawyer.

Do not forget that it is not the amount of the bill that is important; rather, what is important is the client's perception of the value received. And the more the client understands the extent to which you are going to solve his problems, the more he will value your service.

§ 16.05 When Should Bills Be Prepared?

Time records should be prepared as the work is done. Studies have shown that if time passes between when the work is done and when it is noted, a certain percentage of the time worked never gets recorded. The amount of such lost time can amount to one-half to one hour per day. Losing one hour per day, multiplied by a billing rate of $100 per hour, equals $500 per week, or $26,000 per year in gross billings lost!

Time records should be gathered regularly, preferably on a daily basis. By reviewing these records at the end of the day, you will have the greatest chance of remembering work that may have slipped through the cracks.

Also, daily time record reviews give you a chance to monitor your progress in achieving your billable-hours-per-day planning goals. And by reviewing a summary of your time records at the end of each week, you will reinforce your success in reaching your billable-hours goal or determine the reason(s) for failing to achieve it. This may also point out any inadequacies in your marketing efforts to bring in additional work.

To allow enough time in preparing billing statements, you must determine how much time your office requires to collate and record all unrecorded time records at the end of the cycle. If time records are recorded daily, then this element will require very little time.

Print or tally all time records by client and matter. Prepare and print a "prebill," or draft of the billing statement, for each client. Review the prebills and make changes as may be appropriate. Revise the prebills and print the final billing statements.

§ 16.06 When Should Bills Be Sent?

Billing statements should be mailed so that they reach the client on or before the first day of the month. Clients normally process their bills in the first few days of the month. While this does not guarantee payment of your bill in the current month—payment depends on the client's cash flow and many other factors—prompt receipt does guarantee that your billing statement will be considered at the front of the line.

All statements received after about the fifth of the month are usually considered for payment in the following month. This delay adds thirty days to what would have been the normal accounts receivable time frame for the client. (Tip: Send a self-addressed, stamped envelope with the bill; it encourages the client to send the payment that much more quickly.)

§ 16.07 Responses from Clients

Client response is the second part of the two-way communication process. Each alternative response from the client is telling you something, if you only take the time to listen.

The response that you expect, of course, is payment for the billing amount, which probably means that the client is satisfied with your work.

But you can also learn something if there is no check in the mail. You may fail to receive payment because (1) the client is unhappy with the size of the bill or the quality of the work performed, (2) the client did not ask for or expect the work that you performed, or (3) the client simply cannot—or does not want to—pay the bill.

Since you cannot know which of these three reasons is the one responsible for the silence from the client, you need to investigate further (for a more complete description of what is called the "dial-and-smile" technique, see chapter 17). Ask questions to probe and find out exactly what the problem is.

When you do not get paid, there is obviously something wrong, and failing to listen to clear signals from the client will only cause further problems for you. After all, do you want to continue working for a client who does not want the work in progress, does not think that the work is adequate, or cannot continue to pay for it? Legal work should become pro bono only at the discretion of the lawyer, not at the discretion of the client.

§ 16.08 Action Plan

- Prepare billings describing achievements for the client.
- Send statements periodically, at least monthly.
- Follow up with the client if prompt payment is not received.

FIGURE 16.1

Simple Statement

Jane Lawyer, Esq.
500 Attorney Way
Billing, California 00000
000-111-2222

January 25, 2013

Joe Client
400 Corporation Way
Billing, California 00000

STATEMENT FOR LEGAL SERVICES

Balance due per previous statement .... $
Less amount received on account .... $
Balance due: .... –0–
Retainer due on February 10, 2013, per agreement in connection with legal services rendered .... $
Balance due: .... $

Thank you for the opportunity to serve you.

Sincerely yours,

Jane Lawyer

FIGURE 16.2

Time Breakout of Activities with Brief Descriptions

Jane Lawyer, Esq.
500 Attorney Way
Billing, California 00000
000-111-2222

Page 1
Invoice # 5-041272
Date 6/25/2013

Joe Client
400 Corporation Way
Billing, California 00000

Re: 1031 Exchange Tax Matters

For Professional Services Through May 31, 2013:

5/06/13	Telephone Conference with Realty Attorney Re Escrow Instructions.
	Review Escrow Instructions and Changes in Final Section 1031 Deferred Exchange Regulations.
	Conference with Mr. XXXXXXXX Re Escrow Instructions.
5/15/13	Review Proposed Exchange Agreement; Analyze Section 1031 Final Regulations and Revise Agreement.
	Telephone Conference with Mr. XXXXXXXX Re Tax Comments on Exchange Agreement.
5/16/13	Analyze Tax Issuse Presented by Facts Outside Exchange Agreement.
5/22/13	Telephone Conference with Messrs. XXXXXXXX and XXXXXXXX Re Exchange Agreement Revisions.
5/23/13	Draft Security Agreement Provisions and Escrow Instructions.
5/28/13	Revision of Security Agreement Provisions.
5/29/13	Telephone Conference with Mr. XXXXXXXX Re Security Agreement; Legal Research Re Agency Issue.
	Total Services 10.00 hours @ $265.00 per hour $2650.00

5/31/13	Telecopy Charges	20.00	
	Duplication Expenses		7.80
	Total Expenses		$27.80
		Total This Invoice	**$2677.80**

FIGURE 16.3

Narrative Bill

Jane Lawyer, Esq.
500 Attorney Way
Billing, California 00000
000-111-2222

January 25, 2013

Joe Client
400 Corporation Way
Billing, California 00000

STATEMENT FOR LEGAL SERVICES RENDERED

12/4/12
Telephone conference with Jane Smith, CPA: discussed the importance of concluding the settlement negotiations by December 31 and ramifications to both parties if the previously mutually acceptable dates were not met.

12/12/12
Telephone conference with opposing counsel: discussed spousal support and the tax consequences to each party of various amounts suggested on behalf of both parties; further discussed child visitation and the needs of the children to feel settled in one base. Issues still remain to be resolved, but progress appears to have been made.

12/18/12
Court appearance on motion to modify earlier court order in which spousal support had been set; court granted our motion for reduction and encouraged the parties to continue negotiations for full settlement of all remaining issues.

15 hours @ $200 per hour $3,000

Balance due: $3,000

CHAPTER 17

Credit and Collections

The urbane activity with which a man receives money is really marvelous, considering that we so earnestly believe money to be the root of all earthly ills, and that on no account can a monied man enter heaven. Ah! how we cheerfully consign ourselves to perdition!

—Herman Melville, *Moby Dick*

Chapter Checklist

- o Giving Credit Where Credit Is Due
- o Collecting Your Money
- o Steps to Decreasing the Need to Worry About Collections
- o Steps to Increasing Your Collections When Clients Don't Pay
- o Action Plan

Credit and collections are two intertwining aspects—phases one and two—of the same subject: receiving the cash that is owed to you for the services that you provide. First, you extend credit to clients as a good-faith gesture with the expectation that you will be paid at a specific time in the future. Then, after you have performed the work, you move into phase two: actually collecting that money. Let's look more closely at these complementary concepts.

§ 17.01 Giving Credit Where Credit Is Due

When the economy is tight, more small service companies, including law firms, try to reel in cash. The problem is, your clients are conserving their cash, too. And that means that they are taking advantage of credit terms by paying as slowly, or as late, as possible. Although receiving payment of bills when they become due is the best scenario, you do not want to discourage sales by denying credit altogether. Thus, it is important to establish a formal credit policy that spells out effective, but fair, credit terms.

The process of establishing or revising credit policies can be unpleasant for many. The thought of laying down the law with customers smacks of negativity, leading many law firm owners to avoid the task altogether. But now is the time to overcome that discomfort so that your firm can maximize income and minimize bad debts.

In reality, conscientious customers will view your credit policy in a positive light. Your willingness and ability to extend credit reflects stability and a long-term commitment to the marketplace. These attributes are valuable to potential customers, who must invest time and money in establishing a relationship with your company. The credit policy lets them know that you are committed to sound business practices and that you plan to be there to meet their future needs.

Avoid using your credit policy as a sales tool, however. You may be tempted to extend credit when business is slow to get more customers to buy your services, but you will be sorry when they cannot pay the bills.

An effective credit policy requires instituting a client approval process, deciding on credit limits, and setting interest rates.

§ 17.01.1 Approve Clients

The first thing that you have to do is approve clients for credit. By spending a small amount of time up front evaluating customers' creditworthiness, you will save a lot of time and money down the road trying to collect bad debts, or dodging the deadbeats.

Check clients' credit history by devising *and using* a credit approval form designed to capture basic information about any company or individual applying for credit. Ask for name, address, federal ID number (if a corporation) or Social Security number (if an individual), driver's license number, business and residence addresses, three trade and personal references, and bank references. Information about loan balances, repayment performance, and the banker's general impression of the customer's business are invaluable in evaluating a client's creditworthiness. You can also check customers through LexisNexis, Dun & Bradstreet, the National Association of Credit Management, industry trade reports, and credit-rating services such as TRW Credit Services.

§ 17.01.2 Determine Credit Limits

Determine the client's credit limit in advance and stick to it unless, after careful review, there is cause to change the limit. Failure to set the limit in advance will place you in a feverish frenzy when the question arises in the midst of performing some sensitive task for the client—a time when either you will not want to walk away from the work or the court will not permit you to withdraw. Involuntary servitude begins with a failure to set appropriate credit limits.

§ 17.01.3 Set Interest Rates

Set interest rates in advance for outstanding balances owed on bills. Remember that each jurisdiction has different maximum interest rates that you are legally entitled to collect. Frequently, rates also differ based on the status of the client, whether individual or corporate.

Although it may be helpful to set interest rates, the fact remains that if a client fails to pay the amount billed, he is unlikely to be able or willing to pay the interest. Charging interest in advance of a judgment that carries a statutory interest rate may be futile and a bookkeeping nightmare.

§ 17.02 Collecting Your Money

In the best of all possible worlds, soon after you have sent out a bill, you will receive an envelope in the mail that contains a check for payment in full. However, since most of us do not live in this perfect world, chances are that you may not receive a check for payment in full. In fact, you may not receive a check at all.

Late payment or nonpayment of bills is a direct result of tough economic times when everyone is trying to hold onto their money as long as possible. Law firm economics in general are in a state of flux, and the changes are being felt by all lawyers, at large and small firms alike.

Are collections really that important? You bet! Uncollected billings that are never seen again—the worst-case scenario—represent monies that should have gone into your pockets but are now a lost cause because all hope of collecting them has gone. They are revenues that now must be offset by more work.

The amount of new collected billings required to offset every dollar lost in uncollected billings depends upon your gross margin. Gross margin is the relationship between funds available for distribution to lawyers (which is what is left over when operating expenses are subtracted from revenues) and total revenues received. It is usually expressed as a percentage (distribution to total revenue). It is one way of determining how efficient the firm is at distributing "profits" to lawyers. The higher the percentage, the higher the proportion of the firm's revenues that go to the lawyers as salaries or draws.

Let's say that your gross margin is 10 percent. Then you would have to collect $5,000 in new billings to offset $500 in uncollected billings. If your gross margin is 35 percent, you would need to collect $1,429 to offset a $500 loss.

Since uncollected billings mean that you are working for free, your goal is to have them approach zero.

§ 17.03 Steps to Decreasing the Need to Worry About Collections

"An ounce of prevention is worth a pound of cure" is an apt expression in the realm of collections. In other words, you can take steps to minimize the chances that any particular client will become a nonpaying client.

§ 17.03.1 Fees and Budgets

One of the most important prerequisites for ensuring payment is discussing your fee and establishing a budget with the involvement of the client before beginning an engagement.

Budgets significantly increase the chances of collecting fees because they help clients understand what to expect in terms of events, money, and time; and clients agree to the process outlined. In addition, they demonstrate to clients that the firm is sensitive to their needs and reinforces that the firm provides value and not just a block of hourly time.

Furthermore, budgets keep lawyers on track. Too many lawyers focus on the task at hand and the end result without planning the path to get there or getting the buy-in from the client before starting. Often, lawyers start working without thought to whether the client has adequate capital to pay for what's ahead. Budgets help lawyers develop an appreciation of those areas where costs can be controlled and those areas where costs are inherent. In short, they help lawyers do a better job for their clients—and satisfied clients are more likely to pay.

Client involvement is critical in the creation of a budget. Without client buy-in and approval, budgets and collection terms are meaningless. The budgeting process, including all subsequent communication, must be a collaborative effort. If the parties can't trust one another—if the client and the lawyer behave as adversaries—the representation will likely be unsuccessful, and there will likely be difficulty in collecting the fee.

As part of the budgeting process, prepare a written fee agreement, to be signed by both you and the client. The written agreement should explain all charges to be made and the need for timely payment of each bill by the client. This agreement, and each statement mailed to the client, should have language similar to the following: "If you have any questions concerning this statement, please contact the law firm immediately. If the firm does not hear from you within ten days, you agree that the statement is accurate and valid."

§ 17.03.2 Other Communication Considerations

In addition to discussing compensation and budgets, communicating about other aspects of the lawyer-client relationship will improve your chances of collecting fees.

Create a manual or monograph itemizing each of the various collection procedures, form letters, and related documents so that clients have a clear understanding of your expectations.

Do not promise work product sooner than realistically possible after considering the complexity of the matter and the workload of your office. Lawyers must do the work promised in the time promised. If, for any reason, the work cannot be performed in the manner and in the time promised, you need to communicate with the client. The client must be kept informed of the progress of the matter. A friendly secretary or other staff person can effectively convey the message. The client will accept change if told in advance of the due date.

Tell the client what to expect each step of the way. Do not "hype" the client. If possible, include a tentative or expected timetable of events. The client's perception of the legal problem frequently is different from the reality determined by the lawyer. Educate the client. Unless the client has a thorough understanding of the problem, the efforts of the lawyer and the services rendered will not be fully understood or appreciated. Failed expectations cause many problems, in particular unpaid bills. And unpaid lawyer bills tend to stay that way—unpaid.

Finally, make sure that you capitalize on the communication potential of statements. The statement that you send to the client is your primary communication explaining what was done for him during the preceding period of time (hopefully, no more than thirty days since the previous statement) and what the charges are for that service. A communicative statement helps the client appreciate the value received for the fee being billed.

§ 17.03.3 Retainers

You should increase your retainer, consistent with market pressures, to the point that a substantial portion of the initial phase(s) of the task to be accomplished will be covered by the retainer in the client trust account. The larger the retainer, the larger the portion that is nonrefundable (consult your local regulations and practices to determine how large the nonrefundable portion can be). This effectively reduces the risk of collection problems.

Indicate in the written fee agreement that a portion of the retainer will be placed in the trust account and will remain there until computation of the final billing for the client. In the interim, monthly statements will be sent to the client, and the amount billed must be paid monthly. The "extra" sum improves your chances of being paid fees when billed. It can be compared to a security deposit that a tenant delivers to a landlord when renting real property.

§ 17.03.4 The Billing Cycle

Shorten your billing cycle. If you remain on the monthly billing cycle, be sure that your clients receive your statements on or before the first day of the following month. To do this, your billing cycle must end on or about the twenty-fifth of the month.

The theory is that most people pay their bills on or about the first of the month. If a statement reaches the client after this time, the statement is normally placed in the pile of bills to be paid in the following cycle. That means a delay for payment of your statement by as much as seventy-five days. The first thirty days you are doing the work; the second thirty days is the missed payment cycle of the client; the last fifteen days is the minimum amount of time it takes for the client to write and mail the check and for the mail to reach you. If the client delays payment even further, the time extends beyond seventy-five days. Thus, anything that you can do to shorten the cycle will be that much better for you.

Another tactic is to change your billing cycle. Bill one-fourth of the alphabet each week. In this manner, you will receive money from clients on a regular basis, probably weekly rather than once per month.

§ 17.03.5 Time Your Statements

Send statements after a particularly beneficial psychological event, even if it is somewhat before or beyond the normal billing date. For example, after you have won a motion in court, prepared a draft of an important contract with which your client is pleased, or closed the negotiation on a deal that favors your client, send a billing of services rendered to date. This will place the client on the peak of the "client satisfaction curve," the time of least resistance for payment of fees. Later, the client will invariably forget how important you were to the favorable result and wonder why the bill is so high. Once the client is in that state of mind, the statement for services will sit unpaid until some future date.

§ 17.03.6 Make It Easy to Pay

Use remittance envelopes, preaddressed and stamped, and mail them with your statements. This saves the client time and effort in mailing your payment and frequently saves at least one day in the time it takes for you to receive payment.

Also, accept payment via credit and debit cards, PayPal accounts, and electronic deposits of checks.

§ 17.03.7 Discounts for Timely Payment

Consider a discount for clients who pay promptly. A percentage discount (for example, 2 percent ten days, net thirty days) may feel less than professional. An alternative would be to lower your hourly rate by $10 to $25 for the next month's billings as a reward for the client who pays within thirty days of original billing.

§ 17.04 Steps to Increasing Your Collections When Clients Don't Pay

Despite lawyers' best efforts, some clients still resist paying bills. In such cases, lawyers frequently wonder how to collect money: "We have some difficult clients. How can we collect our accounts receivable? The accounts receivable are higher than they have been at any time in the history of our firm, and they need to be collected now! How do we do it?"

First, let's define *difficult*. Usually, a difficult client means one or more of the following:

- The client is not doing what the lawyer wants—that is, paying the bill.
- The client owes a large amount of money.
- The client has owed the bill for an extended period of time.
- The client has ignored the many requests for payment.

Clients may not pay for a variety of reasons. These reasons run the gamut from anger concerning the quality or price of the legal services rendered to the client's inability to pay not only the legal bill but other bills as well. The reason for a client's failure to pay is important; this information should assist you in determining the approach to take for future collection efforts relating to that client.

Collecting unpaid fees is never pleasant. By employing the following suggestions, however, you can make the task easier. And, most important, the client will be more satisfied, will believe that he is receiving legal services of the highest quality, and will be a walking advertisement for you.

§ 17.04.1 Communication

Maintain an accurate listing of accounts receivable. Age and review the accounts receivable weekly. *Aging* means that the amount owed by each client is spread over time by month created. (Refer to the discussion of aging and to Figure 14.1 in chapter 14.) It is essential to know what your clients owe, and aging this listing of accounts receivable is how you can spot if and when a payment problem exists. Determine who the "problem" clients are and gather information about the nature of their problem. Determine a strategy for dealing with the clients and their particular issues. Do not wait long to address and solve each client's issue. Communicate with those problem clients to resolve their unpaid bills (see section 17.04.2, "Dial-and-Smile").

Your client also communicates in a number of ways with a variety of messages. Even when you do not think so, the client is communicating with you, loudly and clearly. In particular, when a client does not pay his bill, he is communicating (see the discussion of the billing process in chapter 16). Many lawyers fail to listen, however. Start listening, and you might see more success with your collections.

§ 17.04.2 "Dial-and-Smile"

Try the "dial-and-smile"[1] technique. To really make use of the two-way communication process between you and your clients and to find out what the clients are *really* saying if they are not paying their bills, use this procedure.

1. This effective "dial-and-smile" technique was first suggested to me by Eric Shaw, president of New York Credit, based in Marina del Rey, California.

First, call the client. That is, have someone else at your firm call; never call the client yourself. The lawyer should not call the client to collect the outstanding amount owed. Successful businesses do not send their salespeople to their customers to collect; that is handled by a separate credit department. If the lawyer contacts the client for payment, the client may be too embarrassed to continue working with the lawyer. Now, not only has the bill not been paid, but the lawyer has lost a client. Worse still, this client will not refer other potential clients because of his embarrassment.

Hire someone (a part-time accounts receivable clerk from a local college or a retired bookkeeper) to help you collect. The cost of this person will be less than the money received as a result of his efforts. Have the person review each file, contact each client as may be necessary, and pursue collection. The caller should always be friendly and smiling on the telephone (hence, the term *dial-and-smile*). The caller should, under no circumstances, be accusatory or in any way hostile to the client even if the client fails to honor one or more commitments for the payment of money due.

Have the caller ask the client whether he *received* the statement. If the answer is no, fax, deliver by messenger, or send a copy of the statement to the client immediately. If the answer is yes, have the caller ask the next question, which is whether the client *understands* the statement. If the answer is no, the caller should tell the client that the lawyer will call shortly to answer any questions. And be sure to call the client as soon as possible to clarify any misunderstandings that the client may have. If the client does understand the statement, have the caller ask whether there is any problem with the bill. If the answer is yes, have the caller get the information about the nature of the problem and deal with the issue appropriately under the circumstances. If the client says, "No, there is no problem with the bill," then the caller should ask the next question: "When can we expect to receive payment in our office?" (not "When will the check be mailed?").

Normally, the client will make a commitment for a certain (even if for only a partial) payment. The caller should mark the calendar for that date. The caller should attempt to get a commitment of no more than ten days out. If the check does not arrive on time, the caller should call the client the very next day and go through the same set of questions. Each set of calls should be approximately ten days apart. The caller should complete this process several times over a period of not more than six to eight weeks.

After this time, if the bill is not paid or at least reduced substantially, you must decide whether to continue working for the client or to terminate the lawyer-client relationship—and then whether to sue for fees earned to date but not paid.

Be sure that the client's responses are noted in the file. This will build a record that no complaint was ever registered by the client and unanswered in the event that either you sue to collect fees or the client, at some future date, brings a case for malpractice.

§ 17.04.3 Plan for Payment

A payment plan may be suggested if the client does not offer anything concrete or acceptable. One such plan may involve payment on a current basis (essentially, COD) with some additional sum being applied toward the old bill (plus a fair rate of interest). At least the bill accrued to date will not increase, and you will receive additional business. Another approach may be to agree that a sum certain will be paid monthly. That amount can be calculated by estimating the total fee and the time for concluding the matter: divide the total by the number of months to determine the monthly payment.

Deposit all checks from clients even if the amount received does not match the amount due per the statement. Make a photocopy of all checks received in the office, especially where the amount of the check differs from the billing statement. Reasonably soon after your office deposits the check, the accounts receivable manager/clerk should call the client. This person needs to have a pleasant demeanor and inquire as to why the client paid an amount different from the bill. The answer may be simple, such as an oversight. The answer may be troublesome, such as the client didn't ask for certain work to be done or didn't agree to the billing/cost rate charged. If the former, there is no problem; your staff person can make arrangements to receive the difference. If the latter, the lawyer will need to get involved and reconcile the client's position with that of the lawyer. You will (hopefully!) ultimately reconcile the amount paid with the amount due; however, in the meantime, you will have deposited the amount sent to you and will continue to receive the benefits of that deposit.

§ 17.04.4 Last Resorts

Stop work! If the client does not participate in the process by keeping a promise to pay as billed, do not continue to work for the client. Either notify the client or, in certain circumstances, make an appropriate motion before the court to be removed from the case.

Sue! Some statistics show that the lawyer/creditor is successful in more than 95 percent of litigation against a client/debtor. Malpractice cross-complaints or counterclaims are not automatic responses. Of course, when litigation occurs between a lawyer and a client, it is obvious that there will be no future relationship between the two—an automatic loss of future business.

§ 17.05 Action Plan

- Establish a policy of credit.
- Take steps to ensure that no client becomes a difficult client.
- Communicate with the client if prompt payment is not received.
- Create a new payment plan with the client if necessary.

CHAPTER 18

Banks and Loans

You want 21 percent risk-free? Pay off your credit cards.

—Andrew Tobias, *American Way*

Chapter Checklist

- o Financial Needs
- o Types of Loans
- o Selecting a Bank
- o How a Bank Selects Borrowers
- o Developing a Good Relationship with the Banker
- o Action Plan

Let's say, for example, that your firm is not collecting on its accounts receivable as quickly as anticipated. This is particularly apt to happen in today's business environment when many clients of law firms (small and large) are experiencing sales downturns, causing the clients to stretch out their payments.

Or maybe—and for quite the opposite reason—the firm is growing quickly. During a period of expansion, the firm will need to hire new personnel (including lawyers) and to purchase new facilities and/or equipment. Periodically, new equipment must be purchased to replace old equipment.

For example, the law firm might need to install a new computer or telephone system.

A common denominator in each of these situations is that the cash needs exceed the firm's own cash-generation ability. When that happens, the firm must have a source from which to obtain the extra cash that it needs in the form of a loan.

There are several loan sources available. The least expensive is the partners themselves, who can advance additional capital to the firm. But normally the partners of a small firm do not have extra cash on hand. Therefore, the firm must borrow the additional cash elsewhere. Relatives of the lawyers are one source of cash, but lawyers usually avoid this route. Borrowing money from relatives is often viewed by lawyers as unprofessional or as an admission of failure.

Under these circumstances, then, it is nice—and sometimes crucial—to have a good relationship with a bank. Banks have the marvelous capacity to lend money to deserving borrowers to help them get over the periods when their cash flow is less than expected. Lawyers and law firms are generally attractive customers for banks desiring to grow. Banks believe, and rightly so, that good lawyers have the ability to both stay employed and accumulate a substantial net worth. Lawyers, aside from being good customers themselves, tend to be opinion leaders in the business community and are viewed by the bank as a rich source of referrals (networking).

This chapter includes some tips, considerations, and important factors for lawyers needing a bank loan.

§ 18.01 Financial Needs

Law, like any other business, requires money to operate. The kinds of money or cash that may be needed are numerous. Here are some examples:

- *Seed money*. This is the initial money that you need to get you started in planning a new business. Consider it "earnest money." It is the financial outlay that proves you are serious about this endeavor.
- *Start-up capital*. This is what pays for the equipment and other initial expenses of getting the firm under way. This is the money that really gets the firm going—but barely. Vendor terms (buying on credit) are also considered a form of start-up money.
- *Working capital*. Working capital is money used to finance accounts receivable and operating expenses. These are the funds that keep you afloat until the cash flow from the business starts flowing in your direction.
- *Growth capital*. These are funds used for expanding sales (and the increase in accounts receivable), purchasing additional equipment to handle larger demand for your services, and adding new people to supplement existing staff. Usually, growth is financed from the profits

of the firm, but the profits may be too narrow or the growth may be too great to be handled by the existing level of profits.

The next obvious question is, How much money do you need? The key word here is *need*, not *want*. Think only about what your firm needs to survive; do not—at this point—think about how much you are going to take out for personal pleasure, comfort, or peace of mind.

Here are some factors that determine this financial need:

- *Sales volume*. The greater the billings, the greater the need for cash in the firm. Why? Nationally, the average time between when you bill someone and when you receive the payment is approximately four and one-half months. This means that the greater the billings, the greater the amount of cash needed to hold you through this waiting period. Some firms actually limit their capital needs by limiting their billings. One way to do that is by raising prices—and, thus, effectively reducing the number of clients.
- *Growth rate*. Faster-growing firms require more money; these can be real "money eaters." By increasing your accounts receivable and your workload, you increase the need for more personnel, more office space, etc. And although your clients may take over four months to pay you, your staff, landlord, and outside vendors expect to be paid now. Growth must be managed very carefully or the entire "ship" may sink.
- *Gross margin*. Gross margin is what is left over after you subtract operating expenses from revenues. It reflects the degree of "profits" that the firm generates and that are distributed to the lawyers as salaries or draws. The lower the margin, the greater the need for additional outside funds. The larger the margin, the higher the profits of the firm and the smaller the requirement for additional funding or sources of funds.
- *Conversion cycle of assets*. This is often called *capital turnover*, or how often the invested assets of the firm are being returned in revenues. The higher the rate of turnover, the more sales that can be produced on the same amount of assets. In professional practices, the net effect of this concept is to understand the cycle of accounts receivable turnover—that is, how soon you can get paid by your clients after you bill them.
- *Lead times*. The longer it takes to get something accomplished (e.g., training an associate to take on more sophisticated matters), the more money that is required.
- *Terms of sale*. The main thing to remember is that you are not in the banking business. When you bill clients, you are extending them credit. The more lenient you are in the credit terms that you extend to clients (see more about this in chapter 17), the greater the risk that you will not be paid and the more money that you will require to stay in business. The sooner you get paid, the sooner you can use your profits

(revenue minus costs) to finance your own growth. Do not become your client's banker!

§ 18.02 Types of Loans

The following are the types of loans typically extended by banking institutions to lawyers and law firms:

- *Line of credit or revolving line of credit.* The amount of the loan is dependent on each bank's perception of the total loan package. Some banks limit a loan to three times the monthly expenses, excluding partner draws. In the case of a line of credit, the borrower may borrow and repay at will up to the amount of the "line"; the bank usually prefers that the borrower be "clean," or out of debt, for at least thirty days to ninety days each year. The line of credit is then reviewed annually and extended, increased, or terminated as circumstances warrant. In the case of a revolving line of credit, the borrower usually obtains a designated sum of money over a period of time. The revolving line of credit is then converted to a term loan and is repayable over a period of two, three, or five years.
- *Equipment term loan.* The amount of the loan will normally be no more than the depreciable life of the equipment, usually three to five years. Some borrowers may be able to obtain loans for a longer period, but this is usually when the equipment being financed is expected to last longer than equipment typically acquired for use by a law firm.
- *Term loan.* These loans can be as long as seven to ten years for a large law firm and three to five years for a smaller firm. Most such loans involve leasehold improvements and furniture and equipment purchases. Frequently, the term loan is drawn down over a period of six to nine months; the payback period begins within three months of the final draw. The periodic payments may be structured to be equal payments until paid in full, or the loan may provide for a balloon payment at the end of the term.

§ 18.03 Selecting a Bank

Not every lawyer can properly represent every client. So, too, not every bank is appropriate for every lawyer. It is important for lawyers to know the prospective banker, know the types of loans that the bank prefers, know the type of customer base that the bank is seeking to build, know the general pricing structure of the bank, and know how flexible the bank will be in seeking new ways of helping the lawyer or firm with its future plans.

Lawyers should look for a bank that gives them the types of services and responsiveness that they want. A bank can effectively handle not only the needs of the firm but also personal banking needs.

For example, banks typically offer the following types of services for law firms:

- Credit arrangements to finance office relocation, leasehold improvements, capital expenditures and capital contributions, and other aspects of the firm's cash needs
- An online financial network to facilitate cash management, such as the opportunity to set minimum and maximum cash balances in the firm's general account, with "extra" funds being transferred daily to money market, interest-bearing accounts and cash advances being drawn from a line of credit in the event that the general account falls below the minimum
- A lawyer's investment account (also known as a client trust account), which can simplify the management of clients' funds and consolidate record keeping and year-end Internal Revenue Service report preparation
- Payroll administration, including tax reporting and record keeping
- Banking services for staff of the firm
- Short-term investment instruments such as certificates of deposit, business money market accounts, commercial paper, U.S. government agency repurchase agreements, and other portfolio options
- Pension plan administration

Banks offer the following types of services for individuals:

- Personal loans
- Home mortgages
- Interest-earning deposit accounts
- Discount brokerage
- Custody (trust) services
- Trust and estate services
- Personal financial planning

The foregoing lists of services are frequently not available all at one bank. However, the larger banks in metropolitan areas do offer all of the foregoing and more. The needs of the lawyer and the law firm will determine the bank to be selected as the bank of the firm.

§ 18.04 How a Bank Selects Borrowers

The old saying was that banks lend money to those who do not need it. Actually, this was never true. Of course, it is unreasonable to expect anyone—including a bank—to lend money unless the borrower has something at risk. Thus, a bank will make a loan only if the borrower has a contribution or money in the deal.

If you need money, it is hard to get a bank to open its coffers. Thus, it is important to establish a banking relationship and to learn—before funds are needed to avoid a catastrophe (e.g., missing the week's payroll)—what factors banks use to determine to whom they will lend money.

§ 18.04.1 Areas of Concern

Bankers require that borrowers have a good understanding of their businesses. Thus, you can expedite the loan process by meeting with your banker on a regular basis and inviting him to your office to see that your business is well managed and that you have good controls in place.

There are four areas of concern that a banker will definitely quiz you on. The better prepared you are to address these concerns, the more confident the banker will be.

- *Financials.* Can your business be characterized as a financial success? Why or why not? How does your company compare financially with its competitors? Is your performance solid and consistent? Do you recognize financial shortcomings and understand their origin?
- *Marketing.* Is your marketing approach effective? How do you measure this effectiveness? Do you understand the link between marketing and financial results? Do you manage your marketing resources efficiently?
- *Management.* Is your firm well managed? Does it incorporate a good mix of management skills? Do the managers have quantitative and qualitative problem-solving capabilities? Describe any weaknesses.
- *Product.* Does your product (providing legal services) provide any benefits beyond those of your competitors? Are perceived product benefits accounted for in your pricing? Do your staff members understand product differentiation? Does management know how to price the services, balancing market factors with costs?

§ 18.04.2 The Four C's

Beyond these areas of concern, banks make loans based on "The Four C's": character, capacity, capital, and collateral. The average banker will weight these factors in the decision-making process as follows: character (80 percent), collateral (15 percent), and capacity and capital together (5 percent).

- *Character.* The first question that the bank asks itself is whether the ethics, business practices, and general reputation of the prospective customer/borrower are such that the bank is comfortable. Does the bank want to do business with this lawyer? Without this threshold question being answered in the affirmative, there is no further discussion. The elements of character are honesty, integrity, and ability.
- *Capacity.* The next question is whether the cash flow of the law firm is sufficient to justify the confidence that the loan carrying costs (interest and related charges) and the principal amount of the loan will be paid back at the appointed time. A cash flow statement (not just an income

or revenue and expenses statement) *must* be submitted to the bank for its consideration.

- *Capital.* The bank wants to know what the funds are being used for. If the loan proceeds will be used to purchase an asset, the bank wants to know how much of the cost of the asset will be purchased by the law firm with assets of the firm, or, in other words, how much equity (or debt-to-equity ratio) the law firm will have in the asset. Banks do not want to be the only party investing in the given asset; they want to know that the law firm has a substantial stake in the purchase. Bankers are willing to take risks, but their risk is that their borrower will not repay the loan. The risk the bankers do not want to take is that their loan to the law firm (or to any borrower) places them in the position of being the only investor in the purchased asset. The risk that the purchase will accomplish the intended objective is or should be on the borrower, not the banker. The banker wants the bank's risk to be limited to the analysis of the law firm's ability to repay the loan even if the ultimate purchase does not work out or does not produce the income expected. If the law firm has an adequate capital base in the investment, the bank is more comfortable in assisting the firm (borrower) in the completion of the purchase. As a side note, it has been said that law firms often need working capital loans. Technically, the advance of funds under a loan does not change working capital. The more correct statement is that the loan is being made to help the law firm meet its liquidity or cash needs. The bank must be assured that there is sufficient equity in the law firm to repay the loan in accordance with the terms of the loan.
- *Collateral.* Despite the bank having been as careful as it can be in its examination and review of the borrower (due diligence), there still may come a time when the loan will go into default. If all else fails, how will the bank's outstanding loan be repaid? The "back door," as some bankers call it, is the value and adequacy of the collateral that was given to the bank to secure the payment of the debt in accordance with the terms of the loan. What type of collateral will be given to secure payment? Is it a house, another piece of real estate, equipment used in the operation of the law firm, a personal guarantee by someone of significant wealth who will be able to honor the guarantee should it be necessary, or some other asset of substantial value? In law firms that are organized in the partnership format, there is joint and several liability for the bank loan. Therefore, the partner with the greater asset base may want to insist that there be substantial collateral or, alternatively, may want to request that the potential profit should be greater than for the other partner(s) by virtue of the greater exposure to risk. If the loan is unsecured, the bank has given up the fourth C (collateral). In today's economic environment, this would be very unusual and would occur only with the best of the bank's customers.

§ 18.04.3 Documents That the Bank Wants to See

The following documents should be prepared for presentation to the bank in order to enter into a new banking relationship:

- Partnership agreement
- Annual fiscal year-end statements prepared by an accounting firm acceptable to the bank (two to five years)
- In-house quarterly statements after the last year-end statement
- Aged accounts receivable schedule
- Cash-flow projection, sometimes considered to be an annual budget, for the next twenty-four months
- Personal financial statement of net worth of the principals
- Personal tax returns of the principals (two to five years)
- Law firm tax returns (two to five years)

Additional documents, such as a business interruption insurance policy and disability and/or life insurance policies, may be required. Further, these instruments may have to be assigned to the bank as additional collateral to secure the payment of the loan.

§ 18.04.4 Additional Information to Discuss with the Bank

In addition to furnishing the documents to the bank, be prepared to discuss with the banker the following issues that help complete the picture concerning your law firm's viability and future growth prospects:

- *Financial statements.* Are your statements prepared on an accrual or cash basis? Most business statements are prepared on an accrual basis, and most law firm statements are prepared on a cash basis; be sure that your banker understands the difference between the two. If the law firm's financial statements are prepared on a cash basis, be sure to submit schedules of liabilities (accounts payable, etc.) and accounts receivable, neither of which will show up on a cash-basis financial statement.
- *Capital adequacy.* How much of the law firm's capital is permanent? What are the payout and pay-in policies of the firm?
- *Hidden assets.* Are there any hidden assets of the firm, such as a lease that has increased significantly in value? Are there significant billable hours that have not yet been billed? Are there contingency cases that are ripe for settlement or promise to be winners in a forthcoming trial?
- *Billing practices.* What are your billing rates? How do these rates compare with the industry? How frequently are statements delivered to clients? What are the aging, reserve, and write-off policies of the firm? How quickly are receivables collected (turnover rate)?
- *Litigation risk.* Does the firm carry an errors and omissions insurance policy? What are the deductible and premium?

- *Cost controls.* What is the gross profit margin of the firm? Are there any major cost-containment programs in effect? Are there any major cutbacks or expansions planned in the near future?
- *Partner control.* Does any one partner or group of partners control a significant percentage of the firm's business? Does any one partner control the business decisions of the firm?
- *Client base.* What type of client is attracted to the firm? Is the client relationship based on transactions or on relations with the lawyer or law firm? Is the firm focused on one area of practice, or is it a diverse practice?
- *Management.* How is the firm governed?
- *Financial strength.* Review ratios of liquidity, leverage, and debt capacity. Review profits per partner and revenue per lawyer.

§ 18.05 Developing a Good Relationship with the Banker

Lawyers should think of the bank as a supplier. Suppliers provide lawyers with the goods and services that allow the law firm to deliver quality legal services. Good banking relationships provide the necessary funds and services that allow a law firm to maintain itself and grow.

The banking relationship must be open, candid, and built on trust. Good bankers are creative people who will find a way to assist a good customer of the bank. The banker can be more creative if he fully understands your goals and circumstances. In time, your banker could prove to be a valuable source of information, advice, and possibly even new business.

§ 18.06 Action Plan

- Determine financial needs.
- Select a bank.
- Prove yourself to be a worthwhile candidate for a loan.
- Create a good working relationship with the banker.

CHAPTER 19

Equipment Lease Financing

Ready money is Aladdin's lamp.

—Lord Byron, *Don Juan*

Chapter Checklist

- o Advantages of Leasing
- o Other Leasing Considerations
- o Action Plan

At a recent seminar, one of the entrepreneurial vice presidents of a Big Six accounting firm related the story of a client who was opening French bakeries in several shopping malls. He initially had $600,000 in cash. Four months before he was scheduled to open his outlets, he spent $500,000 for the specialized French ovens that were going into the locations. By the time he was ready to open, he had no money left for his start-up food stocks or to set up his initial payroll, pay permits, utilities, etc.

The moral is that in business, long-term assets should be financed long term and short-term expenses and assets should be financed with available cash or other short-term methods of credit.

The equipment that the baker purchased had a useful life of over ten years. If he had obtained long-term financing, the equipment would be earning money on a daily basis, and the income from the use of the equipment could easily cover the monthly payments for a financing transaction.

In lieu of bank financing, an attractive, fiscally sound financing option for long-term assets is leasing. Leasing is one form of renting. The funds for leasing can often be obtained from the maker of the equipment or an independent finance company. In the practice of law, the computers, telephones, copiers, fax machines, and even automobiles that are scheduled to be utilized for two, three, or four years can be leased.

Lease financing is, in fact, good business. No prudent businessperson would pay an employee three years' wages in advance, so why would anyone pay the entire cost of a piece of productive machinery in advance rather than letting it earn its cost on a monthly basis?

§ 19.01 Advantages of Leasing

More and more professionals are utilizing equipment (and auto) leasing as opposed to outright purchase. The main reasons for leasing are as follows:

1. Leasing is flexible and practical.
2. Leasing is cost-effective.
3. Leasing has tax advantages.
4. Leasing helps conserve operating capital.

§ 19.01.1 Leasing Is Flexible and Practical

Equipment leasing can generally be tailored to the situation at hand. Normally, leases are structured for one to five years. However, assume that you have a three-year lease for a computer and then six months into the lease you want to upgrade your printer. Frequently, the equipment leasing company will suggest that you structure a thirty-month add-on to the computer lease so that all of the financing will end at the same time. One of the other features of equipment leasing is that sometimes you can have reduced or staggered payments to take advantage of peak seasons in a business cycle or to allow for start-up costs and time needed for the practice to get going before the full payments begin.

§ 19.01.2 Leasing Is Cost-Effective

Leasing is cost-effective because it generally consists of 100 percent financing compared to a bank loan of only 60 percent to 80 percent with additional collateral required. Standard brand-name equipment such as copiers and computers are usually financed at the same 100 percent.

The only requirement is that the leasing company will typically take one or two payments (first and last) up front, which will be applied to the total number of payments or may be treated as a security deposit. It is best to have the up-front payment characterized as *payments* because it may be tax deductible, whereas a security deposit is not treated as an expense at the time it is made and may not be deducted. However, as an exception, if the company is attempting to set up a "true lease," the security deposit may be the only alternative to meet the rules of accounting standards.

Another reason for leasing's cost-effectiveness is that the lease of a productive and useful asset permits the computer or piece of machinery to earn the revenue to make the payments as it is being financed. For example, a computer may be utilized to produce wills or other legal documents for which lawyers charge on a daily or monthly basis. The computer's total cost does not have to be paid up front and then recovered later by the lessee. Instead, it is a working asset that is ideally producing more income than its cost to lease.

§ 19.01.3 Leasing Has Tax Advantages

It is often said that leasing can be a 100 percent expense with certain tax advantages. If the equipment lease is treated as a capital lease, then generally the tax consequences would be only the deduction of the "imputed interest rate" and the depreciation of the asset over five or more years. If the lease is an operating or true lease, then 100 percent of the lease payments may be deducted each month as an expense, much like office rent or utility bills. A lawyer would have to consult with a tax expert to determine how best to treat equipment leases in terms of taxes.

§ 19.01.4 Leasing Helps Conserve Operating Capital

Many times, a lawyer will obtain a line of credit or other loans from the local bank. Leasing, however, is "off-balance-sheet financing" that does not affect your line of credit or other banking relationships. Leasing is more flexible. Lawyers may wish to conserve their lines of credit or other bank financing for emergency situations and handle their normal growth and acquisitions through equipment leasing.

§ 19.02 Other Leasing Considerations

§ 19.02.1 Types of Leases

A lease is considered to be either a capital lease (more like an installment sale) or a true lease. A capital lease is booked as an asset by the company and is depreciated by the lessee. A true lease is characterized more as a rental and may be 100 percent deductible, much like the office rent or the utility bills.

Leases are generally capitalized under two sets of rules: accounting rules and IRS rules. Because of these different rules, it is not surprising to find a lease characterized as a capital lease for the company's books but also set up as an operating lease, or true lease, for IRS purposes.

The definition of *accounting* is found largely in the Financial Accounting Standards Board's opinion and its amendments (FASB 13). The IRS rules change periodically and are found under the "Business Deductions" topics within the *Internal Revenue Code*. Generally speaking, the classification of a lease is determined by the lease rate and the end-of-lease buyout.

One type of buyout is the $1 buyout, which is rarely ever billed. However, the wise lessee should actually send the dollar to the leasing company or pay that up front. Why is this a good idea? If there are late charges at the end of the lease or if the lessee does not make an election within some time period, the lease may continue on a month-to-month basis at the same or at some reduced rate. An institution could claim, for example, that if the personal property or insurance taxes or some late charge is not paid, the lease continues until these nominal charges are paid, and only then would the lease end. While this practice is considered unethical within the industry, it does happen.

The second buyout is termed *fair market value*, which, under the strictest observance, means that at the end of the lease an appraisal takes place, and the lessee may buy out the equipment at its then-determined fair market value. True fair-market-value determinations are usually conducted on a higher level of leasing at, say, hundreds of thousands of dollars worth of equipment. They are usually done to satisfy the strict requirements of a true lease and may be the subject of government contracts ordered by subcontractors or other government contractors. Most fair-market-value leases are set forth as "fair market value not to exceed 10 percent." Fair market value generally will also include sales and use taxes.

The lessee should always make sure that the buyout is stated in writing. If the buyout is not on the face of the lease document itself, it should be the subject of a side letter between the leasing company and the lessee.

§ 19.02.2 Approval Decisions

Unlike most bank financing, leasing companies (especially those doing nationwide business) oftentimes will make a financial decision of up to $100,000 based only on an application. This means that the applicant need only fill out a simple application listing the name of the company; the name, address, and Social Security number of the principal owner; the vendor; the type of equipment; a bank; and three trade references, one of which is usually the landlord. The lease company then processes the application, makes a few calls to the bank, may or may not check all of the trade references, and runs a credit check on the owner. Based on this simple process, approvals or turndowns are usually granted within twenty-four to forty-eight hours.

One of the major leasing companies at a credit scoring seminar indicated that it routinely makes decisions in six seconds using automatic machine scoring on lease applications up to $25,000. There are not many banks or even senior loan officers that would make a credit decision on such a small amount of information. However, the track record of leasing companies suggests that if they pick the right criteria, their overall credit decisions are just as good if not better in machine scoring than having some individual analyst pore over reams of financial information related to the lessee.

For larger transactions, the leasing company may require a personal financial statement of the owner, corporate or business financial statements, or business tax returns going back for the last two years.

§ 19.02.3 Property Taxes

Most lease agreements require that the lessee pay any personal property taxes that may be levied within the state or local jurisdiction. These jurisdictions generally will bill the leasing company, and the leasing company through its contract will bill the lessee and seek reimbursement. In some instances, depending on how the local tax jurisdictions work, the lessee will be asked to declare any equipment under lease or equipment that is being owned or purchased under an installment contract. There is some flexibility as the lessee may declare the property as being on a "lease to purchase option" and pay the taxes directly to the taxing authority.

It is unusual for the leasing company to build into the lease rate the local and state taxes and the personal property taxes on the leased equipment. In almost all cases, the contract requires that the lessee reimburse the lessor for this expense.

§ 19.02.4 Use Taxes

Most lease arrangements in states that require sales and use taxes also apply the same rate to each lease payment. However, when the equipment is purchased by the leasing company from the vendor (note that title remains with the leasing company until the purchase option is exercised), the leasing company will issue the vendor a tax-exempt certificate, which means that the sales price at the time the equipment is purchased will not have sales tax added to the large amount. The same will apply to the lease payments throughout the life of the lease. Therefore, what the leasing company will have in its contract is the lease payment for the equipment plus the sales and use tax, which will then equal the total monthly payment.

§ 19.02.5 Insurance

The leasing company will require that the lessee obtain fire and casualty insurance to cover the equipment during the term of the lease. Many leasing companies offer a simple add-on casualty insurance policy for $3 to $5 a month in addition to the normal lease payment. It is generally more advantageous for the lessee to handle his own insurance and furnish an "additional insured loss payee clause" to the leasing company to cover the equipment in question.

§ 19.02.6 Personal Guarantee

In the small-leasing arena of computers and copiers, the general rule is that the leasing company will require the principal stockholder or partner to guarantee the lease even though a company may be a limited liability corporation or a partnership. Very rarely will this requirement be waived unless the lessee is a major company, a publicly traded company, or a firm with annual billings of millions of dollars.

§ 19.02.7 Rentals

There are many equipment rental companies that rent additional computers, typewriters, and copying machines on a daily or weekly basis. The rates are generally high, but they may be needed for a law office's one-time seminar or special project. Obviously, it is best to avoid rentals unless they are absolutely necessary. Planned management of financial resources that includes long-term equipment leasing is a better alternative.

§ 19.02.8 Lease Rates

Lease rates are often quoted as "lease factors." The vendor of the equipment or the leasing company will oftentimes have a lease factor sheet depending on the term of the lease, the number of payments that are made up front, and what the buyout is at the end. These factors are set forth as a four- or six-decimal point lease factor. In simple terms, these lease factors are interest rates considered as a monthly payment factor based on $1. Take, for example, a $1,000 piece of equipment with a lease factor of .0365 for a thirty-six-month lease. When that factor is multiplied by the cost of the equipment, you get a lease payment of $36.50 per month.

The lease interest rates are generally in the range of lower to medium credit card rates, which are generally higher than bank financing. The important fact to remember is that the security for the lease is generally owning the equipment that is being leased with no other collateral required.

§ 19.02.9 Warranties

Even though the leasing company is buying the equipment directly from the vendor and leasing it to the lessee through the term of the lease, most lease contracts indicate that all warranties and maintenance will be assigned to the lessee to be utilized directly between the lessee and the manufacturer or vendor.

§ 19.02.10 Soft Costs

Most leasing companies will not knowingly lease the large percentage of "soft costs," which can include maintenance, installation, and training. These will often be stripped out, with only the pure equipment costs remaining to be financed. Some leasing companies will go up to 30 percent to 40 percent for software and some cabling and wiring along with the hardware.

§ 19.02.11 Maintenance Contracts

When you buy a maintenance agreement from the vendor, be sure that the warranty period has been subtracted before the maintenance agreement begins. Frequently there is a ninety-day warranty period offered by the vendor on all copying machines, typewriters, and computers; in some cases, the warranty will go as long as a year. The maintenance agreement should not start until the warranty period ends; otherwise, you will be paying twice for the same protection.

In dealing with copying machine dealers, it is wise to separate the cost of the equipment from the service agreement. In this way, you will know what each costs. Oftentimes, copying machine companies will offer the machine at an artificially low price and make up the difference with a service contract. The wise lawyer shopping for equipment will compare pure equipment costs among a series of vendors along with any warranty or service to be priced separately. In this way, you can be sure that you are getting the lowest price possible for the equipment before you turn to the financing of that item through leasing or other financing arrangements.

§ 19.02.12 Leasing and Rapid Changes in Technology

A frequent mistake in equipment financing is the failure to consider the useful life of the equipment or the effect that new technology may have on the equipment's life span.

For example, the first users of the car telephone paid up to $3,000 and financed the equipment over a three-year period with monthly payments in excess of $150. This was fine for a while, but then technology caught on. The price of car telephones dropped dramatically within the next eighteen months, and car telephones then cost less than $1,000, with monthly payments on a three-year financing plan down to $45. Users were looking at better technology at one-third the price. They rapidly became dissatisfied with their financing arrangements because they had failed to appreciate the effect of technology changes on the term of their financing.

Likewise, computers are technologically obsolete within three or four months after they are purchased, although they still can be productively utilized for three or four years. No one is content with using antiquated equipment. Therefore, you should always consider what the useful life of the asset is and when you will want to upgrade it or trade it. This is most important in determining the length of time to finance or lease your equipment, and it is especially true when you want to upgrade your computers within two to three years of the initial acquisition. The financing on the computers should be sized to match the useful technological life of the computer as well as its machinery lifetime.

Since copying machines tend to wear out after three years, it is foolish to have a financing plan for such equipment extend beyond that.

§ 19.02.13 Early Buyouts and the "Rule of 78s"

Often, the lessee may wish to buy out the lease early for any number of reasons.

Be sure that there is no "prepayment penalty" associated with the equipment lease. The worst case would be a noncancelable lease under which the lessee would have to make the total of all of the lease payments on a forty-eight-month lease even if the lessee bought out the lease after twenty-three months. These clauses are rare in lease documents, but, to be sure, you should consult the "fine print" in the contract.

So, how are buyouts calculated? Bank loans are usually, but not always, set up on a true amortized basis, with a percentage of each payment going toward principal and a decreasing percentage going toward interest. The changes with each payment may be very small, but the effect is that you only pay the interest (at the agreed rate) on the remaining principal balance of the loan. A graph illustrating this effect would show a straight line on a 45-degree angle separating the principal portion of each payment and the interest portion. At the start of the loan, the interest would be higher and dwindle down toward a small amount near the end of the payment schedule.

There is, however, another widely used method of calculating the buyout amount, and it is the commercial "Rule of 78s." It is a formula built into many financial software programs, and it utilizes the number of months within the term to determine the amount of interest versus principal on any particular payment. The name *Rule of 78s* is derived from assigning a number to each month of the year and adding all of the numbers together. For example, January is 1, February is 2, and so on through December at 12. The total of these numbers, 1 through 12, is 78.

That number is now used as the denominator in these formulas. Accordingly, if a lessee prepays at the end of month one, the lessor has earned 12/78 of the total charge, and the refund is 66/78. At the end of six months, the lessor has earned 57/78 of the total charge (12/78 plus 11/78 plus 10/78 plus 9/78 plus 8/78 plus 7/78). The same theory works with leases of two, three, or more years; the denominator just gets bigger.

While the sum total of all of the interest and principal amounts of any lease or loan utilizing a regular amortization formula or a Rule of 78s calculation is the same, the effect is that the Rule of 78s creates more interest due on each payment at the beginning of the lease than would be earned on a regular amortization. Where the graph on a normal amortization lease/loan is a straight 45-degree angle over the term of the loan, the Rule of 78s creates a "bow" in the line at the beginning in favor of the interest portion of the payment. Most lease contracts do have a clause that an early buyout will be thus calculated and is not considered a "prepayment penalty."

§ 19.03 Action Plan

- Where appropriate for you, consider leasing as a viable financial-management tool.
- Make sure that you understand the various aspects of leasing that might impact your decision to lease.

CHAPTER 20

Risk Management for Lawyers

Great successes never come without risks.

—Flavius Josephus

Chapter Checklist

- o Insurance Needs
- o Disaster-Recovery Plan
- o Action Plan

There are two types of law firms: those that have experienced a disaster and those that will. "Disaster" for a law firm is not a question of if but rather when. The only unknowns are the type of disaster, when it will occur, and how bad it will be. A hurricane or a disease epidemic are disasters, but so, too, are a burst water pipe or a computer system meltdown to the unprepared. To manage such risks, every law firm should do two things: (1) assess insurance needs and purchase adequate insurance and (2) implement a disaster-recovery plan.

§ 20.01 Insurance Needs

In a law firm, the costs of operation are relatively fixed. The big-ticket items, such as rent, staff, and lawyers, are generally stable with little room for negotiating reduced pricing. But one area in which a great deal of flexibility does exist is risk-management, or insurance, coverage. Buying insurance to reduce the potential catastrophic impact of a disaster is one area to inspect carefully.

The purpose of insurance is to protect against specific catastrophes, not to make a profit. Balancing the need for insurance coverage and the cost of obtaining it is not easy. Careful consideration must be given to the likelihood of occurrence compared to the cost and the cash reserves that you maintain. Until disaster strikes, you may feel foolish spending money on something that is so intangible. But when the disaster does occur and you have the proper insurance coverage, you will be seen as wise. Business and personal insurance programs must be carefully coordinated to transfer risk whenever possible or, if transferring risk is not possible, to manage and insure risk as necessary.

Always make sure that you understand thoroughly how much and what kind of coverage you are actually purchasing by examining the policy documents, not relying on representations by an agent.

The following sections detail the basic types of insurance that lawyers should consider.

§ 20.01.1 Property and General Liability Insurance

This is probably the most common and the first choice of insurance policies to be purchased. These policies protect against general liability, fire, and theft. Subcategories include business auto, fidelity and employee sabotage, business interruption, workers' compensation, and umbrella.

Business auto insurance offers protection for nonowned and hired autos. A separate policy is written for business auto insurance and carries coverage different from personal auto insurance.

Fidelity and employee sabotage insurance offers protection against employee embezzlement. Frequently, this is a rider to another policy and becomes part of an office package. When someone else handles the funds of your law practice, this may be important coverage. The expense is nominal, especially when compared to the protection offered.

Business interruption insurance covers your business (practice) when it is interrupted by a natural disaster, and future sales and revenues are scaled down or at zero. This insurance will pay an amount equal to the net profit and keep you "alive." Three specific types include business income, which replaces income that would otherwise have been earned by the business had no loss occurred; extra expense, which pays for necessary expenses incurred during the period of restoration of the property that would not have been incurred if there had been no physical loss or damage to the property; and contingent business interruption, which covers loss of income incurred due to a property loss at a key client location.

Workers' compensation insurance is generally mandated by the state. Employee accidents that occur at the place of business are covered by this policy rather than by a traditional personal injury/liability policy. The premium is set by law with a minimum amount required.

Umbrella insurance picks up additional coverage on top of other policies' coverage and increases the policy limits provided. The cost of this coverage is relatively nominal, and it should almost always be included.

§ 20.01.2 Cyberinsurance

A disaster can jeopardize computer files, which frequently include confidential client records and work product. Such disasters can result from a computer breakdown or a breach by a hacker. These computer security risks generally are not covered by most insurance. An effective cyberinsurance policy can handle the first-party and third-party liabilities that your firm faces due to a computer security disaster. First-party liabilities include revenue lost during system downtime, the cost of recovering data, and even the ransom demands of hackers. Third-party liabilities involve client losses from compromised or misused data and lawsuit judgments for those harmed by denial-of-service attacks and viruses sent out over their system.

§ 20.01.3 Life Insurance

The primary goal of life insurance is to provide business associates and family with enough protection (money) to allow them to hire and train a replacement for the deceased or to pay the taxes on the estate of a loved one. There are many forms of life insurance, including "key man," whole life, and term. Proof of good health is essential when individual policies are purchased; joining a group plan with guaranteed insurability may be necessary if your current health will not qualify you otherwise.

§ 20.01.4 Disability Insurance

Disability insurance provides a flow of revenue while the insured is either temporarily or permanently disabled and unable to handle financial responsibilities. This coverage is not always easy to purchase because of the need to demonstrate actual past earnings and future earnings capacity. Disability insurance is particularly important if you are without adequate cash reserves or if a family member cannot step in to help in a time of need. The income flow may not be exactly the same as before, but it can prevent a catastrophe.

§ 20.01.5 Health Insurance

With the big debate these days about health maintenance organizations (HMOs), preferred provider organizations (PPOs), and the like, it is hard to know where to turn for health insurance. Also, proof of good current health is required. As in the case of life insurance, participation in a group plan may be required if your personal health is in doubt. If you are unable to find a policy that is reasonably priced and that offers the benefits you desire (for example, the right to select your own doctor), check with your local bar association or the American Bar Association. If you are still unsatisfied with what you find, check with one of your corporate clients to determine if you can be covered under its policy.

§ 20.01.6 Errors and Omissions Insurance

Errors and omissions insurance provides protection against malpractice and is becoming increasingly important in our litigious society. Countering the importance of this insurance, however, is the trend toward increasing numbers of lawyers who are "bare," or without this coverage. For example, in California in 2009, approximately 18 percent of the state's lawyers—some 30,000—did not have malpractice insurance, according to an insurance committee of the state bar.

The reason normally given for the absence of this coverage is the high cost. Annual malpractice premiums usually range from $3,000 to $7,000 per lawyer, often well beyond the ability of small firms and solo practitioners to purchase. The results of a study in California correlated with similar studies in other states and found that 25 percent of active, private practitioners earn less than $50,000 per year; and 50 percent earn less than $100,000 per year. These lawyers, for whom 1 percent to 1.5 percent of gross revenue spent on malpractice premiums would be reasonable, might feel that they cannot afford to spend 10 percent or more of their income on a product that they believe they are likely never to need.

Experience with state disciplinary boards suggests, too, that many lawyers cannot obtain the insurance because of the state bars' disciplinary action against the lawyers. Check in your jurisdiction to determine whether this insurance is mandatory. If so, the risk will be spread out among all the lawyers in the state. This means that even if claims do exist, coverage cannot be denied.

§ 20.01.7 Employment Practices Liability Insurance

This insurance—which includes wrongful termination, wrongful demotion or discipline, invasion of privacy, discrimination or harassment, and sexual harassment—is relatively new and may be the least known type of insurance coverage today. Except for intentional acts, this insurance will provide significant protection for employment-related practices. Suits for wrongful termination and sexual harassment are becoming all too frequent, so it would be wise to invest in this type of insurance.

Policies from the various carriers include different conditions, but most policies include defense costs, settlements, and judgments arising from claims made by employees, leased workers, or temporary workers. Policies from the various companies may have a varying range of deductibles, coinsurance, and policy limits. Some carriers may also provide risk-management assistance, handbook development, and hotlines for legal counsel.

§ 20.01.8 Personal Auto Insurance

This is the most common type of auto insurance, but there are still those who do not have it. Make sure that both you as an individual and the firm are listed as insureds under the policy.

§ 20.01.9 Employee Benefits

While a business is not required by law to provide life insurance, disability coverage, and other benefits—and while the status of mandatory health insurance coverage is still in flux—careful consideration should be given to designing a program of what benefits to offer and when to offer them. In particular, offering staff protection under a health insurance policy may be competitively necessary in today's employment marketplace.

A piecemeal approach can lead to expensive and less-than-adequate coverage. Cafeteria plans, premium-only plans, employee contributions, self-funding, and partial self-funding are all important and expensive decisions that should be thought out and made within the scope of a well-defined plan that can be implemented in totality or in stages as the business is able to provide benefits.

§ 20.02 Disaster-Recovery Plan

Risk management is about more than insurance; it should also include a disaster-recovery plan. The goal of disaster planning is making a recovery that ensures the survival of the firm. Your energy on such efforts is like insurance: "useless" and expensive when not needed, and priceless when needed.

Law firms that plan for disaster remain the exception rather than the rule, but even these firms typically make the mistake of focusing on *things*—insurance policies, alarm systems, and backup servers. Such a focus is doomed to failure because disaster recovery must include a plan encompassing the firm's people. Making sure that a firm's people are involved and prepared is the best way to make sure that the law firm survives. Administrators responsible for disaster-recovery planning should keep these people concerns uppermost in mind.

§ 20.02.1 Create a Task Force

Developing a disaster-recovery plan would be an overwhelming task for one person. You will need acceptance, involvement, and support from a broad cross-section of the firm to create the plan. All key firm stakeholders and leaders must be involved or at least lend their full support.

Do not, however, make the mistake of creating a large, unwieldy group to create the recovery plan on the assumption that the more people involved, the more acceptance there will be. As in most organizational efforts, such groups merely produce inertia rather than results. Instead, put together a small task force populated with people who have power to make decisions, plus young and innovative firm members who are known as people who get things done.

§ 20.02.2 Create a Management Structure

The best way to make a disaster-recovery plan viable is to create a management structure along functional lines, such as the following:

- *Executive director*. This person will have overall responsibility for disaster planning, including the coordination of all components of the plan.
- *Chief financial officer*. This person will have responsibility for protecting and recovering the firm's financial assets, including securing emergency funding and continuity in the collections process.
- *Chief information officer*. This person will have responsibility for all aspects of protecting and recovering the firm's information assets and communication capabilities.
- *Facilities director*. This person will have responsibility for protecting and recovering the firm's offices, office equipment, and other physical assets.
- *Human resources director*. This person will have responsibility for all aspects of protecting and reestablishing the people who work for the firm as well as visitors and anyone else on-site.
- *Managing partner*. This person will have responsibility for recovering or otherwise providing for matters in progress, protecting the interests of clients, and ensuring that the full firm supports the recovery of the overall practice.
- *Marketing director*. This person will have responsibility for the communication process during recovery, including communication with clients, the profession, and the general community.

§ 20.02.3 Create a Communication System

Disaster recovery begins when communication is reestablished after a disaster, and that means a good communication plan must be in place before disaster occurs. Execution of your communication plan should utilize the time and talents of your full disaster-recovery team. The makeup of this team is central to your preparation. Choosing people who will keep their heads and actually perform the tasks is crucial; and there should be a backup for each in case of absence, illness, or panic on the part of the primary designee.

Several people on your emergency team should be trained to send broadcast voice mails to all mailboxes. If people can access the phone system, this is an efficient way to reach them. Designate people to send broadcast e-mails to everyone from and to both office and home e-mail systems. Establish the capability to do this from home PCs and laptops if the network is down.

§ 20.02.4 Test the Efficacy of the Plan

No matter how good a disaster-recovery plan is on paper, it *must* be regularly reviewed and tested. Once you do create a plan, review and revise it regularly to keep it from going stale and becoming useless. More importantly, the firm must periodically pretend that there is a disaster, implement the elements of the plan, and change those aspects that don't work as well as desired.

§ 20.02.5 The Plan in Action

Once the nature and severity of the event is evaluated and an assessment of damage is made, the decision makers can determine whether operations can continue (perhaps in a reduced capacity) or if relocation to an alternate facility is required. When decision makers have decided the course of action, the information should be given to the emergency team by the most feasible method available.

§ 20.03 Action Plan

- Review insurance needs and options.
- Balance personal and professional/business insurance needs.
- Engage the people in your firm to create a disaster-recovery plan.

CHAPTER 21

Client Trust Accounting the Easy Way—with QuickBooks*

To be trusted is a greater compliment than to be loved.

—George MacDonald

In God We Trust: All Others Pay Cash.

—Jean Shepherd

Chapter Checklist

- o IOLTA Basics
- o "Rule of Five"
- o Accounting Theory
- o QuickBooks for Windows
- o Summary of Tasks
- o Action Plan

Suppose you receive a phone call from a state bar investigator who informs you that your bank has notified the bar that a check written on a client trust account, or IOLTA account, has been returned because of insufficient funds. The investigator now wants to review the records of your client trust accounts to determine whether you are in compliance with the current rules. Will you

*QuickBooks is a registered trademark and/or registered service mark of Intuit Inc., or one of its subsidiaries, in the United States and other countries.

be able to provide up-to-date reports for every penny of client funds for which you are personally responsible?

This phone call need not create alarm or cause stress to the solo practitioner or to the small law firm. You do not need to employ a full-time bookkeeper to maintain your trust records. New accounting software is both affordable and relatively easy to learn.

An outstanding software program that can be designed to keep track of every client trust transaction, produce reports as required by the standards, and perform monthly bank reconciliations is QuickBooks.[1] Maintaining these records on the computer and on backup media provides the added assurance that this vital information will be available for the mandatory period of retention (from the date of the last disbursement) and can be reproduced on printed media within a matter of minutes (the required retention period may differ for the Internal Revenue Service and for the state bar; check your jurisdiction's rules and ethics opinions).[2]

§ 21.01 IOLTA Basics

IOLTA (Interest on Lawyer Trust Accounts) trust accounting is one of the most fundamental financial and ethical concerns of any law firm. IOLTA accounts, or client trust accounts, are public service programs regulated by states and the American Bar Association; the accounts earn interest, which is used for civil legal aid for the poor and for improvements to the judicial system.

Managing an IOLTA account, or client trust account, involves highly technical issues that center on depositing into the account a client's payment for work that will be performed and withdrawing that payment from the account and depositing it into a lawyer's general account when the work has been performed. Funds in IOLTA accounts belong to the client and must be strictly safeguarded until the lawyer and firm are entitled to them by virtue of services performed. When the lawyer is entitled to make the transfer, the lawyer *must* make the transfer or be guilty of commingling personal and client funds, which is prohibited by the rules of professional conduct. The ABA *Model Rules of Professional Conduct* Rule 1.15 specifically addresses the impermissibility of commingling the lawyer's own funds with client funds.

The method of pricing that you use impacts this discussion. If you charge a flat fee and agree that it is earned on receipt, trust account withdrawal probably cannot be questioned. It may be better, however, to deposit the flat

1. QuickBooks can generally be purchased at any major software retail store. Currently, you can also purchase QuickBooks or QuickBooks Pro directly from Intuit, http://www.intuit.com (last visited Aug. 1, 2013). Prices are subject to change.

2. This chapter and the methodology described for client trust accounting was originally created in response to California State Bar Rule 4-100, related to accounting for client trust accounts. Since that time, several states have either adopted or utilized the California rules in drafting their own state bar rules. Therefore, although the focus of this chapter is on rules in California, the concepts in other states are the same or similar. It is absolutely mandatory, however, that you contact the state bar of the state in which you are licensed to obtain the rules for your state. If the rules of your state are different from California rules, you may need to modify the use of the methodologies and software described herein.

fee into a client's trust account and withdraw it when reaching specific events: a date certain, the filing of a complaint, or the signing of a settlement or merger agreement. Retainer fees, too, can be deposited into a general account if the agreement says that the retainer is not for future work but for the lawyer specifically being engaged—and thus taken off the market. In other words, there is a valid charge for not being available to others. If you receive a retainer for future work, however, it would seem best to put this into your client's trust account and have the engagement agreement provide for withdrawal of the funds upon realization of a certain date or event. With respect to flat or fixed fees, a case can be made that hours involved are irrelevant. If, however, you compute the flat fee based on the number of hours that you anticipate and discuss that with the client (suggesting that the fee will increase if actual hours exceed the estimate), the billing arrangement looks like hourly billing. Traditionally, when hourly billing fees are involved, the retainer must be deposited into the trust account first, and then withdrawn and deposited into the general account once the fee has been earned.

Under every state's rules of professional conduct in the realm of IOLTA accounting, the lawyer is a fiduciary who, working with the appropriate firm administrator, must keep accurate accounting records of IOLTA account transfers. This fiduciary duty to properly account for clients' funds is intended to prevent misappropriation or negligence. For any lawyer, law firm, or firm administrator with any account-management responsibilities, to do anything other than use an effective software accounting program—such as QuickBooks, detailed in this chapter—or an outside accountant to reconcile trust and bank account records each month is to invite error, inquiry, and trouble. Banks are required to notify the appropriate bar authority of any suspected theft or negligence, and a bounced check from an IOLTA account brings bar examiners into the lawyer's office almost instantly. A failure to maintain and provide accurate accounting records means very bad news for the lawyer—a sanction or even loss of a license to practice law. Simple human error may be an explanation for trust account problems, but it is never an excuse where a lawyer's professional responsibility and liability are concerned.

§ 21.02 "Rule of Five"

The minimum trust record requirements (mandated by the ABA) are summarized by the "Rule of Five":

1. A written "ledger" for each client, setting forth the name of the client and identification of the bank account; the dates of each activity; the amounts received and from whom; the amounts disbursed and to whom, and current balances of funds for each client, each month, or as of any date the report is required
2. A written "journal" for each client trust account identifying the name of the account (including the bank and account number), the date of each transaction, each debit and credit to the account, the names of the sources of each deposit and the names of each person receiving a payment, and the current balance in the account

3. Copies of all bank statements and canceled checks for each client trust account
4. Monthly reconciliation of each of the above items
5. A journal of other properties, such as securities, jewelry, valuable coins, art, etc.

Although a number of good computer software programs are available to assist you in doing client trust accounting, QuickBooks by Intuit stands out as the most flexible and inexpensive program available. QuickBooks has been well used for years, and Intuit has a solid reputation for support and annual updates.

§ 21.03 Accounting Theory

Client funds held in trust are a liability of the law firm to the client. These are balance sheet transactions, not income and expense transactions. For example, funds received in settlement of a personal injury case are credited to the client's liability account and are not income of the law firm until services are performed and invoiced. Therefore, the accounting records of the law firm should reflect two additional accounts in the law firm chart of accounts. The first account is a bank account titled "Cash in Bank—Client Trust." The second account is a liability account titled "Client Trust Liability." In QuickBooks, a separate subaccount will be set up under "Client Trust Liability" for each client matter in which funds will be held in trust. This creates a separate ledger for each and every client matter.

The important concept here is that client funds held in trust must be kept in an entirely separate bank account and cannot be commingled with other law firm funds. Furthermore, the record keeping for client funds will be based solely upon the activity in the client trust bank accounts and will produce totally separate accounting records just for the trust funds. (It is also possible to set up the entire trust accounting as a separate company, which will only account for the client trust transactions. If you set up the client trust accounting as a separate QuickBooks company, the client trust bank account and liability account will not appear on the law firm financial statements. The separate company setup is not required but may be useful if you want to separate the duties of the law firm accounting from the client trust accounting.)

§ 21.04 QuickBooks for Windows

We will focus on QuickBooks for Windows.[3] (QuickBooks no longer sells or supports the DOS equivalent.) All versions of QuickBooks and QuickBooks

---

3. The method of utilizing QuickBooks software to account for client trust funds was developed by the author of this chapter, not QuickBooks, Intuit, or any of their employees. QuickBooks customer support personnel are most likely not familiar with any state bar rules for client trust accounting or the methodologies described in this chapter. Questions regarding the use of QuickBooks itself should be directed to Ed Poll (see contact information in the preface). *See also* LYNETTE BENTON, LAW PRACTICE ACCOUNTING USING QUICKBOOKS: AN ATTOTNEY'S GUIDE TO USING QUICKBOOKS IN A LAW PRACTICE (2011); ANNETTE FADNESS, QUICKBOOKS FOR ATTORNEYS: THE DEFINITIVE USER'S MANUAL FOR LAW FIRMS (2014).

Pro utilize the same features that affect the method of accounting for client trust funds described in this chapter and are referenced together as QuickBooks. QuickBooks is a very simple and well-supported accounting software package.

QuickBooks will save you time because most information, such as payees and sources of settlement funds, is entered only one time if done properly. The next time you write a check to a payee, the name pops up automatically as you type. The program automatically records the name and address so that mailing labels can be generated. If you bill for services on an hourly basis, you will be able to take advantage of the accounts receivable and invoicing system included in the package. There is also a payroll package available that is sold separately.

The advantage of QuickBooks is that you are able to write checks and record deposits directly on the computer and at the same time record all other aspects of the transaction automatically. By printing the client ledger report in advance of disbursing the checks and by obtaining your client's signature on the report, you will avoid client conflict and possible overdrafts on your client's trust account. The reporting abilities are amazingly flexible and allow you to filter information in the reports based upon multiple criteria that you specify. You can immediately generate up-to-date reports for your entire trust account journal and individual client ledgers whenever your client or the state bar calls for the information.

Bank reconciliation reports must be printed each month when the reconciliation is performed, however, and cannot be easily called up for reprinting without considerable effort. And although QuickBooks does not require extensive accounting knowledge, basic computer and accounting skills will be necessary to set up the books, maintain them, and issue the reports required. Furthermore, you must take the time to learn how the program works. QuickBooks has excellent instruction manuals and helpful support staff; however, no matter how good the program, as with any other computer program, "garbage in equals garbage out." Entering data must be done precisely, and each entry must be properly categorized—otherwise you cannot get the reports required.[4]

Before I explain how to use this program for client trust accounting, a word of caution is in order. QuickBooks is a valuable tool that makes client trust accounting easier and more efficient. However, this is a personal responsibility of the lawyer that cannot be delegated. Although you may use

4. The initial setup of the QuickBooks bank account and trust liability account is simple and can be done in very little time. However, discovering the best method of entering data and customizing reports to meet the state bar requirements may be confusing and take several hours. To simplify the process, an instruction manual and a setup/sample disk are available at LawBiz, http://www.lawbiz.com (last visited Aug. 1, 2013). They describe in detail exactly how information should be entered and how to set up the customized reports. The setup and application of client trust accounting has never been tested or attempted with QuickBooks Online.

staff to assist you, the lawyer who receives client trust funds bears all of the responsibility to account for every penny.

§ 21.05 Summary of Tasks

§ 21.05.1 Receiving Funds

When you receive funds in trust, you record the date, name of the deposit source, deposit amount, and a brief memo (for example, "Full Settlement") directly in the check register for the client trust bank account. QuickBooks provides a pop-up window ("Edit/Split") in which to enter the details of the deposit with a space provided to designate the name of the client (customer/job), amount of deposit, the client's trust liability account ("From Account"), a memo field to describe the transaction, and optional fields for method of payment and class of transaction. Upon completing the deposit, the client's ledger is automatically updated.

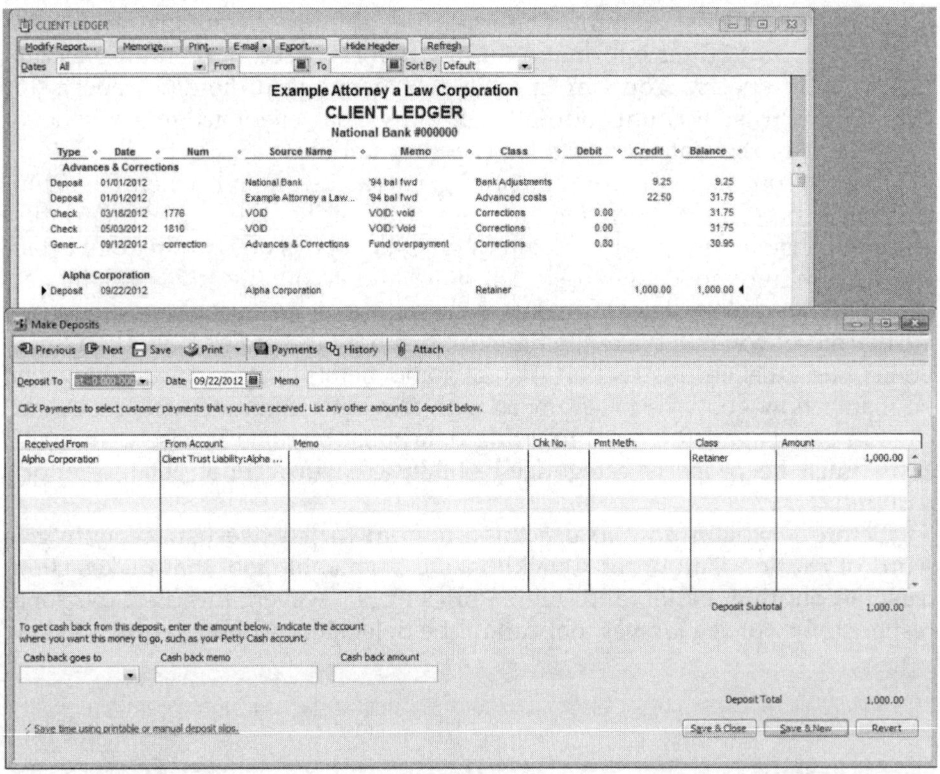

§ 21.05.2 Disbursing Funds

QuickBooks provides the ability to either print checks on the computer or write them manually. Whether you print a check or record the manually written check, the client's ledger is automatically debited for the disbursement. In the "Write Checks" window, there is a space provided in which you designate the name of the client; a memo field to describe the transaction; and a field for the date, payee, and amount of the disbursement. Upon completing the check form, the client's ledger is automatically updated.

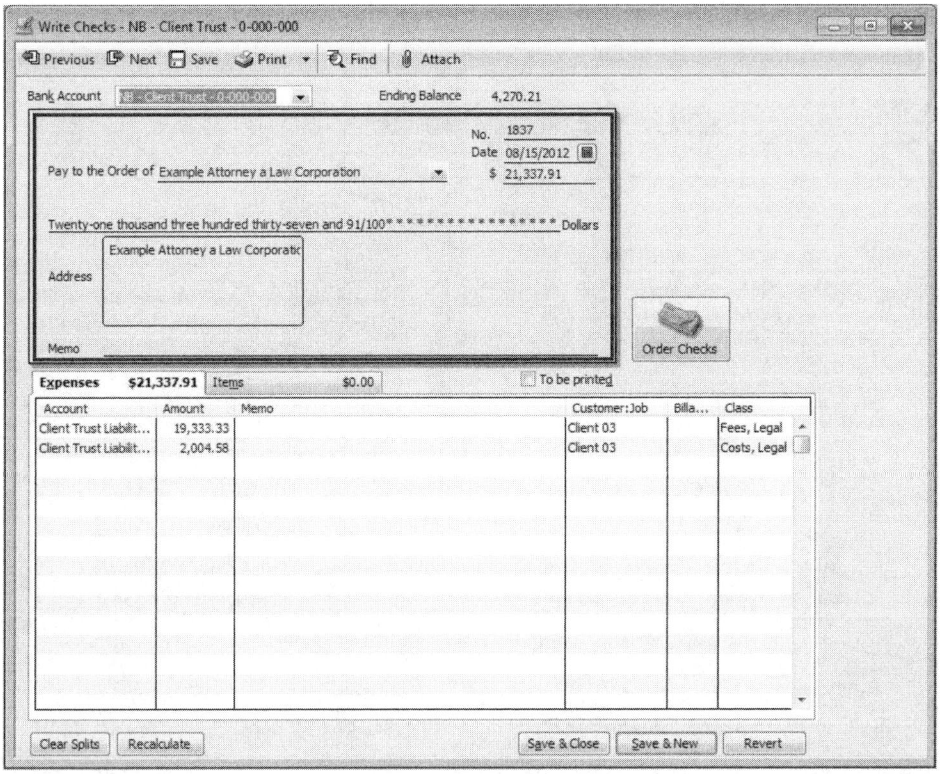

§ 21.05.3 Reports

QuickBooks can generate a number of reports, which you create and save in "Memorized Reports."

The reports are as follows:

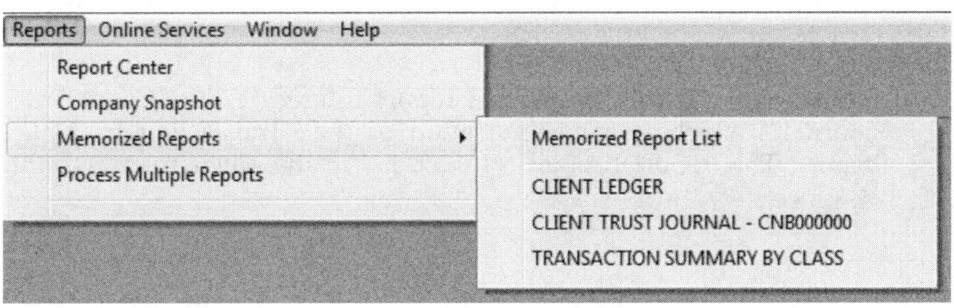

- *Client ledger.* After the deposits and checks are properly entered, reports are printed that display the type of transaction, date, amount, payee, source of deposit, purpose of the transaction ("Memo"), and balance of funds held for the client. This report is known as the "Client Ledger" and is a customization of the "Transaction by Customer" report.

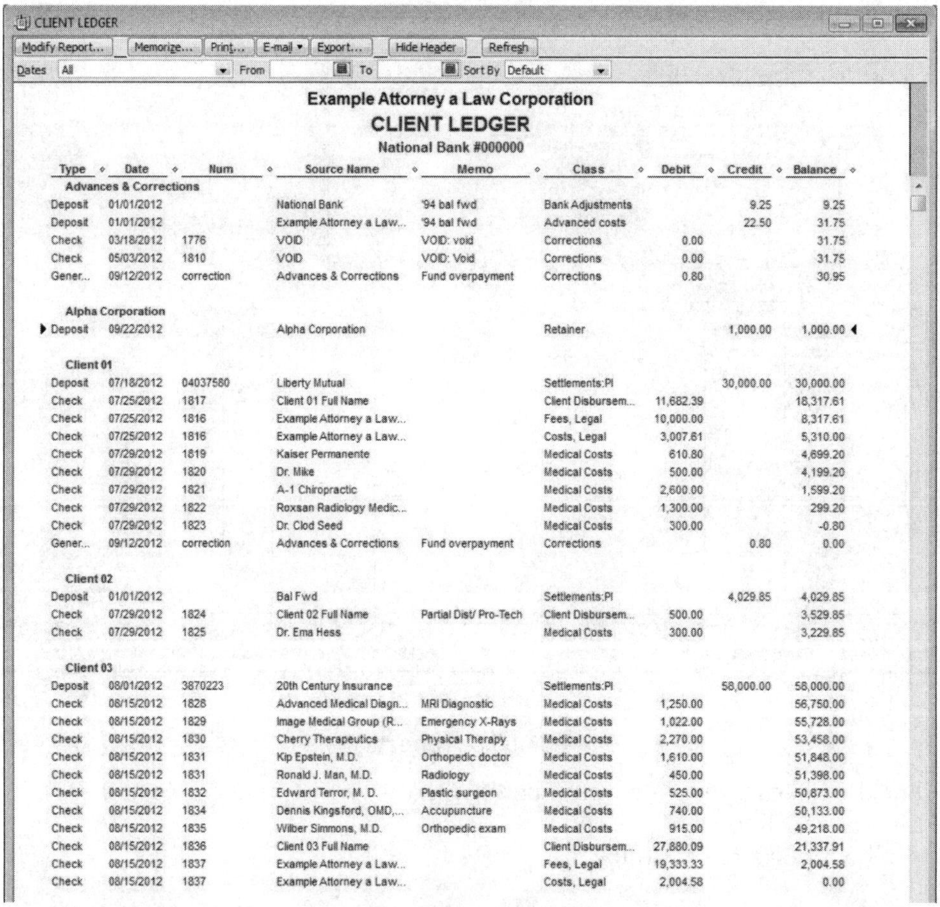

CLIENT LEDGER

Modify Report... | Memorize... | Print... | E-mail | Export... | Hide Header | Refresh

Dates All | From | To | Sort By Default

Example Attorney a Law Corporation

CLIENT LEDGER

National Bank #000000

Type	Date	Num	Source Name	Memo	Class	Debit	Credit	Balance
Advances & Corrections								
Deposit	01/01/2012		National Bank	'94 bal fwd	Bank Adjustments		9.25	9.25
Deposit	01/01/2012		Example Attorney a Law...	'94 bal fwd	Advanced costs		22.50	31.75
Check	03/18/2012	1776	VOID	VOID: void	Corrections	0.00		31.75
Check	05/03/2012	1810	VOID	VOID: Void	Corrections	0.00		31.75
Gener...	09/12/2012	correction	Advances & Corrections	Fund overpayment	Corrections	0.80		30.95
Alpha Corporation								
Deposit	09/22/2012		Alpha Corporation		Retainer		1,000.00	1,000.00
Client 01								
Deposit	07/18/2012	04037580	Liberty Mutual		Settlements:PI		30,000.00	30,000.00
Check	07/25/2012	1817	Client 01 Full Name		Client Disbursem...	11,682.39		18,317.61
Check	07/25/2012	1816	Example Attorney a Law...		Fees, Legal	10,000.00		8,317.61
Check	07/25/2012	1816	Example Attorney a Law...		Costs, Legal	3,007.61		5,310.00
Check	07/29/2012	1819	Kaiser Permanente		Medical Costs	610.80		4,699.20
Check	07/29/2012	1820	Dr. Mike		Medical Costs	500.00		4,199.20
Check	07/29/2012	1821	A-1 Chiropractic		Medical Costs	2,600.00		1,599.20
Check	07/29/2012	1822	Roxsan Radiology Medic...		Medical Costs	1,300.00		299.20
Check	07/29/2012	1823	Dr. Clod Seed		Medical Costs	300.00		-0.80
Gener...	09/12/2012	correction	Advances & Corrections	Fund overpayment	Corrections		0.80	0.00
Client 02								
Deposit	01/01/2012		Bal Fwd		Settlements:PI		4,029.85	4,029.85
Check	07/29/2012	1824	Client 02 Full Name	Partial Dist/ Pro-Tech	Client Disbursem...	500.00		3,529.85
Check	07/29/2012	1825	Dr. Ema Hess		Medical Costs	300.00		3,229.85
Client 03								
Deposit	08/01/2012	3870223	20th Century Insurance		Settlements:PI		58,000.00	58,000.00
Check	08/15/2012	1828	Advanced Medical Diagn...	MRI Diagnostic	Medical Costs	1,250.00		56,750.00
Check	08/15/2012	1829	Image Medical Group (R...	Emergency X-Rays	Medical Costs	1,022.00		55,728.00
Check	08/15/2012	1830	Cherry Therapeutics	Physical Therapy	Medical Costs	2,270.00		53,458.00
Check	08/15/2012	1831	Kip Epstein, M.D.	Orthopedic doctor	Medical Costs	1,610.00		51,848.00
Check	08/15/2012	1831	Ronald J. Man, M.D.	Radiology	Medical Costs	450.00		51,398.00
Check	08/15/2012	1832	Edward Terror, M. D.	Plastic surgeon	Medical Costs	525.00		50,873.00
Check	08/15/2012	1834	Dennis Kingsford, OMD,...	Accupuncture	Medical Costs	740.00		50,133.00
Check	08/15/2012	1835	Wilber Simmons, M.D.	Orthopedic exam	Medical Costs	915.00		49,218.00
Check	08/15/2012	1836	Client 03 Full Name		Client Disbursem...	27,880.09		21,337.91
Check	08/15/2012	1837	Example Attorney a Law...		Fees, Legal	19,333.33		2,004.58
Check	08/15/2012	1837	Example Attorney a Law...		Costs, Legal	2,004.58		0.00

- *Client trust journal.* The second report printed is the "Client Trust Journal," which is a customization of the "Transaction by Date" report. This report lists all transactions in the client trust account.

The aggregate balance of each individual client ledger should equal the balance listed in the client trust journal. If they do not agree, it is an indication of an error in recording one or more of the transactions. You must reconcile and correct these errors to comply with state bar rules.

CLIENT TRUST JOURNAL - CNB000000

Modify Report... Memorize... Print... E-mail Export... Hide Header Refresh

Dates All From To Total By Total only Sort By

04/11/13

Example Attorney a Law Corporation

Client Trust Journal

National Bank # 000000

Type	Date	Num	Source Name	Memo	Class	Debit	Credit	Balance
Deposit	01/01/2012		National Bank	Interest	State Bar Transaction		28.71	28.71
Deposit	01/01/2012		Bal Fwd		Settlements:PI		3,052.50	3,081.21
Deposit	01/01/2012		Bal Fwd		Settlements:PI		4,029.85	7,111.06
Deposit	01/01/2012		National Bank	'94 bal fwd	Bank Adjustments		9.25	7,120.31
Deposit	01/01/2012		Example Attorney a Law Corporation	'94 bal fwd	Advanced costs		22.50	7,142.81
Check	01/03/2012	adj	IOLTA - State Bar disbursement	Payment	State Bar Transaction	28.71		7,114.10
Deposit	01/31/2012		National Bank	Interest	State Bar Transaction		26.31	7,140.41
Check	02/03/2012		State Bar of California - IOLTA Account	Payment	State Bar Transaction	26.31		7,114.10
Deposit	02/28/2012		National Bank	Interest	State Bar Transaction		9.34	7,123.44
Check	03/03/2012		State Bar of California - IOLTA Account	Payment	State Bar Transaction	9.34		7,114.10
Deposit	03/10/2012		Farmers Insurance		Settlements:PI		5,500.00	12,614.10
Check	03/18/2012	1776	VOID	VOID: void	Corrections	0.00		12,614.10
Deposit	03/31/2012		National Bank	Interest	State Bar Transaction		26.01	12,640.11
Check	04/01/2012		State Bar of California - IOLTA Account	Payment	State Bar Transaction	26.01		12,614.10
Deposit	04/19/2012		Insurance Company		Settlements:PI		15,000.00	27,614.10
Check	04/28/2012	1802	Mercury Insurance Co.		Subrogation	1,526.25		26,087.85
Check	04/28/2012	1805	Dr. Sandor		Medical Costs	430.00		25,657.85
Check	04/28/2012	1808	Dr. Eugene		Medical Costs	825.00		24,832.85
Check	04/28/2012	1801	Example Attorney a Law Corporation		Fees, Legal	1,914.50		22,918.35
Deposit	04/29/2012		National Bank	Interest	State Bar Transaction		24.96	22,943.31
Check	05/02/2012		State Bar of California - IOLTA Account	Payment	State Bar Transaction	24.96		22,918.35
Check	05/03/2012	1809	Western Imaging Center Med Group	Radiology	Medical Costs	424.00		22,494.35
Check	05/03/2012	1810	VOID	VOID: Void	Corrections	0.00		22,494.35
Check	05/17/2012	1812	Client 05 Full Name		Client Disbursement	3,207.75		19,286.60
Deposit	05/23/2012		20th Century Insurance		Settlements:PI		3,500.00	22,786.60
Deposit	05/31/2012		National Bank	Interest	State Bar Transaction		22.60	22,809.20
Check	06/01/2012		State Bar of California - IOLTA Account	Payment	State Bar Transaction	22.60		22,786.60
Check	06/07/2012	1813	Client 04 Full Name		Client Disbursement	9,894.00		12,892.60
Check	06/07/2012	1814	Tarzana Sports Injury & Ortho Grp		Medical Costs	845.00		12,047.60
Check	06/07/2012	1815	South ValleyPhysical Therapy		Medical Costs	1,500.00		10,547.60
Check	06/07/2012	1816	Example Attorney a Law Corporation		Fees, Legal	5,875.00		4,672.60
Check	06/07/2012	1816	Example Attorney a Law Corporation		Costs, Legal	386.00		4,286.60
Deposit	06/30/2012		National Bank	Interest	State Bar Transaction		9.41	4,296.01
Deposit	07/18/2012	040...	Liberty Mutual		Settlements:PI		30,000.00	34,296.01
Check	07/25/2012	1817	Client 01 Full Name		Client Disbursement	11,682.39		22,613.62
Check	07/25/2012	1816	Example Attorney a Law Corporation		Fees, Legal	10,000.00		12,613.62
Check	07/25/2012	1816	Example Attorney a Law Corporation		Costs, Legal	3,007.61		9,606.01
Check	07/29/2012	1819	Kaiser Permanente		Medical Costs	610.80		8,995.21
Check	07/29/2012	1820	Dr. Mike		Medical Costs	500.00		8,495.21

- *Bank reconciliation.* Monthly bank reconciliations are almost effortless. After all transactions are entered, you select the "Reconcile" activity and complete the screen. All that is required is to mark those items that appear on the bank statement and enter the state bar interest on client trust accounts (IOLTA) credited and remitted.

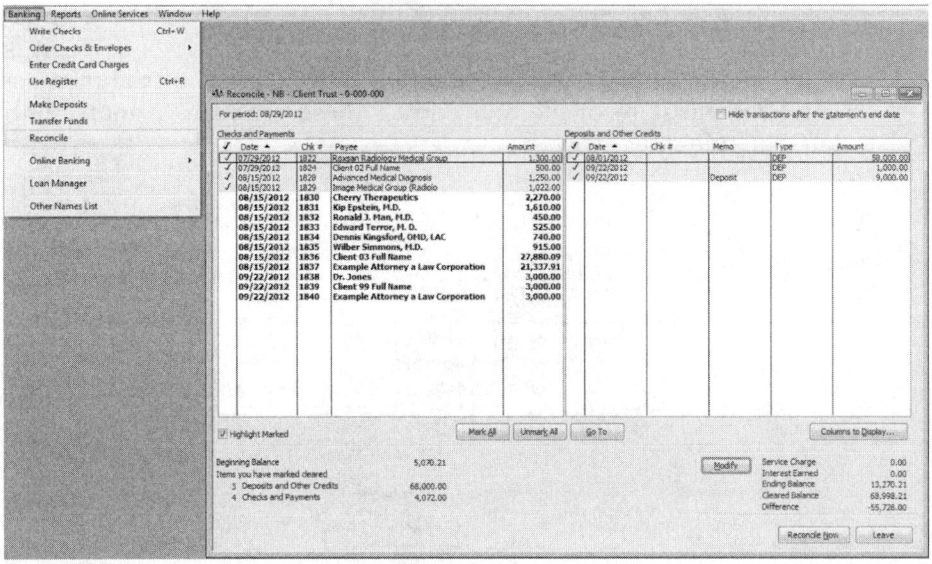

- *IOLTA interest.* Interest income due to the state bar is accounted for each month when reconciling the trust bank account. A separate sub-account is set up for the IOLTA interest received and paid. These amounts are calculated and reflected on your bank statement.
- *Property account journal report.* A "Property Account Journal" report is merely a list of all property received on behalf of a client and held in trust. It is possible to set up a journal in QuickBooks for this purpose by creating an "Other Current Liability" account for each client; however, it would be simpler to use your word processor or spreadsheet to create this list to report other property held in trust.

If a state bar investigator calls you, he will be pleased to know that you can fully comply by using QuickBooks for your client trust account record keeping. And if you are diligent, you need never again worry about issuing an overdraft check on a client trust account.

§ 21.06 Action Plan

- Understand the basics of IOLTA.
- Follow the Rule of Five.
- Use QuickBooks to keep track of client trust transactions.
- Verify that deposits have cleared before releasing trust account charts.

CHAPTER 22

Improving Your Bottom Line

Learn all you can from the mistakes of others. You won't have time to make them all yourself.

—Alfred Sheinwold

Chapter Checklist

- o Banking
- o Office Services
- o Rent
- o Diversity
- o Revenues Versus Expenses
- o Personal/Professional Expense Hierarchy
- o Action Plan

Following are some tips, techniques, and strategies that you can implement to help you improve your bottom line. Browse through them and pick and choose the ones that are applicable to your situation. (If you have any tips that you would like to share, please send them to Ed Poll at the address listed in the preface.)

§ 22.01 Banking

Maintain a high "average daily balance." Most banks today calculate the average daily balance in your bank account. This is one of the most significant bits of information with which a bank works in analyzing a loan request. Thus, you want to maintain as high a balance as possible. This can be done either by keeping a large sum of money in the bank or by keeping limited funds in the account for a longer period of time. You can keep funds in the account longer by depositing revenue immediately upon receipt and spreading the payment of bills throughout the month. Do not pay your bills all at once; this will cause an exaggerated dip in your account balance rather than provide an even flow of funds.

Do not wait until the end of the week to deposit checks. This rule of cash flow management not only helps you maintain a high average daily balance but also prevents the possibility that the check will be worthless by the time you deposit it. While the check is "cooling its heels" in your desk drawer, too many catastrophic events might occur. The client may, in the interim, become angry for whatever reason and stop payment on the check. The check may reach your client's bank at a time when the account is overdrawn. The client may have been named as a defendant in a lawsuit for which attachment procedures are available, and the client's bank account may have been attached and "marked" for a sum that is large enough to cause the presentation of the check you are holding to be rejected. In each of these cases and many others that you can imagine, had the check been deposited immediately upon receipt, it most probably would have cleared the client's bank account.

Reconcile your bank statements immediately upon receipt so that any bank mistakes can be corrected right away and any mistakes made by you will be known and corrected before any embarrassment with the bank or your payee results.

Consider using Quicken or QuickBooks for financial information gathering on the computer. They are the best-selling computer programs of their kind and will write your checks, keep track of your check register, and prepare reports. They will even develop future budgets based on past operating results. And more than one bank account can be operated from the same program. One of the advantages of Quicken is its simplicity: you can master enough of it to be able to write checks and prepare reports in ten to twenty minutes. Also, review other software now available that has similar capabilities.

Be sure that you sign all checks. Do not delegate this authority. You must know the present status of your business at all times.

Mail accounts payable bills on their due dates. Creditors usually accept payment as timely according to the postmark rather than time of arrival (credit card companies are the exception).

Do not commingle trust funds with general funds. Bar associations generally have taken the attitude that even $100 of personal funds in a client trust account is considered commingling of the lawyer's and client's funds and, therefore, a violation of the rules of professional conduct. (See chapter 21 about using QuickBooks for client trust accounting procedures.)

In some states, by agreement between the bar and banks, a trust account can be maintained even with a zero balance, and charges normally assessed by the bank will be taken from the general account. In earlier days, a lawyer had to deposit an "extra" $100 into the client's trust account. These funds were used to open the client's trust account and then retained in the account to be sure that the bank would not close the account or remove clients' funds when charging fees and costs related to the account rather than the individual client. Today, most banks no longer require a $100 deposit to open or maintain a trust account. Therefore, there is no reason to keep this extra money in a trust account. The bank can be instructed to pay bank charges from the lawyer's general account. In addition, the bar frowns, to say the least, on overdrafts in a trust account. There is no excuse for an overdraft in a trust account. In California, for example, all overdrafts in a trust account are reported by the banks to the State Bar of California and will likely result in an immediate investigation. Further, some state bars will make random audits of client trust accounts. (The American Bar Association House of Delegates approved Report 119, which deals with a model disciplinary rule on random audits. More states will soon adopt this procedure.) Lawyers must now be sure that their trust account records are in good order and available for immediate inspection.

Maintain separate payroll and general accounts (of course, keep a separate account for clients' trust deposits/withdrawals). Either use an outside service or place in the payroll account the full amount of gross payroll (including the employee portion of taxes) on the day that payroll is due. The general account should be maintained with only those funds necessary to cover the checks that are presented to the bank that day for collection.

Consider an "automatic bank sweep." Banks today provide for an automatic sweep on a daily basis after you establish the initial minimums and maximums (you can modify these instructions at any future date). Establish a minimum amount of money to remain in your general account, such as $2,500. The exact sum depends on the amount of checks and deposits that pass through your bank account each month. Then, instruct the bank to segregate all funds in excess of this amount at the end of each day and "sweep," or transfer, those excess funds into a money market (interest-bearing) account until needed. Likewise, the bank can be instructed to automatically transfer funds back into the general account from the money market account in the event that the balance goes below the established minimum amount. The better approach, however, is to request the bank to call you on any day during which the balance of your account goes below the minimum amount established by you. This latter approach, as contrasted with the automatic sweep into the money market account, forces the one responsible for these activities to know rather than guess the status of the cash balances at every given moment.

Make bank deposits personally until you know the bank personnel. Get to know the manager of the branch, the operations personnel, and the loan committee. These are the people who can help you the most when you have a need at the bank. Only when you are on good terms with the bank personnel should you either bank by mail or allow someone else in your office to make deposits.

Negotiate immediate access to deposits. Some banks place a hold on funds deposited with them until the funds have cleared through the banking system. Analyze the "availability of funds" schedule at your bank.

Depending on your bank's policy, you may not be able to draw out cash against checks in your deposit for as long as seven days. This problem (which benefits the "float" of banks) was serious enough that Congress enacted regulatory provisions that require banks to make public and announce their "availability of funds" schedule. Determine the number of days that your bank will restrict your use of the funds in your deposits. Banks will negotiate a lesser number of days for a valued customer. If you are a valued customer of the bank and can negotiate either immediate access to funds or a shorter "hold" period, this will enhance your earning power. Even if you do not use the funds now released by your negotiation with the bank (or, in rare cases, the bank's own very short hold period), these funds will be available for placement into an interest-earning account with the same bank.

Negotiate for a lockbox with the bank. In earlier times, the maintenance of a lockbox frequently meant that the accounts receivable had been assigned to a "factor" (commercial finance service) or other accounts receivable financier. Today, however, this is not the prevailing perception since banks have been advertising and heavily marketing the availability of lockboxes as one of their premier services. The bank picks up the remittances several times a day, records them, and then sends details of the transactions to the bank customer within several days. Modern technology allows the bank customer to be made aware of the deposit on the same day or the day following the deposit. This saves the time of opening the mail and processing the deposit. If a lockbox is not cost-effective, be sure that remittances that are received are deposited with the bank on the same day—an absolute rule!

§ 22.02 Office Services

Use special electronic devices to monitor facsimile and photocopy machines if you choose to bill clients for these costs. Recapturing these costs, while not universally accepted, can add up to a large amount. Even faxes sent from and received at your computer can be monitored for billing purposes.

Use a frequent-copier card. Most public law libraries have photocopy machines available where you do research. Rather than bringing a large amount of nickels, dimes, and quarters with you, buy a card with a predetermined number of photocopies available to the purchaser of the card. This card can be renewed from time to time. It provides a good record of photocopies for billing purposes.

Get the best possible credit terms from your suppliers, such as the office supplies distributor and the library provider. See chapter 29 for ideas to increase your knowledge resources while reducing your expenditures. Negotiate for extended credit terms wherever possible.

§ 22.03 Rent

Negotiate a reduction in rent. While this expense may be "fixed" under normal conditions, rent becomes a "variable" expense during times of economic difficulty. Landlords are generally thrilled to maintain their occupancy level as high as possible and prefer to avoid litigation over broken leases whenever possible. Therefore, under the right circumstances, landlords will frequently grant rent concessions if you make a fair and reasonable proposal, taking into consideration all of the factors, including (1) fair market rental value of your premises as currently occupied, (2) fair market rental value of comparable premises, (3) the financial condition of the landlord and his ability to absorb a lower revenue flow, (4) your financial condition and the urgency of the need to reduce costs wherever possible, (5) the landlord's perception of your needs, and (6) the existing relationship between you and the landlord.

You may consider showing the landlord your business plan, demonstrating that expenses are being controlled in all areas and that he is not the only source being asked to contribute to your successful handling of tough times. If you are reluctant to show your complete business plan, you may want to give the landlord a modified or shortened version of your plan in order to convince him of your future viability (the plan, of course, would not disclose the names of clients).

The next time that you renew your office lease, think about taking along your lawyer and brokers. Many companies are hiring outside brokers at renewal time to generate competition between landlords struggling with escalating vacancy rates and developers of new buildings.

Consider hiring a law or auditing firm that specializes in lease audits. These audits verify that the escalations or pass-throughs in a commercial lease are not excessive. Such an audit could save you a significant amount of money in rent.

§ 22.04 Diversity

Spread your clients. No more than 10 percent of total revenues should come from any one client. Otherwise, you are at that client's financial mercy when he wants something, and you will suffer severe consequences if and when the client's business departs.

§ 22.05 Revenues Versus Expenses

Increase revenues before lowering expenses. By the old rule of thumb, the expense-to-revenue percentage used to be 50 percent. At the start of the new millennium, that ratio for many lawyers became closer to 70+ percent. In other words, for every $1 of collected revenue, $0.70 goes to operate the office. Thus, there is less left over for the lawyer than previously. Your goal should be to lower your firm's expense-to-revenue percentage.

In a tight economy, your first reaction is probably to cut expenses. While this may be appropriate, expenses tend to be static and fixed. Be sure that you are not cutting the meat of your operation, which will prevent you from taking on a new client later.

Revenue increases provide the most dramatic impact. Start by collecting old accounts receivable. Then, go out and get new business, first from existing clients and then from new clients.

§ 22.06 Personal/Professional Expense Hierarchy

An important expense item that has a significant impact on cash flow is the partner's draw or lawyer's salary. This is a touchy area for most lawyers because a lawyer's personal style of living and expenses become an important consideration in any successful cash flow budget. To help small-firm and solo practitioners in thinking about what they need to take out of a firm as an owner, I have developed an expense hierarchy:

Personal/Professional Expense Hierarchy*	
Practice Needs	$
Personal Needs	$
Savings for the "Valleys"	$
Savings for Emergencies/Retirement	$
"Gravy"	$

*All figures are per month.

The expense hierarchy shows five boxes representing the basic categories of cash expenditures. These boxes, or levels, represent the needs for cash in the order that a solo or small-firm practitioner should prioritize for the health of the firm and his own livelihood.

First come the needs of the practice. This box contains all of the expenses associated with the practice of law and the operation of your office. Why is this first? Because without the practice, there is no source for personal needs. For a hypothetical one-lawyer firm, let's say, as an example, that such number is $8,000 per month.

Second are the lawyer's personal needs as reflected by the draw or salary. What are all of the expenses required by you and your family to maintain your style of living? This is the box that should be the most flexible; that is, if the practice produces sufficient income, then you can increase the standard of living. But the better approach is to avoid committing yourself to extensive obligations from which you cannot retrench in time of need. Let's give our hypothetical solo lawyer with a small family $12,000 per month.

The third box is allocated to savings for the "valleys" of the practice. During each month, some funds should be set aside to carry the practice through those leaner times experienced by every lawyer and law firm regardless of size. These valleys are typically temporary interruptions of revenues caused either by a transitory shortage of funds by clients or a temporary lull in their legal requirements that shows up as an unsteady flow of funds to the lawyer. Our lawyer puts aside $2,000 during each of six "peak," or fat, months.

The fourth box is for personal savings for unexpected emergencies or for retirement. Too few of us are independently wealthy or maintain a second business activity that will provide ready funds for unanticipated uses down the road. Therefore, the best approach is to set aside a small sum each month and forget about it. Without getting bogged down in investment theories, interest rates, and the like, suffice it to say that because of the power of compounding interest, some sort of regular savings of even a small sum of money can grow significantly over several years. A quick rule of thumb is the "Rule of 72." Take an interest rate and divide it into 72. That is how many years it will take for the money to double in amount. Our lawyer socks away $200 per month for ten years.

The last box is for "gravy." After setting aside funds for each of the above categories, the balance should be considered a bonus. This is the money to reward yourself with a trip, a purchase of something special for you or the business, a speculative investment, a charitable contribution, etc. So, our hypothetical solo practitioner is spending approximately $21,000 per month in the first four boxes. If he pulls in, say, $24,000 each month in revenue, then there is an excess of $3,000 per month in gravy. If, however, our lawyer is collecting only $18,000, then something has to give, and probably it will be the variable draw (Box 2: Personal Needs).

§ 22.07 Action Plan

- Be aware of the impact on your practice from the financial policies that you do or do not implement.
- Keep track of fax and photocopy costs.
- Negotiate rent.
- Do not base your business on one client.
- Focus on increasing revenues instead of lowering expenses.
- Put the needs of your business before your personal needs.

CHAPTER 23

Playing the Slow Economy Game

Have patience, and endure.

—William Shakespeare, *Much Ado About Nothing*

Chapter Checklist

- o Temporary Slowdown
- o Downsizing
- o Demerger
- o Liquidation
- o The Great Recession
- o Action Plan

Temporary slowdown, downsizing, demerger, and liquidation—these are all different reactions of law firms to a difficult economic environment.

Since law is a business and since business is often equated with the playing fields of sports, football is an appropriate metaphor for the downturn strategies of law firms during a slow economy. Think of your firm as the team and the economy as the opponent. Since the game is never over until the last play, the goal of any team is to stay in the game. There are many strategies that football teams use to position themselves to keep playing and ultimately win. In the legal profession, slowdowns, downsizing, demergers, and even liquidating the firm are not necessarily last, desperate acts but defensive strategies. They are different ways that law firms can play the slow-economy game.

§ 23.01 Temporary Slowdown

Early in a football game if a team is not gaining enough ground, it will usually punt, or kick, the ball to its opponent. The team knows that it will eventually recover the ball, but for now it is best just to get rid of it and take up a defensive posture. In any game, there are numerous changes in ball possession that are considered a normal part of play.

So, too, with your law firm. There are many peaks and valleys in a firm's life cycle, and solo practitioners and small firms face the valleys of lean times frequently, sometimes more than once each year. Take advantage of the extra time of slow business to work on your marketing efforts to get more clients and/or to get more work from existing clients. Economic valleys are part of professional life. Expansion will occur later when market forces are once again appropriate and opportunities present themselves.

§ 23.02 Downsizing

At the start of each season, a football team has more prospective players than it can use. There is a culling-out period when marginal team members are "cut." These cuts are needed—and, in fact, required by league officials—to bring the team to its most efficient size.

In the medical profession, good doctors first review the least intrusive medical treatment. In the business world, good businesspeople review the strategy that will cause the least disruption to the unit. For lawyers, the strategy that will cause the fewest "injuries" to the team is downsizing, or cutting—not just eliminating people but saving in other areas, too. Here is a list of cuts—in order of increasing severity—that the law firm needs to consider to increase its efficiency in a slow economy:

- Postpone expansion plans.
- Postpone capital expenditures.
- Postpone bonuses.
- Postpone staff raises.
- Postpone, where possible, equipment and facilities repair and maintenance.
- Reduce partners' income somewhat.
- Lay off some staff members.
- Lay off additional staff members.
- Lay off some associate lawyers.
- Reduce partners' income further.

But be cautious when downsizing. You must preserve and protect the team and maintain a strong resource base. You still want and expect to win the game. You need to be ready to respond to the economic recovery that is always around the corner.

§ 23.03 Demerger

In football, teams reorganize by trading players to improve and strengthen their position. Law firms can also reorganize themselves.

Large law firms grow larger via merger or acquisition. But in a shrinking economy, the opposite can also work. A merged practice can be split up ("demerged") into its premerger units, especially if the separate corporate cultures are still intact.

Alternatively, you may need to cut an area of practice that is not profitable, or you may want to take on a new area of practice that is the sudden rage of the community (elder law, environmental law, bankruptcy practice, etc.).

Finally, segments of a firm or practice or even individual lawyers can break off to form a new boutique or specialty practice.

Another football analogy here is the lateral pass. There has been no loss of yardage, just a delay in reaching the goal line. No ground has been gained, but there is still plenty of time remaining in the game.

§ 23.04 Liquidation

When there are only a few minutes remaining on the clock and the situation looks gloomy, a football team resorts to more drastic measures in order to win. The "Hail Mary" play is an example. In this last-gasp effort, the quarterback throws a long pass toward the goal line and hopes that one of his teammates will catch it for the winning touchdown. It is normally a risky maneuver, but at this late stage, there is nothing to lose.

When the law firm's future is in doubt, it may be time to throw the big bomb and consider liquidation. While the firm will cease to exist, it is not the end of life for the individual lawyers. There is still hope in the destruction of the firm. Individual lawyers can join another team (there are, after all, other teams in the league) or create a new firm. You can begin a new game and start playing again.

When liquidating, be sure that all clients are notified of the situation. Unless there is an agreement among all lawyers, communicate with those clients whom you expect to continue representing. Get a formal, written authorization from each of those clients to take files with you from the sinking firm.

§ 23.05 The Great Recession

The Great Recession that began in 2008, and has yet to conclusively end, definitively showed law firms that, like any other sector of the economy, they cannot ignore the fundamental rules of business. These rules are nowhere stated in the statute books, but they are unquestionably part of a lawyer's responsibility. Understanding the economics of law practice is a necessary part of the fundamental principles under which lawyers must offer their professional services because law firms are governed by the same formula that defines all business success: P = R – E, meaning Profit equals Revenue collected less Expenses.

Before the economic crisis hit, too many large and even midsize firms went their own merry ways for years, happily assuming that high associate salaries and partner draws, rising rates, and leveraged mergers with other firms was a pattern that would continue indefinitely. But the Great Recession has forced law firms to sit up and pay attention to the consequences.

Most lawyers still enter law school with an undergraduate degree in the liberal arts. Law school curricula have little business focus. The problem is too often perpetuated throughout a lawyer's lifetime by a lack of professional training in management and client service issues. Lawyers learn the rules in these areas from the school of hard knocks, and the recession has provided the equivalent of a graduate school course. With every crisis, though, there comes opportunity, and firms that have learned the lessons of the Great Recession will find the most opportunities for winning touchdowns in the postrecession game.

§ 23.06 Action Plan

- Get a coach to help you evaluate your options.
- Stay in the game.

PART V

Employee Issues

CHAPTER 24

Hire Is Not a "Four-Letter Word"

A man isn't a man until he has to meet a payroll.

—Ivan Shaffer

One man's wage rise is another man's price increase.

—Harold Wilson

Chapter Checklist

- o Determining Your Staffing Needs
- o Considering Preemployment Consultation
- o Writing the Job Description
- o Choosing an Advertising Venue
- o Setting Up a Screening Funnel
- o Preparing Before the Interview
- o Conducting the Face-to-Face Interview
- o Hiring Temporary Employees
- o Action Plan

"If I want the job done right, I have to do it myself." "I can't find good help." "I can't afford to hire anyone right now." Sound familiar? If so, you may be acting like a Lone Ranger.

Today's solo practitioner is most likely "hooked up" and "hooked into" Facebook, LinkedIn, and every kind of smartphone and pad available. With all of this, who needs to hire a legal secretary or paralegal? **You do!**

The underlying fiction is that solo practitioners are supercompetent human beings who can accomplish incredible feats on their own, never asking for any help and never showing any signs of difficulty.

Regardless of what you think your production needs are or how much work you think you can handle, look at the data. Track your actual daily rate of productivity and the output of your law practice for no fewer than four weeks. Don't forget to include all of the telephone calls that you are picking up, all of the voice mails that you are answering; and all of the mail sorting, postage metering, client intakes, and hospitality that you are managing.

The hours that you spend "working the parameter" do not make you money; they are costing you money. And being sleep deprived, overstimulated, and exhausted can significantly affect a lawyer's work product and can literally throw a lawyer's competence levels into the bureaucratic hands of the state bar disciplinary system. Hiring an employee is a positive (and I believe necessary) step toward managing your law practice effectively—and increasing revenue.

§ 24.01 Determining Your Staffing Needs

If your practice is at a crossroads or you are experiencing a personal or professional transition, hiring an employee may not be a timely solution. For instance, if you are in the process of making a decision to expand your practice area, you may not know what your production needs will be until the actual change occurs. If your personal life is in transition due to family matters such as a divorce, a death in the family, retirement, or an uncertainty as to whether or not you want to continue practicing law, you may want to postpone making the decision to increase expenditures and responsibilities until your personal situation settles.

Barring these types of situations, it might be time to consider hiring an employee. Ask yourself the following questions:

- "How much time do I spend on each task?"
- "What tasks and/or responsibilities could be delegated?"
- "Where can I make efficiency-minded changes?"
- "Why do I feel anxious about meeting deadlines?"
- "Who can I really rely on to meet the growing demands of my firm?"

The Staffing Needs Survey at the end of this chapter in Figure 24.1 is designed to offer a realistic and objective method of identifying your law practice's staffing needs.

§ 24.02 Considering Preemployment Consultation

Let's presume that you have decided not to go it alone and that it's time to hire an employee. What next? Before you place your first ad or interview the first candidate, I encourage you to hire an experienced and qualified human resources consultant or employment lawyer to advise on the lawful and unlawful preemployment procedures and inquiries. This is not the time to fall back into the Lone Ranger syndrome! It is prudent to hire a consultant for advice and to draft a human resources manual *before* you hire anyone. In addition, it would also be wise to confer with your accountant, financial adviser, or certified public accountant about the economic considerations of hiring employees.

§ 24.03 Writing the Job Description

Now that you have conducted your skill-based production needs and engaged a preemployment consultant, you are ready to explore the next exciting step in the hiring process: how to write the job description. A job listing should accurately describe the nature of the work, level(s) of responsibility, specific and general duties, salary, and hours per week. This entails determining what qualifications you are looking for in an employee and how to classify the position that you want to fill.

First, take the time to think about the requirements for the job. You want to determine what will differentiate a person who will be really good at the task from someone who will probably not succeed. Ask yourself, "What kind of knowledge am I looking for? What sort of skills? What kind of behaviors do I need to see?" For example, if you are a transaction lawyer who wants to bring a strong litigator into the firm, it may be irrelevant whether the litigator has business development skills ("a finder"). In this example, you want a lawyer who is an expert in the litigation process and can take care of the existing clients ("a grinder").

Next, determine the job title that will encompass these qualifications. Do you know the difference between a legal assistant, a legal secretary, and a paralegal? Before you hire support staff, make sure that you understand the differences and distinctions among job classifications.

Keep in mind that each law office differs and that many tasks and responsibilities can and do cross over into more than one job title, but the following descriptions of each type of law firm employee should assist you in determining your production needs and the most appropriate job classification for the employee that you need to hire. (The descriptions are based on a litigation-oriented firm whose employees engage in e-filing, Internet skills, and e-communications.) One important caveat: Employees who assist lawyers in any capacity prefer the title of *paralegal* regardless of the tasks actually performed on the job. For the sake of this discussion—and to rescue you from this sensitive issue in the future with your staff—let us agree that the following job titles as described are accurate and true.

§ 24.03.1 Legal Assistant

Giving your employee the title of *legal assistant* is a generalist term and may cause confusion for you, your employee, and your clients. Here's why.

First, a legal assistant can be an individual who has on-the-job training in a law firm but has not earned a professional certificate or degree as a paralegal. Second, a legal secretary could prefer the title of *legal assistant* to *legal secretary*. And third, the state that you practice in, such as California, may have regulations surrounding the paralegal profession that set criteria for paralegal hires.

§ 24.03.2 Legal Secretary

A legal secretary is typically college educated and/or has at least three years of experience as a legal secretary. If not, the classification can be *legal secretary assistant*. A certificate of completion from a training program is admirable but not indicative of competence. *Always* give the candidate a comprehensive test and a practical skills exercise before hiring.

Tasks and/or Responsibilities

- Prepares and/or assembles legal documents for court filing
- Reproduces documents
- Knows pertinent rules of court and filing procedures, fees, etc.
- Organizes legal documents for lawyer service
- Communicates with lawyer service, vendors, and court personnel
- Maintains court and office calendar
- Creates, organizes, and maintains client files
- Takes and relays intelligent messages for lawyer
- Prioritizes lawyer's daily work product

Office Skills

- Computer literacy
- Keyboarding 85+ words per minute
- Dictation/note taking

Abilities

- Excellent English grammar, punctuation, and spelling skills
- Excellent proofreading, editing, and business communications skills
- Works well under extreme pressure of deadlines and unexpected demands
- Highly organized, neat, and professional

§ 24.03.3 Paralegal (Certificated)

A paralegal is typically college educated and/or has at least one year of experience as a paralegal in the same or similar type of practice area. A certificate of completion from an accredited educational institution is extremely important. Do your own independent research on the educational institution—do not blindly rely on "ABA-approved" status as the only consideration. As law schools differ, so do paralegal schools. Be advised that there are many educational institutions that use the term *legal assistant* instead of *paralegal*. Go to the school's website to review its paralegal program's curriculum, faculty, program length, and accreditation status. Before hiring, always give the candidate a comprehensive and thorough test on your local rules of court and civil procedure in addition to a practical skills exercise pertinent to your practice.

Tasks and/or Responsibilities

- Handles initial client-intake processes
- Organizes and analyzes files and prepares chronologies
- Drafts, files, and prepares service of process for summons and complaints, answers, and other defensive pleadings
- Conducts or supervises fact investigations
- Constructs and/or prepares documents (or prepares responses) for all phases of litigation (commencement of the lawsuit, discovery, law and motions, trial and posttrial motions, and appeals)
- Summarizes depositions
- Performs legal and legal-related research
- Drafts settlement documents, including releases and dismissals
- Coordinates with outside vendors for trial preparation and discovery matters
- Creates, organizes, and maintains client files and handles document management (retention)
- Communicates effectively with clients

Office Skills

- Computer literacy
- Keyboarding 55+ words per minute
- Dictation/note taking

Abilities

- Excellent English grammar, punctuation, and spelling skills
- Excellent proofreading, editing, and business communications skills
- Works well under extreme pressure of deadlines and unexpected demands
- Highly organized, neat, and professional
- Understands and analyzes legal issues
- Writes clearly and concisely

§ 24.03.4 Independent Contractor

Whatever you do, please do not make the mistake of classifying your new employee as an "independent contractor." Only in very rare circumstances do these positions fall under the Internal Revenue Service's definition of *independent contractor*.

The IRS has very clear guidelines as to the criteria for determining whether a hired individual is an "employee" or an "independent contractor." An individual is an employee for federal employment tax purposes if the individual has the status of an employee under the usual common law rules applicable in determining the employer-employee relationship. Guidelines for determining such status are found in the following three substantially similar sections of the Employment Tax Regulations: 31.3121(d).1, 31.3306(i).1, and 31.3401(c).1. These sections provide that an employer-employee relationship generally exists when the person for whom the services are performed has the right to control and direct the individual who performs the services not only with respect to the result to be accomplished by the work but also with respect to the details and means by which that result is accomplished. That is, an employee is subject to the will and control of the employer not only as to what shall be done but as to how it shall be done.

§ 24.04 Choosing an Advertising Venue

In today's world, there are many options for advertising venues. Maximize your resources. You can save time and money by seeking robust networking channels for prospective candidates such as local/regional/state bar association meetings, networking groups, colleagues, and general word of mouth. Utilize online search websites such as Craigslist, LinkedIn, or the like. Many professional paralegal and legal secretary associations post free virtual job boards as well.

§ 24.05 Setting Up a Screening Funnel

If you have a large number of résumés coming into a firm, you need to set up a "screening funnel" to manage all of the applications. The goal is to take the many candidates coming in at the top end of the screening process and gradually narrow them down so that by the time you get to the bottom of the funnel, you are dealing with only the two or three most qualified ones for an in-person interview.

At the top of the funnel, use a "résumé screen" to weed out people who are obviously not qualified or who you know are not going to make the final cut. You can set up a process very quickly for rating a résumé based on the job requirements that you have already set up. Verify the candidate's prior work history, professional references (minimum of three), and educational credentials. In today's highly competitive market, people may misrepresent and/or embellish the content of their résumé in order to become gainfully employed. If this sounds like a process with which you are not comfortable, then consider hiring a consultant or company that specializes in background and reference checks.

On a related note, weed out anyone who sends you a "boilerplate" cover letter. Cover letters are one of the quickest ways of qualifying, or disqualifying, a candidate. By requiring a customized cover letter with the résumé, you are testing the candidate's abilities in terms of grammar, composition, organization, and clarity. A well-written cover letter, which responds to the details listed in the advertisement, adds another layer to the résumé and can be compared to the writing sample in that it ensures proficiency.

At the next level, you can try a "telephone prescreen"—that is, you spend five to ten minutes to go over a short checklist with the applicant to make sure that he is in the right salary range, has the right technical qualifications, and has the right attitude. A telephone prescreen allows the interviewer to actually "hear" the individual without the possibility of a visual bias. You will instantly be able to recognize whether the candidate possesses enthusiasm and interest for the position, as contrasted with the dreaded "I just need a job" attitude. And if you like what you hear, the face-to-face interview will probably be much more relaxed since you and the candidate have already "met" each other over the phone. In addition, the telephone prescreen is beneficial because if you find that you cannot understand the potential candidate, your clients, colleagues, vendors, and the court clerk will not be able to understand him, either.

These two early screens are very effective because they do not require much time or money, and they allow you to focus on the remaining, better-qualified candidates.

An optional final screen, helpful if you can whittle the number of applicants down to a reasonable size, is some sort of testing. One approach is a general ability test: if, for example, you are looking for secretarial or office staff, you evaluate the candidates' word-processing skills, including words per minute, error rate, etc. If you are looking for a mid-range professional, you might want to see written samples of his work. In order to assess the candidate's ability to interact effectively with clients and/or to manage staff, you could suggest a hypothetical client relations scenario and ask applicants to write a description of how they would respond, or you could ask them to tell you in writing what staff situations were difficult for them in their previous employment and how they handled the situations.

The advantage of using a paper-and-pencil or job-simulation type of test is that it is different from a formal interview. It has been proven that the more different kinds of screens you can use, the broader the picture you will get of the candidate and the more likely you will make the best possible decision.

§ 24.06 Preparing Before the Interview

Before you actually sit across the desk from those applicants whom you have decided to interview in person, there are a few things to consider:

- *Give clear and easy directions.* When scheduling the first interview, make sure that the candidate knows where your office is located. Always pay for the candidate's parking fees, if any—and make sure you tell him in advance so that he doesn't park three blocks away.
- *Be honest about time.* Even though the actual interview may take less than one hour, make sure that the candidate is aware that it may run

longer. Be sensitive to the fact that the candidate may already be employed and interviewing with you before work or on his lunch break.

- *Image is everything.* Potential employees form an impression from the moment they step off the elevator and walk into your office until the time they leave the interview. Thus, if you are dressed in casual clothes (no tie, jeans, sandals, shorts, etc.), this gives the impression that the office is casual. This may or may not be the image that you want to communicate. Similarly, on the day of the interview, make sure that your office is professional—that is, tidy and no food odors. Remember, the candidate is interviewing you, too!
- *Make every effort to see the candidate "on time."* While we can agree that life and work interrupt the best of intentions, please consider texting or calling the candidate if you're running more than ten to fifteen minutes late. Everyone's time is valuable.
- *Be prepared.* Study each candidate's résumé and have your interview questions (open-ended questions that elicit the candidate's qualities and skill levels) written before the interview. Prepare a rating rubric. If a practical skills test is in the interview mix, administer it to the candidate upon his arrival so that the results of the test can be discussed during the oral portion of the interview. In addition to a résumé, you may also want to consider having the candidate complete an application. Why? Because the application requires a candidate's signature asserting that all information is "true and correct," it can be used later as a disciplinary/termination tool if the candidate chooses to be untruthful. It happens.

§ 24.07 Conducting the Face-to-Face Interview

The structured face-to-face interview is the mainstay of the hiring process. (However, if geographic distance is a factor, "face-to-face" interviews may be conducted virtually—via Skype, for example.) The goal is to acquire a more in-depth understanding of the best remaining candidates and choose someone who is going to be with you and productive for the long term. This process will not, however, help you find the "perfect" employee. Since perfection is not possible, the perfect employee does not exist. The goal is to find the "ideal" employee—one who is professional, competent, highly skilled, resourceful, smart, congenial, and easy to work with.

By nature, lawyers are intuitive and can assess character and personality styles of judges, potential clients, opponents, witnesses, and juries. There is not much difference when interviewing potential employees. When selecting the person who will be in the office to assist you daily, give attention to each candidate's personality, as well as skill sets, in order to find that ideal employee. Thus, although education and related work experience are tremendously important, you must look beyond the résumés and assess personality and work style in order to determine who would best be suited as your employee. This is what human resource professionals call "a good fit." These qualities can reveal themselves in the actual interview process vis-à-vis the interview questions.

§ 24.07.1 Do's and Don'ts of Interviewing

The problem is that interviewing is not a very effective screening tool as it is commonly applied. Most employers conduct an "unstructured interview." That is, they sit down and just throw questions at the candidate off the top of their heads. The evidence shows that the prediction of success from this type of interview is almost zero. It just does not work.

There are a number of things, however, that can be done to make interviewing an effective hiring tool. A little forethought and planning will go a long way to make you more efficient in the hiring process and more effective, not just lucky, in selecting the right person the first time.

Do's

- Remember to make the interview job related. If you have identified the job requirement areas discussed earlier, now is the time to use them. The questions to the candidate should be open-ended (yes or no answers are not very revealing) and designed to elicit specific traits and (objective) qualities such as professional ethics, integrity, honesty, maturity, intellect, tactfulness, confidence, congeniality, respect for authority, preparedness, timeliness, and organization.
- Put your interview questions into two categories: the "can-do's" and the "will-do's."
    - The can-do's relate to the knowledge areas that a person needs to have: "Are you familiar with the laws in a given area?" and "Do you have the following word-processing skills?" The answers to these questions will give you a good sense of whether the person has the core knowledge that he needs.
    - The will-do's are more behavioral-type questions that elicit information such as whether the candidate will show up for work on time, whether the candidate will treat clients well, and whether the candidate will interact effectively with coworkers. These questions require the candidate to use "situational judgment." You give a person a hypothetical situation—hopefully one drawn directly from the job setting—and ask, "How would you handle this?" A variation would be to ask the candidate to identify specific experiences related to the behavior in question. For example, if one of the skills that you are looking for is a client-service attitude, you may want to ask the candidate to describe a situation in the past in which his client-service attitude was displayed in a trying situation, maybe in dealing with a difficult client or when

a client was demanding a quick answer. These questions will result in "critical incidents," which are examples of behavior that indicate whether a person will perform very well or very poorly in the job.

- Beware of the candidate who, right out of the gate, asks, "How much vacation time and health insurance would I get?" Salary and benefits can be discussed at the point of the job offer as part of the negotiations.
- While not always convenient, conducting the interview with someone else on your "team" usually renders a better outcome.

Don'ts

- Don't ask odd or potentially problematic questions, such as "How do you get along with your mother?" or "When was the last time you saw a horror movie?"
- Don't ask very general and vague questions: "What are your strengths?" or "What are your weaknesses?" These questions produce very little of value, and it is easy for the interviewee to have a stock answer ready.
- Don't ask questions that are illegal. As a general rule of thumb, these are questions that have no obvious reference to the specific job performance or that would be in violation of one of the employment laws. Without going into detail, you cannot ask candidates, for example, how many children they have or what their marital status is or if they have been disabled in the past. Not only will such questions turn off a prospective employee, but also they risk a lawsuit.
- Don't talk too much during the interview. Sometimes lawyers want to rescue an uncomfortable candidate by providing an answer or by talking about their firm. Ask your questions, and then get out of the way and let the interviewee talk.

§ 24.07.2 Sample Questions

Here are thirteen examples of questions for your consideration:

Objective: Integrity/honesty/trustworthiness
Question: "If you saw a coworker doing something dishonest, would you tell your supervisor/me? What would you do about it?"

Objective: Personality/temperament/ability to work with others
Question: "What are two or three examples of tasks that you do not particularly enjoy doing? Indicate what motivated you to complete those tasks."

Objective: Past mistakes
Question: "If you had the opportunity to change anything in your last (or current) job, what would you have done (do) differently?"

Objective: Creativity/creative thinking/problem solving
Question: "Assume that you had to meet two different deadlines given to you by two or more people. What approach would you take?"

Objective: Communication skills
Question: "How would you solve a problem where there were no established guidelines?"

Objective: Conflict and flexibility
Question: "Was there ever an occasion when your first approach to something didn't work and you had to try something different? Tell me about it."

Objective: Independence/resourcefulness/protocol
Question: "Under what circumstances do you think independent decision making is appropriate?"

Objective: Initiative
Question: "What types of work projects have you initiated, and were the outcomes successful?"

Objective: Interest in learning
Question: "What do you expect to learn from this position?"

Objective: Planning/time management
Question: "How do you set and prioritize work-related tasks?"

Objective: Ability to handle stress
Question: "Tell me about a work situation that was especially stressful. How did you manage it?"

Objective: Written communication/technical knowledge/professional knowledge
Question: "May I see some writing samples that highlight your knowledge in the field?"

Objective: Work standards
Question: "How do you go about meeting deadlines? Give me an example of what you had to do to get a project done on time."

There are, of course, a number of traditional questions to throw in for good measure, such as the following:

- "How has your education and experience prepared you for this position?"
- "What is important to you in a job?"
- "What do you think it takes to be successful in a firm like ours?"

And a perennial favorite:

- "What questions do you have for me?"

§ 24.08 Hiring Temporary Employees

An alternative to hiring a permanent full-time or part-time employee is "going temp." The American Staffing Association reported that the temporary employee industry is continuing to grow.[1]

People of all ages and economic, educational, and social backgrounds actually choose temping as their preferred work style or a pathway to gain practical experience.

By hiring temporary employees, firms can realize significant savings to their "bottom line" because they can hire staff as needed, avoid costly employee-related expenses, reduce exposure to employee-related risks, have candidates prescreened and pretested by experts, and add staff with one click of an e-mail or phone call. From solo practitioners to large firms, many engage temporary help to manage discovery and trial preparation.

If you are considering taking this route, choose an employment agency that specializes in legal temporary placements. Know your exact production needs. Do not order a legal secretary if you only need a receptionist—rates increase in accordance with skill levels.

Ask for a detailed rate sheet, including any fees involved. Agencies may quote odd rates, such as $16.23 per hour instead of $16. This may sound like only a few pennies on the front end, so always do the math. An additional $0.23 per hour can add up over time!

Also ask for printed information about the agency, a current client list of law firms/lawyers, a current list of references to call, and samples of the agency's entrance testing (for the position you want to hire) and its requirements for employment.

§ 24.09 Action Plan

- Decide if you need a new employee.
- Write a job description for the position you want to fill.
- Prepare for the interview of the applicant.
- Ask open-ended questions.
- As a professional courtesy, call or send an e-mail to those not selected to thank them for their time.

1. Am. Staffing Ass'n, *Staffing Employment Grew 8% in 2011*, Staffing Today, Mar. 6, 2012, http://staffingtoday.net/2012/03/06/daily/.

FIGURE 24.1

Staffing Needs Survey

Rate each of the following according to how often it occurs.

1 = Never occurs
2 = Rarely occurs
3 = Occurs from time to time
4 = Occurs with some frequency
5 = Occurs frequently

1. The business phone is mostly answered by voice mail.
2. I have difficulty returning phone calls within one hour of the original call.
3. I have difficulty returning phone calls within two hours of the original call.
4. I have difficulty keeping track of phone messages.
5. I am not in the office between 8:00 a.m. and 8:30 a.m. Monday through Friday.
6. I am not in the office between 8:30 a.m. and 9:00 a.m. Monday through Friday.
7. I am not in the office until after 9 a.m. due to court or other conflicts.
8. I open, read, sort, and file all incoming mail and documents.
9. I read current court decisions to keep up on legal updates and changes in the law.
10. I read media content online to help my practice succeed.
11. I attend local bar association CLE meetings on a regular basis.
12. I attend civic organization meetings/events on a regular basis.
13. I attend networking and other business-oriented meetings/mixers/events.
14. I meet with potential/existing clients in my office.
15. I meet with potential clients outside my office.
16. My work product is timely and complete.
17. I am able to file court documents well in advance of the deadline.
18. I file court documents myself.
19. I have difficulty planning and preparing for the unexpected.
20. I have difficulty in tracking and/or recording billable hours.
21. I make it a practice to inform my clients of the progress of their matters.
22. I feel that I have complete control over my calendar and conflict schedule.
23. I ask my colleagues how much staffing costs "these days."
24. I advertise for help but cannot find anyone qualified.
25. I have hired staff members but find them to be incompetent.

Here's how to score:

100–125 Congratulations! You suffer from the Lone Ranger Syndrome.

75–99 You are at a crossroads and/or transition with your practice needs and should consider hiring, perhaps a part-time employee.

50–74 Maybe you should work on your marketing and networking.

25–50 What do you do anyway?

CHAPTER 25

The Law Office as Equal Opportunity Employer: Rights, Risks, and Responsibilities

I celebrate myself, and sing myself,
And what I assume you shall assume,
For every atom belonging to me as good belongs to you.
—Walt Whitman, *Song of Myself*

Chapter Checklist

- o The Foundation of Equal Employment Opportunities
- o The Legal Framework
- o Preemployment Selection
- o Discrimination in the Workplace
- o Action Plan

Law offices, through their managers (typically partners or firm administrators), have many responsibilities in managing the workplace effectively. One important responsibility is ensuring that discrimination does not exist in the workplace.

When there is an opening for a position, managers make selection decisions from among many individuals who all claim to have the needed skills, knowledge, and abilities. They usually rely on résumés, applications, interviews, references, and sometimes preemployment tests to make a selection decision. If knowledge, skills, and abilities were the only factors used in distinguishing among applicants, discrimination in the workplace would not be a major issue. The large number of discrimination claims made each year to the Equal Employment Opportunity Commission (EEOC), though, suggests that discrimination *is* a major concern for employers, including law firms. Managers must ensure that characteristics other than an individual's skills, experience, and knowledge do not become factors in making employment decisions.

Since 1964, with the passage of expanded civil rights legislation, employers have been obligated to maintain a discrimination-free workplace. The equal employment opportunity statutes, specifically Title VII, prohibit discrimination against any individual based on gender (sex), race, color, religion, or national origin. In addition, other federal statutes have expanded the rights of individuals to be free from unlawful discrimination in the workplace on bases such as age and disability. Managers are responsible for understanding equal employment opportunity requirements and striving for enforcement of these requirements in their particular work environment.

§ 25.01 The Foundation of Equal Employment Opportunities

The premise of all federal equal employment opportunity legislation, and many parallel state statutes, is that an employer must not permit its managers or supervisors to make employment decisions such as hiring, compensating, training, disciplining, evaluating, supervising, and terminating on the basis of an applicant's or an employee's gender, race, color, religion, national origin, age, or disability. Likewise, individuals who fall within "protected groups" are entitled to be free from harassment and other unlawful forms of discrimination by coworkers. Law office managers not only must avoid discriminating in their own employment decisions but also must ensure that all workplaces that they supervise are bias free. This may include appropriate action against other employees—even nonmanagers—whose conduct creates a discriminatory environment.

The term *protected group* is used to describe the individuals who are protected under a particular discrimination law. Law office managers must keep in mind that although minorities and females are protected by many of these statutes, Caucasian males may also fall within a protected group on the basis of race, age, or disability. In fact, they may be the victims of discrimination because of their gender, which is also unlawful under Title VII.

§ 25.01.1 Areas of Concern

There are five primary areas of concern for law offices in maintaining an equal opportunity workplace. Stated another way, law office managers must avoid discriminating on any of the following bases:

- *"Intentional" discrimination/disparate treatment*. This occurs when the manager (or a coworker) purposely treats an applicant or employee differently. *Intent* does not necessarily mean "malice" or "ill will"; intent to make the employment decision is sufficient when discrimination exists. Disparate treatment can fall into four categories:

- *Overt.* This category includes, for example, rejection of all Latino applicants because of a stated concern that one or more of them may be an illegal alien.
- *Special rules.* This category includes enforcement of a special employment rule against employees or applicants who are members of a particular protected group, such as preventing women of childbearing age from attaining certain jobs while allowing men to perform those jobs.
- *Harassment.* Slurs, epithets, comments, or jokes about a person's gender, race, color, ethnic origin, religion, or disability encompass this category.
- *Subtle stereotypes.* This category includes special rules or disparate treatment based on stereotypes or assumptions. This falls under the "intentional" category even though the manager may be well-intentioned and not malicious or bigoted.

- *Adverse impact.* Adverse impact includes enforcing an employment practice or policy that is neutral by its terms but that has a discriminatory effect on a protected group. This occurs in two settings:
  - Where an employer has no intent to unlawfully discriminate but establishes qualification criteria that are not related to a business necessity and that have a disproportionately adverse impact on women, people of color, older workers, or disabled individuals
  - Where an employer sets seemingly neutral qualifications that have an adverse impact on minority groups, such as requirements for a high school diploma, a certain number of years of experience, an acceptable credit rating, or reading and writing ability (to prevent adverse impact, these requirements must be job related)
- *Perpetuation of the effects of past discriminatory policies and practices.* This area of concern can include, for example, having a policy of hiring people referred by employees before hiring other applicants. This may appear to be neutral and not have an adverse impact on any protected group; however, the EEOC has found that if the existing workforce is entirely Caucasian or male because of past discrimination, use of employee referral hiring tends to perpetuate the all-white nature of the workforce.
- *Harassment or hostile work environment.* Such an atmosphere permits insults, pranks, innuendos, slurs, derogatory comments, and embarrassing or humiliating jokes that target gender, age, race, religion, or ancestry of individuals or groups.
- *Retaliation/reprisals/intimidation.* Retaliation is a *separate* basis for a discrimination claim. It arises when an employee makes a complaint of discrimination (formal or informal) and then is penalized or "punished" for raising the claim. Other employees who are witnesses or are otherwise "participants" in the resolution of an employment discrimination

claim are also protected from retaliation. The two types of retaliation include the following:

- *Direct retaliation.* Direct retaliation can include adverse performance appraisals, differential or punitive work assignments, refusals of requests for training, demotion, discipline or discharge, and supervisor threats or intimidation.
- *Indirect retaliation.* Sometimes called *subtle reprisals,* indirect retaliation can include ostracism, ridicule, taunts/threats, hazing, and other interpersonal indignities created or performed by supervisors or coworkers.

§ 25.01.2 Defenses to Discrimination Charges

Law offices, like all employers, are entitled to certain defenses in the context of some discrimination charges. The primary defenses are as follows:

- *Bona fide occupational qualification.* Bona fide occupational qualifications (BFOQs) apply where gender, age, race, national origin, religion, or disability are reasonably necessary to the normal operation of a particular business or enterprise. The BFOQ defense is extremely narrow and does not include employment discrimination based on stereotyped characterizations.
- *Business necessity.* The test for determining a business necessity is very stringent. The defense is not applicable unless there is an overriding legitimate business purpose—that is, the practice is necessary for safe and efficient operation of the business. In adverse impact cases, the business purpose must be sufficiently compelling to override any adverse impact.
- *Undue hardship.* This defense applies in a disability discrimination case where the disabled applicant or employee requires a "reasonable accommodation" but the accommodation poses an undue hardship on the employer due to cost, necessary restructuring of the work site, or business necessity.
- *Objective, job-related standards.* In addition to statutory defenses, a law firm employer may also defend on the ground that the particular decision was not discriminatory and was based on objective, job-related standards that were consistently applied.

§ 25.02 The Legal Framework

There are several federal and corresponding state statutes with which employers must comply. The purpose of this section is to acquaint you generally with these laws and to provide a framework for discussion. The federal statutes discussed below apply to employers with fifteen or more employees unless otherwise noted. Some state laws apply to employers with five (or more) employees.

Sometimes it seems that we are prohibited from doing so many things that there is very little we *can* do. Yet, the underlying intent of the laws is to provide a sense of fairness in the workplace for everyone, not just those who previously worked for caring and sensitive employers. Thus, it is more important for us to acknowledge and operate in accordance with these precepts.

§ 25.02.1 Title VII of the Civil Rights Act of 1964

Title VII is the most widely enforced antidiscrimination statute. The statute prohibits employers from discriminating in employment on the grounds of gender, race, color, religion, or national origin. In addition, the Pregnancy Discrimination Act of 1978 established that Title VII must treat adverse employment decisions based on pregnancy, childbirth, or pregnancy-related medical conditions as unlawful gender-based discrimination (commonly called *sex discrimination*).

Title VII protects job applicants and employees in any of the above-mentioned groups from discrimination in hiring, compensation, all terms and privileges of employment, and termination of employment. Claimants who allege that they have been discriminated against in employment must first file an administrative claim with the EEOC. Following an investigation, which may be bypassed in some jurisdictions, the EEOC may elect either to proceed with an administrative or judicial complaint or to close the investigative file. If the EEOC closes the case, it issues a "right to sue" letter, and the applicant or employee may then proceed with a lawsuit in a civil court.

Title VII specifically makes it an unlawful employment practice to discriminate or retaliate against any individual (whether or not a member of a protected group) because that individual has opposed any employment practice that is unlawful under Title VII or has filed charges, testified, or otherwise participated in such a proceeding, investigation, or hearing.

- *Sex discrimination.* Title VII prohibits discrimination in employment against any individual, male or female. When the gender of an individual is a factor upon which an employment decision is based, the resulting decision is unlawful. Sex discrimination claims typically arise in five contexts:
  - Refusal to hire, promote, or train an individual for a certain job based on gender
  - Termination, demotion, or other adverse employment actions based on gender
  - Disparate treatment based on pregnancy or childbearing capability
  - Sexual harassment or gender targeting
  - Retaliation against people who participate in good faith in a sex discrimination investigation or complaint process

  There are two general exceptions to the use of gender as a factor in employment decisions:

    - *BFOQ.* In very narrow instances, gender may be either an appropriate qualifying or disqualifying factor. Gender must be reasonably necessary to carry out a particular job function for the normal business operation, such as the need for male and female roles for authenticity in a theatrical production. The EEOC has strongly indicated that the BFOQ defense is reserved for those jobs, such as wet nurse, where the sex of the employee is a biological prerequisite.
    - *Business necessity.* The U.S. Court of Appeals for the Fifth Circuit has stated that the word *necessity* requires that the court apply a business *necessity* test, not a business *convenience* test. Discrimination is valid when the essence of the business operation would be undermined by not hiring members of one sex exclusively. Discriminatory criteria based on generalizations, protective policies, or paternalistic motives are invalid. This defense is primarily used when necessary for safety on the job or at the work site. This defense is rarely applicable to sex-based discrimination and has been rejected even in instances of concern for fetal protection for pregnant employees in very high-risk work environments.
- *Race/color discrimination.* Title VII prohibits discrimination in employment decisions by federal government agencies on the basis of race or color. When race is a factor, any resulting hiring, termination, promotion, demotion, training, or other employment decision is unlawful. This applies to members of both minority and majority races. Racial discrimination typically occurs in four contexts:
    - Refusal to hire, promote, or train an individual for a certain job based on the individual's race or color (applies when discriminatory decisions are made between people of the same race when complexion or skin color is a factor)
    - Harassment, such as racial jokes, slurs, and other offensive verbal or physical conduct
    - Aptitude or other employment tests or evaluation mechanisms that disproportionately disqualify applicants of a particular race
    - Retaliation against people who participate in good faith in a race discrimination investigation or complaint process

  Defenses to claims of racial discrimination may be based on a BFOQ or business necessity, but these are rarely upheld.
- *Religious discrimination.* Title VII defines *religion* as including all aspects of religious observance, practice, and belief. This includes atheists and agnostics. Religious discrimination occurs when an individual is required by an employment rule or policy to choose between abandoning a fundamental precept of religion or losing an employment opportunity. Religious discrimination typically occurs in five contexts:
    - Employment policies, such as overtime pay, that result in a disadvantage to employees who observe a Sabbath other than Sunday
    - Denial of employee requests for reasonable accommodations for dress or grooming requirements that are based on the employee's religion

    - Failure or refusal of an employer to provide a reasonable accommodation when an employee notifies the employer that a training program or technique conflicts with the employee's religious beliefs
    - Religious harassment, such as jokes, insults, and epithets or a manager, supervisor, or other employee promoting a particular religion or religious belief
    - Retaliation against people who participate in good faith in a religious discrimination investigation or complaint process
- *National origin discrimination.* Title VII also bans employment practices that foster national origin discrimination. The term *national origin* includes members of all national groups and groups of people of common ancestry, heritage, or background. It must be distinguished from race or color discrimination because certain factors other than race identification or skin color may be the basis of a claim of national origin discrimination. For example, English-only rules and certain weight and height restrictions often have a disparate impact on certain ancestral groups. National origin discrimination typically occurs in five contexts:
    - Refusal to hire or promote an individual with a foreign accent when the accent does not interfere with the applicant's or employee's ability to perform the essential requirements of the job
    - Harassment, such as ethnic slurs, jokes, and other verbal or physical conduct relating to an individual's national origin
    - Height and weight requirements that are not based on a reasonable business necessity
    - Aptitude or other employment tests or evaluation mechanisms that disproportionately disqualify applicants of a particular national origin
    - Retaliation against people who participate in good faith in a national origin discrimination investigation or complaint process

  Defenses to claims of national origin discrimination may be based on a BFOQ or business necessity, but managers must be especially careful to ensure that their determinations of essential job requirements and preemployment testing criteria do not—even unintentionally—disproportionately exclude protected individuals. The EEOC and civil courts will scrutinize each employment criterion to determine whether it is truly a BFOQ or business necessity.

§ 25.02.2 Age Discrimination in Employment Act of 1967

The Age Discrimination in Employment Act of 1967 (ADEA) is a federal statute that applies to all employers with twenty or more employees. It prohibits discrimination against individuals age forty and over. When originally enacted, the federal law applied to people age forty to sixty-five; amendments in 1978 raised the ceiling to seventy years of age, but the maximum age of seventy was eliminated in 1986 with very narrow exceptions. Any adverse employment decision in hiring, terms and privileges of employment, training, discipline, or firing that is based on the individual's age is prohibited by the ADEA. The ADEA also prohibits mandatory retirement policies.

The underlying thrust of the ADEA is that age may not be used as a factor in making an employment decision regarding a member of a protected group. To hold an employer liable under the ADEA, an age discrimination plaintiff must show that age was "a determining factor" in the challenged employment decision.

Although they were exempt from the original act, U.S. citizens working abroad are now protected by the provisions of the ADEA, as amended effective October 9, 1984. However, these employees remain unprotected if the employer is a foreign person not controlled by an American employer.

Job applicants and employees forty years of age and older are protected from employment discrimination in all aspects of employment, including hiring, compensation, benefits, pensions, discipline, appraisal, training, and termination. Under the ADEA, individuals who make a successful claim of age discrimination have a wider array of remedies, including certain forms of compensatory damages, than victims of gender, race, religion, or national origin discrimination under Title VII.

Age discrimination typically occurs in four contexts:

- Refusal to hire, promote, or train an individual for a certain job based on the individual's age (especially prevalent when managers make subjective hiring, training, and promotion decisions based on characteristics such as energy, ability to be trained, and flexibility, using preconceptions concerning older workers)
- Age harassment, such as "ageist" comments, innuendos, conduct, jokes, and insults (e.g., sending black balloons on a fiftieth birthday)
- Mandatory retirement or other unlawful exclusions of older workers from continued job benefits
- Retaliation against people who participate in good faith in an age discrimination investigation or complaint process

§ 25.02.3 Older Workers Benefit Protection Act of 1990

The Older Workers Benefit Protection Act of 1990 (OWBPA) clarifies and extends age discrimination standards in benefits, pensions, and health insurance. It also provides that an individual may not waive any right or claim under the ADEA unless the waiver is "knowing and voluntary." The OWBPA provides procedural requirements for obtaining releases in cases of involuntary terminations or reductions in force.

§ 25.02.4 1990 Americans with Disabilities Act

The 1990 Americans with Disabilities Act (ADA) prohibits employers from discriminating against qualified individuals with physical or mental disabilities. (Note: The ADA consistently uses the term *disability* rather than *handicap* as used in the Rehabilitation Act and cases interpreting that act. The terms are intended to be interchangeable, but use of the word *disability* is preferred because it reflects greater sensitivity toward the contributions of disabled employees. Indeed, in many contexts, managers find that use of terms such as *physically challenged* rather than *handicapped* or *disabled* conveys a greater understanding of the value of diversity in the workplace.)

The ADA defines *disability* broadly to include chronic illnesses; disfigurements (i.e., severe burns); certain emotional conditions (i.e., history of depression); past drug or alcohol dependencies; and sight, hearing, and physical impairments. AIDS-infected and HIV-positive individuals are also included. A disabled individual is a person who has a physical or mental impairment that substantially limits one or more of the person's major life activities *or* who has a record of such impairment *or* who is regarded as having such an impairment:

- *A physical or mental impairment that substantially limits one or more of the individual's major life activities.* Physical or mental impairment includes any psychological disorder or condition, cosmetic disfigurement, or anatomical loss affecting one or more of the following body systems: neurological, musculoskeletal, special sense organs, respiratory, cardiovascular, reproductive, digestive, genitourinary, hemic and lymphatic, skin, and endocrine. The term *physical or mental impairment* also includes, but is not limited to, diseases and conditions such as cerebral palsy, epilepsy, muscular dystrophy, multiple sclerosis, cancer, heart disease, and diabetes. People with a history of chemical dependencies, such as alcoholism or drug addiction, are covered *if they have been rehabilitated.* Current users of alcohol and/or illegal drugs are specifically exempted from coverage.
    - Physical impairments, such as the ability to sit, stand, walk, talk, see, hear, move, manipulate with hands or feet, and/or work, must be permanent and not transitory (broken limbs or temporary back injuries would not be covered as a disability under the ADA, but if they are work related, workers' compensation will apply).
    - Mental or cognitive impairments, such as the ability to learn, reason, or analyze, include learning disabilities such as dyslexia and attention deficit disorder, mild retardation, organic brain syndrome, Alzheimer's disease, and related syndromes. Also included are some mental disorders, such as depression and some forms of dementia caused by AIDS.
- *A record of such impairment.* Examples include a record of treatment for cancer, kidney disease, HIV-related illness, AIDS-related syndromes, other chronic illnesses, and drug and/or alcohol dependencies (through a certified rehabilitation program).
- *Being regarded as having the impairment.* Conditions that are not *in fact* disabling (because they do not actually impair a major life function) but that the employer or supervisor may *erroneously perceive* to be disabling fall under this category. Examples include hypertension; heart disease;

diabetes; epilepsy that is medically controlled; and physical appearance, such as burns or other disfigurements. "Front-office appearance" requirements will be carefully scrutinized. All individual applicants and employees must be objectively evaluated to determine whether they can perform the essential functions of the job with or without reasonable accommodations. "Patronizing" attitudes ("we're protecting him from danger or ridicule") will be unacceptable, according to the EEOC.

To be protected under the laws, a person must be both disabled and be "otherwise qualified" by education, skills, or experience to perform the job. But beware. The phrase *qualified individual* means a person who, with or without *reasonable accommodations*, can perform the essential functions of the job that the individual either currently holds or desires. This definition thus requires an assessment of whether a person, though disabled, nevertheless can be accommodated under the ADA.

The phrase *essential functions* means the fundamental duties of the employment position that a person holds or desires. Such duties do not include marginal functions of the position. A job function may be considered essential for any of the following reasons:

- The position exists to perform the function.
- There is a limited number of employees available among whom the performance of the function can be distributed.
- The function is highly specialized, and the incumbent in the position was hired for his expertise or ability to perform the function.

In addition, to be considered a qualified person with a disability, a person must not pose a direct threat to the health or safety of himself or others when performing the essential functions of the job. *Direct threat* means a significant risk of substantial and imminent harm that cannot be eliminated or reduced to an acceptable level by reasonable accommodation. A threat that is remote or theoretical is not sufficient to conclude that a person is not a qualified person with a disability. The assessment of whether or not a person poses a direct threat must be made on a case-by-case basis, taking into account the following factors:

- The duration of the risk
- The nature and severity of the potential harm
- The likelihood that the potential harm will occur
- The imminence of the potential harm

An employer may not refuse to hire a disabled individual who is otherwise qualified for the duties and responsibilities of the job. Likewise, existing employees may not be denied privileges of employment—including training and benefits—or fired because of a non-job-related disability.

Disability discrimination in the law office may include the following:

- Refusal to hire, promote, train, or accommodate an individual because of the individual's disability
- Harassment, such as insults, disparaging remarks, jokes, or innuendos

- Refusal to make a reasonable accommodation so that a disabled employee may perform the essential functions of the job, provided that the reasonable accommodation does not place an undue hardship on the employer, such as extensive costs or danger to other employees at the work site

Reasonable accommodations may include, but are not limited to, the following:

- Making facilities readily accessible to and usable by disabled people
- Job restructuring and part-time or modified work schedules
- Acquisition or modification of equipment or devices used on the job
- Appropriate adjustment or modification of examinations
- The provision of readers and interpreters and other similar actions

The burden of proving inability to accommodate is on the employer.

§ 25.02.5 Family and Medical Leave Act of 1992

The federal Family and Medical Leave Act of 1992 (FMLA) provides for a wide variety of circumstances in which an employee may take an unpaid leave of absence with full job and benefit protection and reinstatement rights. The act covers employers with fifty or more employees. An employee is covered if the employee has worked continuously at least 1,250 hours during the past twelve months and works at a location with fifty or more employees in a seventy-five-mile radius. Technically, it is not an antidiscrimination statute but rather a mandated leave-of-absence statute. However, because of the strong provisions barring discrimination in reinstatement rights following an authorized leave, coupled with strengthened nonretaliation provisions favoring eligible employees requesting a leave or following their return to work, it is referred to here in the equal employment opportunity context.

Covered employees are entitled to take up to twelve weeks of unpaid leave in each twelve-month period under two circumstances, and twenty-six weeks of paid leave in an additional circumstance.

First, men or women may take leave for the birth or adoption of a child. The leave must be taken in a single block of time up to twelve weeks.

The second, and more difficult, challenge for employers is the medical leave provisions. Employees who themselves have a "serious medical condition" that interferes with their ability to perform their job, or who must care for a close family member with such a serious condition, are entitled to take (in each twelve-month period) up to twelve weeks of unpaid leave and may take such leave intermittently as the need for medical or related treatment arises. Increments of leave time may be as small as thirty minutes. Employers may obtain appropriate medical certifications but may not deny leave time on the sole ground that it interferes with work shift scheduling.

Third, employers must provide up to twenty-six weeks of unpaid leave to an employee because of a qualifying exigency arising out of the fact that the spouse, domestic partner, son, daughter, or parent of the employee is on active duty, or has been notified of an impending call to active duty status, in support of a contingency operation ("military exigency leave").

This may affect enforcement of employers' existing attendance policies. Supervisor awareness training will be helpful to the company in developing and enforcing consistent attendance and workload policies that meet business needs without violation of an employee's FMLA rights.

§ 25.02.6 Comparison/Contrast of FMLA and ADA

The FMLA differs from the ADA in two important respects. First, a serious medical condition may or may not be a covered disability under the ADA. Second, under the ADA, an employer may have an "undue hardship" defense to a disabled employee's "reasonable accommodation" request for a flexible work schedule (even if it is unpaid); but undue hardship is not a defense to an otherwise proper leave under the FMLA.

Under the FMLA, an employer cannot discriminate in granting such leaves of absence and cannot refuse to reinstate an employee returning from such a leave to the employee's own or a comparable position. Further, an employer cannot discriminate in benefits or fail to maintain benefits in effect during an authorized family or medical leave or a military exigency leave.

As with the ADA, every employer must post required notices informing employees of their rights under the FMLA. They are available in English and Spanish from the U.S. Department of Labor, which is the enforcement agency for handling FMLA complaints.

Appendixes G–J detail the similarities and differences between the ADA and the FMLA in terms of essential provisions, overlap and conflict, employer actions, and effect on workers' compensation.

§ 25.03 Preemployment Selection

A law office must select employees—both professional and clerical staff—in a nondiscriminatory manner. This applies to all aspects of employee selection, including application forms, advertising, recruiting, making preemployment inquiries, and conducting personal interviews.

§ 25.03.1 Recruitment and Advertising

It is improper to advertise or solicit a position for a certain sex, age, race, or other improper characteristic or past "protected practice." At the preinterview stage, it is unlawful to describe an opening in a manner that excludes entire protected groups from consideration:

- "A one-*man* office"
- "*Young, female* receptionist"
- "*Junior* secretary"
- "*Girl* Friday"
- "Single *man* for extensive deposition travel"

- "Without *family* problems"
- "Applicant must arrange for suitable *child* care"
- "Healthy, robust *man*"
- "No *foreign* accents"

All of these descriptions, whether in classified advertising or stated verbally, would be unlawful discrimination. In essence, at this stage of selection, an employer cannot rely on preconceived determinations such that applicants with specific characteristics cannot, under any circumstances, qualify for the job. Unless the job absolutely requires exclusion of specific groups because of a BFOQ or business necessity, predefined exclusions are not permitted.

The EEOC and many courts have determined that advertisements during the recruitment stage that specify particular exclusions or characteristics are improper because they may discourage a qualified applicant from applying for the job. For example, a man prevailed in a Title VII sex discrimination case against an airline because an advertisement for a "stewardess" inhibited him from applying. Accordingly, even though the advertisement included the legend *an equal opportunity employer*, the court ruled that the gender-specific advertisement effectively deterred men in the industry.

Keep in mind that the goal is to hire applicants who are qualified to meet the job-specific performance requirements due to their skills, education, and/or experience. Employers must ignore stereotypes and are not permitted to make assumptions about how certain groups will perform, as the following examples illustrate:

- A law office employer may not assume that a female file clerk cannot handle a job that requires bending, lifting, and/or stretching unless the individual's skills and experience are examined against the *specific* requirements of the position. An employer also cannot generalize that working mothers will be unable to devote full time or attention to the job or meet billable-hour requirements.
- Partners should not assume that a lawyer over age fifty will have difficulty adapting to change or that a male cannot fill a job role that traditionally may be viewed as "female," such as receptionist or word processor.
- Employers should not assume that a sight-impaired or physically challenged law clerk cannot "fit" into the work environment. Accommodations for wheelchairs or jobs suitable for sight-impaired employees may be appropriate.
- Decision makers may not assume that foreign-born or ethnically diverse support staff will be unable to effectively perform jobs requiring verbal and/or written communication skills.

The key requirement for managers is to determine precisely the characteristics, skills, education, and experience required for the position and then to assess each applicant against those specific criteria. The entire process is accomplished without reference to protected characteristics. Thus, one of the essential factors in avoiding discriminatory preemployment screening is the existence of comprehensive job descriptions. Every manager and supervisor who will be developing a job solicitation or interviewing a prospective employee should thoroughly understand the essential functions of the job and the standards by which applicants will be evaluated. This process accomplishes several important functions:

- It provides an objective set of functions for the job that can be quantified. Example: "Position requires lifting boxes of files weighing 70–100 pounds 60 percent of the time" (*not* "Job requires heavy lifting").
- It forces managers to focus on precisely what knowledge, education, skills, or experience will be required to meet the essential functions of the open position. Example: "Successful candidate will be responsible for caseload of fifty active files and will work two weeks each month in New York and two weeks in our Los Angeles office" (*not* "Available for extensive travel").
- It requires managers to accurately assess the physical and/or mental functions of the job—in objective rather than subjective terms.
- It promotes consistency in job standards for various positions.
- It promotes consistency in comparing prospective employees because every applicant is judged against the same objective criteria.
- It increases the likelihood of placing an individual who can competently perform the requirements of the job.
- It facilitates good documentation of the essential functions of the job and the experience, education, skills, and/or knowledge required.

Let's look at a couple of examples that illustrate how objective job descriptions will ensure that employers do not engage in unlawful stereotyping and thus discriminate:

- *Objective job description:* "Position requires regular attendance five days per week, 8:30 a.m. to 5:30 p.m. Position requires extensive trial practice."

  With this job description, the manager conducting the interview is able to inquire specifically about the applicant's ability to fulfill the precise requirements of the job: "This job requires attendance five days per week, between the hours of 8:30 a.m. and 5:30 p.m. Can you fulfill this requirement?" "You will be expected to provide all appropriate work during trials, which may involve late hours and weekend work. Can you fulfill these expectations?" If attendance during the particular hours is a critical component of the job, it is a business necessity. Thus, if the applicant cannot meet the requirements because of outside obligations (whether child-care or unrelated obligations), the applicant may be excluded from consideration. The objective job description precludes the possibility that a manager will ask improper questions—such as "Do you have adequate child-care arrangements?"—that are based on the subjective assumption that a working mother may have spotty attendance or will not fulfill client obligations.

- *Objective job description*: "Position requires that employee lift boxes weighing approximately 70 pounds and take them to court. This lifting and loading is 25 percent of the job responsibility; the other 75 percent is managing the firm's file room."

  This job description allows the manager to ask appropriate questions, such as "This position will require you to lift boxes weighing 70 pounds. That part of the job takes up one-quarter of the day. The remaining three-quarters is inventory control. Can you lift seventy pounds for this percentage of the day? If not, is there any reasonable accommodation that will allow you to do so [such as using a cart or mechanized lifting equipment]?" In this example, a very precise job description permits the manager to properly screen prospective applicants without violating the provisions of the ADA. The applicant is not a "qualified individual" unless the applicant can meet the objective job-performance criteria, with or without reasonable accommodations. Rather than making an assumption that a person with a prior back injury will not be able to carry case files or large trial exhibits—and asking such improper questions as "Will your prior back injury prevent you from lifting heavy things?"—the manager has a precise, objective standard upon which to measure *all* prospective applicants.

Naturally, there are some "judgments" that an interviewing manager must make about the way a prospective employee will perform in a given job, particularly when filling a management-level position. However, the more subjective the decisions, the greater the opportunity for subtle discrimination.

§ 25.03.2 Criminal Background Screening and/or Credit Checks

The EEOC believes that the improper or overzealous use of criminal background screening and credit checks has a disparate impact on individuals based on race and national origin. For that reason, the agency requires that employers adopt a background screening policy that is justified for specific job positions based on the nature of the job requirements. Credit checks are permissible only for certain positions, such as those involving access to cash or confidential proprietary information. Similarly, criminal background screening requires individualized consideration depending on the nature of any prior offenses by an applicant or employee and the nature of the job requirements. It is no longer acceptable according to EEOC guidance to routinely screen out every candidate with a criminal background. While background screening can be very helpful in weeding out dishonest and unqualified applicants depending on the results, it is critical to use experienced employment counsel in developing a protocol for how to use any information obtained through the screening process.

§ 25.03.3 The Personal Interview

Decision makers should always determine whether the applicant has the relevant job-related background, skills, education, experience, knowledge, and/or capabilities before excluding that person from consideration for an open position. One way to do this is by interviewing the individual involved.

Every person interviewed must be asked the same job-related questions. Appendix K details examples of lawful and unlawful preemployment interview questions in the areas of questioning that are primarily of concern to employers. The list is not exhaustive. Any question, inquiry, or test that improperly solicits information about sex, age, race, religion, national origin, and/or disability status for purposes of preemployment selection is improper.

In addition, the ADA requires employers to make reasonable accommodations in the preemployment interview and testing process. This includes prohibiting facilities and "neutral" tests that do not test tasks required in the job (such as reading) and that create a disparate impact for sight- or learning-impaired job applicants.

§ 25.04 Discrimination in the Workplace

Areas of prohibited discrimination include the following:

- Sex, including pregnancy, childbirth, related medical conditions, and marital or family status
- Sexual orientation (in some states, such as California)
- Race or color
- National origin, including ethnicity, English language proficiency, and detectable accents
- Religion or creed, including bona fide religious and consistently held belief systems
- Age
- Disabilities, including physical, cognitive, and emotional disabilities; chronic illnesses; and records of past impairments
- Past use of legal protections, including taking leaves protected by law (medical, family, pregnancy, workers' compensation)

§ 25.04.1 Sex Discrimination

Once employees are hired, they may not be discriminated against on the basis of their gender. This relates to decisions regarding all privileges and benefits of employment, training opportunities, performance appraisals, promotion and demotion considerations, discipline, and termination.

Overt, intentional discrimination still exists in some workplaces, particularly in environments where females are filling nontraditional roles, such as law enforcement and some construction trades. However, much sex discrimination is not overt. Rather, it is based on subtle assumptions about the interaction between men and women and the roles that they play in the workplace. In essence, equal employment opportunity laws prohibit unequal treatment of applicants and employees even when the inequality is created by long-standing or widely accepted societal assumptions.

Marital status, pregnancy, and childbirth remain the areas of most "subtle discrimination." For example, failure to promote a qualified woman to a position requiring extensive travel because she has four children is unlawful. Differential treatment, firing, and threats of discipline for women who are pregnant are also impermissible. Likewise, failure to promote a woman or treating her differently because she has exercised a right to a pregnancy leave or has had a pregnancy-related medical disability leave violates the law.

Remember that men may claim sex discrimination, too. This occurs in situations where women are preferred for secretarial, word processing, or receptionist positions. It also occurs with regard to sexual harassment.

The following is a brief summary of the legal guidelines involving sex discrimination and job acquisition:

- Marital and family status are irrelevant.
- Discrimination on the basis of past or anticipated future pregnancy or childbirth is improper.
- Height and weight considerations are inappropriate unless clearly job related. Do not assume that women should not be considered for warehouse, technical, construction, or manufacturing jobs.

The following is a brief summary of the legal guidelines involving sex discrimination and job placement and benefits:

- Equal employment opportunity laws prohibit an employer from restricting, excluding, or classifying jobs on a discriminatory basis. Examples include the following:
  - In the absence of job-related physical restrictions, an employer may not limit certain positions to men.
  - Drawing such narrow job specifications that an employer excludes all women in the particular workforce is discriminatory because of the adverse impact it has on a protected group.
- Employers must provide equal pay without regard to an individual's sex where equal work is performed under similar working conditions in jobs requiring equal skill, effort, and responsibility. This mandate stems from the Equal Pay Act of 1973.
- Women may not be refused promotions or other advancements for gender-related reasons. Examples include the following:
  - Work-related travel requirements
  - Child-care responsibilities
  - Spouse's job status
  - Potential for pregnancy
  - Fear that female employees of childbearing age are placed at unacceptable physical risk (fetal protection policies)
- The use of height and weight requirements that discriminate against either sex is unlawful. So are tests of physical agility or strength, unless job related.

§ 25.04.2 Age Discrimination

"Ageism" is an emerging concept in the workplace. Like "sexism" (sex discrimination) and "racism" (racial or ethnic discrimination), discrimination against an applicant or an employee because of age (age forty or over) is unlawful under the ADEA. There has been a significant increase in the number of age discrimination claims brought before the EEOC. Thus, this is an area where managers should continue to update their awareness of circumstances that may result in discrimination complaints.

Age discrimination is sometimes overt, such as in the following examples:

- A decision by a supervisor not to promote a fifty-six-year-old employee in favor of a thirty-five-year-old individual based on the difference in salary requirements, the anticipated length of future service, or the desire to place a more "energetic" or "forward-thinking" person in the position
- An EEOC action against a county prosecutor's office for age-related comments written on rejected applicants' résumés, including *all washed up*

A law firm may not justify different treatment of older workers on the grounds that older workers cost more to employ. Moreover, if an employment practice, including a test, can be shown to have an adverse impact on individuals who are protected by the act, an employer may only justify the practice as a business necessity. (In addition, employment agencies that serve employers covered by the ADEA may not refuse to refer an individual for employment or otherwise discriminate against an individual because of age.)

A law firm is not in violation of the ADEA if it can show that its employment decisions regarding older workers were based on reasonable factors other than age. EEOC regulations state that if an employer uses age as a factor in making employment decisions, it may not argue that its practice is justified by a "reasonable factor other than age." This argument has been raised in many "pretext" cases, in which the claimant alleges that the stated reason for an adverse employment decision is merely a pretext to mask the age-based reason for the decision. Employers who claim to have made employment decisions on the basis of reasonable factors other than age must show that the factors actually exist and are directly relevant to their business.

When decisions are based on objective job-related criteria and specific examples are given to the employee about the employee's performance, age discrimination cannot be established. It is necessary for supervisors to consider and communicate the following in every employment decision (formal appraisals, informal feedback, and other decisions affecting employment):

- The objective fact of excellent, marginal, or unacceptable performance by the employee
- The supervisor's assessment of why the objective fact meets, exceeds, or falls below the performance standard
- What the employee can and/or must do to improve
- The consequences of failure to improve in a reasonable time

The ADEA specifically provides that an employer may discharge or discipline an individual for "good cause." This includes, of course, objectively established misconduct, lapses in judgment or integrity, dishonesty, and related violations. It may also include poor or unacceptable performance. The supervisor should be able to document and support such a decision with objective, consistently applied, job-related performance standards.

§ 25.04.3 Religious Discrimination

A law office employer has a duty under Title VII to make reasonable accommodations for the religious needs of its employees. This accommodation requirement was instituted to militate against employer policies, neutral on their face, that affected the ability of employees with sincere convictions to comply with the policies.

In applying this provision, the U.S. Supreme Court has ruled that an employer need only "reasonably" accommodate the employee's needs—and only as far as such accommodation does not cause undue hardship on the conduct of the employer's business. The concept of undue hardship with relation to reasonable accommodation of employees' religious needs under Title VII is a different and lesser standard than undue hardship under federal disability bias laws, according to the EEOC (ADA employment regulations (403 FEP Manual 1561)).

Some basic considerations of the courts in determining whether employers have made reasonable efforts to accommodate their employees' religious practices include the following:

- *The nature of the job.* If the job is specialized or unique, the employer may discharge or refuse to employ a person whose religious practices conflict with its needs.
- *The size of the law office.* If the employer is a large company, it may well be required to explain why it cannot transfer the employee to a different operation.
- *The effect of transferring the employee to a different job.* If a transfer means a substantial reduction in pay, the employer may be required to show that no other method of accommodation is possible.
- *The employee's efforts in reaching accommodation.* If an employee fails to inform an employer of the employee's needs or refuses to cooperate with the employer in trying to reach an accommodation, the employee may have given up the right to reasonable accommodation.

§ 25.04.4 Disability Discrimination

Employers may not discriminate against qualified individuals with a physical or mental disability with regard to hiring, promotion, training, retraining, advancement, other terms and conditions of employment, and privileges of employment. This includes such instances as when an employer limits, segregates, or classifies a job applicant or employee in such a way that it adversely affects the individual's employment opportunities or status.

The emphasis of most ADA publications is on preemployment selection. Indeed, this is an area of great concern because of the restrictions on the information that may be obtained regarding existing or past disabilities. However, managers must keep in mind that they make placement decisions about existing employees as well as job applicants.

Areas of prohibited discrimination in placing existing (as well as new) employees include the following:

- Physical impairments, such as the ability to see, hear, walk, talk, stand, sit, move, manipulate, run, or exercise
- The applicant's or employee's use of a device such as a cane, wheelchair, walker, brace, sight dog, or hearing aid
- The need to take medication or treatments
- The applicant's or employee's emotional impairments, including a history of depression and/or past treatment by a physician, psychiatrist, psychologist, or therapist
- Cognitive disorders, such as dyslexia, attention deficit disorder, and other learning disabilities
- Past treatment for drug or alcohol dependencies (providing that there is no *current* use or dependency)
- History of treatment for chronic disorders, such as chemotherapy or kidney dialysis
- Current chronic conditions: cancer; diabetes; epilepsy; and HIV, AIDS, and related illnesses

There are some stereotypes about disabled individuals in the work environment that, when used negatively in the employment setting, may give rise to a claim of discrimination. It is the responsibility of managers to dispel these myths:

- Disabled employees are not reliable because they require time off for health reasons.
- Disabled employees present an unacceptable risk to their own safety or the safety of others during emergencies (such as a fire or earthquake).
- The presence of disabled workers will create a morale problem for the workforce.
- Integrating disabled employees into the workforce will present "reverse discrimination" problems—for example, when nondisabled workers are not provided flexible schedules.
- Providing reasonable accommodations to disabled employees is necessarily cost prohibitive.
- Disabled employees will be made uncomfortable by the reactions or attitudes of vendors, customers, visitors, and other people over whom the employer has no control. Accordingly, for their own protection, they should be excluded.

An employer not only is required to refrain from discriminating against applicants and employees but also must accommodate the reasonable needs of these individuals where an accommodation can be made without the employer incurring significant difficulty or expense to its business. (The defense of undue hardship may be asserted by employers in limited situations.) Employers must provide reasonable accommodations in all aspects of employment for the disabled. This includes training, benefits of employment, and access to *all* facilities used and enjoyed by able-bodied employees (including lunchroom, break facilities, and off-site work-related functions).

An obligation to reasonably accommodate a disabled worker's needs may include any of the following:

- Making existing facilities accessible
- Job restructuring
- Establishing part-time or modified work schedules
- Reassigning the worker to a vacant position
- Acquiring or modifying equipment or devices
- Appropriately adjusting or modifying policies, examinations, and training materials
- Providing qualified readers and interpreters (for sight- or hearing-impaired workers)

Some examples of cases that found reasonable accommodations include the following:

- An employer who purchased a telephone headset that allowed an insurance salesperson with cerebral palsy to write while talking
- An employer who supplied a visually impaired receptionist with a light probe that allowed her to determine which telephone lines were ringing, on hold, or in use
- An employer who obtained a timer with an indicator light so that a deaf medical technician could perform lab tests required by her job
- Employers who have installed ramps and other devices for workers who must use wheelchairs

With regard to occupational injuries, employers should view the ADA as an opportunity to reduce or eliminate the costly "vocational rehabilitation" component of the current workers' compensation system. For example, an employee returning from a disability may only be able to do 80 percent of the prior job instead of 100 percent. A reasonable accommodation may require job sharing or shifting of responsibilities so that the returning employee may still perform the same job.

Any consideration or decision about existing employees for promotion, advancement opportunities, or expanded job responsibilities is now covered by the ADA. The following circumstances can occur:

- *A disabled employee seeks a promotion to a job that will require a different accommodation (consideration for promotion or lateral transfer falls into this category).* The same standards will apply: an employee cannot be questioned on the disability except as it relates to performance of job-related tasks or reasonable accommodations.

- *A disabled employee is being reasonably accommodated and the job changes.* For example, introduction of new technology or reductions in force that add tasks to remaining employees' position descriptions must be carefully considered under the ADA.

§ 25.05 Action Plan

- Review the guidelines set forth in the present laws, both federal and state (consult your jurisdiction standards).
- Compare the guidelines with the actual conduct in your office.
- Change or modify your current firm practices or course of conduct as necessary.

CHAPTER 26

Conducting Effective Performance Appraisals in a Law Office Setting

Choose a job you love, and you will never have to work a day in your life.

—Confucius

Chapter Checklist

- o Setting Objective Performance Standards
- o Specific Performance Appraisal Considerations
- o Conducting a Performance Appraisal Conference
- o Action Plan

Performance management is one of the most significant challenges for employers, and law firms are no exception. Giving concrete feedback to improve performance problems or to identify marginal performers is both unpleasant and time-consuming. Partners rarely make the time to provide candid, constructive criticism of employees—from associates to support staff.

The consequences of avoiding this feedback can be more than productivity problems. When employees are not clearly told about relevant performance requirements, about where their performance needs improvement, and—most important—about the consequences if they fail to improve, they may resort to legal action following an adverse action.

§ 26.01 Setting Objective Performance Standards

One of the essential factors in avoiding discriminatory performance reviews is the existence of comprehensive performance criteria. Appraising employee performance with reference to a set of written standards that mirror the job descriptions is a valuable approach. Employers should develop specific position descriptions to comply with the Americans with Disabilities Act (ADA) and to reflect the essential functions of each job. Every person who will be evaluating an employee's performance on behalf of the employer should thoroughly understand the essential functions of the job and the standards by which applicants should be evaluated.

§ 26.01.1 Purpose

This process accomplishes several important functions:

1. It establishes an objective set of functions for the job that can be quantified.
2. It forces appraisers to focus on precisely what knowledge, education, skills, or experience will be required to meet the essential functions of the open position.
3. It requires those who evaluate performance to accurately assess the specific physical and/or mental functions of the job—in objective rather than subjective terms.
4. It promotes consistency in job standards for all positions.
5. It promotes consistency in comparing an employee's performance with acceptable performance criteria because every employee is judged against the same objective criteria.
6. It increases the likelihood of placing or keeping an individual who can competently perform the requirements of the job.
7. It facilitates good documentation of the essential functions of the job as well as the experience, education, skills, and/or knowledge required.
8. It documents that employment decisions, such as decisions to terminate employment, withhold pay increases, or promote one employee over another, were made fairly and without illegal prejudice.

§ 26.01.2 Specifics of Creating a Standards-Based Appraisal System

Every position should have performance standards. To say that written standards cannot be prepared for a position is to say that the supervisor does not know what to expect of an employee and that the employee's work cannot be objectively evaluated.

Standards should cover specific positions, not broad classes of positions. Even though certain employees may have the same job title, different standards should apply for these employees if significant differences in operating practices or working conditions exist. For example, a clerk typist in accounting and one in public relations would perform different work, probably in different quantities. Only when the duties and working conditions of positions are identical should a single set of standards apply to them.

Standards should apply to specific, significant tasks of the position. A task is a major unit of work or significant component of the job. Task/responsibility statements need to be written or reviewed before standards can be written so that one or more performance standards can be set for each task. The task statement should be broad enough to serve as a significant tool for evaluating an employee's performance, but not so broad that it becomes burdensome or impossible to develop standards for the task.

- It is important to avoid overly broad statements such as "Does routine clerical work," which may, in the case of a clerk, describe the entire job. Statements of overall responsibility do not give enough help in defining a job. In general, statements with words such as *supervises, coordinates,* or *directs* probably describe overall responsibilities rather than tasks.
- Overly narrow statements should also be avoided. For example, "Places correspondence in file folders" is only a subtask of the major task "Maintains correspondence files."
- Temporary or unusual responsibilities or relatively minor tasks should be omitted since this would make the standards too long, complicated, and difficult to communicate and administer. Remember, though, that what is a major task for one employee may be a minor task for another employee. For example, the maintenance of correspondence files, while a significant task for a clerk, is only a minor task for a civil engineer.

For ease in rating, most jobs should be described in terms of four to eight major tasks.

Standards should reflect a fully acceptable or a satisfactory level of performance. Standards should be attainable and should reflect what is expected of a fully trained and competent employee. Standards must be high enough for the work unit to accomplish its objectives and low enough for competent employees to reach them.

Standards should be expressed precisely. If the employee's responsibilities are expressed in vague, general language, it will be difficult—perhaps impossible—to write clear, meaningful standards for the job. Wherever possible, tasks should be expressed in concrete terms that describe definite actions that the employee takes. The more precisely standards are stated, the easier it will be to evaluate performance and give employees guidance on what is expected of them. For example, "Responds to requests for estimates in accordance with established deadlines" is not as precise as "Responds to requests for estimates within two days of receiving a request." Vague or general words or phrases, such as *reasonable, seldom,* or *rapidly,* should be replaced with more precise terms whenever possible.

§ 26.02 Specific Performance Appraisal Considerations

Partners and firm administrators can take several concrete steps to ensure consistency, objectivity, accuracy, and fairness throughout the performance appraisal process:

- *Perform candid appraisals.* Do not avoid poor performance ratings due to fear of discrimination charges. Instead, address performance issues consistently for all employees on a timely basis. Be accurate and objective in your performance ratings. Rate poor performance as well as good performance. A failure by the manager or supervisor to identify poor performance allows the problem to continue. The obvious problem is that the employee is not made aware of the performance deficiency and therefore cannot correct it. In addition, failure to document poor performance can create a liability for the employer in legal claims of discrimination or wrongful discharge.
- *Communicate expectations.* Communicate standards or expectations to employees, and clearly identify each aspect of required performance. Communicate the relative importance of each aspect of performance. Employees should be told in advance what is expected of them. Examples of performance on the different job criteria should be provided to the employee. Employees should understand the criteria upon which they are assessed.
- *Stick to objective job-based criteria.* Focus performance evaluations on objective job-related criteria. Examples of objective criteria that have been upheld by the courts include quantity of work, quality of work, and completion of job-specific performance objectives. Avoid rating employees on items that are irrelevant to job performance. When items are irrelevant or of marginal relevance, indicate *not applicable.* Consider the full rating period. Avoid the tendency to be swayed by performance events that occurred in the last month. Compare the employee's performance to a norm or performance standard rather than the performance of other employees.
- *Record and memorialize.* All evaluations should be in writing, and any verbal feedback made during the evaluation period should be included. The language used on written appraisals should be as simple and easy to understand as possible.
- *Be as specific as possible.* Review appraisals to ensure that high and low ratings are documented with anecdotal information showing what the employee did or did not do to earn the rating. Avoid vague or descriptive personal criteria that may be misinterpreted or subjective. Examples include adaptability, bearing, demeanor, manner, and social behavior (except to the extent that interpersonal skills are an appropriate element of job-related performance).
- *Confront performance problems positively and constructively.* Discuss and/or deal with performance problems at the time they occur. If the employ-

ee's performance is unsatisfactory, the manager or supervisor should immediately either counsel the employee on deficiencies and suggest concrete ways to improve performance or get the human resources department involved to assist. Management's motive in a poor performance discharge may be questioned if the incident prompting discharge occurred substantially prior to the time of the discharge.

- *Consider reasonable accommodations where necessary.* Where performance is unsatisfactory due to inattentiveness, failure to follow directions, excessive absenteeism, or inability to concentrate or where performance declines suddenly, the employer should consider the possibility of a medical or disability-related problem and act accordingly. Follow the employer's policies with respect to medical examinations or evaluation of necessary reasonable accommodations.
- *Specify consequences of nonperformance.* Clearly specify a final warning on the performance appraisal if performance is so poor that a discharge may occur.
- *Strive for consistency.* Be consistent with performance appraisals and corresponding pay adjustments. If poor performance is evident, document it as a basis to delay or deny a pay adjustment. Inconsistency will reflect poorly in any subsequent legal proceeding.
- *Plan your documentation.* Avoid making any notes on appraisal forms that may be deemed discriminatory or reflect a "mixed motive." Avoid contrived or pretextual statements. Avoid unreasonably harsh treatment of the employee in order to cause resignation as this may be deemed a constructive discharge. Think about having the appraisal enlarged and viewed by jurors who do not know you or the employee. Can it be misinterpreted?
- *Never backdate appraisals. Never* attempt to document something that did not occur. Always attempt to document events as they occur.

§ 26.03 Conducting a Performance Appraisal Conference

Probably the most crucial part of the entire appraisal process is the meeting with the employee in which the appraisal is discussed. If handled well, the discussion can lead to a better understanding between the employee and the supervisor. Ideally, any problem will be identified, and the employee will come to understand what is required to improve performance. If the meeting is not conducted properly, the employee may feel resentment rather than a desire to improve. Honestly and appropriately appraising employees' performance and suggesting the paths that they should travel toward improvement are essential to achieving optimum performance; and receiving the best performance from those in your firm, both lawyers and staff, is the surest way to succeed.

The following suggestions will ensure a beneficial performance appraisal conference:

- **Preparation**
  - Determine in advance what you are going to say in the conference.
  - Decide on your major goal for the meeting.
  - Determine what is the most important matter to be considered, and steer the discussion to address that point.
- **Timing**
  - Tell the employee in advance, preferably by several days, when and where the formal appraisal conference will take place.
  - Schedule enough time for a meaningful exchange.
- **Location**
  - Arrange for a quiet location.
  - Be sure that you have privacy, and avoid interruptions.
- **Conduct of the Meeting**
  - Proceed to discuss all aspects of the job; go over each area of the appraisal separately. Although you must point out both strengths and weaknesses, it will probably be more effective to discuss positive aspects of performance first.
  - Focus on performance rather than personality.
  - Review defined goals or objectives that were discussed at the start of the rating period. Note which were achieved.
  - Review the immediately preceding performance appraisal to determine whether performance has improved, declined, or stayed the same. Praise improvements, and suggest attention to areas that still need improvement.
  - Be constructive rather than destructive. If there are weaknesses, point them out, but emphasize what can be done to rectify the situation. Discuss a specific plan for improvement with a timetable for follow-up evaluation.
  - Discuss advancement possibilities and what the employee can do to move upward. Be careful, however, not to make promises that cannot or may not be kept.
  - Welcome any questions or complaints that the employee may have.
- **Summary**
  - Briefly review the important points of the appraisal.
  - Carefully restate the details of any proposed courses of action that you have recommended.
  - Be sure that the employee has had sufficient opportunity to say everything that he intended.
  - At the end of the interview, allow the employee to read the written appraisal and fill out the employee comments section.
  - Have the employee sign the form to verify that he has read it.

§ 26.04 Action Plan

- Set job performance standards.
- Periodically appraise the performance of your staff, and discuss the results with them in a constructive manner that encourages continuing improvement.

CHAPTER 27

Preventing Workplace Harassment and Retaliation in the Law Office

Law is order and good law is good order.

—Aristotle

Chapter Checklist

- o What Is Workplace Harassment?
- o Myths and Facts About Workplace Harassment
- o High-Tech Workplace Harassment and Abuses of Electronic Messaging
- o Retaliation as a Separate Form of Discrimination
- o Responsibilities of Supervisors
- o Developing Enforceable—and Defensible—Policies
- o Action Plan

Harassment in employment is one of the major challenges for employers. Law firms are no exception.

Sexual harassment in particular has been a challenge. News media accounts of high-profile cases, such as *Jones v. Clinton*, 990 F. Supp. 657 (E.D. Ark. 1998), have to some extent provided conflicting messages to employees and their administrators. Yet, the U.S. Supreme Court has ruled that the definition of *sexual harassment*, based on a hostile work environment, is very broad under Title VII of the 1964 Civil Rights Act and its 1991 amendments.

Although sexual harassment has captured most of the attention, other forms of workplace harassment are still in the news—and in the courts. These claims range from allegations of targeted remarks to retaliation and hostile or abusive investigations of employee misconduct. As the demographics of the workplace change and employees become more diverse (by age, race and ancestry, and physical/mental abilities), the potential increases for inappropriate interpersonal behavior that targets specific individuals or groups.

Administrators and supervisors must be alert to the issues so that they can enhance morale, maintain the highest degree of productivity, and decrease liability. Case after case upholding liability emphasizes three common legal violations:

- Absence of separate workplace harassment policies and reporting procedures
- Inconsistent or ineffective enforcement of existing policies/procedures
- Inappropriate response by partners, administrators, or investigators, such as failure to take a complaint seriously, attempts to discourage the claimant from coming forward, threatening or abusive behavior, acts of retaliation, or condoning coworker retaliation

A law firm's commitment to preventing workplace harassment is critical to its success in defending against lawsuits. To effectively and legally handle issues of workplace harassment, an administrator must know what harassment is and develop and enforce policies to offer a harassment-free work environment.

§ 27.01 What Is Workplace Harassment?

The Equal Employment Opportunity Commission (EEOC) is the federal agency that enforces the federal antidiscrimination laws, specifically Title VII of the 1964 Civil Rights Act. The EEOC, in various guidance statements, has defined *harassment* and *sexual harassment*.

§ 27.01.1 Harassment

Harassment is defined as "unwelcome conduct that is based on race, color, religion, sex (including pregnancy), national origin, age (40 or older), disability or genetic information."[1]

Harassment rises to the level of illegality "where (1) enduring the offensive conduct becomes a condition of continued employment, or (2) the conduct is severe or pervasive enough to create a work environment that a reasonable person would consider intimidating, hostile, or abusive." In addition, antidiscrimination laws "prohibit harassment against individuals in retaliation for filing a discrimination charge, testifying, or participating in any way in an investigation, proceeding, or lawsuit under these laws; or

---

1. U.S. Equal Opportunity Employment Comm'n, Prohibited Employment Policies/Practices: Harassment, *available at* http://www.eeoc.gov/laws/practices/harassment.cfm (last visited June 18, 2013).

opposing employment practices that they reasonably believe discriminate against individuals, in violation of these laws."[2]

In order for the conduct to be considered unlawful, "it must create a work environment that would be intimidating, hostile, or offensive to reasonable people." Examples include "offensive jokes, slurs, epithets or name calling, physical assaults or threats, intimidation, ridicule or mockery, insults or put-downs, offensive objects or pictures, and interference with work performance." Such behavior as "[p]etty slights, annoyances, and isolated incidents (unless extremely serious)" are not illegal.[3]

The following situations constitute harassment:

- "The harasser can be the victim's supervisor, a supervisor in another area, an agent of the employer, a co-worker, or a non-employee."
- "The victim does not have to be the person harassed, but can be anyone affected by the offensive conduct."
- "Unlawful harassment may occur without economic injury to, or discharge of, the victim."[4]

§ 27.01.2 Sexual Harassment

Sexual harassment is defined as

> [u]nwelcome sexual advances, requests for sexual favors, and other verbal conduct of a sexual nature when:
>
> 1. submission to such conduct is made either explicitly or implicitly a term or condition of an individual's employment,
> 2. submission to or rejection of such conduct is used as the basis for employment decisions affecting such individuals, or
> 3. such conduct has the purpose or effect of unreasonably interfering with an individual's work performance or creating an intimidating, hostile, or offensive working environment.[5]

Conduct is not unlawful sexual harassment when

- the conduct is not "unwanted" (consenting romantic attractions);
- the conduct is not "of a sexual nature";
- the conduct is not "offensive, intimidating or hostile" (the *victim*'s perception sets the standard, unless wholly unreasonable; the standard in a hostile environment case is whether a "reasonable woman" or a "reasonable man" who is victimized would be embarrassed or find the work environment hostile); and
- the conduct, if of a verbal nature, is not persistent or continuing (single episodes of isolated behavior).[6]

---

2. *Id.*
3. *Id.*
4. *Id.*
5. *Id.*
6. *Id.*

Many instances of sexual harassment have their roots in the use and abuse of power. Partners, supervisors, and administrators have power over all aspects of their subordinates' jobs—and their work climate. Sexually offensive behavior—including jokes, innuendo, physical conduct, and unwanted e-mail—encompass the new wave of harassment claims sweeping through the nation's courts. Actionable hostile environment harassment occurs when an employee is forced to work in an environment that is offensive, intimidating, or hostile because of sexually explicit or demeaning behavior.

Sexual harassment is not confined to female victims. In many industries, the 1980s and 1990s brought unprecedented opportunities for advancement for women. It also brought the power relationship to female supervisors who control the livelihood and working conditions of both men and women. Just as *some* men abused their power over females in demeaning and sexually explicit ways, *some* women have done the very same thing to men. And when this occurs, sexual harassment claims follow. Male employees confronted with unwanted sexual behavior from their supervisors do not like it any more than female employees do.

There are two basic types of sexual harassment:

1. *Quid pro quo or conditional harassment.* This is the most easily understood type of sexual harassment. This occurs when an employment benefit is conditioned, for example, on sexual favors: "Sleep with me or else . . ." It also occurs when an employment detriment is suffered or threatened as a result of refusal to engage in sexual conduct: "I'm the one who writes your performance appraisal."

   Under the U.S. Supreme Court rulings in *Faragher v. City of Boca Raton*, 524 U.S. 775 (1998), and *Ellerth v. Burlington Industries*, 524 U.S. 742 (1998), quid pro quo as a distinct form of harassment is now minimized. The basis for recovery against an employer for the harassing acts of a *supervisor*—a power holder—does not depend solely on the existence of job-related threats or whether a threat against the job was carried out. Rather, the employer will be liable *unless* it had an enforceable policy and internal complaint procedure, it had trained supervisors on harassment prevention, and the victim *unreasonably* failed to use the internal complaint procedure.

2. *Hostile work environment harassment.* The conduct may include the following:

   - Physical: touching, pinching, blocking passage in aisles/walkways, leering, gestures, and/or suggestive body language
   - Verbal: jokes, insults, comments of a sexual nature, innuendo, and repeated use of terms of affection
   - Visual: cartoons; posters; pinups; written materials; and more subtle conduct, such as compliments, touching, repeated requests for dates that are declined, or any sexually suggestive behavior that may not be easily recognizable but that is perceived negatively

Such unlawful conduct can occur on or off the work site. Often, conduct occurs at parties and social functions where drinking has occurred. Sexual harassment may exist where the work environment is so "sexually charged" by consensual relationships that a nonparticipant asserts "hostile environment." Even nonemployees (customers, vendors, members of the public) may create a sexually harassing environment, and the firm is responsible for preventing such a hostile, offensive, or intimidating environment.

§ 27.02 Myths and Facts About Workplace Harassment

The following are some myths and facts about workplace harassment:

1. *Myth:* The firm's nonharassment policies protect only women and nonmanagement employees.
   Fact: Both sexes and employees *at all levels* are protected from all forms of workplace harassment, including sexual, racial, religious, age, disability, ethnicity, and sexual orientation.
2. *Myth:* An employee whose conduct creates an offensive environment for a coworker must *intend* to offend.
   Fact: "Intent" is not a relevant consideration in determining whether the conduct is inappropriate. The firm, through its human resources (HR) department, must treat every situation seriously and investigate all complaints or reports of offensive, abusive, or intimidating behavior. Appropriate corrective action must be taken where necessary.
3. *Myth:* An employee who is offended or intimidated by a coworker's conduct must first tell the offender that the behavior is unwelcome before asking for assistance from an administrator or the HR department.
   Fact: Firm policies must provide several ways for employees to request that unwelcome harassing behavior be stopped, including complaints to administrators, partners, and/or the HR department. While employees may choose to discuss their discomfort with a coworker's behavior with that person in a professional manner, they are not required to do so.
4. *Myth:* In order to correct a hostile or offensive environment, an employee must make a formal complaint against the offender.
   Fact: All employees can expect an administrator or the HR department to conduct a neutral inquiry into the circumstances and to take corrective action where warranted. It is not necessary to make a formal complaint, but all employees should be encouraged to voice concerns when issues arise.
5. *Myth:* Abrasive, bullying, sarcastic, or threatening behaviors by coworkers or administrators are not prohibited by workplace harassment policies.
   Fact: These types of conduct, particularly when persistent or repeated, may create an intimidating work environment. This is not productive

and may interfere with employees' abilities to perform their jobs. The firm must investigate and take appropriate action where necessary to correct inappropriate behaviors of this nature.

6. *Myth:* An employee who laughs at a joke is not offended.
   Fact: Because levels of comfort may vary by individual, circumstances, and context, any employee may object to unwelcome conduct that creates, for him, an offensive, intimidating, hostile, or abusive environment. Circumstances include individual background, experiences, and comfort zones.
7. *Myth:* Nonretaliation policies protect only the person making a complaint about workplace harassment.
   Fact: Every person who participates in an HR investigation is protected from all forms of retaliation. This includes the person reporting the incident, the person whose conduct is the subject of the report, and any coworker or administrator who may have knowledge of the events or issues being investigated.
8. *Myth:* The firm is not responsible for the conduct of vendors, customers, or other nonemployees if they create an offensive or abusive environment for employees.
   Fact: The firm is responsible for maintaining a harassment-free work environment and must encourage employees to alert an administrator or the HR department to inappropriate behaviors by third parties in the workplace. The firm must investigate and take corrective action where appropriate.
9. *Myth:* Workplace harassment only occurs when there is a tangible job detriment.
   Fact: In some situations, simply working in an environment that is offensive, intimidating, or hostile is sufficient to require a report and appropriate corrective action.
10. *Myth:* The purpose of workplace harassment policies and disciplinary actions is to punish employees who behave inappropriately at work.
    Fact: While the effect of discipline may be punishing, the purpose of policies is to create a work atmosphere in which every employee is comfortable raising his concern with an administrator or the HR department so that it can be promptly addressed.

§ 27.03 High-Tech Workplace Harassment and Abuses of Electronic Messaging

A major problem faced by employers in the new computing environment is that employees generate, and the computer system saves, a variety of electronic files that can impose liability.

Users of electronic messaging systems, including e-mail, voice mail, and multimedia messaging, assume that their messages are private, will not be saved, and will never be seen by anyone who was not an addressee of the original message. (*Multimedia messaging* refers to a set of capabilities that allow users to add audio, video, and still-photo messages to their electronic messages.) Based on incorrect assumptions of privacy, employees use computer systems to send electronic messages that would never appear in a formal interoffice memo and certainly never would be saved. Many electronic communications contain ill-considered, uninformed, off-the-cuff, offensive, obscene, or startlingly candid comments.

These electronic messages may be attributed to the firm, particularly in discrimination or slander cases, and may constitute damaging evidence in litigation. Pick up a newspaper, and you are apt to see a reference to explosive e-mail evidence. Discriminatory language, racial/sexual harassment, threats, and abusive or retaliatory messages are fertile sources of liability. Examples include the following:

- Chevron Corporation paid $2.2 million due to sexually explicit and racially insensitive e-mail messages exchanged on its system by employees.
- The *New York Times*, First Union Bank, Dow Chemical, and others have fired or disciplined employees for abuses of the company's e-mail policies, including exchange of sexually graphic pictures.
- A major law firm in England was embarrassed when one of its top associates forwarded a lewd message from his girlfriend to six friends, and the content ended up on millions of computers around the world. It also became front-page headlines, with the firm prominently identified.

In other cases, employees used workplace computer systems to store their personal journals or diaries, including those revealing sexual fantasies, sometimes about coworkers or other company representatives. Computer stores are full of digitized pictures, as is the Internet, that can be loaded onto computers and distributed via text-based e-mail; sexually or racially charged images, as well as photos of coworkers or anything else that can be scanned into the computer, often are modified and manipulated using simple "paint" programs and other techniques to achieve a variety of predictable effects—many of which can embarrass the employer or give rise to liability. Continental Airlines was slapped with a $600,000 verdict in favor of a flight attendant who was subjected to sexual harassment when a pilot took a digital picture of her, altered it to make her appear nude, and then displayed the image as a screen saver in the workplace.

Electronic evidence is fast becoming a central focus of litigation. Specialized computer consultants now have the power to process electronic data in ways that were previously unimaginable. E-mail and other electronic data evidence have become more prevalent and critical in employment litigation. Given current trends, it appears that electronic materials will become the primary type of documentation utilized by all parties to court cases. This reality makes it more important than ever to develop and consistently enforce a method for electronic data management.

§ 27.03.1 Unwelcome E-Mail Messages

E-mail provides opportunities for unwelcome messages or attached materials that may offend coworkers. Even when unintentional, this can lead to a hostile environment. Users should not assume that messages are private or will not be seen by others.

Examples of inappropriate or inflammatory content include the following:

- Offensive or obscene e-mail messages or attachments
- Racial or sexual content downloaded from the Internet and forwarded to other employees (when not welcomed) or displayed
- Angry or abusive messages or gossip
- Explicit or demeaning jokes, pictures, cartoons, or graphics
- Displays of offensive or improper materials via screen savers or other audiovisual presentations

Examples of unwelcome personal messages of a sexual, racial, or religious nature include the following:

- Persistent personal messages or invasive questions
- Graphic gossip about coworkers or ridicule of others
- Disclosure of personal or private information about another employee
- Transmittal of unwelcome religious or political material

Examples of misuse of technology include the following:

- Digital alteration of coworkers' photographs
- Pranks involving the Internet, including registering coworkers for mail lists from sexually explicit sites on the Internet
- Alteration of, or tampering with, e-mail messages
- Alteration or sabotage of computer files

§ 27.03.2 Myths About Explosive E-Mail

It is important to understand that the following statements are not facts but myths about e-mail:

- Employee e-mail messages are private because they are password protected.
- Deleted e-mail is gone from the system and cannot be used as evidence against the law office in litigation.
- Employees always have a reasonable expectation of privacy in their e-mail and can sue the law office for invading that privacy if the employer monitors e-mail.
- Informal personal messages exchanged between employees are not official business records.
- Electronic communications that are not printed in hard copy need not be produced in response to a subpoena or request for production of documents.

- E-mail cannot be used as evidence against the law office unless it relates directly to the subject matter of the lawsuit or administrative proceeding.
- Harassing or inflammatory e-mail messages are limited to jokes, pictures, or other material downloaded from the Internet.
- Sexual harassment is the only form of unlawful harassment that can be created or distributed on law office e-mail systems.
- A single, isolated act of harassment via law office e-mail can never create a hostile work environment.
- The person who sends an inflammatory e-mail must intend to offend or discriminate.
- The recipient of an unwelcome inflammatory e-mail message must specifically tell or inform the sender that he is offended and ask not to receive similar messages before proceeding with an internal complaint or external legal action.
- The law office is not responsible for workplace harassment via e-mail unless top management knows about the behavior or the employee has complained internally.
- To avoid liability, law office employers should have a blanket policy requiring immediate deletion of all e-mail messages, even if it conflicts with regular document-retention policies.

§ 27.03.3 Reasons for Monitoring Employee E-Mail

There are several reasons that law firms should consider monitoring employee e-mail:

- *E-mail messages (even those deleted) provide crucial evidence in criminal and civil cases.* The law office may be compelled to provide e-mail information to auditors, third parties in litigation, government regulators, and law enforcement authorities. In legal proceedings, employers often must produce copies of documents related to the issues being litigated. This includes both hard copies and electronic files. The law office's e-mail system creates a large amount of potentially discoverable information. More parties are demanding access to e-mail during pretrial discovery, especially since e-mail messages are often informal and contain statements that sometimes would not be committed to formal paper correspondence.

  If confidential or privileged documents are exchanged on e-mail systems, special issues may arise regarding the need to protect those documents from discovery. In general, to protect the confidentiality of records and to protect the lawyer-client privilege, the law office employer would need to demonstrate to the court that he has taken appropriate precautions to protect such materials. This includes confidential markings and restricted distribution of such materials, similar to what is done with hard-copy equivalents.

At a minimum, law offices should take active steps to keep information—especially lawyer-client privileged material and proprietary information—from widespread distribution. Maintain a strict need-to-know basis for this information. Also, be especially careful when transmitting electronically between offices or to groups of people in the same office. If people without a need to know have access to your information, you may lose your privilege. In addition, the law office should train employees using the system to preserve such confidentiality.

Finally, partners and administrators should establish firm file-retention periods for e-mail messages. This will reduce the time and expense if legal discovery proceedings require production of all messages even remotely related to the legal issues in the pending case.

- *Racial, sexual harassment, or retaliatory messages exchanged between employees can be grounds for employer liability, particularly when courts believe that the employer should know what is on its own system.* This can have serious legal repercussions. For example, employees who use e-mail to send messages with racial or sexual content or regarding coworkers' personal activities could expose the organization to claims of discrimination, harassment, or defamation.

  One company faced six claims of sexual harassment because an employee downloaded an "adult bulletin board" to the company's computer system and programmed it to display the offensive material on employees' screens when they accessed their mail. Still another is being sued for firing an employee after discovering an e-mail message that identified him as a male stripper.

  In another case, confidential communications between an executive and the HR department regarding a planned disciplinary action were inadvertently disclosed on the e-mail system. Similarly, there is a danger that confidential medical information about an employee will fall into the wrong hands when exchanged or referenced via e-mail messages.

§ 27.03.4 Development of an E-Mail Monitoring Policy

The following are guidelines for developing an e-mail monitoring policy:

1. Define the "rules" of the e-mail system:
   - The e-mail is owned by the law office. All messages created, sent, or received using the system remain the property of the law office.
   - The e-mail system is for business communications only. Personal business is unauthorized and should not be conducted at any time.
   - Offensive or disruptive messages are prohibited.
   - Access to messages received by or transmitted through the e-mail system is limited to people with a "need to know" the information. Employees should disclose information or messages only to authorized employees.

- Specifically reserve the right to review, audit, intercept, access, and disclose any business or personal messages created, sent, or received on the e-mail system.
- The use of passwords does not indicate that a message is confidential or that the firm will not be able to intercept it. All passwords must be disclosed to an authorized representative of the law office.
- The deletion of a message does not give an assurance that it will not be retrieved or read. Until the message is written over on the hard disk drive, it is retrievable and the law office has the technical tools to do so and so reserves that right.

2. Define appropriate—and impermissible—content. Incorporate a nondiscrimination policy regarding e-mail content and tie the e-mail policy to general nondiscrimination policies. Expressly prohibit the following:
   - Messages containing insensitive language, racial, sexual, ethnic, or religious material (in common e-mail terms, *flaming* involves an inflammatory remark or message)
   - Abusive or vulgar language, gossip, or insults in business communications
   - Downloading of sexual, racial, religious, or otherwise discriminatory or offensive material from the Internet
3. Establish specific and objective disciplinary policies and apply them consistently to all employees.

§ 27.03.5 Enforcement of the E-Mail Monitoring Policy

Establishing a policy is only the first step in limiting liability when monitoring e-mail. Equally important is enforcing the policy in a manner that makes it fully effective in eliminating employees' alleged reasonable expectations of privacy.

Systematically and regularly enforce the policy. Employers should regularly exercise the rights it reserves or claims under the policy. Failure to do so could result in waiver of the employer's rights (such as employees alleging that they expected privacy because the law office was known never to enforce its monitoring policy and was also known to be aware that employees were exchanging personal or private e-mail messages).

Some tactics to make the policy more enforceable in the eyes of the law include the following:

- Make the policy consistent with existing policies or procedures.
- Put the policy in writing. Over the last several years, many courts have ruled that when employers enact specific policies, they may be creating contractual promises. As a result, employers have become reluctant to adopt written policies because they fear creating unintended rights or enforcing policies inconsistently. This reluctance may actually come back to bite partners because many areas of employer discretion must be preserved and communicated in writing to be enforceable.

- Obtain written acknowledgement signed by each employee acknowledging awareness of the policy and authorization to search, monitor, obtain, use, and disclose e-mail communications.
- Create an electronic disclaimer that is triggered each time the individual logs on to the e-mail system or accesses a personal e-mail mailbox to establish that the employee has no reasonable expectation of privacy:

  This computer network, including all data, files, and applications, is the property of Law Office of ABC. All materials and information created, transmitted, or stored on this system are the property of Law Office of ABC and may be accessed by authorized personnel. Users should not have any expectation of privacy with respect to the material and information stored in the system. Users should store, input, and create only communications that are for legitimate business transactions in the ordinary course of business for the Law Office of ABC.

- Monitor only where necessary to protect legitimate business purposes:
  - What are the law office's needs to retain—and the user's need to access—e-mail?
  - Is the information needed by the law office transactional or content information?
  - How does the law office employer anticipate using the information, and to what extent does it want or need to disclose the information to others?
- Train partners and administrators on enforcement issues.
- Establish and consistently enforce a business-appropriate, document-retention policy for electronic communications.

§ 27.03.6 Limits on Employees' Privacy

The question of whether a law office's "intrusion" concerns a sufficiently private matter and is objectionable depends upon whether the employee has a reasonable expectation of privacy. If an employee is found to have a privacy interest, that interest is then balanced against the employer's business justification for the intrusion.

In determining whether a reasonable expectation of privacy exists, courts take into account all surrounding factors. These include, but are not limited to, the following:

- The fact that the employee has the exclusive use of an office, desk, and computer
- Whether coworkers are able to and permitted to access one another's e-mail
- Whether supervisors or administrators are permitted to and routinely do access an employee's e-mail
- Whether the e-mail system provides a way of labeling messages as private

- Where passwords are necessary to access e-mail mailboxes, whether the password was provided by the employer or is known only to the employee

Some actions by employers may jeopardize their ability to monitor e-mail exchanges. For example, an employer who knowingly permits employees to exchange private e-mail messages without opposing or managing the process may be creating an "implied agreement" under which employees have a reasonable expectation of privacy in their electronic communications. Secondly, the issuance of private passwords to employees in order to restrict outside access to these systems may cause the employees to believe that their e-mail and voice mail messages are private.

§ 27.04 Retaliation as a Separate Form of Discrimination

Retaliation—sometimes called *reprisals*—is a separate form of discrimination. It arises when an employee makes a lawful, good-faith claim of discrimination in the workplace. That claim is protected by law, and Congress has taken the position in federal civil rights legislation that every employee's right to make claims of discrimination under the statutes (Title VII, ADEA, ADA, etc.) is protected by public policy. The remedies under these statutes would be hollow if employees had to fear retribution, adverse treatment by supervisors or coworkers, or other harmful results from making a good-faith claim of discrimination.

Retaliation is the most rapidly increasing type of discrimination. The EEOC estimates that fully one-third of all discrimination claims include an element of retaliation.

Direct retaliation may include the following:

- Adverse performance review
- Differential assignments
- Negative or abusive treatment by supervisors or administrators
- Improper denial of promotion
- The "3 D's": discipline, demotion, discharge

Indirect retaliation may include the following:

- Ostracism by administrators, partners, or associates who have management responsibilities for support staff
- Ostracism by coworkers that is ignored, tolerated, or incited by administrators
- Ridicule or sabotage of work
- Taunts, threats, or other coercive activities

Retaliation through e-mail messages exchanged with remote locations, including derogatory gossip or threatening communications, has also been found to be actionable discrimination. This occurs even where the *recipient* of the e-mail message is not harmed in the employment relationship. If the *subject* of the message is the victim of retaliation, the employer may be liable.

Claimants, witnesses, and even the accused person are protected from retaliation. This means that anyone who participates in a discrimination complaint process can do so free from fear that he will be the object of adverse treatment as a result of participating in a protected activity.

The number of cases involving retaliation—in whole or in part—is growing rapidly, and damages for retaliation may include substantial punitive recovery because of the strong public policy issues involved. Administrators need to be alert to situations where their reaction (or that of other coworkers or other administrators) may create even more potential legal exposure.

§ 27.05 Responsibilities of Supervisors

The following is a review of the responsibilities of supervisors, including partners and firm administrators, in preventing workplace harassment:

- *Always* conduct objective performance reviews of employees at the earliest possible time to minimize the potential that they will claim that an adverse action is harassment or retaliation.
- A supervisor or administrator must take steps to ensure that all employees are aware of the prohibition against sexual and other forms of workplace harassment and what this means. Explain and provide employees with a copy of the firm's policies and discrimination complaint procedure.
- If supervisors or administrators become aware of conduct of a sexually harassing nature, they must act even though no formal complaint has been made. The conduct must be stopped even if not a single victim files a complaint or if a single victim withdraws the complaint or leaves the work environment because the perpetrator may engage in similar conduct against future victims.
- Appropriate action must be taken whenever a complaint of *any* workplace harassment is made. Supervisors should comply with the specific firm policies.
- In addition to cooperating in the investigation of complaints and implementing appropriate discipline, the firm (through the appropriate department) must take steps to ensure that the complaining party is not subject to any retaliation, direct or indirect. Retaliation may include discharge, discipline, transfer, demotion, denial of promotions, lack of challenging assignments, and even ostracism or unwarranted criticism.
- As an administrator, when an employee brings a complaint of sexual harassment to your attention, you should notify the EEOC office immediately.
- Address inappropriate attitudes—expressed or implied—by a person in a position of authority in a sexual harassment setting.

- The following are examples of inappropriate comments made to the complainant:
  - "Boys will be boys."
  - "You must have misunderstood."
  - "You're being overly sensitive."
  - "You must be exaggerating."
  - "You must have asked for it by dress, conduct, or mannerisms."
  - "Nobody will believe you."
  - "You just have to get used to our workplace culture—we act this way all the time and have done so for years."
  - "Nobody else has complained. Why are you causing trouble?"
- The following are examples of inappropriate comments made to the alleged harasser:
  - "Management will protect you even if the allegations are true."
  - "We'll take care of it quietly."

§ 27.06 Developing Enforceable—and Defensible—Policies

A forceful preventive program should include an explicit policy against harassment that is clearly communicated to employees and effectively enforced. The objectives of any policy should be to discourage acts considered to be harassment, to encourage employees to report incidents that they consider to be harassment at the earliest possible time, and to provide protection for the work site against claims of unreported harassment.

To achieve these goals, the policy should familiarize all employees with the definition of *sexual harassment* and the forms that it can take, clearly state that harassment is prohibited and that violators will be disciplined, and instruct employees on available avenues for reporting incidents. A harassment policy must be carefully tailored to the needs and circumstances of the specific work environment. The language should be understandable to employees at all levels of the workforce.

The policy must, at a minimum, define the types of harassment that are prohibited and describe those who are protected under the policy. (See section 27.01.2. See also section 27.04 for a discussion concerning retaliation.)

§ 27.06.1 Clear and Effective Reporting Procedures

Every law office should develop a reporting procedure for employees to register complaints. Recognizing that many employees will be reluctant, embarrassed, or fearful to complain about harassment, the procedure should be calculated to encourage victims to come forward with a complaint. EEOC guidelines emphasize that employer procedures should ensure confidentiality as much as possible and protect victims and witnesses against retaliation. Employers should consider incorporating a statement to this effect in their written policies to encourage prompt reporting of perceived harassment.

The policy should make it clear to all employees that complaints of harassment need not be in writing and can be brought to the attention of a designated management representative *other than the employee's immediate supervisor*. This is particularly important since the immediate supervisor may, in fact, be the harasser.

By creating a sexual harassment policy and complaint procedure, employers comply with federal requirements. The policies must be enforced consistently to provide the law office maximum opportunity to prevent harassment before it occurs, to take immediate and appropriate corrective action where warranted, and to defend its actions from legal challenge.

Employers may defend successfully if a victimized employee unreasonably fails to avail himself of the complaint procedure. Case law strongly suggests, however, that an ineffective investigation process or the existence of actual or threatened retaliation against employees who complain may affect the reasonableness issue.

§ 27.06.2 Effective Training to Avoid Other Liabilities

In *Weeks v. Baker & McKenzie*, 63 Cal. App. 4th 1128 (1998), a high-profile lawsuit against one of the largest international law firms, the jury's award to a legal secretary, Rena Weeks, exceeded $6 million, much of it in punitive damages against the firm for failure to handle the inappropriate behavior of a senior partner for years before Weeks ever entered the firm. In the *Weeks* case, the secretary was subjected to a sexually hostile environment for less than seventy days. However, the trial judge found that the firm had facilitated the harassment by ignoring a series of similar, prior complaints about the same high-level offender over a period of several years. The case—and the independent liability of the firm as employer—was upheld on appeal. In upholding more than $3 million of the original award, the trial judge found that the firm failed to meet its legal obligation to take immediate and appropriate corrective action to stop the offending behavior. Had the firm done so, new employees such as Weeks would not have been confronted by a legally hostile work environment.

In other words, it is not so much the original behavior—unwelcome verbal, physical, visual conduct of a sexual nature—that creates massive liabilities. Many of these behaviors occur in workplaces every day. Rather, it is the way that management handles the issue, or fails to deal with a complaint, that subjects the employer to significant legal exposure. The underlying conduct merely triggers the complaint. The employer's legal responsibility to conduct an immediate investigation and then to take immediate and appropriate corrective action is the focus of many cases today. Accordingly, you may be called upon to design management training that successfully avoids or minimizes these real legal risks.

Although you may distribute written policies that prohibit harassment and offer employee training on the issue, you can be held liable if a supervisory employee is charged with harassment. For this reason, it is especially important to conduct effective sexual harassment prevention training for partners and administrators.

One of the major challenges you may face in presenting sexual harassment programs is resistance by the participants. Many simply do not want to be there. The best way to gain and retain their attention is to explain the concept of personal liability. Begin with your organization's policy as well as all of the pertinent laws and regulations. A review of the range of personal consequences for employees can include potential disciplinary actions for violations.

Sexual harassment is hard to define and even more difficult to explain. You may find some philosophical resistance to government "regulation" of interpersonal behavior. Trainees often have trouble with the legal definition of *sex discrimination* as a form of "harassment" because much of the behavior is socially acceptable outside the work setting (such as at parties and "happy hour").

The false notion that discrimination must be motivated by ill will, malice, or other intentional conduct is hard to overcome. Employees often feel threatened by the fact that unintentional behavior, such as joking or compliments, can be unlawful discrimination based on the perception of the person who claims to be offended (in legal parlance, the *victim* of discrimination). Issues of gender identity, sexuality, and sexual interaction are uniquely personal and emotional, and the differences in reactive perception are compounded by cultural, spiritual, and other life experiences.

Because of the difficulty in defining *sexual harassment* and the fact that a partially subjective standard (perception of the reasonable "victim") applies, many organizations approach the training from an "awareness" perspective. This approach is based on the belief that if employees, partners, and administrators are sensitized to the issues involved with sexual harassment, they will make efforts to question whether their own behavior and that of others could possibly be construed as offensive or could be found illegal.

§ 27.06.3 Training Guidelines

Effective training starts with these guidelines:

- *Carefully consider mixing management and staff in the same program.* Cautiously approach the decision to train management and nonmanagement employees together. The advantages to training employees of all levels together are that everyone will be reading the same materials and nonmanagement employees will witness firsthand that management has knowledge of how to properly handle such matters. Disadvantages include the risk that partners in the session will *not* be knowledgeable and will show their ignorance to employees who report to them or even make comments that can exacerbate an environment that is already hostile. Likewise, employees may feel intimidated and not ask questions, particularly about incidents that they feel management may not have handled appropriately.

- *Obtain support from the highest levels of management.* Top management must support the programs and make attendance mandatory. Monitoring complete attendance helps make the content available to everyone and serves the legal purpose of documenting the employer's efforts to prevent harassment in its workplace.
- *Consider content issues carefully.* The training should reinforce participant awareness and provide practical examples for development. Some specific content that is critical to legal compliance includes the following:
  - Educate management participants in understanding how to create an environment that encourages recipients of unwelcome behavior to talk with the harasser or employer.
  - Clarify the specific differences between compliments and sexually harassing behavior.
  - Encourage an environment in which sexual harassment is taken seriously and where men and women are not afraid to interact when addressing the issue.
  - Clarify the employer's, management's, and employees' responsibilities to create a sexual-harassment-free workplace and to take appropriate corrective action if a sexual harassment situation occurs.
  - Encourage participation with a nonjudgmental attitude. If a participant's behavior is inappropriate or if a trainee advocates an action that is unlawful or that violates company policy, the trainer must clearly say so and explain why.
- *Use only qualified trainers.* The trainer must be professional at all times and take the issue seriously because he is the role model for how sexual harassment is handled in the training program. In addition, the presenter should know the audience, history of sexual harassment situations, sexual harassment policy, complaint process, and any unique issues that may affect the program's effectiveness.
- *Use effective methodology, designed for maximum understanding, and application of skills to enforce legally defensible behaviors throughout the workplace.* Your curriculum design should provide for a variety of learning styles by using lecture, group discussion, small-group exercises, and case studies. Role playing is also extremely useful for management training. Highly interactive sessions build upon individual attitudes, behaviors, and knowledge.
- *Carefully approach the issue of videotaping sessions.* Since sexual harassment training must be provided periodically (and to all new hires within a reasonable period of time), employers may seek to reduce their costs by videotaping sessions for later use. Carefully consider this decision. While it is cost-effective, there are two problems. First, the camera may cause some employees to withdraw or fail to seek clarification of issues that they do not understand. The value of interaction and discussion—so important with this topic—is thereby diminished. Second, the law in this area changes frequently. Unless you assign someone to continually monitor the content, you may find yourself providing outdated (and inaccurate) information.

§ 27.07 Action Plan

- Review attitudes and actions of lawyers and staff of the firm.
- Review existing policies of the firm relating to workplace harassment.
- Revise or create policies that will enable the firm to address any future workplace harassment.
- Revise or create defensible policies to prevent future workplace harassment.

CHAPTER 28

Should You Hire an Executive Director?

There was a time when a fool and his money were soon parted, but now it happens to everybody.

—Adlai E. Stevenson

Chapter Checklist

- o The Executive Director's Job
- o A Profit Center for the Firm
- o Measuring Benefits
- o Action Plan

Small firms and solo practitioners are spending precious time managing their firms when that time could be better spent lawyering. Law is a business, and lawyers are asking themselves serious questions about the economics of their practices. One such question is, "How can I better manage my practice?"

One answer to the question of how to better manage a practice, even a solo practice, is to increase the lawyer's team of players providing additional expertise. The traditional lawyer's team consists of the lawyer, a secretary, and perhaps a paralegal. The team may also have a part-time bookkeeper or accountant. The added team member would be an executive director. Hiring a part-time executive director is one way that a solo or small firm can better manage the practice, deliver higher-quality legal services, and make more money doing it.

§ 28.01 The Executive Director's Job

An executive director manages the firm. He helps the lawyer identify the problem areas of the firm, suggests and creates solutions to the problems, arranges for the personnel to be trained to handle the solutions, and provides follow-up involvement and guidance.

Within this general framework, the specific tasks that an executive director performs are many, and they are as varied as are lawyers who practice law. These tasks include facilitating and participating in the process of preparing a business plan; preparing or facilitating the preparation of a marketing plan; preparing or facilitating the preparation of cash flow projections; collecting accounts receivable; establishing and maintaining good relations with the firm's creditors, including, but not limited to, the firm's banker; organizing the office routine; hiring necessary employees as the firm grows or as new personnel are required to replace retiring personnel; facilitating and arranging for the training of employees, both at the staff and professional levels; buying new equipment; creating purchasing procedures for supplies; leasing new facilities; and all the other, myriad details of running a practice as a business.

Executive directors should have management skills as a result of education and training. They also need good people skills (especially when it comes to interacting with other employees) and good organizational skills. Firms that want to hire an executive director should look for one with references from other law firms or other service businesses.

When discussing the functions of an executive director, most people imagine a full-time, on-site employee. However, all of the above tasks can be performed by someone on a part-time basis, either on-site or from the office of an independent contractor. In fact, there is a burgeoning industry of hands-on management of the administrative tasks of small law firms and solo practitioners by independent consultants.

§ 28.02 A Profit Center for the Firm

In a law practice, the lawyer is the revenue center. The executive director will not produce revenue. However, the executive director will produce—or cause the production of—profits. This is accomplished in several ways.

First, the executive director can do tasks, as noted, that the lawyer would otherwise have to do. If you can turn your attention to doing more lawyering (normally a higher per-hour value than managing), the total revenue will increase and the total profit for the firm will increase. If you do not do more lawyering but, rather, do marketing for the firm, the firm's future will be assured as the marketing produces more business.

Further, the executive director will be sensitive to the costs that the firm is incurring for maintenance of the firm's library, health insurance, malpractice (errors and omissions) insurance, and other big-ticket costs. The executive director, by taking more time than is normally available to the lawyer to focus attention on reducing costs to the firm, can usually facilitate a reduction of costs or at least "hold the line" on increases that might otherwise occur.

By reducing costs, creating efficiencies within the firm, and allowing the lawyer a greater opportunity to do more lawyering, the executive director is a direct contributor to the profit (as contrasted with revenue) of the team.

§ 28.03 Measuring Benefits

The professional approach to managing the firm that is brought by a qualified executive director can be an important, profit-producing factor in the delivery of quality legal services.

Most lawyers, especially solo practitioners, concede that they spend ten to twenty hours per week doing what they consider to be management activities. Assuming a billing rate of $100 per hour (a very modest rate, to be sure) and fifteen hours per week, the value of the time expended by a lawyer in management activities would be $1,500 per week, approximately $6,500 per month, and approximately $78,000 per year.

If 50 percent of these management activities were performed by an executive director, resulting in time saved by the lawyer, $39,000 gross would be saved annually. The actual savings would be less because the firm would incur the cost of the executive director, but the cost of this employee for however many hours per week would be substantially less than $39,000 per year no matter how much the part-time executive director might cost. The net difference is profit to the firm. (Another consideration would be the increased quality of the management effort from a professional manager, the executive director, who will add new dimensions to the firm.)

Therefore, you can measure the prospective gain to be anticipated by hiring an executive director. Of course, if the time presently spent by you on management activities is greater than fifteen hours per week or if the billing rate exceeds $100 per hour, the net savings will be even greater.

By hiring an executive director, the lawyer, especially the solo practitioner, benefits by having a better-run organization and an organization that will be poised to accept growth and deliver higher-quality legal services to the clients of the firm. As long as the lawyer is either lawyering in the present or marketing for the future, an executive director will be valuable to the team.

§ 28.04 Action Plan

- Calculate the number of hours per week that you spend on management activities, exclusive of marketing.
- Consider engaging someone to administer your management functions.

PART VI

Technology

CHAPTER 29

Technology and the Legal Information Age

The big difference between computers and humans is that computers can't think ... but they know it.

—Gene Perret, *Business Humor*

Chapter Checklist

- o The Open-Access Movement
- o E-Books
- o Going Mobile: Apps
- o Improvements in Legal Databases
- o Action Plan

One of the biggest technological changes affecting the legal profession and the way lawyers work has been the World Wide Web coupled with the mainstreaming of electronic media and electronic devices. With the worst recession since the Great Depression hitting the legal sector in 2008, new legal business models have evolved that have forced law firms to respond to clients with less expensive ways to access legal information and increase the productivity and efficiency of the way lawyers produce their work products of legal documents. The open-access movement of free legal information, the e-book phenomenon in legal publishing, and the mobile devices and their applications allowing lawyers to provide faster, improved client services that are demanded in today's competitive legal environment will be discussed in this chapter, along with the resources that you need to be part of the "new normal."

§ 29.01 The Open-Access Movement

The open-access movement of free legal information, which began in the 1990s, was a result of individuals and organizations taking free government data, paid for by the public's tax dollars, that legal publishers had turned into profitable legal databases and providing the same basic data for free or a lower cost than what fee-based legal database publishers charged.

As clients became more sophisticated about free web offerings in legal information, they began to push back on billing for legal research via legal databases, once a big profit center for law firms. Many firms can no longer bill clients for legal database use because many clients believe that library overhead such as books and legal and business databases should be part of a firm's billing rate. Savvy firms have quickly adjusted to these changes by training their lawyers and paralegals to use these alternative resources before going online to access the fee-based databases of major legal publishers.

For law firms interested in accessing free legal and investigative resources, the one reference book that should be in everyone's arsenal is Carole A. Levitt and Mark E. Rosch's *The Cybersleuth's Guide to the Internet: Conducting Effective Free Investigative and Legal Research on the Web*, available at www.netforlawyers.com/ in both print and e-book editions. The following subsections detail some of these resources.

§ 29.01.1 Open-Access Legal Portals

A legal portal differs from a search engine or directory. Search engines return their results by an automated program. A legal directory categorizes websites by areas of law jurisdiction and provides links to those websites. Free legal portals are usually sponsored by different groups that have their own reasons for support and sponsorship, such as companies having related pay products or services, government entities making their documents more accessible to the public, or academic institutions using their sites to further scholarship and learning. The legal portal is one way to access full-text legal information.

One of the best free legal portals is **Justia** (http://www.justia.com). The portal provides users with free federal and state case law, federal and state codes, and regulations (see the "U.S. Regulation Tracker" link). Justia can even display cases by causes of actions filed. Many of you who have federal practice areas such as bankruptcy, securities regulation, or intellectual property use the government's PACER service at ten cents per printed page. Justia can help eliminate some of these charges by providing access to the U.S. district court dockets (civil only) and U.S. court of appeals dockets back to 2004. To find this feature on the database, you must access the "More" drop-down menu. Using the advance search mode, you can search by judge, party name, court in which the case is located, or type, which mimics PACER's "Nature of Suit." Many of the docket results are in summary form, but if there is a gavel icon, the opinion and orders are available for free. To stay current, Justia's dockets are available in RSS feed, meeting the criteria that you specify. Justia also has many value-added features, such as its free court opinion summary newsletters for federal appellate and state supreme courts and its weekly practice area newsletters. To subscribe, go to http://law.justia.com/subscriptions.

Another good general portal is **WashLaw** (http://www.washlaw.edu/), a free service of Washburn University School of Law. It has entries for all areas of federal law, including, among others, the office of the president, agencies, administrative law, Congress, federal courts, and the Supreme Court. State law resources cover basic state information such as demographics, state directories, historical documents and news, state agencies, information on the executive and judicial branches, and court decisions and rules. There are also international resources and a subject index.

A portal that focuses strictly on state law resources is **Open States** (http://openstates.org), a project of the Sunlight Foundation. In production for the past several years, it currently has state legislative data for all states and the District of Columbia.

Oyez (http://www.oyez.org/) provides not only Supreme Court opinions dating back to 1793 and the Court's calendar and dockets but also audio and text synchronization from 1981 to 2012.

Law.com (http://www.law.com/jsp/law/index.jsp) is a portal owned by American Lawyer Media. The portal concentrates on the business aspects of the practice of law in a variety of ways. The most common feature is the daily newswire of major cases and practice area news; best practices; and well-known legal blogs of vetted authors in different practice areas of law, such as Robert Ambrogi's blog (http://www.lawsitesblog.com/). The newswire covers legal events such as legal technology and makes available free text articles from the *National Lawyer, Corporate Counsel*, and *Law Technology News*. These should be required reading.

The **Legal Information Institute** (LII) is a portal created by Cornell Law School (http://www.law.cornell.edu/). Besides having information from other websites, there are many value-added items created by faculty at the law school. The website is searchable by keyword. Highlights of the database include federal law, the *United States Code*, the *Code of Federal Regulations*, the Supreme Court, federal rules, state law statues by topic, the Uniform Commercial Code, the *Uniform Laws Annotated*, and international law. There is a free legal dictionary and a free legal encyclopedia (http://www.law.cornell.edu/wex/) created by a collaboration of the LLI and legal experts. If you are an expert in an area of law, this is an opportunity to share your knowledge with others. (Hint: A quick way to find more localized information is to sign on to your state bar association's website. Some association websites have not only codes, cases, and regulations but also online discussion groups and bar publication articles.)

Another useful portal is offered by the **American Bar Association** (http://www.americanbar.org/aba.html). While some of the content is restricted to membership in the various sections, the ABA has plenty to offer not only to a nonmember attorney but to the public as well. There are free daily law articles posted hourly. The current *ABA Journal* is available in full text. Under the particular sections, there are various related practice aids and articles available as well as ABA surveys and studies. Rounding out the portal are podcasts to listen to and blogs to read. In addition, there is a web store to purchase new and classic book titles.

Several years ago, Google launched **Google Scholar** (http://scholar.google.com/), probably the best-known open source database, which not only provides legal opinions but also legal articles, including patents. All opinions from state appellate and state supreme courts go back to 1950; federal district, appellate, tax, and bankruptcy court opinions go back to 1923; and U.S. Supreme Court opinions go back to 1791. Searching Google Scholar is just like searching Google, with phrase, Boolean, and proximity search.

Google Scholar also has a citator tab. Caveat emptor: We strongly advise you to only use citator services in LexisNexis and Westlaw as accurate citation sources. In a 2012 white paper by Internet for Lawyers, Inc., entitled *Are All Citator Services Created Equal? A Comparison of Google Scholar, FastCase, Casemaker, LexisNexis, Westlaw, and Bloomberg*, authors Carole A. Levitt and Mark E. Rosch tested the citation services of free and low-cost legal databases Google Scholar, Fastcase, and Casemaker against Westlaw, LexisNexis, and Bloomberg and found that only LexisNexis and Westlaw produced accurate results. To read the white paper, go to http://tinyurl.com/citators.

By using the Advanced Scholar Search feature in Google Scholar, you can find cases by federal court, circuit court, or district court. You can find the name of a case using the "with the exact phrase" feature and the "where my words occur" feature, with which you can choose "anywhere in the article" as an option. Cases are displayed in full text with highlighting of your search terms, which can be removed if you wish. You can even set up alerts about any cases or topics from a chosen court to key current issues in your area of practice, saving costs if you subscribe to a fee-based legal database. To search articles, again go to the Advanced Scholar Search page. You have the option of choosing an author or publication when you specifically know what you are looking for. Otherwise, go to the collection and check "Articles (include patents)." To pinpoint what you want if it is a legal article, check "Social Services, Arts and Humanities." If you know what time frame you want to limit your search to, insert the year(s).

One drawback of using Google Advanced Scholar Search for articles is that you can only limit the search by year, not by month or day. Another limitation is that not all journals are on Google Scholar, and there is no directory of contents or date limitations; you must use other sources, such as the *Index to Legal Periodicals and Books*, to ensure that you are doing a complete search. Finally, only articles that have open source licenses can be printed in full from Google, but using Google Scholar for legal and other articles is a time- and cost-saving way to start a legal research project.

§ 29.01.2 Government Portals

FDsys (http://www.gpo.gov/fdsys/) grew out of the Government Printing Office's effort to change its website and function. This is a one-stop portal for the legislative, agency, and executive branches of government. Featured collections include the budget of the U.S. government; Code of Federal Regulations; presidential documents; congressional bills, calendars, documents, hearings, records, and reports; U.S. Constitution analysis and interpretation; economic indicators; *Federal Register*; public and private laws; *United States Code;* and U.S. court opinions. Additionally, you can search and browse all government publications and find out information about federal depository libraries, which is important when seeking historical documents to aid you in such practice areas as products liability, medical malpractice, environmental law, and just about anything else of a historical nature. There is even a "Locate a Library" link within your search results, which will guide you to the library that has your document of interest!

Congress.gov (http://beta.congress.gov/) is an emerging website with information on current and past legislative activities and members of Congress. It has a searchable database by topic, bill number, or public law number. Featured near the top is a list of the bills with the most views as well as the bills introduced in the current year. This website is still under construction and will eventually replace www.thomas.gov as the source of federal legislative information online. Congress.gov aims to improve upon the THOMAS site with its upgraded searching capabilities, more intuitive design, and mobile device support. In the future, it plans to incorporate the *Congressional Record,* House and Senate calendars, and the *Congressional Record Index*.

The **Guide to Law Online** (GLO) (http://www.loc.gov/law/help/guide.php) is an annotated collection of links to information on the law and government useful to lawyers having an international practice. It is put together by the Law Library of Congress Public Services Division and covers both U.S. and international law. It features general and specific information on laws in every country, as well as full texts of U.S. federal court decisions, laws, and regulations. The GLO even provides research assistance through the website for international, foreign, state, and federal law, but a response can take up to five business days.

§ 29.01.3 Collaborative Websites

RECAP (https://www.recapthelaw.org/) is an independent project of the Center for Information Technology Policy at Princeton University (https://citp.princeton.edu/). It is not affiliated with PACER or the U.S. judiciary system. RECAP provides partial federal district court dockets and bankruptcy court dockets only. It is an extension for the Firefox web browser for PACER account holders that improves PACER users' searching and downloading experience while helping them contribute and build a free open-access repository of public court records. Chrome and Internet Explorer work successfully as search tools, too, according to *Internet for Lawyers* (http://www.netforlawyers.com). A user with RECAP installed will notice no difference in the experience except that when a document is available for download, there is an icon next to the official PACER link. The user then has the choice between downloading the free RECAP version if one is available or paying for the PACER version. As you use PACER, RECAP will upload docket files and PACER-downloaded PDFs to the RECAP Archive (http://archive.recapthelaw.org/) for others to download for free. By using RECAP, you are contributing to the growing open-access collection of free legal court documents. You can subscribe to an e-mail alert for new case activity.

All attorneys are asked on occasion a question that is not in their practice area. The Center for Computer-Assisted Legal Education, **CALI** (http://elangdell.cali.org/), offers free e-books for legal education through its eLangdell Press. It can be a big money saver for attorneys or law firms to have basic textbooks as ready reference tools in areas of law where they are not experts. Best of all, a firm can really cut its expenses by downloading CALI's court rule books. CALI offers *Federal Rules of Civil Procedure, Federal Rules of Criminal Procedure, Federal Rules of Evidence,* and *United States Bankruptcy Code and Rules.* As the center is nonprofit, all it asks for is a donation of these works so that it can continue to provide open-access materials on an ongoing basis.

Inforuptcy (https://www.inforuptcy.com/) is a collaborative website where lawyers, trustees, creditors, investors, and buyers can gain information to benefit each other in the bankruptcy context. There is a search capability for filings across all circuits and districts nationwide. If your case is not in the system, you are referred to PACER, where PACER charges apply. Next, there is a marketplace section for bankruptcy assets and claims. There are full-page ads, pictures, and locations that a user can enter with social sharing links automatically integrated. Information usually includes the designation of an asset as personal property or real property, price, location of asset, date listed and expiration date, seller, buying format, court, and chapter. There is free online news and a collective community page where questions and answers can be exchanged. Also, investors and buyers can securely collaborate with each other while going through the site. With Inforuptcy, there are costs involved. Creditors can list for free, but there is a small commission upon sale.

§ 29.02 E-Books

For the last decade, legal publishers and bar associations have been rapidly moving away from the print industry. They have been migrating their print treatises, monographs, law journals, and multivolume sets onto their database platforms with enhancements for the end user. Doing so has been a profitable course for publishers with digital content rights in subscription contracts. The costs associated with producing hardback books and paperback supplements have been replaced with electronic sets of books whose advantage is that no one ever has to go looking through an entire law firm for a missing volume needed for THE project that needs to be finished by the end of the day.

What is the real difference between an online book available from your legal publisher or already in your library computer and an e-book? Simply, an online book is a fully searchable electronic format equivalent accessible through your legal publisher research platform. The user must have a username and password to gain access to the information. The benefit of online books is that you can search for relevant keywords or phrases. There can be multiuser access depending upon the licensing agreement that the firm has with the publisher. Usually there are hyperlinks to statutes, cases, or other documents depending upon the legal publisher's research platform. And, of course, there is a savings in the lack of physical space requirements.

An e-book, according to Wikipedia, is "an electronic book (e-book, ebook, digital book, or e-edition)" that "is a book-length publication in digital form, consisting of text, images, or both, and produced on or published through and readable on computers or other electronic devices."[1] E-books sometimes are the equivalent of a conventional printed book, but e-books can be born digitally without a printed equivalent. E-books were historically read on dedicated e-book readers or tablets, but in the legal sphere, personal computers, mobile phones, and almost all smartphones employ applications to read anything from court rules to noted treatises.

§ 29.02.1 Pros and Cons

There are many benefits of acquiring e-books for your firm's attorneys. It is an easy distribution model to a particular set of attorneys in particular practices within a firm. Users have access as soon as payment is confirmed. Users like e-books because of the currency of information and instant access to full-text search. Many publishers have added features allowing users to electronically bookmark important paragraphs; annotate what they think is important; electronically highlight text; and, like online books, copy and paste relevant text into documents and have instant access to additional content. Some e-books have software applications that allow users to adjust font type or size of text for the size of their device or for their reading comfort. The format of an e-book is portable and can be used anywhere in the world where the attorney may be working with an Internet connection. E-books also eliminate the need for and expense of loose-leaf filing services or clerical staff to unpack and shelve new books.

While this sounds very promising, e-books currently present challenges to different departments of a law firm. For example, there will be more

---

1. Eileen Gardiner & Ronald G. Musto, *The Electronic Book*, *in* Michael Felix Suarez & H. R. Woudhuysen, The Oxford Companion to the Book 164 (Oxford Univ. Press 2010).

reliance on your IT department to upload e-books to a multitude of devices for users in the firm. While many of the legal publishers are making their e-books hardware neutral, one of the biggest issues in the legal e-book industry is the lack of standardization of the platforms on which to deliver the information to lawyers and their staffs. In addition, the publishers will have to address different scenarios for solo firms; medium to large firms; and institutional law libraries, e.g., law schools and government entity law libraries. Furthermore, where there are multivolume sets with many lawyers needing access, the challenge for the publishers is to provide access to parts of the content as well as the entire content with easy access points, without the attorney having to follow too many steps to get what he needs. Thus, not only must e-books deliver functionality to the lawyers, but they must also offer administrative solutions to those managing the "library," whether it be a law librarian and his library staff, a paralegal, or an IT department.

§ 29.02.2 E-Book Purchases

One of the challenges that firms face in using e-books is determining which legal resources in their libraries they want or need to have in electronic format. For those who want to purchase e-books from their legal publishers, there are plenty of offerings. Major legal publishers such as the American Bar Association, Bloomberg BNA, LexisNexis, PLI, Wolters Kluwer, and West have begun the transition by now, providing formerly bound volumes and supplements and pocket parts to their publications in e-book format. The **LexisNexis Digital Library** (http://www.lexisnexis.com/en-us/products/digital-library.page) has over 1,200 primary law books, desk books, code books, treatises, and other titles. **Thomson Reuters ProView** (http://thomsonreuters.com/site/proview/) has 431 law titles that directly link into WestlawNext with its productivity benefits, and it will be releasing more titles throughout the year. **PLI** (http://www.pli.edu/) offers PLI Discover Plus, a collection of 1,600 treatises and course handbooks and access to the transcripts of seminars and the forms in course handbooks, which can be downloaded and used with your work product. **Wolters Kluwer** (http://www.wolterskluwer.com/Pages/Home.aspx) has over 60 titles in the areas of law and business and is strong in the tax and benefits fields. **Fastcase** (http://www.fastcase.com/ebooks/) currently has 50 e-book advance sheets available with plans for hundreds more—all free. Most new offerings eventually will be in e-book format only.

Another challenge will be how the firm will choose the formats in which the information will be made available to its attorneys and paralegals. While it is assumed that each desktop computer in an attorney's office will have protected access to these resources, will the firm also have a policy of making the format available on mobile devices of the employee, or will it have secure devices on loan for when an attorney is working out of town, going to court, or wants to work from home because of illness or a deadline? Work with your management committee or IT department to make sure that there is a consistent policy on BYOD (Bring Your Own Device) to use e-books.

Here are some useful questions to ask your various legal publishers before purchasing e-book titles:

- "What is the browser and device compatibility?"
- "Is special software or a plug-in required?"
- "Are you planning in the future to use EPUB (an open and free e-book standard compatible with most e-reader devices)?"
- "What is the scope and content of the individual e-book or collection being offered?"
- "Is there a print or online equivalent? Is there a difference between the e-book and its print equivalent?"
- "How often is the content updated?"
- "Are there tutorials?"
- "What happens to prior editions of e-books?"
- "Is there an embargo period from when a title is published and when it is made available?"
- "Can the end user copy and paste text into documents?"
- "Can text and font be expanded or contracted?"
- "Are there printing limitations?"
- "May a user download free or with a charge for off-line reading?"
- "Can a user annotate important passages?"
- "Are there saved search features?"

§ 29.02.3 E-Book Cost and Licensing Considerations

Unlike print book subscriptions, e-books have a different business pay model. The attorney or law firm never owns an e-book. The e-book as well as new editions and supplements are on a leased subscription format. Once the e-book is purchased, some publishers will not let you return it for credit. There can be single-user or multiuser licenses depending upon the DRM (digital rights management) policy of the publisher. These clauses are in your subscription, usually under the terms of use. Some publishers do not let you share data with a nonsubscriber. This ensures that copyright laws are being enforced and that both the author and publishers are compensated fairly. In almost all cases, once an e-book is uploaded to a device, a user can access it as many times as needed. One thing to pay attention to in your contract is the responsibility of the attorney or law firm if the e-book device crashes or is lost or stolen. Some publishers will let you download another copy, but always check your contract. A good rule of thumb is to always work with your publisher's representative to have a clear understanding of the firm's contract obligations and to make sure that these understandings are conveyed to the attorneys and paralegals in a clear and concise format.

§ 29.02.4 A Possible Future Model for E-Books

Currently, there are few large firms or law libraries that have embraced e-books due to technical issues, cost, licensing, and compliance issues.

However, recent lending agreements might be a blueprint for a future business model. For example, under the new agreement between the New York Law Institute (NYLI) and NYLI members, the institute has made its 56,000 e-books available to NYLI members free of charge as a member benefit. The requirement that a law firm have an EOS (electronic online system), however, will bar many smaller or solo practitioner firms from using it. The law firm of Debevoise & Plimpton LLP is the institute's first e-book client to merge the NYLI's catalog with its own catalog holdings for the benefit of its attorneys. Cooley LLP is using Matthew Bender titles through its LexisNexis contract on Overdrive, an electronic lending platform for e-books; and other firms are using PLI's Discover Plus product. True, many of the legal publishers have not allowed their offerings to be part of this public law library development because of the licensing restrictions on their contracts, but time will tell if this business model changes as more large bar association and county law libraries adopt e-book lending programs.

§ 29.03 Going Mobile: Apps

When the *2012 Am Law Tech Survey* (http://www.americanlawyer.com/PubArticleTAL.jsp?id=1202575625114&interactive=true) was published in November 2012, it was no surprise to learn that lawyers, in rapidly increasing numbers, have quickly adopted mobile devices as a way to provide better service to their clients as well as increase their personal productivity in their practices. Although the smartphone environment has quickly changed in the last few years—a preference for the BlackBerry dropped from 46 percent of smartphone users in 2011 to 31 percent of users in 2012, iPhone usage increased from 31 percent in 2011 to 44 percent in 2012, and Android phone usage increased to 16 percent—the thing that has not changed is that smartphones and now tablets are being used in many capacities. Lawyers use these devices for the following functions: accessing documents out of the office, doing virtual research anywhere, and drafting and sending documents.

What does this mean for law firms and their law libraries in terms of apps? Mobile apps come in all shapes and colors, so to speak. Some are free, others are low cost; some work on selected devices, others are device neutral. Every attorney has his personal favorites. Each firm needs to decide whether there should be a standardized list of firm-approved (and firm-tested) apps to use so that all people in the firm can relay the same information to one another and to their clients and so that there is standardized training among the support staff in receiving data from their attorneys and paralegals on the go.

It is imperative for the IT department, the law firm librarian, or the paralegal in charge of information and research within the firm to convey to the attorneys and staff information about new apps to improve work project management and flow. Before news of a new app is distributed by the library or firm in the form of a newsletter, e-mail, or presentation in practice group meetings, the app needs to be tested so that all of its nuances can be passed on to the attorneys.

How do lawyers and law firms find the apps that they need? The following subsections detail apps that law firms might find useful. (Be aware that many apps, especially from nonlegal publishers, may not be updated as frequently as sources of law from established legal publishers, and they may not offer authenticated versions of the law. *ALWAYS* double-check information against official sources.)

§ 29.03.1 Ready Reference Apps

Every lawyer on the go should have a collection of ready reference apps on his smartphone or tablet. The following well-known apps, most of them free, will enable lawyers to be more efficient in conducting legal research and producing work product on the go and should be your go-to tools:

- **Bing** (free—Google Play, iTunes): a voice-activated search engine
- **Budget of the U.S. Government** (free—mobile website (http://m.gpo.gov/budget/)): a copy of the yearly budget optimized for mobile phones
- **DK The Human Body** ($6.99—iTunes): over 200 full-color and zoomable high-resolution images
- **Google Earth** (free—Google Play, iTunes): a virtual look at domestic and international locations
- **Merck Manual** ($34.99—iTunes): a digital version of the medical textbook used to diagnose and treat medical disorders
- **National Geographic's World Atlas HD** ($1.99—Google Play, iTunes): a 2013 atlas with high-resolution maps and an interactive 3-D globe feature
- **Weather Time Machine** ($1.99—iTunes): detailed weather conditions dating as far back as 1960 for 40,000 locations in the United States and Canada
- **WebMD** (free—Amazon, Google Play, iTunes): information about medical conditions, medications, and what to do in case of a medical emergency
- **Wikipanion** (free—Google Play, iTunes): access to the entire Wikipedia database
- **Wolfram Alpha Lawyers Professional Assistant** ($4.99—iTunes): a full legal dictionary, statute of limitations for every state, investigative information, financial computations, information on the weather, company information, IP lookups, and a blood alcohol calculator

§ 29.03.2 Legal Research

The following apps are useful for legal research:

- **eDelaware** (free—iTunes): access to Delaware state laws and case law summaries
- **Fastcase** (free—Google Play, iTunes): the largest free law library app

- **FDA Lawyers News & Updates** (free—Google Play, iTunes): current issues, debates, and decisions of the FDA
- **GAO** (free—Google Play, iTunes): the latest reports, testimonies, and legal decisions from the Governmental Accountability Office
- **Google Search** (free—Google Play, iTunes): searches the web using text or voice commands
- **Lawstack** (free—iTunes): the U.S. Constitution and various federal rules; state codes added for a fee
- **MyCongress** (free—Google Play, iTunes): information on U.S. congressional members, including how they vote and how to contact them
- **Patents** ($2.99—iTunes): uses a patent number to retrieve information on a specific patent, bookmarks patents, and compares multiple patent texts
- **Real Time Congress** (free—iTunes): live updates from the House and Senate
- **The Congressional Record** (free—iTunes): a daily update of the *Congressional Record* with records dating back to January 1995
- **The Constitution** (free—iTunes): a digital copy of the U.S. Constitution
- **U.S. Code by Shawn Bayern** (free—iTunes): all federal statutes accessible through your Apple device

§ 29.03.3 Legal Publisher Apps

The major legal publishers have apps for their customers to conduct legal research when out of their offices. The following is a summary of what is currently available. Be sure to regularly check your legal research provider web page for announcements of new apps, and discuss with your representative as well as your law librarian the costs involved in using apps—that is, whether they are covered in your contract or instead will incur an extra charge to be accessed.

- **Bloomberg**
  - **Bloomberg Law Reports** (free—iTunes): access to the *Daily Labor Report*, *Daily Tax Report*, *Daily Report for Executives*, and *United States Law Week*
  - **Court Directory** ($9.99—iTunes): the 2011 edition of the *BNA Directory of State and Federal Courts, Judges, and Clerks*
  - **Law Officer's Pocket Manual** ($9.99—Google Play, iTunes): the latest Supreme Court decisions on defensible police practices
  - **Quick Tax Reference** (free—Google Play, iTunes): calculates taxable income and shows tax rates for the year of your choice
- **LexisNexis**
  - **LexisNexis Get Cases & Shepardize** (free—iTunes): allows users to conduct legal research and Shepardize cases from an iPhone
  - **LexisNexis Legal News** (free—iTunes): access to a constantly updating feed of legal news from numerous sources of websites,

  videos, blogs, and Twitter accounts; basic version of the app allows open-web content for free
  - **LexisNexis Legal News Briefs** (free—iTunes): legal news from top publications every day, sortable by the publication or by subject-specific legal topic
  - **LexisNexis Tax Law Community** (free—iTunes): the latest tax law analysis, commentary, and news
  - **Lexis Advance HD** (free—iTunes): access to all of the Lexis Advance features in HD
- **Westlaw**
  - **Black's Law Dictionary App for iOS and Android** ($54.99): a mobile version of *Black's Law Dictionary*
  - **WestlawNext App for Android** (free): the WestlawNext website specifically optimized for Android devices; can be downloaded from Google Play, the Amazon Appstore, or the BlackBerry App World
  - **WestlawNext for iPad** (free): essentially the WestlawNext website on an iPad; will sync with both the mobile and full-size WestlawNext automatically

§ 29.03.4 Productivity

The following apps will increase lawyers' general productivity:

- **AppBox Pro** ($0.99—iTunes): a "Swiss army knife for your digital life"—includes a secure wallet, alarm clock, currency calculator, event diary, flashlight, all holidays, mirror, ruler, translator, and unit converter, among many other useful features
- **Awesome Note** ($3.99—iTunes): allows users to quickly take notes, make memos or lists, keep a journal, or track ongoing projects
- **Buffer** (free—Google Play, iTunes): schedules social network updates throughout the day and includes analytics to see what links people have clicked in your posts
- **Days** ($2.99—iTunes): keeps track of important dates from the past or counts down to events in the future
- **Documents to Go** ($9.99/$14.99—Amazon, Google Play, iTunes): creates Word, Excel, and PowerPoint files
- **Dragon Dictation** (free—iTunes): voice-recognition software that allows you to speak to your phone to write a text message or e-mail
- **Dropbox** (free—Google Play, iTunes): allows users to save files and access them on the go
- **Evernote** (free—Google Play, iTunes): allows users to take notes or pictures, create to-do lists or voice reminders, and sync the files on all devices used
- **GoodReader** ($4.99—iTunes): handles large text files, including PDFs, and allows annotation on the files
- **Instapaper** ($3.99—iTunes; $2.99—Google Play): saves web pages offline in a text-only format to be read at a later time

- **Jotnot Scanner Pro** ($0.99—iTunes): turns an iPhone into a scanner that automatically removes shadows, adjusts white balance, and corrects contrast on scanned images
- **LinkedIn** (free—Google Play, iTunes): allows users to keep in contact with people in their business network, read news, and share content on the go
- **Notes Plus** (7.99—iTunes): allows users to take notes with a stylus or keyboard, convert handwritten text to typed text, and insert text or pictures from websites
- **OmniFocus** ($19.99/$39.99—iTunes): organizes tasks by project, date, person, or place
- **PDF Expert** ($9.99—iTunes): allows users to read and annotate PDF documents, fill in PDF forms, highlight and underline text, create typed notes, and draw on the document with their fingers
- **PrintnShare** ($6.99—iTunes): prints documents from any WiFi or network printer and transfers and stores files at your convenience
- **Quick Charts** (free—iTunes): creates, saves, and e-mails pie charts
- **Quickoffice** ($14.99—mobile; $19.99—Google Play, iTunes): allows users to edit Microsoft Office documents and access cloud storage
- **QuickVoice2Text Email** ($2.99): allows users to send e-mails by talking instead of typing and create voice memos or their own ringtones
- **Reeder** ($2.99—iTunes): allows users to read RSS news feeds and add news feeds to blogs or websites
- **Speaktoit Assistant** (free—iTunes): answers questions, finds information, and performs tasks such as sending e-mail—all through voice recognition
- **SpeakWrite** (free/$0.0125 per word—Google Play, iTunes): a voice recorder that uses real typists to transcribe audio, making it more accurate than Dragon Dictation
- **Text Expander** ($4.99—iTunes): allows users to create custom text shortcuts or abbreviations that expand into full text when typed
- **ZeroTap** (free—iTunes): allows users to type text on their computer keyboard and send it to their iPhone as a text message or note

§ 29.03.5 Trial Practice

The following apps are specific to trial practice:

- **American Arbitration Association** (free—Google Play, iTunes): searches through rules, protocol, codes, and contact information
- **Fed. R. Civ. Pro. by Cliff Maier** ($2.99—iTunes): the most commonly used parts of the U.S. Code
- **iJuror** ($9.99—Google Play; $19.99—iTunes): allows users to choose jurors and track jury information
- **JuryTracker** ($4.99—iTunes): allows users to take notes on the individual reactions of jury members using built-in emoticons and gestures; all notes are time stamped so they can be compared to the transcript

- **Mobile Transcript** (free—Google Play, iTunes): allows users to view case transcripts, highlight and e-mail important testimony, and keep track of billable time
- **Rulebook** (free—iTunes): federal and state court rules and *The Bluebook* (with a charge for accessing each book or rule)
- **The Deponent App** ($9.99—iTunes): 300 deposition questions, which can be customized for a case
- **TrialDirector** (free—iTunes): allows users to manage and present evidence during a trial
- **TrialPad** ($89.99—iTunes): allows users to present evidence to the jury directly from an iPad using AppleTV and import, organize, and annotate trial documents

§ 29.03.6 Keeping Current

The following are sources of information to help lawyers keep current with new developments in law firm apps and mobile technology:

- **Annual Surveys**
  - **2012 Am Law Tech Survey** (http://www.americanlawyer.com/PubArticleTAL.jsp?id=1202575625114&interactive=true)
  - **ABA 2013 Legal Technology Survey Report** (http://tinyurl.com/ABA-survey)
  - **ABA Legal Technology Resource Center** (http://tinyurl.com/aba-legal-tech)
  - **Law Practice Today** (http://tinyurl.com/law-today)
- **Legal Blogs**
  - **Inter Alia: Tom Mighell's Technology Blog** (http://www.inter-alia.net/blog/)
  - **iPhone JD** (http://www.iphonejd.com/)
  - **LawBiz Blog** (http://www.lawbizblog.com)
  - **LLRX.com** (http://www.llrx.com/)
  - **Technology Law and Legal Technology: DennisKennedy.com** (http://denniskennedy.com/)
- **Vendor Online Newsletters, Demos with Reps, and Databases**
  - **Bloomberg BRIEF** (http://www.bloombergbriefs.com/)
  - **CCH** (http://www.cch.com/)
  - **LawBiz Tips** (http://www.lawbiztips.com)
  - **Lexis Advance** (http://tinyurl.com/lexis-news)
  - **LoislawConnect** (http://tinyurl.com/loislaw-news)
  - **Mobile Apps for Law** (http://tinyurl.com/law-apps)
  - **The Grant Company** (http://www.intelliconnect.net/)
  - **Westlaw Edge** (http://tinyurl.com/westlaw-news)

§ 29.04 Improvements in Legal Databases

Due to the proliferation of open-access online legal and business resources, the major legal publishers are easing out of the content business. Instead, given the work environment that demands its customers provide legal and work product faster, cheaper, and more efficiently, the main legal publishers Bloomberg BNA, LexisNexis, Thomson Reuters (West), and Wolters Kluwer have been concentrating on developing law practice management and work-flow solutions to help lawyers and law firms better meet the needs of their clients. The "Google-ization" of legal research and new infographic technologies have changed the way that attorneys search and absorb results in their online research—much to the chagrin of law librarians and older lawyers. A population schooled with computers coupled with advances in education technology has resulted in the major providers of legal databases developing their products in innovative ways for the new and future generations of lawyers. Basic single-search functions are now "Google-ized" or based upon algorithms instead of the strictly Boolean searching of yesterday. The interfaces of the research systems now cast a wider net over the entire contents of the database, allowing for the prefiltering of primary and secondary news sources and more content to save a searcher's time. Special features have components of artificial intelligence that help a user pick the correct words and terms to get the best search in the system or that even suggest related sources.

Some of the databases have graphic features that help the searcher remember what has been done in the thought and work-flow process, so time is not wasted if the searcher needs to revisit his research. Even the citation services present their findings in an easy-to-read chronological or hierarchical infographic format. Most legal publishers provide a free viewing of what matches your search query in summary format. Some systems have abolished the per-search charge; instead, users pay for what they select to look at in full text, resulting in cost-effective search results. Other publishers charge an up-front search fee, and then an attorney pays for what is actually utilized for his work product.

The real technological advance has been marrying all of this with advanced legal-management tools to help organize and produce better work flows. Results from the legal research can automatically be saved into chart/project folders that can be shared with colleagues for collaboration. Some of the systems automatically update the research in the folders at specified times, relieving the user of this task. Most legal publishers allow users to have access to the work saved in the folders as many times as they want for free; others will charge after a one-year period. Other integrated work-flow features of these law practice management systems include time/billing features with preloaded ABA billing codes, calendars, automated legal forms specific to practice group and jurisdiction, e-mail integration, task lists, and more.

Most of these ancillary products are not part of your basic contract, so choose carefully. Develop a working partnership with the provider's representatives and your IT department. Have in-house demonstrations, read reviews, and take your time in making the choice that is best for your firm and your clients.

The following list contains contact information for legal publishers:

- **Bloomberg BNA** (http://www.bna.com/)
- **Casemaker** (http://www.casemaker.us/)
- **LexisNexis** (http://www.lexisnexis.com/en-us/home.page)
- **The Grant Company** (http://www.intelliconnect.net/)
- **Thomson Reuters (West)** (http://thomsonreuters.com/)
- **Wolters Kluwer** (http://tinyurl.com/loislawconnect)

§ 29.05 Action Plan

- Familiarize yourself with open-access sources and e-books.
- Be aware of the variety of apps available for your mobile devices.
- Use the technological advancements to improve client services and your bottom line.

CHAPTER 30

Financial and Ethical Implications of Technology

It's not the computer that makes a difference. It's how you use it. That's pretty much the way it used to be with your head.

—Gene Perret, *Business Humor*

Chapter Checklist

- o Financial Implications of Technology
- o Ethical Implications of Technology
- o Action Plan

Perhaps no other area of starting or maintaining a law practice offers as much promise—and is as complicated—as information management.

Before the widespread use of personal computers, lawyers relied on secretaries and paralegals for the majority of their information management. Today, maintaining a practice without some type of automation simply is not an option. The world of the law is more than ever the world of the computer.

In general, technology offers many benefits for lawyers. However, along with the benefits are issues to address—in particular, financial and ethical issues.

§ 30.01 Financial Implications of Technology

The recent death of Apple founder Steve Jobs brought a spate of stories about how his flair for sleek design combined with his innovative thinking to create products that the marketplace perceives as "cool." Law firms are not immune to the cool factor in their technology purchases. Firms want new technology not only because it helps them do more, more quickly but also because it's attractive or fun. Firms also have a strong competitive streak, and they either want to be the first to tout using a new technology or don't want to admit that others are using it and they are not.

However, technology expenditures should not be based on emotion. They must be made because they provide an adequate return on investment (ROI). Technology must increase service levels and work volume if it is to lead to more client work assignments. No matter what the reason for purchase or replacement cycle, higher ROI on the technology expenditure must be the result. The ROI for technology purchases is maximized when the firm defines its technology needs and makes purchases to fill those needs according to a budget, not according to emotion fueled by what's cool. There is no one right or correct rate of return, but maximizing it is essential. The return selected or expected will be a function of personal choice, client demands, available alternatives, and investment resources.

§ 30.01.1 ROI and Cash Flow

Awareness of what technology can consume from a firm's cash flow, as well as from lawyers' billable time, gives a true picture of the return that the firm gets on its technology spending.

Here is a typical way to calculate ROI. Say the slated expenditure is $1,000 and the expected savings or the expected increase in net revenues is anticipated to be $100 annually. Taking the savings as the numerator and the expenditure as the denominator, the ROI of the purchase is 10 percent per year. Another way to look at this is to figure that the $100, if it occurs each year, will result in a "recovery" of the entire investment after ten years; or, said another way, the "payback period" is ten years. A 10 percent return is usually considered too low to make the purchase (investment) unless there are other factors involved, such as new services that it allows the firm to offer or greater efficiency that it provides.

Because there are invariably a number of technology expenditures competing for priority, using ROI helps to rank them in the order of financial preference. Then, depending on the budget and resources available, the most productive or profitable investment can be made first.

§ 30.01.2 ROI and the Replacement Cycle

Don't automatically assume that a new computer or software will greatly increase lawyer or staff productivity, with a resulting increase in profitability. Projected ROI is often thwarted by human considerations: support staff and lawyers can resist change, be afraid of the new technology, or have no emotional investment in its use. Fear of how much time it takes to negotiate the technology learning curve can be another factor. In any of these circumstances, the technology can languish until it becomes obsolete, with little of the expected savings or profits.

Such concerns keep too many small firms and solo practices behind the technology curve, even to the point of not using e-mail or not keeping electronic files of client records. Those that do use technology often do not spend enough or maintain upgrades to keep it current. This is done at their peril for two reasons. First, such firms are in danger of violating the ABA *Model Rules of Professional Conduct*—specifically, Rule 1.1, which requires lawyers to meet the standard of care in the local community and today is generally assumed to mean using technology effectively for trial support, case management, and the like (see section 30.02.1 in this chapter). And second, if a lawyer contemplating retirement has not kept the practice's technology up to speed, the firm's value is going to be diminished in negotiations once a potential purchaser realizes that a substantial IT investment will be necessary.

In contrast with the four-, five-, or even six-year technology replacement cycle at small firms, larger firms typically make technology a bigger focus of dollars and time. In a survey that I conducted several years ago of selected large firms, 66 percent of respondents allocated 2 percent or less of their gross revenue for hardware purchases; 75 percent of the respondents allocated an additional 2 percent or less of their gross revenue for software purchases. These numbers aren't large percentages but represent large numbers of dollars. Furthermore, 67 percent of the respondents age out their computers and related technology before the end of a three-year cycle (17 percent in two years), guaranteeing a continual cycle of expenditures. Thus, the amount of dollars committed to technology purchases in a large firm can be substantial.

§ 30.01.3 ROI and Financing

To pay for an upgrade, firms typically pursue one of several options:

- *Cash*. This is typically done only for a small purchase (a single computer and its software licenses). It eliminates finance charges and fees, but even the few thousand dollars required are enough to be a deal breaker for some firms.
- *Leasing*. Leases facilitate more frequent upgrades, protect a firm's credit, and can even offer tax advantages. However, lease arrangements are typically limited to computer hardware, still leaving the firm to come up with cash for software and implementation.
- *Manufacturer financing*. This can include items such as technology and services that are usually not covered in lease packages, and it may be for as short a period of time as two years. But such programs still are loans with organizations, often not as flexible as banks. Bank financing for technology purchases may be through a line of credit, equipment loan, or term loan.

The cost of such loans varies. Factors include the firm's bank balance, other services purchased, and credit rating.

The reason that bank financing is not usually pursued is because the minute that software or computers are purchased, their obsolescence is assured. Their value to the bank isn't nearly as great as a hard asset like real estate, no matter how expensive the technology is. Thus, bankers are nervous when it comes to financing IT purchases. Banks may accept technology as collateral but will not put a high value on it. The prospective borrower must provide as much safety to the bank as is possible, especially by contributing both capital and collateral to the overall financing package.

Whatever financing method is used, thinking through the purchase and getting as many people as possible committed to using the technology before it is purchased is the best way to achieve the level of usage that produces a higher ROI.

§ 30.01.4 ROI and Efficiency

In the law firm marketplace, as profit pressures increase, those firms that can take advantage of the time savings, efficiency, and commoditization of routine tasks and services afforded by computers and other electronic technology will profit. Such firms will use a marketing strategy emphasizing technology tools that allow for greater efficiencies that can reduce clients' legal costs while maintaining or increasing the law firm revenue through higher volumes of work. Three tools in particular can be effectively leveraged for business development: client relationship management (CRM) systems, knowledge management (KM) systems, and e-discovery software.

- *CRM systems*. Shared CRM databases on computer desktops can make available to all firm members the contact history and service requirements of any client or prospect, bringing far greater efficiencies to client service functions. This is the type of information that used to be stashed away in individual Rolodexes and address books or in hard-copy marketing files. With a CRM system, information can be entered and viewed by anyone authorized to do so. But if partners zealously, jealously guard data rather than share it because they fear that sharing information on "their" clients will negatively affect their compensation and bonus, the incompleteness of the firm-wide data will make the CRM a wasted investment with little useful return.
- *KM systems*. Investing in a KM system poses a challenge similar to that of CRM systems. KM systems combine the work product of all lawyers into a single unified database that can be accessed for the financial benefit of all clients. The old KM concept involved looking in file cabinets and pulling out the paperwork of the most recent deals or pleadings. The heart of the KM process is to identify precedent documents that can be used in future matters and ensure that they are both identified and easily accessible. The KM process only works when the information is classified and categorized consistently and frequently.

Many lawyers believe that this is not billable time, particularly after a transaction or case is completed, and so they either do not do it or do it incompletely. No matter how sophisticated the database, KM only works when all knowledge is shared in a way that all lawyers can access it.

- *E-discovery software.* In litigation, e-discovery software can analyze documents required for litigation discovery in a fraction of the time, for a fraction of the cost, when compared to using lawyers for the task. Some programs have the power to search electronic files and find documents with relevant terms at high speed. They also extract relevant concepts and deduce patterns that would have eluded lawyers examining paper copies. Inescapably, hours that used to be spent conducting document review will no longer be billable. Profitability for the firm will come from the ability to swiftly analyze the millions of equivalent paper pages that electronic documents represent, thus allowing the firm to take on more clients.

Increased profit by increased efficiency through the use of CRM, KM, and e-discovery software technology is the firm's secret weapon to turn legal knowledge into a high-volume commodity. But being able to maintain and expand billings while becoming more efficient requires yet another marketing innovation—changing the billing system to embrace value-based, alternative fee arrangements. This is a new business development dynamic, one that every law firm should understand. The Great Recession caused corporate America to revolt against the traditional American law firm model with its annual hourly price increases, and few firms of any size can afford to ignore the way that global technology flattens the cost of legal service. There is inevitable pressure to reduce fixed fees and squeeze the firm's profit margins. Thus, maintaining billings while becoming more efficient requires changing the billing system to embrace alternative fee arrangements. The premise of any such billing system is that time is not the relevant issue to determine the fee. A new fee dynamic focused on value can create an environment of sharing the efficiencies offered by technology—an environment in which both the lawyer and the client will benefit.

§ 30.02 Ethical Implications of Technology

Firms have a duty to meet standard of care responsibilities under the ABA *Model Rules of Professional Conduct* when it comes to the computer. The *Model Rules* noted here are, of course, advisory, but most states, including California, adopt and incorporate them into their own rules of professional conduct.

Compliance is the lawyer's requirement, but management of computer and information technology is typically viewed as a staff function, which makes it a responsibility for administrators with technology control. Thus, it is vital that firm administrators act as the link between technological advancements and ethical requirements under the *Model Rules*.

§ 30.02.1 Meet the Standard of Care

It has long been held that lawyers who do not use technology effectively for client files, trial support, case management, and the like are willfully less competent than their peers—a clear example of malpractice. In 2012, the American Bar Association clearly identified technology as an area of competence by adding a comment to Rule 1.1 ("Competence") that "to maintain the requisite knowledge and skill," a lawyer "should keep abreast of changes in the law and its practice, including the benefits and risks associated with relevant technology."

This is particularly a concern for smaller firms. Surveys have found that while the majority of large law firms upgrade their computers and software every two to three years, many small firms and solo practitioners go as long as six to eight years between upgrades. They cite cost, time to learn and implement the new technology, and lack of certainty that new technology will increase efficiency and work quality. None of these reasons will protect a firm against a client who claims that outdated technology led to incompetent representation, violating Rule 1.1. Firms with obsolete technology should beware.

§ 30.02.2 Safeguard Files

Rule 1.15 ("Safekeeping Priority") states that lawyers have a professional duty to "appropriately safeguard[]" all documents relating to clients. Failure to keep files safe is a failure in the duty to act competently in the best interests of a client. (The rule does not stipulate a minimum time frame. The rules and specific time periods for storing or destroying client files vary by jurisdiction. Some states, for example, require a lawyer to securely store a client's file for ten years after completion or termination of the representation unless the lawyer and client make other arrangements.) Clearly, this implicates electronic documents.

In addition, the Federal Rules of Civil Procedure, since 2006, have required producing not just paper but all electronic documents and data for trial. Defendants and their counsel must carry out this duty to preserve and provide electronically stored information (ESI) or face penalties from the court.

In the past, file management and retention involved boxes of paper documents. Now, however, electronic technology is the lawyer's ally in taming the records beast. From generating electronic files on personal computers to scanning paper files to storing electronic records in a remote "cloud" location, computers have made records retention more manageable—yet at the same time more complex. Particularly in terms of safeguarding records, law firms must be alert to the perils as well as the promise that electronic technology brings to records management and retention.

It is a given that every law firm should be backing up electronic data regularly—every day, if at all possible—and storing backup data files off-site. This site should preferably be in another city or region to mitigate the impact of widespread disaster. It also goes without saying that there should be clear requirements for what is backed up and how often the backup procedure is done. As key elements of their electronic systems, firms should verify backups and test the ability to restore files. Make sure the entire procedure works: the physical transfer from the backup storage facility as well as electronic transfer over the Internet.

A first-level records-management strategy is to scan everything, keep the scanned electronic files in multiple locations for security, and then shred everything except important originals like contracts. As always, before embarking on such a strategy, check the rules and specific time periods in your jurisdiction for storing and destroying client files. If the stipulated storage time has lapsed, destroy the paper files by shredding the hard copies through the services of a company that assures security in the shredding process.

It is important to note that with cloud computing, where software and servers are owned by service providers and reside in a remote cloud location, firms have no direct control over data storage. This can be a problem—particularly if specialized legal software is not backed up on different servers—because cloud computing services have already suffered major service breakdowns that make data unavailable.

§ 30.02.3 Maintain Confidentiality

Rule 1.6 ("Confidentiality of Information") details each lawyer's responsibility to preserve client confidentiality. However, in the world of technology, there are many ways in which that confidentiality may be compromised. Your computer system could be hacked or otherwise threatened by criminal activity. An annual survey of businesses and professional organizations conducted jointly by the Federal Bureau of Investigation and the Computer Security Institute found that 90 percent of survey participants suffered a computer security breach. Law firms should examine data security and encryption procedures to make sure that electronic transmission of backup files is protected from hackers and other security breaches.

In addition, the many lawyers using smartphones and wireless laptops potentially expose client information to anyone who can access the wireless connection. Several years ago, the State Bar of California issued Opinion No. 2010-179 to address this issue. The opinion emphasized that wireless connections should have a reasonable level of security, which should include the use of precautions such as file encryption. It is essential to ensure that wireless transmission of client files and messages has legal protection—equal to that for phone calls and stored computer files—against third-party interception and unauthorized access.

Security is also a concern for firms that use cloud computing. Although no major cloud computing data breaches have been publicized, that possibility exists. The firm that uses cloud computing does so knowing that it may have security problems. It's a virtual risk that requires careful evaluation.

§ 30.03 Action Plan

- Maximize information technology return on investment.
- Employ technology to meet, at the least, minimum standards of competence.
- Address issues of file safeguarding and confidentiality.

PART VII

Operating Your Law Practice

CHAPTER 31

A Checklist for Moving Your Law Firm

They're very tight with office supplies in our office. If you need a legal pad, it's easier to hire a lawyer and borrow one from him.

—Gene Perret, *Business Humor*

Chapter Checklist

- o The Decision to Move
- o New-Space Planning
- o Premove Planning
- o The Move
- o After the Move
- o Action Plan

Sooner or later, almost every law firm, large and small, faces the necessity of making an office move. Regardless of the size of the law firm, an office move is a complicated and difficult project and requires considerable thought, preplanning, and coordination well in advance of the actual move. An office move can be compared to preparing a meal for one hundred people or developing a game plan for a sports contest—each has a number of different yet interrelated ingredients or elements that must be present for success. No military leader would consider taking an army into battle without a plan for logistics, troop movement, and battle formation. An office move is a battle, and you must plan well for that battle!

Use this chapter as a checklist of things to consider and do in preparing to move your law firm. This is intended to be a guide. As with any map, you must fill in the gaps based on your own journey.

§ 31.01 The Decision to Move

§ 31.01.1 Establish an Initial Timeline

Establishing a timeline (see Figure 31.1) at the beginning of the move process provides you with a tool to focus your efforts and track the various elements of the move. The timeline at first may consist only of (1) the date the decision to move was made, (2) the expiration date of your current lease, and (3) the anticipated date of the actual move. As you proceed through the moving project, you will add elements as they occur and continue to refine your actual move date.

It will also be useful for you to take some time to "visualize" the move. As you visualize, think about various details or elements of the move (no matter how trivial they may seem) and write them down. Continue to refine your list as you go along through the process and add these elements to your timeline.

The form of the timeline should be whatever works best for you, but consider keeping the timeline in a notebook where you can maintain the supporting details.

Also, think about having a large board that can be posted as a visual reminder to everyone of the status of the move. Note that the actual date of the move is not the last date on your timeline. You will be adding elements that must be considered after the move date—for example, "Inspect old suite after the move."

§ 31.01.2 Locate New Space

You or your firm has decided to move. Your next job is to begin the process of finding new space.

Before you begin, however, you have some homework to do. Prepare a list of the reasons that your firm is moving; be specific. Add to that list the features that your firm is looking for in new space—again, be specific. You might want to conduct a survey of the staff and lawyers asking them about features that they want or do not want in the new space. Specifically, you want their input on such things as the number of electrical outlets in their space, the location of data and telephone cables, and the proximity of copiers and fax machines and other basic functional items. Make sure that all of the "powers" sign off on the list before beginning your search. This list will be a tool to share with brokers and leasing agents as a qualifier for the space that they want to show you. This entire process can be a long and difficult one, and anything that you can do to organize and maintain the direction of the project is necessary.

§ 31.01.3 Negotiate for New Space

As you negotiate for new space, have three factors locked firmly in mind: (1) know exactly what you can afford, (2) know exactly which features you are looking for and which ones are the most critical, and (3) know exactly what your obligations are before you sign a new lease.

Several important items to consider during the space negotiations are as follows:

- *Tenant improvements and betterments (TIBs).* These are the improvements that are made to the space for your occupancy. The TIBs can be paid for by the landlord, by the tenant, or by both. TIBs are a negotiable item.
- *A space planner.* Oftentimes, a landlord will offer the use of its space-planning personnel, but you can negotiate to use your own as well.
- *A contractor.* As with the space planner, the landlord may have a contractor that it uses regularly in the building. This is not a bad option to consider as the contractor will know the landlord and the building, and therefore the work can proceed more quickly and without you having to serve as the go-between.
- *Free rent.* Sometimes, depending upon the availability of space for rent and the rental market in general, you may be able to negotiate for free rent. Essentially this means that the landlord offers you anywhere from a month to several months of occupancy in your space rent free as an inducement for you to sign a lease. Know your rental market before you begin negotiations with a landlord! Check with other law firms that have moved recently to see what they were able to obtain in the way of rents and rent concessions.
- *Tenant broker.* This is a commercial real estate broker who represents only tenants, not landlords. You may wish to consider retaining a tenant broker to provide needed assistance to reduce your commitment of time in locating and negotiating for new space.

Finally, please remember that the terms of the lease, the rent, the TIBs, the space planner, the contractor, and most all other items can be and are subject to negotiation.

§ 31.01.4 Set a Moving Date

Set a tentative moving date. However, the only way that you will be able to establish an accurate moving date is to know exactly when (1) the new space will be available to you; (2) the improvements (TIBs) to the new space will be completed (allow for overruns, changes, etc.); and (3) the utilities (i.e., telephone, fax, network) are actually connected. The size of your firm and the scope of the TIBs are major factors to consider. Usually, the larger the firm and the more extensive the TIBs, the greater the chances are for delays. Plan for them!

§ 31.01.5 Develop a Moving Budget

Any office move has a cost associated with it. That cost represents numerous individual expenses that your firm will incur as part of the move. It is imperative that you develop an accurate and complete budget for the move, or you may find yourself out of money even before you have moved!

Your moving budget will need to include a separate line item for everything associated with the move, including printing, moving company, refreshments for staff and movers, telephones, computer moves, old-space cleanup, repairs for both old and new space, furniture repair, and numerous other items. You must think through each phase of your move and identify each of these expense items and assign an accurate and realistic value to each one. The budget should be developed early in the process, and it should be preapproved by the management committee. You will be required to amend and revise the budget to reflect changes and unanticipated expense items.

§ 31.02 New-Space Planning

§ 31.02.1 Plan New-Space Improvements

You should have already developed some basic information for improvements for your new space from the criteria you developed in conjunction with searching for the space. Now is the time to refine those criteria into the actual improvements that you will require. It is essential that you ensure that your firm will "fit" into the new space. The best way to do that is to work with a space planner who is familiar with commercial space planning and with law firms. You should work closely with the space planner so that the final plan accurately reflects your initial criteria, the tenant improvement budget, and a plan that is practical.

One person in the firm should be given the authority to coordinate with the landlord's representative, the space planner, the contractor(s), and the mover. This person will be the only person who can initiate change orders. It is also essential that you keep the landlord fully aware of the status of tenant improvements.

§ 31.02.2 Establish What Goes Where

The space plan has to account for all of the items that you are planning to move. Make a list of everything that is to be moved and locate the items on a floor plan of your new space. Be sure that you have room for every item that you plan to move (and/or add).

In the course of developing the space plan for the new office, you may find that certain items are not going to fit properly, requiring a decision either to replace them with items that will fit or to dispose of them before the actual move takes place. (Do not pay to move something that you are not going to use; dispose of it before the move.)

§ 31.02.3 Determine Location of Telephone, Electrical, and Computer Hookups

Err in the direction of too many hookups! While this may seem a basic necessity, many firms move into new space and find that the number and location of the various hookups are inadequate. Plan for various scenarios of where desks, computers, and telephones may be located (some last-minute furniture relocations may be a possibility).

If using Wi-Fi for wireless connections, ensure that your current Wi-Fi unit will be sufficient to adequately reach all work spaces in the new location before making the move.

§ 31.03 Premove Planning

§ 31.03.1 Create a Move Manual

In addition to posting the timeline on a bulletin board, you should prepare and maintain a move manual (see Figure 31.2). The move manual will include the supporting documents and information associated with each element of the timeline. The manual should be set up in a logical and detailed fashion. It will be a tool that anyone could pick up in your absence to know quickly the status of each element of the timeline.

The move manual should include a copy of the new lease; a copy of the space plan; individual pages indicating the layout of furniture, computers, telephones, and other equipment; the mover's contract; moving specs; and all details of each element of the timeline.

Publishing a move manual for your lawyers and staff will enable you to keep them informed of the move's status as well as advising them of what is expected of each of them during its progression. If they are informed about the status of the move on a regular basis, you will have fewer questions to answer. In a law firm that is prone to rumors and gossip, a well-informed group usually means a happier group!

§ 31.03.2 Solicit Moving Bids and Hire a Moving Company

When you have established a tentative move date, it is time to interview moving companies. You should develop a list of potential movers and attempt to perform due diligence on each before you contact them.

Have a firm plan in mind for the move, and prepare a schematic of your existing space and new space before you meet with the movers. Obtain from your current landlord and from your new landlord their written requirements for conducting moves, including insurance and bonding requirements, time of moves, loading dock and elevator availability, safety requirements for protecting floors and elevators, and any other related requirements. You should assemble a packet for each potential mover so that each has the same information. (These specifications may change later and will require updating as necessary.)

Prepare a detailed request for proposal (RFP) to be distributed to each potential mover that you contact. The RFP will enable you to evaluate each proposal on an apples-to-apples basis. It can be helpful if you obtain some preliminary information from movers so that your RFP is written in a format that works for the moving companies.

Keep in mind that everything a mover does for you has a cost. Therefore, you must be sure that you understand each mover's proposal completely. Some things to consider are the following:

- Can the move be made in one day?
- Are there any breakdown and setup charges for furniture and equipment?
- What are the costs for packing materials?
- Will there be any special charges by either landlord with respect to the move?
- Will the mover charge for storage if the move cannot be made in one day?
- For what and how will the mover charge you for overtime if the move exceeds the projected time period?

Make sure that you obtain a certificate of insurance from the selected moving company that names the landlords of the current space and the new space as well as your law firm before the day of the move.

§ 31.03.3 Factor in Lead Time for Ordering Furniture, Equipment, and Supplies

If you are ordering any new furniture, equipment, or special supplies, be sure to factor the lead time for delivery into your timeline and moving date. Most furniture, unless stock, has at least several weeks' lead time. Equipment and supplies may vary depending on the level of specialization that you require.

§ 31.03.4 Order Printed Firm Materials

As with furniture, equipment, and special supplies, stationery, business cards, brochures, websites, billing forms, computer macros, and other printed firm materials take time. So, design and order early! Again, factor these into your timeline.

§ 31.03.5 Order Packing Supplies

In your moving RFP, require that the potential movers estimate what packing materials you will need and what the cost will be on a per-item basis. You may then compare their costs with what you might be able to purchase independently of the mover.

§ 31.03.6 Schedule Telephone and Computer Services

It is imperative that you schedule the installation of any mechanical or technical equipment such as computers and telephones far in advance of the actual move date. With probable delays in equipment shipping and installation scheduling, this could be a major factor in determining your actual move date.

Do not delay in setting up your computer and telephone installation dates and establishing the requirements for service. The sooner you establish a plan for the move for these services, the better your chances are of a successful and error-free transition. The last thing you need is to complete the move and then find out that the Internet is not up and running, the telephone system was not installed or the phones are in but all the features are not working, or voice mail is not reestablished.

Making sure that the telephones are installed is not enough. If your phone system and telephone service providers are different companies, get them together and make sure that they both understand what has to happen and when. Make them both confirm it in writing.

Determine if your current telephone switch is adequate for both your current needs as well as future needs; this would be the ideal time to upgrade if necessary. If you are using T1 lines or plan to upgrade to T1 lines, the lead time is important and a critical factor, so coordinate early with your service providers.

If you are changing telephone numbers, leave your old main number active with a recorded message advising callers of the change for an appropriate period of time. And try out any crossover measures; do not just accept that they will work.

If you are maintaining your same telephone numbers, be sure that at least a day or two before the move you change your main voice mail recording to alert callers of the date of the move and give them an alternate number (an answering service or a pager number) to call if they experience problems.

§ 31.03.7 Handle Other Notifications

In addition to telephone and computer service companies, there are a number of other potential groups and individuals that should be included in your notification procedures:

- *Clients.* Even though you may be able to complete your move over a weekend and without interruption to your normal working hours, anticipate the unexpected! It is possible that a client will have an emergency and need to speak to someone immediately while you are moving. With this in mind, let your clients know what you are doing and give them the ability to reach the firm if necessary. Chances are that no client will need the emergency contact number, but if one does, you will be prepared.
- *Insurance agent/broker.* Do not forget to notify your insurance agent/broker of your pending move before the move. Your property

and general liability insurance policy may temporarily cover your move to a new location without notification, but you will probably have new values for furniture, electronic data processing (EDP) equipment, TIBs, valuable papers, and off-site storage that should be changed in conjunction with the move. In fact, you should have already requested your agent/broker to review your new lease before you signed it. Why? Your new lease will have insurance provisions for which you become obligated once it is signed. This obligation may require additional and/or different coverages than what you already have. Sometimes, the newer insurance requirements are difficult to meet. A landlord typically uses a standard lease form that is not changed or altered that often. You might, for example, be required to provide flood and/or earthquake coverage when in fact that coverage is not available. There are other lease provisions that may have an impact on your insurance requirements, such as the new TIBs that are built into your space. Are you required to insure them, or is the landlord? What value is set for those TIBs and by whom? Do you have to insure the full value or an amount that decreases annually? Your insurance agent/broker should be able to review your proposed new lease and provide you with an analysis of the insurance requirements that may be important deal points for the lease negotiation.

- *All vendors.* As part of premove planning, prepare a list of all of the vendors that serve your firm. Using your move bulletin or a letter or some other form of notice, keep your vendors informed of your move. The last thing you want is the bottled water delivery or your coffee service to show up at the old location and not the new one! Keep the vendors on top of any last-minute changes as well. They will appreciate it, and ultimately so will you.
- *Bar associations and law schools.* You should have a list of the various bar associations that your lawyers belong to and the law schools that you deal with in your recruiting program. Let them know when and where you are moving and how to reach you. Give them advance notice so that they are able to change their mailing and computer records.
- *Local media.* Prepare in advance a press release to the local news, business, and legal media. This is an excellent opportunity to obtain some free PR and perhaps to announce your open house at the new space. If you tell people about your new office and invite them to an open house or simply to stop by for a visit, they will come.
- *Others.* Other notifications should include appropriate taxing authorities, all publication providers, Internet listing services, retirees and COBRA participants (insurance purposes), opposing counsel, courts, and post office(s).

§ 31.03.8 Set Up Tagging/Labeling Plan

Develop a plan to color code and tag all files, furniture, equipment, and artwork that will be moved. This plan should include floor plans and diagrams for the spotting of all items to be moved. Share this plan in advance with your mover. Usually, your mover can assist you in setting this up to effect a smooth move for everyone and everything.

§ 31.03.9 Assign New Parking Cards and Building Passes

You should establish a plan to distribute new parking cards, suite keys, building passes, and other related items to everyone before the move. And be sure to collect the old versions of these items. Work with both landlords on setting up this plan as they will have ideas to help make the process efficient and convenient for everyone.

§ 31.03.10 Review Vacations and Personal Days

Review your vacation- and personal-day schedules for lawyers and staff. Obviously, you want to have all hands available for the move. If it is unavoidable that certain lawyers or staff members will be absent, set up your guidelines for packing their things to be moved. You may want to place the responsibility upon them to accomplish the packing of their files before they take a vacation or a personal day. Have a contingency plan for those people who might miss the packing or moving day for inescapable reasons.

§ 31.03.11 Schedule Premove Meetings

As often as necessary, hold premove meetings with all hands or in logical groups to keep everyone current on the progress of the move.

§ 31.03.12 Schedule Premove Inspections of New Space

Try to schedule at least four inspections of your new space prior to the actual move date. The first inspection should include your landlord representative, telephone company representative, computer network installer, and copier/fax equipment representative. The purpose of the visit is to familiarize everyone with the space and which improvements are planned. You will want their input as it pertains to their services.

The second inspection will probably be with the mover(s) that you are considering so that they can better provide you with a proposal. Use your judgment as to whether you meet all prospective movers at the new space together or individually. There should be no problem doing the former if time is a factor for you.

The third inspection should be with the landlord representative, telephone company representative, computer network installer, and copier/fax equipment representative after they have all indicated that their installation work is complete.

The fourth inspection should be made by you and the landlord representative the day before the actual move to ensure that any last-minute details are resolved and that the space is actually ready for occupancy.

By no means should you feel limited to making *only* four visits to your new space. Make as many visits as your particular situation requires.

§ 31.03.13 Schedule an All-Hands Space Visit

Prior to the move, and preferably when the space is ready, schedule an all-hands visit to the new space so that everyone has the opportunity to familiarize themselves with their new home prior to the actual move. This will benefit you from a morale standpoint and also help everyone better visualize where to place their furniture, files, and other equipment.

§ 31.03.14 Obtain Acknowledgments

Be certain that you obtain written acknowledgments from your current landlord and new landlord, mover(s), service providers, and others of the date, the time, and their expectations regarding the pending move.

§ 31.04 The Move

§ 31.04.1 Publish the Moving Schedule

As you refine your tentative moving schedule, you should post or publish it for everyone. When you have a final schedule, publish or post that, too. The final moving schedule should include each person's responsibilities regarding their work space; packing, coding, and tagging instructions; instructions for daily operations other than moving responsibilities; and any other information that will make everyone's transition to the new space a positive experience.

§ 31.04.2 Appoint Move Coordinators

Whether you have one or multiple floors to move, appoint "move coordinators" to assist in the move. The move coordinators should have a copy of the move manual and be as versed in the moving plans as you are. You may want to issue cell phones or some other communications devices to each of them. If you have the personnel, assign one coordinator with a cell phone to stay with the movers, a second one to stay in the old space, and a third to be present at all times in the new space.

§ 31.04.3 Post Color-Coded Floor Plans

At both the old space and the new space, post color-coded floor plans, work space layouts, and file locator plans to assist the movers in both picking up and locating items. This effort will save time, confusion, and extra work on everyone's part.

§ 31.04.4 Determine Optimum Order

You may want to consider staging your move so that computer equipment and other related equipment is moved first and set up in the new space before furniture, files, and other items are moved. This will help make the move flow more smoothly.

§ 31.04.5 Schedule Technicians/Maintenance Staff

On the day(s) of the move, schedule your vendors to have technicians available at the new space to assist with any difficulties that might occur in the course of the move. You may want to consider having maintenance personnel and handyman personnel available to assemble desks and assist with any other minor repairs or cleanup.

§ 31.04.6 Address Security Issues

Depending on your location and situation, you should consider assigning security guards at both the old location and the new one, as well as assigning some form of visible temporary identification during the move.

§ 31.05 After the Move

§ 31.05.1 Clean Up Old Space

The lease for your old space probably will require you to leave it in "broom-clean condition," and it may require you to schedule certain repairs prior to releasing you from the space. Review your old lease and schedule the cleanup and repairs as may be necessary. You may want to have this completed on the moving day after everything has been removed. This will require prescheduling the personnel and/or service vendors. You should schedule a walk-through of your old space with personnel and service vendors before you move so that they know exactly what needs to be done and will have the proper materials on hand.

§ 31.05.2 Inspect Old Space with Landlord

When you feel that you have completed all of the items under the terms of your old lease, schedule a walk-through of the old space with your landlord. Prepare a "punch list" of any items that have to be completed, and then schedule that work. Again, walk through the space with the landlord until the punch list is completed.

§ 31.05.3 Obtain Certification and Release of Old Space

When you and the landlord agree that the punch list items have been completed, certify that fact in writing with the landlord, and request that the landlord provide you with a formal, written release from the space.

§ 31.06 Action Plan

- Develop a plan to move.
- Implement the plan.
- Make your move!

FIGURE 31.1

Timeline for Moving

No.	Item	Due Date	Responsible	Comments/ Status	Completed
I. THE DECISION TO MOVE					
1	Establish an initial timeline				
2	Locate new space				
3	Negotiate for new space				
4	Set a moving date				
5	Develop a moving budget				
II. NEW-SPACE PLANNING					
6	Plan new-space improvements				
7	Establish what goes where				
8	Determine location of telephone, electrical, and computer hookups				
III. PREMOVE PLANNING					
9	Create a move manual				
10	Solicit moving bids and hire a moving company				
11	Factor in lead time for ordering furniture, equipment, and supplies				
12	Order printed firm materials				
13	Order packing supplies				

No.	Item	Due Date	Responsible	Comments/ Status	Completed
14	Schedule telephone and computer services				
15	Handle other notifications				
16	Set up tagging/ labeling plan				
17	Assign new parking cards and building passes				
18	Review vacations and personal days				
19	Schedule premove meetings				
20	Schedule premove inspections of new space				
21	Schedule an all-hands space visit				
22	Obtain acknowledgments				
IV. THE MOVE					
23	Publish the moving schedule				
24	Appoint move coordinators				
25	Post color-coded floor plans				
26	Determine optimum order				
27	Schedule technicians/maintenance staff				
28	Address security issues				

continued

No.	Item	Due Date	Responsible	Comments/ Status	Completed
V. AFTER THE MOVE					
29	Clean up old space				
30	Inspect old space with landlord				
31	Obtain certification and release of old space				
VI. GOING OUT ON YOUR OWN					
32	Review existing partnership agreement				
33	Know your financial obligations				
34	Establish a relationship with a bank and a banker				
35	Select a CPA				
36	Establish a relationship with an insurance agent/broker				
37	Create a business plan				
38	Develop a forms file				
39	Review and select technology				
40	Develop your client and related files list				
41	Determine which clients and matters you will take				

No.	Item	Due Date	Responsible	Comments/ Status	Completed
42	Draft a client contact letter				
43	Prepare substitution of attorney letters				
44	Develop a retainer letter				
45	Develop a retainer agreement				
46	Prepare a letter to colleagues in the firm				
47	Interview staff				
48	Determine list of publications to be ordered				
49	Arrange for off-site storage				
50	Register domain name				
51	Facilitate website development and choose an Internet service provider				
52	Determine type of business to set up				
53	Develop a case file–numbering scheme				
54	Advise firm of departure				

FIGURE 31.2

Sample Move Manual Page

[NAME OF LAW FIRM] MOVING MANUAL		
No.	**Item: Establish a Timeline**	**Due Date**
XX	Responsible: Office Administrator	January 23, 2013
NOTES		
Date	**Comments**	**Status**
October 10, 2012	Working on this now. Expect to have completed on Friday.	Pending

CHAPTER 32

Your Own Island: Opening a Home-Based Practice*

Professor: I'm making notes for a book. It's to be a chronicle of our adventures on the island.... I think it's a book people will want to buy, don't you?

Gilligan: Sure, I'll buy one. I'm dying to find out what happens to us.

—*Gilligan's Island*

Chapter Checklist

- o Packing for Your Trip to the Island
- o Crew on the Island
- o Ethics of the Island
- o Happily Stranded on the Island
- o Action Plan

Technology has changed a lot since the second edition of Ed Poll's book was printed in 2002, making that final chapter on home-based law practice obsolete. To give you some insight, the second edition included a floppy disk at the back of the book—when was the last time that you used a floppy disk?

*This chapter is written in the first person based on the experiences of the contributor. See the About the Contributors for more information on the contributor.

Thus, an update is in order. To find a context for today's law office from home, let's look at *Gilligan's Island*, a television comedy series in the 1960s. Robert Jarvis, a professor of law at Nova Southeastern University, wrote an article in 1998 for the *Santa Clara Law Review* focusing on the legal issues that occurred on and around the island, and he concluded that "one would be hard pressed to find a group of characters more in need of a lawyer."[1] With that in mind, what would a modern lawyer need to practice law from an island?

I worked for a short time as a contract attorney for dependency cases for the juvenile court. When I interviewed with the chief judge, she told me that this job was one "you could do out of the back of your truck." Similarly, with the tremendous technological advances since 2002, there has been a paradigm shift such that a traditional physical law office is not essential. More lawyers than ever before have a virtual law practice—that is, they practice from home offices or alternate working spaces primarily through the Internet.

The concept involves minimal expenditures on physical office space; contact with clients or professional colleagues largely by e-mail, Internet portal, or telephone; and the use of online "virtual assistants" at another remote location for staff support. Although there are some ethical issues to consider in setting up a virtual law practice, a home-based practice can be a cost-efficient, productive, and highly satisfactory and successful experience for both lawyers and their clients.

§ 32.01 Packing for Your Trip to the Island

You will need a few things to properly outfit your virtual law practice.

§ 32.01.1 Computer

Perhaps the most important thing to pack for your trip to the island is a computer, which can be a desktop or a laptop. There are a variety of storage methods for retrieving documents and other files when not at home, so a laptop is not essential. Things change fast in the computer arena, so you should purchase the fastest computer with the most memory that you can afford. Adding more memory will give you the best return for performance. Your processing speed will be largely limited by your disk drive and how fragmented your files are. For a laptop, you want an Intel Core i7 with at least a 2.4 GHz processor, 8 GB in memory, and 750 GB in hard-drive storage. Your operating system will depend on your computer choice (Windows or Mac). You will also need a video card and audio capability. In order to videoconference, it's helpful to have a camera and microphone built in as well. You can custom design your computer to fit your needs, and many

1. Robert M. Jarvis, *Legal Tales from Gilligan's Island*, 39 Santa Clara L. Rev. 185, 204 (1998).

online and in-store sites will help you do this. You can pick the best choice for performance and design and include features such as Wi-Fi and Bluetooth. I suggest that you research this by reviewing websites that have comparisons, such as www.toptenreviews.com, http://reviews.cnet.com, www.pcmag.com, and www.consumerreports.org.

You may also want a mouse since it can be difficult to navigate a laptop with the touch pad, especially for those of us who remember floppy disks.

§ 32.01.2 Internet Connectivity

On our island, or home office, we will also need Internet connectivity in order to make that computer worthwhile. Many cable or Internet providers will set this up for you at your house, along with your television and other services. I have a network at my home with a modem to which more than six computers can connect, either with a cable or wirelessly. Once you have a wireless connection set up with a password, the Internet is easily available for family and friends by sharing your password. You can access this anywhere in your house and even outside. You should have a password so that you don't unwittingly share your Internet and possibly your privacy with your neighbors.

§ 32.01.3 Printer/Scanner/Copier/Fax Machine

Now that you have your computer and Internet connection, an all-in-one printer/scanner/copier/fax machine will be most helpful. You can purchase a machine that is wireless and serves a variety of needs. As long as your computer has a wireless connection to your printer, you can complete documents while lying outside in your hammock and send them to the printer inside the house. Including a fax in this machine is not necessary since there is an online subscription service that allows you to receive faxes and have them sent directly to your computer. Online facsimile technology converts the fax into a readable document on your computer. I found at least five online fax providers in a quick search. I suggest that you use a review service to determine the best choice for you.

§ 32.01.4 Smartphone

In order to be productive inside and outside your home office, I also recommend a smartphone, a camera (which may be in your smartphone), and a tablet or other mobile device. Some mobile devices can be useful for completing tasks at home and then accessing them by storing them in the cloud. Not the fluffy white clouds over our island, but data storage by third-party virtual servers, which you can access remotely with your Internet connection and your storage password. Remember the floppy disk that I mentioned at the beginning of this chapter? With storage in the cloud, you don't need a physical tool such as a USB drive to access your data.

§ 32.01.5 Software Program

An office software program is required. You need one with capability for documents, spreadsheets, and presentations. I use Microsoft Office, and I have taught myself to use it. Community colleges offer classes to make you proficient in different software programs.

§ 32.01.6 Online Services

In order to complete legal research, there are free and subscription services. For example, LexisNexis has a site, http://lexisweb.com, for free online legal research. There are also very good websites maintained by law schools, such as Cornell Law School. Cornell supports the Legal Information Institute, a nonprofit group that provides legal resources at no cost. Many states also provide services to bar members that allow them to complete free legal research. New Mexico is one of those states, and it includes access to New Mexico and federal legal libraries, among others.

Courts now have electronic filing capability, so pleadings can be e-filed from your computer or another location. Electronic filing can be done in federal court and some state courts and with some federal and state agencies. In Arizona, the AZTurboCourt application is available for law firms to file civil documents in certain counties. Check with your state bar association to determine the rules for e-filing.

You also need to be sure to back up your files, and this can be done either with an external hard drive or remotely. There is a plethora of services available in the cloud. These services offer different costs for personal and small-business use. Once again, you need to research different options using comparison sites or online reviews.

§ 32.01.7 Office Furniture

Finally, you should also consider purchasing a comfortable chair, although many people work standing up with a stand-up desk. I found a variety of these chairs and work spaces in an online search.

§ 32.02 Crew on the Island

A virtual assistant should be able to conduct any needed support activity electronically from a remote location. Digital and electronic technology make available highly educated talent, whether halfway around the world or in a nearby city, allowing law firms to reduce by up to 80 percent the cost of the following:

- Transcription of voice files from depositions, trials, and hearings
- Accounting support in the preparation of time sheets and billing materials
- Data entry for marketing, conflicts, and contact management

- Litigation support graphics
- Legal research, including case citation summaries and patent searches
- Review and due diligence of business documents
- Secretarial services

§ 32.03 Ethics of the Island

Certainly there is no formal ethical prohibition against having a virtual office. In fact, the eLawyering Task Force of the ABA's Law Practice Management Section has prepared guidelines for conducting a virtual practice: "To be successful in the coming era, lawyers will need to know how to practice over the Web [and] manage client relationships in cyberspace," the task force stated.[2] The task force further noted that "eLawyering encompasses all the ways in which lawyers can do their work using the Web and associated technologies."[3] Nevertheless, there are ethical concerns involved with a virtual practice. These concerns include service, quality, and confidentiality.

§ 32.03.1 Service

Even if a virtual law office or law practice is acceptable, a virtual lawyer is not. The attractions of a virtual office must be balanced by a consideration of its limitations.

Keep in mind that while the flexibility offered by voice mail, e-mail, and other electronic tools is real, it can become dangerous when used as a replacement for client contact. A major differentiating factor for most clients is the "care and feeding" offered by lawyers. No matter what technology makes possible, it is not the answer if it creates a situation in which the lawyer is either not as invested in or is perceived as not as invested in the client's case.

When it comes to a virtual practice, value is determined by the client, not the lawyer. If lawyers are perceived as inaccessible, fees become an issue, and client complaints increase. The ability to respond quickly is essential to answering the visibility question. Clients may be more inclined to generosity in terms of the location of a solo practice if they have the assurance that they can always get in touch when they need to.

As always, technology is only a tool; it is not the goal. Lawyers with virtual practices must always strategically use technology to address the needs of their clients. In reality, though, doesn't this same principle apply to *all* lawyers?

---

2. Law Practice Mgmt. Section, Am. Bar Ass'n, *What Is eLawyering?*, AM. BAR ASS'N, Nov. 21, 2011, Apps.americanbar.org/dch/committee.cfm?com=EP024500.

3. *Id.*

§ 32.03.2 Quality

Although legal work may be produced remotely and delivered electronically using virtual assistants, as always it is the individual lawyer who bears full responsibility for quality and completeness.

§ 32.03.3 Confidentiality

Along with the responsibility for service and quality comes the need for confidentiality. Wireless laptops and smartphones are prerequisites for virtual practice. But the eLawyering Task Force has emphasized the need for a secure, encrypted website for maintaining client confidentiality in representation, in retainer agreement terms, and in online payment. An inadvertent disclosure of privileged or confidential information or work product through insecure wireless connections would have severe consequences, and you need to guard against this at all costs.

§ 32.04 Happily Stranded on the Island

You can create your own legal career in an environment that makes you happy. With incomes shrinking and access to information on the Internet expanding, many people assume that they cannot afford a lawyer and that they can do just as good a job for themselves using what they find on the web. If lawyers embody the efficiency and low cost of the Internet while bringing their creativity and experience to the table, they will maintain their professional positions even if those positions are virtual ones. My home with my husband and four children is my Gilligan's Island. If I can be productive with four rowdy teenagers, I have the utmost confidence that you will be successful, too.

§ 32.05 Action Plan

- Pack (lightly) for your trip to the island.
- Understand the difference between a virtual law office (good) and a virtual lawyer (not good).
- Address security issues.
- Enjoy the benefits of a virtual practice.

CHAPTER 33

Case Study: Starting a Family Law Practice*

A wise man will make more opportunities than he finds.

—Francis Bacon

The right man [woman] is the one who seizes the moment.

—Johann Wolfgang von Goethe, *Faust*

Chapter Checklist

- o The Advice
- o Implementation
- o Action Plan

Starting my own family law practice ultimately became a destination on a journey with many stops along the way. I started my professional career as a law clerk for a federal district court judge. Following my clerkship, I became an associate at a prestigious "megafirm." After a year there, I concluded that to really learn family law, I needed to be taught by lawyers who practiced only in that arena. The lawyers at my firm were terrific litigators, but they did not have substantive or procedural knowledge of

*This chapter is written in the first person based on the experiences of the contributor. See the preface for more information on the contributor.

family law. Thus, my next move was to join a family law "boutique" firm. During my fifth year as an associate in this family law boutique, I realized that I wanted to move in a direction that would enable me to have more control over my time. I knew a number of lawyers who specialized in family law and who had acquired their practices by associating with senior practitioners moving toward retirement once they had someone in place to take over the existing business. I knew and respected just such a senior practitioner, and we worked out an arrangement that complemented both of our objectives—mine of ultimately assuming an ongoing practice and his of phasing out toward retirement. Unfortunately, unexpected events occurred within a few months of our arrangement that prevented the idea from reaching its implementation.

I now had to revisit the choices of my career path and decide what steps to take next. A number of partners in both larger and solo practices approached me. I was blessed with many options, but none felt exactly right.

So I solicited the input, feedback, and advice of my mentors. Across the board, the advice offered was, "Start your own firm."

§ 33.01 The Advice

What? Where? How? Here, the advice was not unanimous.

One mentor advised that I only handle smaller cases, building a high-volume practice by charging a modest and competitive hourly fee. Others suggested that I "just go for it" and let the firm's profile evolve on its own. I realized that what I really wanted deep down was both to utilize the analytical and litigation skills that I had developed at my former firm and to start my own boutique.

While dancing around the question of what type of practice to establish, I also had to address logistical issues. Where would I locate my office? What type of office? Did I want my own private suite or a suite occupied by other professionals, sometimes described as an "executive suite"? And, if I selected the latter option, did I want to be one of several family law practitioners or unique in my area of service?

§ 33.01.1 Do You Really Want Your Own Firm?

Before you begin to address the specific issues of how to start a law practice, you should evaluate whether or not you are suited for firm leadership. The head of a firm must, by definition, be accountable for everything that occurs within the penumbra of the practice. The errors of secretaries, clerks, paralegals, associates, and associated counsel will be deemed, without exception, the errors of the head of the firm in the eyes of the client, the legal community, and the malpractice insurance carrier. If you are not ready to accept such accountability unequivocally, it might be wise to consider other professional options. In addition, if you are starting your own firm and hope that it will grow by adding other attorneys, you need to have a personality and attitude that will enable you to train and encourage those other professionals who will join you.

§ 33.01.2 Profiling the Desired Practice

In formulating a plan to start a law firm, you need to profile the services that the firm will offer. For example, in the family law field, there are two distinct ends of the spectrum.

At one end is the high-volume practice where lower hourly fees are charged for financially smaller cases with a likelihood of a quick turnaround. The practitioner pursuing this type of practice ideally would excel at and enjoy the procedural ins and outs of keeping a matter on a short-track schedule. For the most part, volume family law practitioners serve as sounding boards and legal advisers to their clients. Clients who do not have large estates and extraordinarily high incomes generally conclude that the cost of conducting discovery often will be greater than the amount of funds in controversy. Additionally, the smaller cases usually do not involve issues that require expert analysis and input. For financial reasons, lawyers who handle smaller cases generally do not engage in extensive correspondence in negotiating deals. It is more cost-effective to streamline the case on a litigation track. It is not uncommon for issues in these smaller cases to be resolved on the proverbial steps to the courthouse between the calendar call and the time that the case is set for hearing. The total fees that are generated by these smaller cases are generally in the low five figures. It is not unusual for a lawyer to be processing many of these cases at any given time. Such a practice demands extraordinary skills at calendaring and procedural compliance.

At the other end of the spectrum is the family law boutique firm, which in the family law context generally and for the purposes of this chapter, can be described as a firm that usually consists of not more than about a dozen lawyers and is dedicated to servicing high-profile, multi-issue divorces. The boutique firm generally has fewer cases than the high-volume firm, and those cases require more time spent on each case due to the magnitude of assets to be allocated, support to be paid, and other sometimes more esoteric issues to be addressed. The parties in these cases often play out their contentious custody issues in the public arena—they can afford to do so, or at least they think that they can.

Cases handled by a boutique family law practice can and often do remain active—that is, in the prejudgment stage—for many months, sometimes even years. A number of pretrial issues, such as the date of separation and date of valuation, may require pendente lite litigation, which can last for days; trials on these issues have been known to last for months. Typically, one or more experts are engaged on behalf of the client, including forensic accountants, mental health experts capable of conducting custody evaluations, vocational evaluators, real property appraisers, personal property appraisers, and so on. The client will need to be consulted frequently to make decisions, authorize a course of action, and otherwise be kept abreast of the status of his case. In the main, each individual case handled in this type of practice is labor intensive. It is not unusual for the fees that are generated in a case handled by a reputable firm to end up in the six- to seven-figure range, exclusive of the fees and costs incurred for the various experts.

Assuming that the goal is to handle high-end cases in a boutique setting (as distinguished from a small-case, high-volume practice), a "team" is generally needed. The team is a matter that should be addressed at the start. A natural solution might be for two or more lawyers to start the boutique firm as partners. However, a partner may not be desired, or a desired partner may not be available when you are getting your firm off the ground.

An alternative way of establishing a team might be to engage outside cocounsel or associate counsel on a case-by-case basis. This allows you to postpone the financial commitment of retaining associates. It also is a valuable means of networking within the family law community. In some cases, the client may engage the outside cocounsel directly, establishing a discrete billing process. In other cases, cocounsel or associated counsel can be retained by the firm on a case-by-case basis. Either way, the newly established firm is able to offer the capacity of team representation to prospective clients, which is especially useful in the situations in which the client requires or believes that there is a need for representation by a group rather than a solo practitioner.

Whether engaging cocounsel or associate counsel as a full-time partner or on a case-by-case basis, extreme care must be given to the potential for conflicts: each attorney involved in the case must be sure that his own client base has been fully reviewed to ensure that there are no conflicts in the representation and that any potential conflicts have been disclosed to the client.

Needless to say, between the strictly volume practice handling smaller-sized cases and the boutique practice handling larger, more complex cases, there is a wide variety of blended practices that accept both categories of cases. And, regardless of the initial evaluation of the case, any family law matter may morph into something else. A modest-income, modest-estate, "no-issues" case can explode at any time and demand lengthy and costly discovery and litigation. On the other hand, a case involving a celebrity spouse, millions of dollars, and children can settle before the petition for dissolution of marriage is filed. As a result, regardless of the practice profile desired for any given firm, you must be prepared to address the client's needs and demands, which could span the spectrum.

§ 33.01.3 Selecting the Location of the Practice

Almost every aspect of operating a new family law firm can be adjusted or otherwise fine-tuned after the firm has started, with one very critical exception: location.

When all else is equal, spouses who engage counsel for a dissolution of marriage want their lawyer to be conveniently accessible. Working clients, especially professionals, often select counsel with offices close to their own businesses. Similarly, homemakers and primary parents will prefer going to an office that does not necessitate crosstown travel.

There is one main exception to the general role that location plays in a client's selection of a lawyer. There have been instances in which wealthier or well-known clients from smaller towns may want to avoid the notoriety that might occur were the dissolution case to proceed in their hometown. And, for whatever reasons, Southern California clients from Palm Springs, San Diego, Orange County, and Santa Barbara on a regular basis retain counsel in Los Angeles.

The selection of a location for the office does not end with the geographic decision, however. There is the need to decide what type of physical office space best presents your desired image. You should be aware of the messages that can be relayed to a prospective client by the setting of the practice. The size of the office makes a statement. A large office with a conference table speaks to the potential need for team meetings. A smaller office might imply that things will be simpler, nonadversarial, more one-on-one. Fee-conscious clients may not want to feel that they are underwriting an imposing setting and might prefer going to a storefront office with free parking, while business moguls and celebrity spouses may find assurances in the prestige associated with a multipurpose, marble-and-glass high-rise with valet parking and might interpret the prominence of their counsel's office as representative of their prowess on the legal battlefield.

The expectations of potential clients play a major role in any lawyer's decision of where to locate an office, but not the only role. Your personal taste and professional style should be reflected in the office setting.

Additionally, you should consider with whom you want to share your work environment. If you intend to open a family law boutique on your own, selecting a suite occupied by other, similar practices may result in some competition, but it does offer easy access when a need arises for brainstorming or a sounding board for a plan of action or a legal interpretation. Additionally, you have a conveniently located pool of potential cocounsel and associated counsel. You are also well placed to take advantage of any referrals from the other family law attorneys in the suite.

One of the drawbacks to be anticipated in family law, however, is that one spouse may be reluctant to hire a lawyer in the same suite as the other spouse's counsel. Right or wrong, most divorcing spouses do not want to witness a friendly rapport between their respective adversaries, and space sharing can be perceived as inconsistent with adversarial acumen. On the other hand, there are divorcing spouses who perceive a benefit from having paired with counsel that do not have their own adversarial agendas to add to the fray.

Finally, keep in mind that technology has enabled the creation of the virtual firm, which enables lawyers to practice together, virtually, even though their physical offices may be located in different buildings or even in their individual homes. A number of office landlords have developed fully equipped offices and conference facilities that may be rented on a daily basis. With technology, this type of business "hoteling" could enable virtual firms to operate quite effectively. Only time will enable us to determine the actual feasibility of this approach and its success.

§ 33.01.4 Staff Considerations

Rarely can a lawyer establish a solo practice or a small firm without some assistance, if for no other reason than that the lawyer needs to focus his time on being a lawyer. Typing, filing, answering telephones, maintaining office supplies, establishing client trust accounts, dealing with equipment and electronic issues, and attending to accounts receivable and payable on a timely basis are all time-intensive. And regardless of how adept you are at providing a variety of routine office services, a potential client may look dimly on a lawyer attending to "nonlawyer" duties.

Part-time and temporary help can be secured directly or through employment agencies. Other ways of securing staff are through advertising and engaging the aid of a referral network (i.e., secretaries working for other lawyers). In addition, such work as document typing can now be outsourced to secretarial services that may be located anywhere in the "cloud," even as far away as India or the Philippines, where overnight word processing for U.S.-based lawyers is becoming commonplace.

If you want to focus exclusively on practicing law and recruiting clients, you might want to consider hiring an individual who has experience in setting up a professional office and overseeing—if not personally providing—the wide range of services needed to make an office run smoothly.

No matter how many staff people are needed—permanent, temporary, part-time, or some combination thereof—it is wise to have a full complement on hand before the first client walks in the door.

§ 33.01.5 Equipment Considerations

Whether you open a freestanding office, rent space in an executive suite, or operate "virtually," you will need to determine whether to address only your current needs or to invest in systems that are designed to handle expansion opportunities.

Keep in mind that in the digital age, file maintenance is going through major changes. Paper files are gradually being replaced by electronic or digital files maintained in on-site servers or in the cloud (off-site electronic file storage facilities provided by third-party vendors).

There are no exceptions to complying with filing deadlines based upon malfunctioning office equipment, and it is safe to assume that a client will not tolerate excuses based upon such limitations. As with the issues of appearance that affect a decision regarding office location and size, the appearance of an office with equipment problems needs to be taken into consideration when planning to open a new firm.

§ 33.01.6 Promoting the New Practice

The promotion of any practice, whether new or well established, is multidimensional. It involves an intertwined and interrelated process of networking, advertising, public relations, and other marketing activities (see parts II and III of this book for more on marketing).

- *Networking referral sources.* Asking a mentor's opinion about establishing a family law practice may be the first promotional act of a lawyer with respect to the new practice. It involves both marketing and networking since the mentor may be both a direct referral source and a networker for other referral sources. Referral sources are critical to the success of any firm. The building of a broad and active referral base can be promoted in a wide variety of ways, most of which are reflective of the personality of the lawyer. It is vital to keep in mind that anyone can be a referral source; therefore, plans to establish a new firm should be shared with every personal and professional contact. In my own experience, some of my best cases have been the result of referrals from hairstylists and other not-so-likely sources. Nurture your referral sources. At a bare minimum, thank them—in writing. Beyond thanks, referral sources need to be assured that you are worthy of their referrals. One dissatisfied client can end a referral relationship. If a client who has been referred from a primary referral source shows signs of wanting to discharge the firm or, alternatively, may need to be discharged by the firm prior to a resolution of the case, the lawyer should be the one to bring to the attention of the referral source the fact that the relationship between the referred client and the firm is not working out, without divulging privileged information.
- *Announcements and other mail pieces.* Printed announcements introducing a new law practice should be formal, regardless of the profile of the practice. The announcement mailing list would ideally include any person who might be considered a referral source. And because referral sources are people, the announcement mailing list should contain the names of individual people rather than merely the names of businesses. When creating the announcement mailing list, keep in mind that the list can be a valuable asset for the ongoing promotion of the firm: mailing holiday greeting cards, announcing professional personnel changes in the firm, and mailing or e-mailing periodic newsletters. Because mailing lists can serve many purposes, it is worth the investment of having the first list processed so that it can be duplicated, updated, and expanded on a frequent basis. The term *mail* in the digital age can mean a variety of things: "hard copies" sent via the U.S. postal system or private document-delivery companies such as FedEx and UPS, electronic mail (e-mail), and even communications via social media such as Facebook or Twitter. It is important to be thoughtful and thorough about getting the word out in the manner that you think works best both for you as the sender and for your recipients, keeping in mind that some recipients may not be as impacted by e-mail and are much more influenced by hard copies that they receive.
- *The public presence.* There are countless opportunities for you as a lawyer to establish a public presence in your community. You can serve as a speaker, volunteer for panels at professional seminars, serve on boards for various professional and charitable organizations, and more (see chapter 5 for more suggestions). Some less traditional ways for

lawyers to establish and maintain a public presence include golfing with a potential referral source and hosting luncheons, a periodic open house, or wine and cheese receptions. Any opportunity to establish or expand a public presence should be considered an opportunity to expand a referral base.

- *Paid advertising*. Paid advertisements in trade and other professional journals and periodicals announcing the formation of a new law firm or the expansion of an existing firm are a standard promotional tool. Because of the individual cost of each ad, it is wise to ascertain whether the target audience of the journal or periodical complements your intended target audience in a cost-effective way. For example, it may be smart for a firm with offices around the country to advertise in a national journal, but a family law boutique would make better use of its resources by advertising in local community or bar publications.
- *Use of promotion specialists*. Lawyers can orchestrate their own promotional or marketing activities, especially on a small scale. However, a lawyer looking for an expanded promotional campaign should consider consulting a promotional, marketing, or public relations expert. Keep in mind that most consultants are reluctant to provide do-it-yourself tips. Usually, the consultant needs to be retained to execute a campaign for a specified budget over a specified period of time.

§ 33.01.7 Expansion from Solo Practice to Partnership

Finding the perfect partner for an expanding business is not unlike finding the perfect partner for your personal life. Regardless of the formulas, tick lists, and other devices that can be used to compute compatibility, the only true test is time. And even time does not ensure enduring success. Nonetheless, there are some matters worthy of advance consideration by someone deliberating the formation of a partnership.

In addition to being compatible on a personal level, it is important that lawyers who are considering forming a partnership have complementary areas of strength. For some, this might mean that each lawyer can handle all areas of representation equally well. For others, it might mean that one lawyer's litigation skills are matched well by the other lawyer's drafting abilities. For still others, the partnership might be a perfect "good-guy/bad-guy" dynamic for both the courtroom and the mediation table.

Prospective partners should share a similar work ethic. If you are a lawyer who sets a high priority on providing top-quality client relations, you need to ascertain the nature of a prospective partner's client-relations skills. Similarly, compare the standards set by each lawyer for approving documents for filing, dress codes, and after-hours availability.

Finally, it is reasonable to anticipate periodic discord between even the most suitable of partners. Any lawyer planning to form or join a partnership should discuss with the prospective partner(s) procedures by which they will address disputes that will surely arise in the future. The more specific the procedure is, the easier it is to put it to work if or when a problem arises between partners. If your process includes arbitration and/or mediation in addressing such disputes, you should consider identifying the arbitrator and/or mediator upon whom you and your prospective partner(s) can agree. Moreover, you will be ahead of the game if your procedures can include the process for selecting an arbitrator and/or mediator if the arbitrator or mediator previously designated is not available or if one has not been designated. If possible, these issues should be addressed in the partnership agreement documents.

§ 33.02 Implementation

One of my mentors reminded me that years before I actually started my own firm, he had asked me if I considered myself an employer or an employee. He told me that I did not hesitate before responding *employer*. Clearly, long before I actually took the plunge, I came to terms with the fact that I was prepared for the responsibility and ultimate accountability that distinguishes an employer from an employee.

The decision to establish a practice without a partner was not difficult for me. It was my belief that I would have more options and negotiating leverage if I established my own niche in the field of family law first and *then* approached prospective partners. I would make this same decision again today.

Once I was committed to establishing a firm with no partners, I was ready to package a business plan and select a banker. This step involved making a number of other decisions, namely, what type of practice to start and where to set up shop.

§ 33.02.1 Profiling My Firm

I knew that with the right assistant, I could handle the types of cases that I had handled at the family law boutique where I had formerly worked—cases involving multi-million-dollar estates that usually involved esoteric issues such as defining and quantifying professional and celebrity goodwill and apportioning a community property interest in intellectual property. I knew the issues, the law, the gray areas, and the cutting edges. I also knew—and was known by—the majority of the forensic experts who had established reputations in their respective fields. These were matters that I had experience in handling and the types of cases to which I wanted to devote my time and expertise.

I also realized that I did not have expertise in handling many of the routine matters that often arise in a high-volume, small estate/income family law practice. I concluded that I did not want a volume practice but rather a practice devoted to the representation of high-caliber clients and one that, hopefully, would evolve into a boutique firm along the lines of the firm with which I had been previously associated.

§ 33.02.2 Selecting My Office

Once the decision to establish a family law boutique had been made, I needed to select an office compatible with the geographic and ambience needs and expectations of the clients I wanted to attract. Additionally, I wanted the accessibility and companionship of other family law professionals. My needs and preferences steered me in the direction of becoming a subtenant in a suite maintained by a high-end family law boutique and occupied by a few subtenants, some who were family law attorneys and others who practiced in other areas of the law. This arrangement functioned in many ways that were similar to an executive suite. I leased my office space not from the building directly but from the suite's master tenant (the high-end boutique family law firm).

This decision proved invaluable for me. For one thing, I was well placed for the referral of matters that did not meet the threshold financial requirements of more established family law boutiques. I also believe that I benefited by a dynamic I refer to as *competence by association*—that is, I *must* be competent if I shared a suite with the best practitioners in my field. Furthermore, by being in proximity to other respected family law lawyers, I was able to tap into valuable resources for purposes of brainstorming or testing the viability of a legal theory that I was developing. In addition, I was able to "borrow" associates of the other firm or otherwise develop cocounsel relationships on a case-by-case basis as the need arose, knowing that the expertise and quality of the lawyers who were working with me were of a level that would meet the high standards required by the clients I was able to attract. With time, I was able to reciprocate, serving as a devil's advocate or sounding board for my suite mates and making cross-referrals. From my perspective, I had all of the benefits of being associated with a larger firm and none of the big-firm drawbacks and headaches.

§ 33.02.3 Staffing and Equipping My Office

While at the family law boutique with which I was associated before deciding to strike out on my own, I had the good fortune of meeting a full-service assistant. This individual had helped other professionals set up new firms and practices and, in addition, had strong secretarial and bookkeeping skills.

Before I took one step toward establishing my firm, I met with this assistant and had her spell out what it would cost for me to have her full time and attention in establishing my practice and serving as my secretary, bookkeeper, and computer guru. I have no regrets whatsoever regarding the extraordinary amount of money it cost me to have this experienced and trusted individual work for me.

The primary guideline I gave my secretary was that I wanted to start with a first-rate operation. I wanted state-of-the-art computers and the "best" software to meet my needs, both at the present time and in the future when expansion was a reasonable likelihood. I wanted furniture that complemented my office. I wanted high-quality professional stationery, billing statements, and other documents that carried my firm's name. I did not want to cut corners.

§ 33.02.4 Outlining a Business Plan

Once I set out on the table what I envisioned for the firm, my assistant and one of my most respected mentors aided me in putting together my comprehensive business plan. Armed with the facts and figures of what my anticipated "fixed costs" would be, my assistant, my mentor, and I evaluated my referral base and referral history. We then were able to make realistic, conservative estimates as to my potential income.

Armed with my business plan, I interviewed a number of banks and finally selected the banker that I felt could best meet both my immediate and long-term needs. With the assistance of this banker, I was able to secure a loan for the full amount of my anticipated cash needs during my start-up phase and a line of credit in the event that I had failed to anticipate a need or did not generate revenues at my projected rate. Because of the detailed time and attention that my assistant, my mentor, and I gave to drawing up my business plan, our financial projections were very accurate. I never had to use my line of credit.

§ 33.02.5 Embracing the Opportunity to Grow

Within the first week after officially starting my new firm, one of my former employers from my first law firm (the full-service megafirm) invited me to cocounsel on any major family law matters that were referred to her firm and offered to refer other matters to me. This invitation confirmed for me the correctness of starting my firm as a first-class operation in terms of location, setting, staff, and equipment.

At this point in time, my office consisted of me and my assistant. I also had access to a paralegal who worked on a contract hourly basis. In addition, I was uniquely fortunate to have in my office my father, who had practiced as a successful lawyer in New York City and had come to live in California.

Within six months of the start of my firm, the senior partner in the prestigious family law boutique located in my suite asked me, as a favor, to hire a friend of the family as a summer law clerk. Before I had the benefit of the clerk's assistance, I did not realize just how much work I, personally, was handling that was not reflected on my billing time sheets.

After the clerk went back to school, I decided that I needed an associate. Because I was not prepared to saddle my firm with the expense of a full-time associate, I hired a relatively novice associate who was willing to work for me on an as-needed hourly compensation basis. Within a year, I had entered into a similar arrangement with another associate who had extensive family law experience. Over the following years, as my firm and its success grew, I was able to constantly upgrade the quality of lawyers working with me, which, in turn, resulted in the opportunity to constantly improve my team.

During this same time, I needed to address the issue of my support staff. Once my office was up and running, I no longer needed the services of an assistant who was able to command a compensation premium for helping establish a new business. I needed and hired a secretary who had experience working for family law lawyers. I also hired a bookkeeper to oversee the accounts receivable, accounts payable, corporate accounts, client trust accounts, and payroll.

At the end of my first year, I recruited the services of a fellow family law practitioner who had recently left a boutique and relocated to another state.

This individual had strong drafting skills and actually enjoyed processing the pleadings needed for ex parte matters. These skills were a perfect complement to my needs, and the opportunity to continue practicing on a part-time hourly basis met my friend's needs. We agreed upon an hourly rate and an availability schedule and started our own telecommunications "extension office."

After nearly three years of managing my own firm as the sole full-time lawyer, I wanted to take a vacation. I knew of many solo practitioners who were members of informal groups that covered for one another during vacations and other absences from the office. However, I knew that I would be too nervous to leave my practice for any length of time unless I knew that there would be someone covering for me who was as devoted to my cases as I was.

I concluded that I needed to find one or more partners. Two other solo practitioners and I considered teaming up as partners. One had worked for me as "of counsel" on a number of my cases, and we formed a partnership. This partnership lasted for approximately one and one-half years.

From the perspective of hindsight, I realize that, while I knew most of the important business points to discuss with a prospective partner, I did not understand the importance of making sure that the person's work ethic was compatible with my own. By *work ethic*, I mean the priority given to a client's needs in relation to the lawyer's personal schedule. I personally maintain a work ethic that puts the client first except on High Holy Days and my children's birthdays. This means for me that I return all telephone calls within twenty-four hours and respond to emergencies on nonreligious holiday weekends. My partner had a different approach, affording a greater priority to her personal life and the needs of her family members. Our different approaches gradually made us incompatible as partners, and we went our separate ways.

In the succeeding years, I formed another partnership that grew with additional partners and, at times, contracted as partners later withdrew.

§ 33.02.6 Where I Am Today

Today, my firm consists of four partners, four associates, an experienced trial lawyer who is of counsel, and a senior paralegal and three other paralegals who double as secretarial assistants. We have a support staff of seven or eight additional full-time employees. We share our suite with the very same boutique family law firm with which I was a subtenant decades ago. Both firms are essentially the same size, and each occupies approximately one-half of the suite. We share the reception room and receptionist, with each firm having a separate entry from the reception area into its own office space.

However established my firm may seem to others, I continue to maintain as one of my priorities the need to network my referral sources, whom I highly value, respect, and appreciate, and to maintain a public presence. I continue to give speeches, write articles and commentaries, and serve on various professional and charitable boards. I serve as a mentor to a number of junior lawyers and clerks. And I have written a book on divorce, now in its sixth printing.

I also continue to promise and deliver to each of my clients my personal attention and leadership with respect to their individual cases. I do my utmost to ensure that every call is returned within twenty-four hours, even if I am unable to return the call myself.

Over the years I have grown from a "baby" associate to a "baby" owner of my own firm to becoming a senior member of the family law community both in Los Angeles and around the country. Owning my own firm began with a vision and grew with sound business advice and management—a career path that is not right for everyone but is within the reach of those who want it and are willing to work for it.

§ 33.03 Action Plan

- Decide if owning your own practice is right for you.
- Focus on a type of practice.
- Make decisions about an office, staff, equipment, and business plan.
- Embrace opportunities to grow.

CHAPTER 34

Overcoming Stress in Your Legal Career

If a cluttered desk is a sign of a cluttered mind, of what, then, is an empty desk a sign?

—Albert Einstein

Chapter Checklist

- o Prioritize
- o Ten Steps to Organization
- o What Not to Do
- o Good Stress
- o Action Plan

High blood pressure is called a "silent killer," and one of its major causes is stress. Lawyers seem to be particularly prone to stress due to an overload of demands on their time.

Would you consider yourself busy these days? Sounds almost like a ridiculous question since most of us are very busy more often than not. In fact, most of us are too busy—that is, we are flat-out overcommitted and still awaiting the arrival of the simple life.

To address this problem, lawyers need to learn to prioritize, to employ the system of ten steps to organization, and to avoid multitasking.

§ 34.01 Prioritize

Stress for lawyers can come from having too much work to do—and the ensuing sense that their practice (and personal life) seems to be spinning out of control.

Most folks who claim that they have too little time generally fall victim to one, two, or all three of the following:

1. They fail to make a list of priorities.
2. They hop around the list.
3. They allow themselves to be distracted by urgent, but unimportant, other tasks.

Time cannot be managed until priorities are set and the top priorities are systematically addressed.

Taking the time to prioritize is the equivalent of a deep breath that restores perspective. This does not have to involve huge steps or major changes. A good start is daily prioritizing. Create a list of priorities for tomorrow. When you go into work the next morning, address the number one item for the day, then the number two item, then the number three item, and so forth. At the end of the day, assess the priorities that were left undone and reprioritize them for the next day. By doing that, you are always at least accomplishing the first priority, moving the ball forward, and creating a sense of achievement that can relieve the stress of uncertainty.

In the context of a law practice, prioritizing is important in particular because there are two types of "law time" hours: those necessary to develop and provide legal advice and those necessary to run the business of law. Both types are required for a financially successful and personally satisfying law practice. Making time for legal matters is usually not a problem; however, that is not the case with matters related to running the business of law.

Taking the time for business management requires setting and regularly reviewing priorities, but far too many lawyers procrastinate on that vital task. They lack confidence in themselves to do the task (never having received either law practice management training in law school or on-the-job training); lack interest in achieving the objective (finding law more interesting, absorbing, and demanding); or put too low a priority on achieving the objective (preferring to emphasize billable time rather than viewing the practice holistically).

With marketing or similar nonbillable issues, priorities are typically approached only after the billable work is done. Unlike with client matters, there are no ethical or financial consequences for not meeting business priorities. There's no threat of a lawsuit for malpractice or complaints from clients to the state bar because you didn't take care of your own financial well-being. Thus, business priorities often simply languish, to the long-term detriment of the firm.

The way to handle priorities here is for the lawyer to define the self-consequences if business priorities are not achieved. However, acting as your own conscience in that way is difficult. The more practical way to address those nonbillable priorities is to work with a legal-business coach. A good coach is not a friend who only compliments and encourages. A good coach is a leader who also pushes and challenges. That is difficult for lawyers to accept. However, the truly successful person wants and needs a target; and when it comes to prioritizing, a coach can sharpen your aim.

§ 34.02 Ten Steps to Organization

Busy people generally have

- too much to do and not enough time to do it;
- too much paper and not enough places to put it or time to work on it;
- too many project commitments and not enough uninterrupted time to complete them qualitatively;
- too many meetings to attend and not enough time to prepare for them or debrief from them;
- too many interruptions in their days;
- too many voice mail and e-mail messages; and
- too much stuff in their garages, closets, drawers, etc.

If you are a busy professional, being organized is a requirement to maximize your productivity as well as to live a somewhat balanced life. How can you achieve optimum levels of organization? There are ten ingredients to this elusive objective called *organization*—that is, ten contributing elements to becoming a more organized professional. These ten points or ingredients for an organized work life have been tried and tested throughout the United States with busy people in leadership and management positions. If you wish to grow as well as succeed, arrive home at decent hours, and feel more balanced in your professional role, give them a try. The results can be extraordinary!

§ 34.02.1 Step One: Unclutter Your Office

During the past several years, much more paper has come into your office than has gone out. When you couple this with the infrequency with which your office has probably been purged, you simply have run out of space to put things. Look around your office—any visible stacks or piles? Open your desk and cabinet drawers—any room for more paper and files? Probably not.

As a result, you are no doubt experiencing what is sometimes called *subliminal screaming*—the feeling that there are hundreds of people clamoring for your attention. Clutter is demoralizing, discouraging, distressing, distracting, and debilitating; and some people even become depressed about the administrative nightmare that they walk into every day. What you really want to feel is *delighted* with the condition of your office, proud of its being uncluttered so that you can concentrate and focus on one thing at a time.

Achieving an uncluttered office requires three major steps:

1. Completely purge your office.
2. Set up an excellent filing system.
3. "Process in" paper every day.

Purging your office requires an initial commitment of at least one to four hours (although you may need more time than this) to completely go through every desk drawer, file cabinet drawer, bookcase shelf, desk and credenza top, and every other place that has stuff on or in it. Then, with ruthless abandon, dispose of (recycle) all unnecessary, unwanted paper and other items. Exceptions include regulatory paper and personal mementos. After about ten minutes, you should find yourself really getting into it and feeling good about the purging process.

An excellent filing system implies that you have two systems working simultaneously: a recurring filing system and a nonrecurring filing system. The recurring filing system is a place to put paper items that you need to see again, but not today (described in step two). The nonrecurring filing system is your current labeled files. Now would be a good time to make sure that your labeled files are organized categorically so that you not only know where things are but also can find any item within twenty seconds without searching.

Now that your office is purged and you have an excellent filing system for storage, you need to allocate time every day to "process in" new paper. This means that you either file, route, or dispose of all new paper that comes into your office every single day. Not allocating time each day for paper-flow management will cause you to be right back where you started (a cluttered office with stacks everywhere) within forty-five days.

§ 34.02.2 Step Two: Set Up a "43" System

The "43 System" is a recurring file method that can work wonders. It is a place to put paper and documents that you need or want to see every day, but not today.

Here is how it works:

1. Convert one of your desk drawers to your recurring file system.
2. Enter into this drawer forty-three hanging files, thirty-one numbered *1* to *31* to correspond to the days of the month, and twelve labeled *January* through *December*.
3. File all needed, wanted documents and items into the appropriate file for the day or month that you next wish to see it. Every day, access the next day's file and plan to accomplish all of the items that are in that file.

This system is virtually guaranteed to create an uncluttered, stack-free work environment for you within a very short time.

§ 34.02.3 Step Three: Employ a U-Shaped Office Layout

The best layout of an office for maximum productivity and efficiency is U-shaped (an L-shaped desk with a credenza behind you). Your desk is your work space, and the only paper items on your desk should be those that are related to the project or task in progress. All other papers should be out of sight; they are distractions.

The return (the small part of the L-shaped desk) is a place for your telephone, calendar, pens, pencils, stapler, etc., allowing easy access to these essential tools.

The credenza is a great place for four-tray systems:

1. One stack tray for the work you need to complete today
2. A vertical tray housing your in-progress projects
3. One stack tray for pending items (awaiting phone or fax response)
4. An out tray

There should be *no* in-box on your desk because that is a significant source of subliminal screaming as well as a dumping ground for most people. The only paper that should enter your office prior to the end of your workday is anything classified as imperative; all other papers should be placed in an outside mail slot for processing at the end of the day.

Additionally, you should not have any meetings at your desk. The ability to concentrate is hampered at your desk; thus, effective listening may suffer. Use a separate conference table or room for all meetings.

§ 34.02.4 Step Four: Spend Time on Daily Planning

One of the most important time-management activities is daily planning, where you allocate and spend thirty minutes at the end of every workday to do the following:

- Recap today.
- Process in all new paper and messages.
- Plan tomorrow.

The reason to do this at the *end* of your workday is because of the stress-management benefit. Wrapping up today and clarifying tomorrow's blueprint for success is a tremendous stress-management tool.

Your daily plan should include a calendar system with the following items:

- Things to do
- People to see
- Places to go
- People to call
- Things to discuss
- Things to delegate

Putting these items in writing, usually in list fashion, will produce feelings of confidence and control that are almost indescribable. It is essential for a daily plan to be written in order to enjoy these implied benefits.

§ 34.02.5 Step Five: Incorporate PWT

A typical week in your life probably includes handling routine operational matters, attending meetings, and dealing with interruptions. Thus, you may have only a small amount of time to work on projects. Not having enough time to work on project commitments will cause undue stress because of fast-approaching deadlines or simply being behind schedule.

PWT (Project Work Time) is the solution:

- Every week, schedule a minimum of five hours to be uninterrupted and inaccessible to work on commitments.
- Decide what you will work on before PWT.
- When the time comes, close your door and turn on your voice mail system so that you are not disturbed.
- Commit to accomplishing what you set out to do.

Giving yourself the gift of PWT will enable you to increase immeasurably your personal productivity per week with stress-management benefits. It is a wonderful activity to engage in.

§ 34.02.6 Step Six: Prepare a Weekly To-Do List

Preparing a list of important tasks and projects to be accomplished in the coming week is also an excellent time- and stress-management technique. It enables you to forecast and plan time for important commitments, and it provides additional motivation for PWT planning.

Every Friday afternoon, Monday morning, or sometime during the weekend, prepare a to-do list of all of the things that you wish to accomplish for the coming week. Include personal-life items in this list as well. After your list is complete, enter next to each item the day that you need or want to accomplish each task. Use this list to guide your daily planning as well as to increase the effectiveness of PWT.

Doing this on Friday afternoon can really reduce preoccupation with work-related items during the weekend. Additionally, having done this planning before the next week starts, you will find that the week really begins on a positive note.

§ 34.02.7 Step Seven: Manage Interruptions

Arguably, the most prominent cause of an unproductive day is interruptions—those constant moments in the day when someone wants something from us. It seems that more and more people are leaving their office at the end of the day with a list of incomplete expectations and stacks of projects that were not worked on.

Interruptions can be put into three categories: imperative, optional, and whenever.

Follow these guidelines to better manage interruptions:

- Understand and accept that the client or customer is never an interruption. The problem is centered on internal interruptions.
- Before interrupting or accepting an interruption, diagnose it. Ask yourself if the interruption is imperative (has to be given or taken at this moment), optional (can wait until a later time or can go to e-mail), or whenever (should be forgotten about completely for now).

Being sensitive to the significant consequences of unjustified interruptions will motivate you to take those five to twenty seconds to diagnose before causing or accepting an internal interruption. It could dramatically change the complexion of the day, increasing productivity and efficiency dramatically.

§ 34.02.8 Step Eight: Assign Numerical Time Frames for Requests

One of the most effective ways to accomplish more is to delegate and request things from other people. The problem is that many busy people do not take the time to clarify their needs properly, thus "dumping" more often than delegating to others. There is an old saying: "Poor planning on your part does not constitute a crisis on mine."

Perhaps the most critical deficiency in delegating is the lack of precision regarding the time frame for completion. Too often we say "as soon as possible" or "sometime today" or make some other vague request. For a request to be understood and agreed to, it must have a numerical time frame. This means that a delegated task should always be accompanied with acute clarity as to when you want it, using specific times, days, dates, etc.

Every day, during daily planning, make a list of what you want/need from others and specifically when you want/need it. Then, using e-mail, voice mail, or a face-to-face meeting, communicate to all of the people on your list what it is you want or need.

You will find that doing this at the end of the workday dramatically reduces the number of one-at-a-time, unjustified interruptions during the day.

§ 34.02.9 Step Nine: Conduct Efficient Group Meetings

Many busy people strongly dislike going to meetings because of how much time they seem to waste while attending. This wasted time could be better used getting current on projects or working on other important items that seem to be backed up.

The problem with meetings is that they are often poorly prepared. Here are the most important guidelines for an efficient group meeting:

1. Agendas are mandatory (no agenda, no meeting!).
2. Always begin and end on time—never wait for latecomers because it is rude to the people who have arrived on schedule.
3. Insist that notes be taken, preferably by a designated note taker whose responsibility is to provide all attendees with a summation of the meeting within thirty-six hours.
4. At the end of a meeting, make sure that everyone is aware of any assignments, with numerical time frames attached.

Following these simple guidelines will dramatically reduce any resentment from attendees. As a meeting leader, you should always take personal responsibility for returning a productive dividend to the time invested by all who attend.

§ 34.02.10 Step Ten: Conduct One-to-One Briefings

The final step is to allocate and schedule fifteen to thirty minutes per week to meet with "direct reports" for a briefing. These very personalized conversations contribute heavily to the productive nurturing of the working relationship. It is an opportunity to touch base, to discuss important but nonurgent issues, and to delegate.

List your direct reports, and schedule each one into a fifteen- or thirty-minute time slot every week. Follow this agenda:

- Updates and progress reports from the direct report
- Discussion of issues needing advice and counsel
- Delegation, with numerical time frames
- Miscellaneous items (family, health, vacations, etc.)

Making these briefings nonnegotiable will create a working relationship that is based on mutual respect, understanding, and professionalism—one that allows individuals to come together to form groups for common purposes. In a word, *teamwork.*

§ 34.03 What Not to Do

Walking and texting or listening to music is a bad combination: pedestrian deaths are increasing even as fatalities from other traffic accidents fall. This is just one confirmation that *successful multitasking* is an oxymoron. We can do only one thing at a time successfully.

This is a particularly relevant warning for lawyers. Those who reach the pinnacle of success in practicing law are able to do many things, but they do them best when they focus on one at a time.

Consider the common scenario of lawyers sitting in a meeting with smartphones in hand, checking text messages or sending new ones while they're ostensibly participating in the proceedings. Such multitasking often results in the individual either reacting too quickly to an e-mail or missing something important in the live dialogue as it is going on. An inattentive lawyer who misses a key point in a meeting risks arousing client ire or making a mistake that could have major negative ramifications. (Certainly, technology facilitates multitasking, but multitasking generally does not facilitate good lawyering.)

Many attorneys claim to have too little time or say that they are overwhelmed by the need to balance client, practice, and personal priorities. Thus, they feel that they should multitask. Yet, attempting to do too many things at once creates self-defeating fear and paralysis as the tasks become overwhelming, producing attorneys who are close to burning out or, at the very least, are unhappy in their day-to-day occupation.

§ 34.04 Good Stress

Is stress always bad? A recent *Los Angeles Times* article featured an attorney who regularly works up to eighty hours a week as managing partner of her firm, a role that entails overseeing the other lawyers, ensuring all work product quality, vetting business operations, and managing her own cases. Nevertheless, she had a marvelous and somewhat unusual perspective on her workload: "There is an excitement about what is around the corner," she said, calling her enthusiasm "a fire that fuels itself."[1]

For the lawyer profiled and others with that same perspective, the article used an unusual term: *engaged workaholic*.[2] Said differently, if you are engaged in what you are doing, the task is not a chore; rather, it generates enthusiasm and passion.

As the article emphasized, stress can hinge on attitudes about work. In other words, if you love what you're doing, it's not work. And if it's not work, you may be exhausted at the end of the day, but you won't be stressed out or feel a lack of control over your environment.

§ 34.05 Action Plan

- Prioritize.
- Organize your office, desk, and files.
- Create a daily and weekly list of priorities. You can manage only your priorities; you cannot manage time.
- Effectively manage interruptions, requests, and meetings.
- Avoid the lure of multitasking.
- Love what you do.

---

1. Kathleen Doheney, *Workaholism: Maybe Not Such a Bad Thing*, L.A. TIMES, Feb. 13, 2012, http://articles.latimes.com/2012/feb/13/health/la-he-workaholics-20120213.

2. *Id.*

APPENDIX A

Cash Flow Projection Forms

Cash Flow Projection Form: Collected Revenue

Revenues	Jan.	Feb.	Mar.	Apr.	May	June	July	Aug.	Sept.	Oct.	Nov.	Dec.	Totals
Cash Retainers Collected for General Account (Not Trust Account)													
Transfer of Funds from Trust Account per Client Instructions													
Contingency Fees Collected													
Collected Accounts Receivable													
Funds Collected from Sale of Assets													
Miscellaneous Collected Funds													
Total Operating Funds Collected													
New Equity Funds Collected													
New Debt Funds Collected													

Note: A cash flow projection can include eighteen months of information. Review and revise the projection on a monthly basis.

Cash Flow Projection Form: Paid Expenses

Expenses	Jan.	Feb.	Mar.	Apr.	May	June	July	Aug.	Sept.	Oct.	Nov.	Dec.	Totals
Employee Salaries													
Employee Taxes													
Partner Draws/Shareholder Salaries													
Rent													
Health Insurance													
General Insurance													
Errors and Omissions Insurance													
Marketing and Public Relations													
Supplies													
Phone/Copy/Fax													
Professional Dues													
Continuing Legal Education													
Library													
Professional Services													
Travel and Entertainment													
Loan Repayments													
Total Operating Expenditures													

Note: A cash flow projection can include eighteen months of information. Review and revise the projection on a monthly basis.

Cash Flow Projection Form: Summary

	Jan.	Feb.	Mar.	Apr.	May	June	July	Aug.	Sept.	Oct.	Nov.	Dec.	Totals
Beginning Cash Balance													
Plus: Increases—Collected Revenue													
Less: Decreases—Paid Expenses													
Ending Cash Balance													
Plus: Short-Term Loans													
Cash Available													
Less: Capital Expenditures													
Balance of Cash													
Plus: Long-Term Loans													
Free Cash Flow													
Less: Savings													
Net-Free Cash Flow													
Less: Extraordinary Use of Cash Flow													
Net-Free Cash Flow Carryover													

Note: A cash flow projection can include eighteen months of information. Review and revise the projection on a monthly basis.

APPENDIX B

Monthly Accounts Receivable Aging Analysis

Monthly Accounts Receivable Aging Analysis

Month: ________

Name of Client	0–30	31–60	61–90	91–120	121–150	151+
Totals						

Accounts Receivable Aging Schedule by Percentage by Quarter

Days Outstanding	1st Qtr. (Jan.–Mar.)	2nd Qtr. (Apr.–June)	3rd Qtr. (July–Sept.)	4th Qtr. (Oct.–Dec.)
0–30				
31–60				
61–90				
91–120				
121–150				
151+				
Totals	100%	100%	100%	100%

Accounts Receivable Aging Schedule by Percentage by Quarter

Days Outstanding	Jan.	Feb.	Mar.	Apr.	May	June	July	Aug.	Sept.	Oct.	Nov.	Dec.
0–30												
31–60												
61–90												
91–120												
121–150												
151+												
Totals	100%	100%	100%	100%	100%	100%	100%	100%	100%	100%	100%	100%

APPENDIX C

Profit and Loss Statement

Profit and Loss Statement
1/1/13 Through 7/31/13

All Accounts

Category Description	1/1/13–7/31/13
INCOME/EXPENSES	
INCOME	
4000-FEE INCOME	$704,081.99
4020-BANK CREDIT MEMO	1,819.82
9999-VOID CHECK	0.00
Income: Other	0.02
TOTAL INCOME $705,901.83	
EXPENSES	
1500-Furniture and Fixtures	$ 1,584.00
5000-Advertising	1,108.70
5010-Accountant	800.00
5020-Attorney Service	1,481.22
5050-Law Library Expenses	14,471.91
5060-Continuing Education	1,845.00
5070-Clients Costs	33,611.74
5071-Court Reporter	2,525.70
5072-Courier Service	4,153.66
5080-Donation: Regular	205.00
5090-Donations: Political	3,600.00
5100-Dues and Subscriptions	6,443.00
5120-Employee Benefits	976,50
5130-Entertainment and Gifts	900.99
5140-Equipment Rental	770.77
5141-Expense Reimbursement	2,002.38
5150-Filing Fees and Court Costs	1,392.00
5160-Insurance	19,518.04
5170-Interest	500.00
5180-Messengers	4,131.36
5190-Office Expense	19,575.42
5200-Outside Labor	13,690.97
5210-Payroll Taxes	100,104.63
5220-Payroll Service	683.32
5222-Federal Tax	650.00
5230-Parking	9,125.00
5250-Professional Fees	4,705.00
5310-Taxes: Other	7,369.77
5320-Telephone	8,482.68
5330-Travel	4,396.41
5350-Postage and Printing	2,645.23

5355-Rent	54,000.00
5360-Repairs	1,478.68
5390-Office Salaries	187,925.05
5400-Officers' Salaries	138,990.00
5450-Bank Debt Memo	3,854.96
9998-Unknown Transaction	1,053.93
Expenses: Other	0.82
TOTAL EXPENSES	$660,753.84
TOTAL INCOME/EXPENSES	$45,147.99

APPENDIX D

Budget Recap Revenue and Expense Forms

Budget Recap: Revenue

Use this form to summarize projected and actual revenues and the amount of difference between the two. Show at least two years to spot any trends or patterns.

Month	Description	2013	2014
Jan.	Projected Actual Variance		
Feb.	Projected Actual Variance		
Mar.	Projected Actual Variance		
Apr.	Projected Actual Variance		
May	Projected Actual Variance		
June	Projected Actual Variance		
July	Projected Actual Variance		
Aug.	Projected Actual Variance		
Sept.	Projected Actual Variance		
Oct.	Projected Actual Variance		
Nov.	Projected Actual Variance		
Dec.	Projected Actual Variance		
YEAR TOTAL	Projected Actual Variance		

Budget Recap: Expense

Use this form to summarize proiected and actual expenses and the amount of difference between the two.

YEAR: ____

Month	Descrip-tion	Salaries	Taxes	Draws	Rent	Insurance	Market-ing and P.R.	Office Supplies
Jan.	Projected Actual Variance							
Feb.	Projected Actual Variance							
Mar.	Projected Actual Variance							
Apr.	Projected Actual Variance							
May	Projected Actual Variance							
June	Projected Actual Variance							
July	Projected Actual Variance							
Aug.	Projected Actual Variance							
Sept.	Projected Actual Variance							
Oct.	Projected Actual Variance							
Nov.	Projected Actual Variance							
Dec.	Projected Actual Variance							
YEAR TOTAL	Projected Actual Variance							

Month	Description	Phone/ Copy/Fax	Professional Dues	Education	Library	Professional Services	Travel/ Entertain.	Loan Repayment
Jan.	Projected Actual Variance							
Feb.	Projected Actual Variance							
Mar.	Projected Actual Variance							
Apr.	Projected Actual Variance							
May	Projected Actual Variance							
June	Projected Actual Variance							
July	Projected Actual Variance							
Aug.	Projected Actual Variance							
Sept.	Projected Actual Variance							
Oct.	Projected Actual Variance							
Nov.	Projected Actual Variance							
Dec.	Projected Actual Variance							
YEAR TOTAL	Projected Actual Variance							

APPENDIX E

General Ledger Information

9/2/14

General Ledger Information

Monthly	Fees Billed	WIP Fees	Fees Nonbillable	Fee Write-Offs	Accounts Receivable
January	$ 68,285.50	$ 1,172.40	–0–	($15,163.00)	$277,574.55
February	$ 54,095.50	$ 88,661.00	–0–	($ 3,509.23)	$270,439.07
March	$ 88,534.00	$ 86,470.50	–0–	($ 99.00)	$243,212.47
April	$ 91,270.50	$ 77,277.00	–0–	$ 8,458.61	$214,823.40
May	$186,103.30	$ 39,993.00	–0–	($43,245.38)	$352,484.08
June	$139,983.36	$122,375.30	–0–	($18,290.58)	$300,192.42
July	$138,116.50	$119,571.00	–0–	($ 5,599.14)	$365,856.60
August	–0–	$ 61,840.50	–0–	–0–	–0–
September	–0–	–0–	–0–	–0–	–0–
October	–0–	–0–	–0–	–0–	–0–
November	–0–	–0–	–0–	–0–	–0–
December	–0–	$ 82.50	–0–	–0–	–0–
Totals	$766,388.66	$597,443.20	–0–	($77,447.72)	N/A

Monthly	Costs Billed	WIP Costs	Cost Write-Offs	Interest Charged	Sales Tax Charged
January	$ 9,798.96	$ 241.75	($1,565.79)	–0–	–0–
February	$ 12,671.59	$ 10,670.33	($1,371.50)	–0–	–0–
March	$ 3,065.82	$ 3,817.88	–0–	–0–	–0–
April	$ 1,996.25	$ 1,997.12	–0–	$ .05	–0–
May	$ 17,239.14	$ 3,933.47	($ 937.77)	–0–	–0–

9/2/14

General Ledger Information

Monthly	Fees Billed	WIP Fees	Fees Nonbillable	Fee Write-Offs	Accounts Receivable
June	$ 8,692.53	$ 5,958.60	($1,561.04)	–0–	–0–
July	$ 8,757.97	$ 7,091.53	–0–	–0–	–0–
August	–0–	$ 3,373.05	–0–	–0–	–0–
September	–0–	$ 69.24	–0–	–0–	–0–
October	–0–	–0–	–0–	–0–	–0–
November	–0–	–0–	–0–	–0–	–0–
December	–0–	–0–	–0–	–0–	–0–
Totals	$62,222.26	$37,152.97	($5,536.10)	$ .05	–0–

Monthly	Discounts Allowed	General Payments	Retainer Payments	Withdrawn from Trust	Deposited to Trust
January	$ 925.65	$118,011.80	–0–	–0–	–0–
February	$ 601.35	$ 68,420.49	–0–	–0–	–0–
March	$ 1,935.95	$116,791.47	–0–	–0–	–0–
April	$ 2,707.70	$127,406.73	–0–	–0–	–0–
May	$ 4,777.80	$ 31,276.08	–0–	–0–	–0–
June	$ 4,842.90	$182,753.05	–0–	–0–	–0–
July	$ 1,961.30	$ 77,866.15	–0–	$100.00	–0–
August	–0–	–0–	–0–	–0–	–0–
September	–0–	–0–	–0–	–0–	–0–
October	–0–	–0–	–0–	–0–	–0–
November	–0–	–0–	–0–	–0–	–0–
December	–0–	–0–	–0–	–0–	–0–
Totals	$17,752.65	$722,525.77	–0–	$100.00	–0–

9/2/14

Quarterly General Ledger, Information

Quarter	Fees Billed	WIP Fees	Fees Nonbillable	Fee Write-offs	Accounts Receivable
First	$210,915.00	$176,303.90	–0–	($18,771.23)	$243,212.47
Second	$417,357.16	$239,645.30	–0–	($53,077.35)	$300,192.42
Third	$138,116.50	$181,411.50	–0–	($ 5,599.14)	$365,856.60
Fourth	–0–	$ 82.50	–0–	–0–	–0–
Totals	$766,388.66	$597,443.20	–0–	($77,447.72)	N/A

Quarter	Costs Billed	WIP Costs	Cost Write-offs	Interest Charged	Sales Tax Charged
First	$ 25,536.37	$ 14,729.96	($2,937.29)	–0–	–0–
Second	$ 27,927.92	$ 11,889.19	($2,598.81)	$.05	–0–
Third	$8,757.97	$ 10,533.82	–0–	–0–	–0–
Fourth	–0–	–0–	–0–	–0–	–0–
Totals	$ 62,222.26	$ 37,152.97	($5,536.10)	$ .05	–0–

Quarter	Discounts Allowed	General Payments	Retainer Payments	Withdrawn from Trust	Deposited to Trust
First	$ 3,462.95	$303,223.76	–0–	–0–	–0–
Second	$ 12,328.40	$341,435.86	–0–	–0–	–0–
Third	$ 1,961.30	$ 77,866.15	–0–	$ 100.00	–0–
Fourth	–0–	–0–	–0–	–0–	–0–
Totals	$ 17,752.65	$722,525.77	–0–	$ 100.00	–0–

Accounts Receivable Aging: 09/02/14

Current	$135,721.40
30–60 Days	$58,383.09
61–91 Days	$55,328.10
91–120 Days	$20,557.32
Over 120 Days	$95,866.39
Total Accounts Receivable	$365,856.60

APPENDIX F

Payment Pattern Analysis

Payment Pattern Analysis (by Averages)

Month of Billing	First Month After Bill	Second Month After Bill	Third Month After Bill	Fourth Month After Bill	Fifth Month After Bill	Sixth Month After Bill	More Than Six Months After Bill
(% for Jan.)							
Jan.	$	$	$	$	$	$	$
(% for Feb.)							
Feb.	$	$	$	$	$	$	$
(% for Mar.)							
Mar.	$	$	$	$	$	$	$
(% for Apr.)							
Apr.	$	$	$	$	$	$	$
(% for May)							
May	$	$	$	$	$	$	$
(% for June)							
June	$	$	$	$	$	$	$
(% for July)							
July	$	$	$	$	$	$	$
(% for Aug.)							
Aug.	$	$	$	$	$	$	$
(% for Sept.)							
Sept.	$	$	$	$	$	$	$
(% for Oct.)							
Oct.	$	$	$	$	$	$	$
(% for Nov.)							
Nov.	$	$	$	$	$	$	$
(% for Dec.)							
Dec.	$	$	$	$	$	$	$
Totals	$	$	$	$	$	$	$

APPENDIX G

Comparison of Essential Provisions of the ADA and the FMLA

Provision	ADA	FMLA
Employers covered	Employers with fifteen or more employees	Employers with fifty or more employees
Employees covered	Qualified applicants and employees with a disability	Employees with one year of service who worked 1,250 hours that year
Enforcement agency	EEOC	U.S. Department of Labor
Cause for leave	Reasonable accommodation, subject to undue hardship defense	Employee's "serious health condition"; serious health condition of spouse/child/parent; child's birth/adoption/placement in foster care
Terms of leave	Unpaid leave, generally for defined period, subject to undue hardship defense; employer not explicitly required to pay benefits during leave	Up to twelve weeks of unpaid, job-protected leave per twelve-month period; part-time leave allowed; up to twenty-six weeks of unpaid military exigency leave; benefits paid by employer
Return to work	Employee entitled to position held prior to leave, subject to undue hardship defense	Employee entitled to job previously held OR equivalent job with equivalent benefits, pay, and other terms of employment
Definition of *disability* or *health condition*	The ADA protects any "qualified individual with a disability," meaning any individual with a disability who, with or without reasonable accommodation, can perform the "essential functions" of the employment position held or desired. The ADA defines *disability* as "(A) a physical or mental impairment that substantially limits one or more major life activities of such individual; (B) a record of such an impairment; or (C) being regarded as having such an impairment."	Labor Department regulations define *serious health condition* as an illness, injury, impairment, or physical or mental condition that involves either "in-patient care" or "continuing treatment by a health care provider." Specifically, the injury, illness, impairment, or physical or mental condition must involve the following: (1) any period of incapacity or treatment in connection with or consequent to in-patient care, such as an overnight stay in a hospital, hospice, or residential medical care facility; (2) any period of incapacity requiring absence from work, school, or other regular daily activities, of more than three calendar days, that also involves continuing treatment by, or under the supervision of, a health-care provider; or (3) continuing treatment by, or under the supervision of, a health-care provider for a chronic or long-term health condition that is incurable or so serious that, if not treated, would likely result in a period of incapacity of more than three calendar days, or for prenatal care.

Provision	ADA	FMLA
Limitations required to support leave under statutory definitions	The phrase *substantially limits* means "(i) [u]nable to perform a major life activity that the average person in the general population can perform; or (ii) [s]ignificantly restricted as to the condition, manner or duration under which an individual can perform a particular major life activity as compared to the condition, manner or duration under which the average person in the general population can perform that same major life activity." With respect to the major life activity of "working," EEOC regulations state that the term *substantially limits* means "significantly restricted in the ability to perform either a class of jobs or a broad range of jobs in various classes as compared to the average person having comparable training, skills and abilities. The inability to perform a single, particular job does not constitute a substantial limitation in the major life activity of working." The term *essential functions* refers to "fundamental job duties of the employment position the individual with a disability holds or desires." A job function may be considered essential, inter alia, because the position exists to perform that function, there are a limited number of employees available among whom the performance of the job function can be distributed, and/or the incumbent is hired for his expertise.	The final interim regulations for the FMLA define *unable to perform the functions of the position* as being "unable to work at all or [being] unable to perform any of the essential functions of the employee's position" within the meaning of the ADA.

APPENDIX H

Examples of Overlap and Conflict Between the ADA and the FMLA

Applicability	ADA	FMLA
Applicants for employment	Yes. All provisions apply.	No. Only employees are protected.
Duration of employment before leave entitlement	None required. Even new employees are covered.	One year of employment with at least 1,250 work hours
When both statutes apply concurrently	When the employee has a covered disability (physical or mental condition) that substantially limits a major life activity	When the disability is *also* a serious medical condition
Employee not disabled/ill but family member is	No discrimination is permitted in hiring, placement, or terms and conditions of employment because employee has a close association with a disabled person (spouse, child, parent, sibling, or living companion), *but* no accommodation in the form of leave is required because it does not "assist the employee in performing the essential functions of the job."	Intermittent or "blocks" of unpaid leave are mandated when the employee is required to care for a close family member with a serious medical condition.
Illness/disability of short duration	The ADA definition of *disability* typically does not include transitory illnesses or temporary, nonchronic impairments of short duration, having little or no long-term or permanent impact, such as broken limbs or gall bladder surgery.	The employee can take up to twelve weeks of unpaid leave for a "serious health condition" if the employee suffers from an illness, injury, impairment, or physical or mental condition that involves either "in-patient care" *or* "continuing treatment by a health-care provider." This leave entitlement applies to an employee who merely stays the night in a hospital, hospice, or medical care facility *or* has any period of incapacity requiring absence from work, school, or other regular daily activities, of more than three calendar days, that also involves continuing treatment by, or under the supervision of, a health-care provider.

Applicability	ADA	FMLA
Substance abuse	The ADA excludes illegal drug users from the definition of *qualified individual with a disability.* The ADA covers, however, those who are participating in a supervised rehabilitation program and are no longer engaging in such use.	The FMLA regulations define *serious health condition* to include treatment for substance abuse when in-patient care is required. Consequently, an employee with a drug condition may be entitled to leave under both the FMLA (when an employee's supervised rehabilitation involves in-patient care) and the ADA (only if the employee is no longer using drugs).
Pregnancy	Pregnancy is specifically excluded from the definition of *disability* by the EEOC *Technical Assistance Manual.*	Up to twelve weeks of *unpaid,* job-protected leave of absence is permitted for pregnancy.
Availability of undue hardship defense for employer	Yes. However, the defense is *very* narrowly construed to arise only with direct, medically documented proof of direct threat to the health or safety of the disabled employee or coworkers or serious economic hardship, making an accommodation impossible.	No. There is one exception: an employer may deny restoration rights to a narrow class of "highly compensated employees" if "necessary to prevent substantial *and* grievous economic injury to the operations of the employer."

APPENDIX I

Employer Actions

Action	ADA	FMLA
Medical examinations	The ADA prohibits an employer from inquiring, including through medical examinations, whether an employee is an individual with a disability and, if so, the nature of the disability, *unless* the inquiry is "job-related and consistent with business necessity"—that is, required for the assessment of the individual's ability to do the job at issue. Information obtained by the employer must be maintained in separate, confidential medical files. Access to medical files must be restricted to statutorily designated individuals who have a specific need for such information (supervisors and first aid personnel).	Under the FMLA, an employer may require an employee to submit a certification from a health-care provider to substantiate that the leave is due to a serious health condition. The employer also may require, as a condition to the restoration of employment, that an employee present certification of fitness to return to work. However, if an employer requires a medical certification, it must comply with the ADA requirement that the examination be job-related and consistent with business necessity. Seeking more information than is necessary to verify the leave request or to verify fitness to return to work may violate the ADA. Likewise, to avoid violating the ADA, employers should keep all information obtained in separate, confidential medical files.
Administration of medical examinations	Under the ADA, medical examinations may be administered by the employer's physician.	The express language of the FMLA limits medical certification, at least the first opinion regarding entitlement to leave and fitness to return to work, to certification supplied by the health-care provider of the employee, not that of the employer. If an employer doubts the validity of an employee's certification, the FMLA allows an employer to require, at its own expense, that the employee obtain a second opinion from a health-care provider designated by the employer. If this second opinion differs from the original certification, an employer may require, at its own expense, that the employee obtain a third opinion from a jointly designated or approved health-care provider. The third opinion is final and binding.

Action	ADA	FMLA
Maintenance of employee health benefits	The ADA requires employers to reasonably accommodate the known physical or mental impairments of an otherwise qualified individual with a disability. Reasonable accommodation may include additional unpaid leave and "job restructuring [and] part-time or modified work schedules." Thus, an employer may attempt to reasonably accommodate a disabled employee by offering the employee a part-time job or a leave with *no benefits*.	The employer **MUST** maintain the health benefits of an employee on FMLA leave. In fact, the employer cannot recover the premium payments paid during the period of leave if the employee does not return to work for reasons beyond the employee's control, such as a serious health condition. Consequently, an employee whose "disability" also constitutes a "serious health condition" could work part-time until the expiration of twelve weeks of leave, with health benefits maintained during this period.
Reinstatement rights of employees	Under the ADA, upon returning from leave, an employee is entitled to the position held prior to leave unless the position is no longer vacant because it would have been an undue hardship to hold it open. Consequently, an employee has greater reinstatement rights under the ADA than under the FMLA where reinstatement to the same job is not an undue hardship.	Under the FMLA, an employer does not have to establish undue hardship in order to transfer an employee to an equivalent position (with equivalent benefits, pay, and other terms and conditions of employment) instead of restoring the employee to the position held prior to leave.

Action	ADA	FMLA
Impact on attendance policies	The ADA may require an employer to make exceptions to its attendance policies as a reasonable accommodation. Under the ADA, the rules regarding attendance policies are relatively ambiguous as neither the statute nor the regulations provide much detail in this area. For example, neither the statute nor the regulations indicate when an employer must grant additional unpaid leave as an accommodation or when it is entitled to refuse such an accommodation and terminate an employee for unsatisfactory overall attendance. The lack of certainty in this area necessitates, when appropriate, looking to Rehabilitation Act cases for interpretative guidance.	The FMLA may require an employer to deviate from its attendance policies by granting an eligible employee intermittent leave and by ignoring FMLA leave in calculating absences for disciplinary purposes. Under the FMLA, eligible employees are entitled to take up to twelve workweeks of unpaid leave per year regardless of the employer's attendance policy. In cases involving a serious health condition that befalls an employee or an employee's family member (such as an employee's spouse, son, daughter, or parent), an employee is allowed to take leave intermittently, in separate blocks of time. This intermittent leave can include leave periods from as short as one hour to as long as several weeks. The FMLA also prohibits an employer from (1) considering FMLA leave as a negative factor in considering an employee for discipline, promotion, or other employment actions; and (2) counting FMLA leave under "no fault" attendance policies. An employer's attendance policy will not be affected often by the foreseeable intermittent leave needs of an employee because an employee is required to give the employer thirty days' notice, or else notice as soon as is practicable. Failure to provide such notice within thirty days without a reasonable excuse may allow the employer to deny the taking of FMLA leave until thirty days after the date that the employee provides notice of the need for leave. Generally, unforeseeable intermittent leave has the greatest potential to implicate an employer's established attendance procedures and policies. Because an employee may take intermittent leave in increments of as short as one hour at a time, such leave can cause serious attendance problems.

Action	ADA	FMLA
Discipline/ discharge of chronically late or absent employee	There is no duty to tolerate excessive absenteeism.	Although neither the FMLA nor the regulations provide clear guidance in situations involving a chronically absent or tardy employee, an employer's ability or inability to discipline or terminate an employee in the following two areas is reasonably clear: (1) *Justified absence or tardiness.* An employee who is consistently late or absent due to an illness or ailing family member whose condition requires *unforeseeable* treatment may not be terminated or disciplined for FMLA-covered absences (an employer may not require an employee to adhere to the employer's internal rules and procedures when FMLA leave is involved). (2) *Unjustified absence or tardiness.* A situation in which an employee is consistently late or absent due to an illness or ailing family member whose condition is *not serious* and requires foreseeable treatment may give rise to the following: (A) *Denial of leave.* If it is clear that the employee had *actual notice* of the FMLA notice requirements and the employee does not have a reasonable excuse for failing to give notice, the employer may deny leave for thirty days after the date that the employee provides notice of the need for leave. (B) *Reassignment.* The employer may require the employee to transfer *temporarily* to an available alternative full-time or part-time position of equal pay and benefits for which the employee is qualified and that better accommodates recurring periods of leave than does the employee's regular position.

APPENDIX J

Effect on Workers' Compensation

Issue	ADA	FMLA
Preemption	Consistent workers' compensation provisions are not preempted. The ADA does not preempt any existing state law that is consistent with the ADA. Thus, a single violation may subject an employer to actions under both the ADA and state workers' compensation statutes. In contrast, the ADA preempts any conflicting provisions under state workers' compensation law. For example, if an employer declines to assign an employee with a disability to a job that may give rise to a long-term risk of injury, in reliance on a state workers' compensation statute that makes it liable for additional benefits if an injury occurs because the employer assigned the person to a position likely to jeopardize the person's health or safety or exacerbate an earlier workers' compensation injury, the employer typically violates the ADA. However, workers' compensation laws may permit or require an employer to exclude the individual with a disability from such a position. Because the ADA preempts these laws, an employer could not assert as a defense to a charge of discrimination that it failed to hire or reinstate an individual with a disability because doing so would violate a state workers' compensation law that required exclusion of this individual (EEOC *Technical Assistance Manual* § 9.6).	The FMLA does not preempt state laws simply because they provide medical leave. The FMLA does not supersede any provision of state or local law that provides greater family or medical leave rights than those provided by the FMLA.

Issue	ADA	FMLA
Interplay between legislation and workers' compensation	The definition of *disability* under workers' compensation laws differs from that under the ADA due to the different purposes of the statutes. For instance, the ADA does not cover nonchronic impairments of short duration with no long-term or permanent impact or minor injuries but does cover disabilities not caused by the job (EEOC *Technical Assistance Manual* § 9.2). In contrast, state workers' compensation laws provide no benefits for disabilities not caused by the job but generally provide benefits to employees not only for permanently disabling job-caused injuries but also for temporary ones. Therefore, if an employee breaks a leg on the job and cannot work for two months but the leg heals normally within a few months, the employee would not be an individual with a disability under the ADA but could receive workers' compensation benefits.	Not all workers' compensation absences are FMLA absences. For instance, an employee who received treatment for a cut hand and did not return to work until the following day would be eligible for workers' compensation leave but would not be eligible for FMLA leave because the injury did not keep the employee out of work for more than three days or require ongoing treatment. However, Department of Labor officials have indicated that the final FMLA regulations likely will contain a provision explicitly allowing FMLA leave and workers' compensation leave to run concurrently if an injury qualifies under both laws. Sometimes employers try to run an employee's workers' compensation leave, FMLA leave, and accrued vacation and sick pay all at once. The final regulations should address this practice.
Reassignment to "light duty" on return from workers' compensation or other leave	The employer's right to reassign an employee to another position that better accommodates FMLA leave is limited by the need to comply with the ADA. For example, the ADA will require an employer to keep the ADA-protected individual in the individual's regular position during periods of intermittent leave where such assignment does not pose an undue hardship for the employer.	If the FMLA entitles an employee to leave, an employer may not, in lieu of medical leave, require an employee to take a "light duty" position. However, the employer certainly may, but under the FMLA is not required to, offer "light duty" assignments as an alternative to leave. In addition, an employer may reassign an employee requesting leave intermittently or on a reduced leave schedule to another position better suited to accommodate that type of leave. Although the new position must offer pay and benefits equivalent to the employee's previous position, the new position need not have equivalent duties. An employer may augment the pay and benefits of an existing alternative position (that typically is compensated at a lower rate) to meet the "equivalent pay and benefits" requirement.

APPENDIX K

Preemployment Inquiries

Area of Inquiry	Lawful Inquiries	Unlawful Inquiries
Name	For access purposes, inquiry about whether the applicant's work records are under another name	Inquiry about whether a woman is a Miss, Mrs., or Ms.; inquiry about maiden name or any other previous name used
Address/housing	Inquiry about place and length of current and previous addresses and applicant's phone number or how applicant can be reached if a number is not available	Inquiry about whether applicant owns a home, rents, or lives in an apartment or house; inquiry about foreign addresses
Age	Require proof of age by birth certificate, *only after hiring*	Inquiry about age or age group of applicant or about *date* of high school graduation; request for birth certificate or baptismal record *before hiring*
Birthplace/national origin		Inquiry about birthplace of applicant or that of the applicant's parents, grandparents, or spouse; any other inquiry about national origin
Race/color	If ability to speak a specific foreign language is a BFOQ, inquiry about whether applicant is fluent in *that* language; inquiry about race/color to indicate that the institution is an equal opportunity employer; inquiry about race for affirmative action plan statistics, *only after hiring*	Inquiry about "native tongue" or foreign language or any inquiry that would indicate race or color (including requiring a photograph)
Sex	Inquiry about sex to indicate that the institution is an equal opportunity employer	Inquiry about anything that would indicate sex (unless job related), childbearing issues, family responsibilities, or maiden name
Marital/parental status	Inquiry about status (married or single) for insurance purposes, *only after hiring*; inquiry about number and ages of dependents and/or spouse for insurance purposes, *only after hiring*	Inquiry about marital status *before hiring* and the number and age of children, who cares for them, and if the applicant plans to have more children
Religion/creed		Inquiry about religion or religious customs and holidays and willingness to work on the Sabbath or any particular religious holiday; request for recommendations from church officials
Citizenship	Inquiry about whether applicant is a U.S. citizen and, if not, whether applicant intends to become one; inquiry about whether U.S. residence is legal and whether spouse is a citizen; require proof of citizenship, *only after hiring*	Inquiry about whether applicant is native born or naturalized, whether spouse or parents are native born or naturalized, and the date of citizenship; require proof of citizenship *before hiring*

Area of Inquiry	Lawful Inquiries	Unlawful Inquiries
Relatives	Inquiry about name, relationship, and address of person to be notified in case of emergency, *only after hiring*	Inquiry about names of relatives working for the employer or the identity of the nearest relative
Military service	Inquiry about service in the U.S. armed forces, rank attained, branch of service, and any job-related experience; require military discharge certificate, *only after hiring*	Inquiry about the type of discharge and about military service in the armed services of any country but the United States; request for military service records
Education	Inquiry about academic, professional, or vocational schools attended; inquiry about language skills, such as reading and writing foreign languages	Inquiry about the nationality, racial, or religious affiliation of schools attended; inquiry about how foreign language ability was acquired
Criminal record	Inquiry about convictions and other misdemeanors	Inquiry about arrests
References	Request for general and work references not relating to race, color, religion, sex, national origin, or ancestry	Request for references specifically from clergy or any other people who might reflect race, color, religion, sex, national origin, or ancestry
Organizations	Inquiry about organizational membership—professional, social, etc.—as long as affiliation is not used to discriminate on the basis of race, sex, national origin, or ancestry; inquiry about offices held, if any	Inquiry about *all* clubs to which applicant belongs or has belonged
Photographs	Require photograph for identification purposes, *only after hiring*	Request for photograph *before hiring*; photographing applicants during interviews
Work schedule	Inquiry about willingness to work a required work schedule and whether applicant has military reservist obligations	Inquiry about willingness to work any particular religious holiday
Disability	Inquiry about applicant's capability to perform the job (burden of proof for nondiscrimination lies with the employer)	Inquiry that excludes disabled applicants as a class on the basis of their type of disability; inquiry about whether applicant has or can qualify for a driver's license where driving is not a BFOQ
Other qualifications	Inquiry about any area that has a direct reflection on the job for which the applicant is applying	Any non-job-related inquiry that may present information permitting unlawful discrimination

INDEX